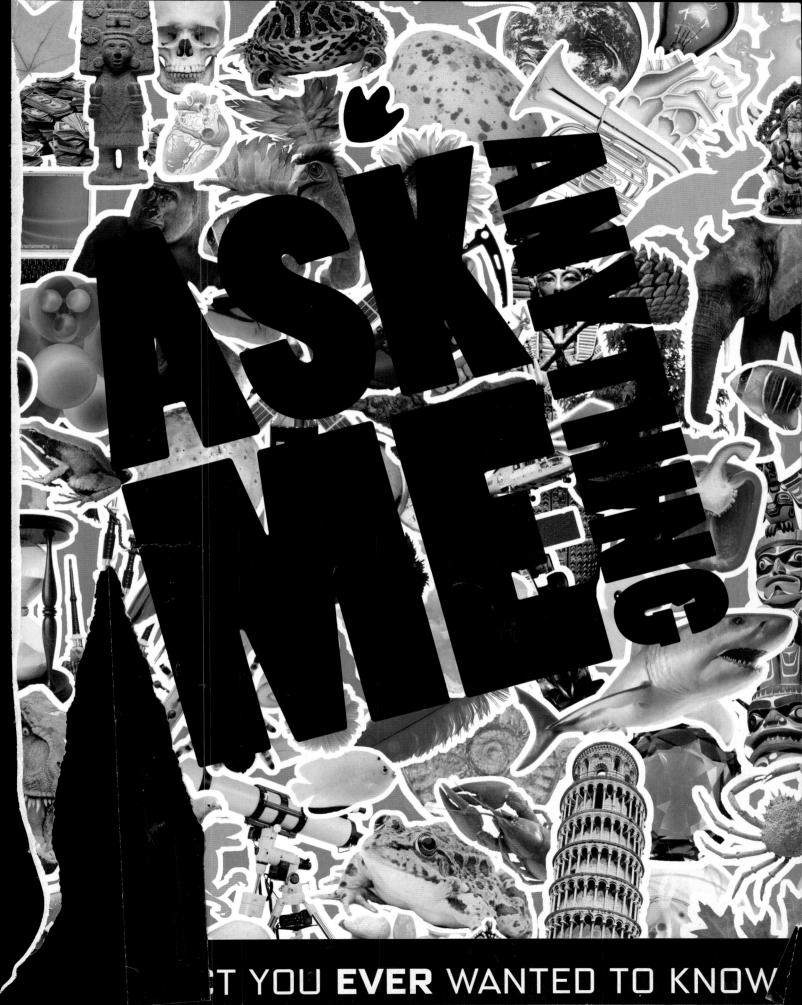

ASK ME ANYTHING

ANYTHING

LONDON, NEW YORK,
MELBOURNE, MUNICH, AND DELHI

Senior editor Julie Ferris
Senior designer Smiljka Surla
Project editors Francesca Baines, Niki Foreman
Art editors Jim Green, Marilou Prokopiou
Editors Ashwin Khurana, Andrea Mills
Designers Dave Ball, Sheila Collins, Spencer Holbrook,
Philip Letsu, Hoa Luc, Johnny Pau, Owen Peyton Jones, Jacqui Swan

Managing editor Linda Esposito
Managing art editor Diane Thistlethwaite

Commissioned illustrations Maltings Partnership
Picture researcher Nic Dean

Publishing manager Andrew Macintyre
Category publisher Laura Buller

DK picture researchers Lucy Claxton, Rose Horridge,
Emma Shepherd, Romaine Werblow
Production editor Andy Hilliard
Senior production controller Angela Graef
Design development Martin Wilson
Jacket designer Junkichi Tatsuki
Jacket editor Mariza O'Keeffe
Jacket manager Sophia M Tampakopoulos Turner

First published in Great Britain in 2009 by
Dorling Kindersley Limited,
80 Strand, London, WC2R 0RL

6 8 10 9 7
LD098 – 04/09
Reprinted in 2011

A CIP catalogue record for this book
is available from the British Library

ISBN: 978-0-143-41457-5

Exclusively marketed and distributed by Impulse Marketing
(For sale only in India, Bangladesh, Sri Lanka, Philippines, UAE, Qatar, Bahrain,
Kuwait, Saudi Arabia and Oman only).

Colour reproduction by MDP, UK
Printed and bound by PWGS, China

**Discover more at
www.dk.com**

ASK ME

Contributors
Kim Bryan, Lisa Burke,
Dougal Dixon, Susan Kennedy,
Jim Pipe, Carole Stott,
Richard Walker, Claire Watts

Contents

Space

How old is the Universe?

The Universe is about 13.7 billion years old. At its beginning it looked nothing like it does today. Yet, everything in today's Universe did exist in some form back then. It all started with the Big Bang, a kind of explosion that would not only go on to produce all the matter in the Universe but also marked the start of time.

Elements in the Sun

The top ten chemical elements that make up the Sun are:

01:	**hydrogen**	71%
02:	**helium**	27.1%
03:	**oxygen**	0.97%
04:	**carbon**	0.4%
05:	**nitrogen**	0.096%
06:	**silicon**	0.099%
07:	**magnesium**	0.076%
08:	**neon**	0.058%
09:	**iron**	0.14%
10:	**sulphur**	0.04%

FAST FACTS

Creation of the Universe

01: At the start, the Universe was a hot and dense ball of radiation energy.

02: In one-thousandth of a second, tiny radiation particles produced tiny particles of matter. These combined to form the first ever chemical elements, hydrogen and helium.

03: Some regions of the young Universe contained slightly more hydrogen and helium than others. These shrank to form the first stars.

04: Nuclear reactions inside the stars produced many other chemical elements, including carbon and oxygen.

05: The elements in the Universe today were produced from elements created in the Big Bang.

How to: create the Universe

01. Start time with a Big Bang – a massive explosion that lasts for less than one trillionth of a second that will create tiny particles of radiation smaller than the size of a full stop.

02. Wait 380,000 years for the first atoms to form a mix that is 76 per cent hydrogen and 24 per cent helium.

03. After 1 billion years check that the first stars have formed, and there are dwarf galaxies throughout the Universe.

Everything in the Universe produces energy – you produce energy when you exercise, and light energy is produced by nuclear reactions inside stars.

WHAT'S IN A NAME?

The term **"Big Bang"** was coined by Fred Hoyle in 1950 to illustrate to his radio listeners the difference between it and his own theory, "Steady State", where the Universe has no beginning.

Hot stuff!

100000000000000000000000000000000000

In the first trillionth of a second of its creation, the temperature of the Universe was **ten billion trillion trillion degrees Celsius**

Looking back

We see objects in space because of their light. Stars produce their own but others, such as the Moon and planets, shine by reflecting light.

Light travels at 299,800 km per second (186,287 miles per second) – faster than anything else.

Distant stars are seen as they were in the past – when the light left them.

The most distant galaxies we see are about 13 billion light years away, and as they were in the early Universe.

Blasts from the past

1931 Belgian Georges Lemaître suggests that all material in the Universe started as a single condensed sphere that exploded

1948 Russian-born physicist George Gamow explains the first elements formed in the explosion

1955 Englishman Fred Hoyle shows how heavier elements are produced by massive stars

1965 American physicists Arno Penzias and Robert Wilson discover cosmic microwave background radiation, the leftover radiation initially produced by the Big Bang

1980 American Alan Guth modifies the Big Bang theory by introducing the idea of inflation – a short period of extra expansion within a split second of the start of the Universe

The Universe is **expanding** by about 70 km (43 miles) every second.

Australopithecus skull

Human origins

5 billion years ago
The Sun formed from hydrogen and helium and small amounts of other elements.

4.5 billion years ago
Some of the material not used up in the Sun joined together to form Earth.

About 3.7 billion years ago
Carbon-containing molecules in young Earth's oceans evolved into bacteria-like cells; the first forms of primitive life.

1 million years ago
The first humans walked on Earth.

Near, far... and really far

Depending on how far away objects are, distances in the Universe are calculated using a variety of measuring units.

★ **Kilometres or miles**
Useful for measuring the distance of relatively near objects in our Solar System, such as the planets, moons, and asteroids.

★ **Astronomical units**
Used for measuring planetary distances within the Solar System. The distance from the Sun to Earth equals one astronomical unit (AU).

★ **Light years**
This measurement is useful for distances within our galaxy, the Milky Way, and across the Universe. One light year is the distance light travels in one year – equal to 9.46 million million km (5.88 million million miles).

05. When 9 million years old, form our Solar System in the Milky Way Galaxy.

04. When the Universe is 3 billion years old, merge small galaxies to form massive ones.

What about me?

All the elements on Earth, including all the elements in your body, were produced in stars.

Bigger **and bigger**

Planets
Earth may feel big to us, but at 12,756 km (7,926 miles) across, it is just a speck in an expanding Universe.

Stars
Planets orbit stars – our star is the Sun. Without it there would be no life. It measures 1.4 million km (870,000 miles) across.

Galaxies
Stars exist in galaxies, colossal star systems that come in a range of sizes and shapes. Earth is in the Milky Way Galaxy.

Cluster
Galaxies exist in clusters – the Milky Way Galaxy is in the Local Group cluster, stretching 10 million light years across.

Supercluster
Galaxy clusters are within superclusters – we are in the Virgo Supercluster, 200 million light years from one side to the other.

Voids
The largest structures in the Universe are chains of superclusters that are separated by huge empty voids.

How many galaxies are there in the Universe?

We don't know. Every time astronomers look into the Universe they discover more galaxies. Some parts of the Universe have not been looked at yet, and there are other parts that telescopes cannot see. The best estimate by astronomers is that there are at least 125 billion galaxies out there.

WHAT'S IN A NAME?

Galaxy comes from the Greek name for the galaxy we live in – the Milky Way Galaxy – and has its origins in the Greek word for milk.

Colliding in space

Adjacent galaxies are typically ten galaxy diameters apart. But galaxies can collide – as this picture of galaxies NGC 6050 and IC 1179 shows.

Common shapes

Spiral galaxy
A disc-shaped galaxy with a central bulge and arms spiralling away from it.

Barred spiral galaxy
A spiral galaxy with a straight bar of stars that runs through the centre, like the Milky Way.

Elliptical galaxy
A collection of old stars that can be shaped like a ball, egg, or cigar.

Lenticular galaxy
This is a lens-shaped galaxy that seems to bridge the gap between ellipticals and spirals.

Irregular galaxy
It cannot be classed into any group due to no regular shape, yet it is rich in gas and dust.

Black holes

singularity

Jets: Particles of disc material are shot out of the hole

Disc: A vortex of hot gas forms around hole

✳ A black hole is a region of incredibly powerful gravity that drags matter towards it and squeezes it into a tiny space or point, which is called a singularity.

✳ They are called "black" because the light that is sucked in cannot get out.

✳ You get black holes when massive stars explode. These explosions are called supernovas.

✳ You also get black holes at the centre of active galaxies, where their mass is equivalent to millions of Suns.

FAST FACTS

Galaxies

01: Galaxies are huge star systems, made of stars and large amounts of gas and dust.

02: They come in a range of sizes and shapes consisting of millions, billions, or even trillions of stars.

03: Some, known as active galaxies, have unexpected amounts of energy that come from star material falling into a black hole.

04: Other galaxies are transformed by galactic collisions.

Galaxy gallery

The vast spinning collections of stars, gas, and dust that make up a galaxy can look truly spectacular. Some galaxies are named after the earthly objects they resemble.

Sombrero Galaxy

Black Eye Galaxy

Cigar Galaxy

Cartwheel Galaxy

Blasts from the past

1784
William Herschel estimates the size and shape of the Milky Way. He wrongly thinks we are at its centre

1917
Observations made with the 2.5-m (8.2-ft) Hooker Telescope on Mount Wilson, California, show that the Andromeda Nebula is a galaxy – the first known to exist apart from the Milky Way

1920
Harlow Shapley discovers that the Sun is two-thirds of the way out from the centre of the Milky Way

1924
Edwin Hubble proves there are other galaxies in the Universe, and later develops a classification scheme based on shape and structure. He also shows the Universe is expanding. The more distant the galaxy, the faster it is moving away

1985
Vera Rubin finds that many galaxies contain dark matter

Orion Arm

Central bar: Arms of stars spiral out from both ends

Disc: Contains arms of younger stars

01. From above
If we could see the Milky Way from above it would look like a big glowing swirl. Our Solar System lies on the Orion Arm.

02. From the side
A side view reveals that the Milky Way is a flat disc 100,000 light years wide and 4,000 light years deep. At the centre, but hidden from view, is a black hole 3 million times more massive than the Sun.

03. From Earth
From Earth, we can look into the plane of the Milky Way disc. We see this as a glowing band across the night sky. There are about 200–500 billion stars in the Milky Way.

Apart from the Milky Way, three galaxies are easily **seen with the naked eye** from Earth – Andromeda, the Large Magellanic Cloud, and the Small Magellanic Cloud.

I don't believe it !

Two irregular galaxies, the Small and Large Magellanic Clouds, orbit the Milky Way. Our galaxy has already pulled material from them. In time they may be torn apart and be incorporated into the Milky Way.

What's in our Solar System

Apart from the planets, the Solar System contains countless objects hurtling through space.

- 1 Sun
- 4 rocky planets
- 4 giant planets
- at least 5 dwarf planets
- more than 160 moons
- billions of asteroids
- thousands of Kuiper Belt Objects and trillions of comets, way beyond Neptune

Pluto
Earth
Mars
Venus
Saturn
Uranus
Ceres
asteroid belt
Jupiter
Mercury
Neptune
Eris

Are all stars the same?

No, every star is unique. With the exception of the Sun, stars are all so far away from Earth that they appear as pinpoints of twinkling light to us. But even though they may look the same to the naked eye, they all have their own characteristics, differing in size, temperature, colour, and brightness, depending on how old they are.

In numbers

45,000°C
(80,000°F) The temperature of the hottest stars

2,500°C
(4,500°F) The temperature of the coolest stars

6 million
How many times more light is produced by the most luminous stars than by the Sun

10 billion
How many years the oldest stars can live

How to: form a star

01. You will need perfect star forming conditions – vast clouds of mainly hydrogen, helium, and dust.

02. Collapse fragments of the cloud and shrink them to form protostars – the first stage of a star's life.

03. Start nuclear reactions in the star's core so that it is able to shine steadily.

STAR LIFE
A star's mass – the amount of material it is made of – determines how long it is going to live; the greater the mass, the shorter the life.

RECORD BREAKER
All stars spin, but some spin much faster than others. The **fastest star** of all is a neutron star identified as XTE J1739-285, which spins around at a head-turning 1,122 times a second.

Closest stars to the Sun

Proxima Centauri

name	distance (light years)
Proxima Centauri	4.2
Alpha Centauri A	4.3
Alpha Centauri B	4.3
Barnard's Star	5.9
Wolf 359	7.8
Lalande 21185	8.3
Sirius A	8.6
Sirius B	8.6

Five brightest **night-time stars**

How bright a star appears in Earth's sky depends not only on how much light it produces – its luminosity – but also on its distance from Earth.

Sirius
Distance:
8.6 light years
Brightness scale
-1.44

Canopus
Distance:
313 light years
Brightness scale
-0.62

Rigil Kentaurus
Distance:
4.3 light years
Brightness scale
-0.28

Arcturus
Distance:
37 light years
Brightness scale
-0.05

Vega
Distance:
25 light years
Brightness scale
0.03

Stellar stunners

Despite their name, planetary nebulae actually have nothing to do with planets or star-forming nebulae, but are mature stars whose outer layers of gas have been pushed out to create a spectacular ring of colour around the white-dwarf remains of the original star.

Failed star

Brown dwarfs are stars that aren't massive enough to start nuclear reactions in their core. Therefore these stars don't shine but are instead a dark reddish brown.

BRIGHTNESS
The brightness of a star seen from Earth is described according to a scale of numbers. The smaller the number, the brighter the star. Those with a value of 6 or below can be seen by the naked eye.

Ant Nebula

Cat's Eye Nebula

Eskimo Nebula

Helix Nebula

04. End the life of your massive star with an explosion, leaving behind a supernova remnant, neutron star, or black hole.

Exoplanets

The Sun is not the only star with planets orbiting around it; more than 330 planets have been identified beyond the Solar System, with new ones being found all the time.

The first exoplanet (planet outside the Solar System) was discovered in 1992.

Exoplanets found so far are mostly Jupiter-like worlds – massive, giant planets.

For a planet to support life it is thought that it needs to be at a distance from the star where the temperature is right for liquid water to exist.

Three ways to search for life in the Universe

01 The Allen Telescope Array in the USA is a group of 42 radio-telescope dishes working as a giant ear listening out for signals from extraterrestrial life.

02 Anyone can take part in the Search for Extraterrestrial Intelligence (SETI) by running a screensaver on their computer that looks for data patterns from the Allen Telescope.

03 In 2015, a spacecraft called *Darwin* will be launched to look for Earth-like planets. Onboard telescopes will then analyze light from the planets for signs of gases that might have been produced by living things.

Will the Sun shine for ever?

The Sun is a star – a vast sphere of luminous gas. Its light is a by-product of gas-fuelled nuclear reactions in its core. It shines steadily now, but in about five billion years it will swell up before dying as a cold, dark cinder in space.

Tell me more: the Sun's surface

Flares: These are massive bursts of energy that explode in the Sun's lower atmosphere

Spicules: Short-lived jets of gas shoot out from the surface

Prominences: Sometimes giant clouds of gas loop out hundreds of thousands of kilometres

Photosphere: The Sun's visible surface looks bumpy here due to hot gas rising up from inside the star

Faculae: The hottest areas, called faculae, look almost white and are highly active regions created by the Sun's magnetic field

I don't believe it !

The Sun is 332,945 times more massive than Earth, and 750 times more massive than all of the planets in the Solar System put together.

In numbers

1.3 million
How many Earths could fit inside the Sun

600 million
The number of tonnes of the gas hydrogen converted to helium every second in the core of the Sun

220 km/sec
(137 miles/sec) The speed at which the Sun is moving around our galaxy's centre

220 million
The number of years it takes the Sun to orbit our galaxy once

Studying the Sun

Watching from space...
Spacecraft have observed the Sun since the 1960s. The Solar and Heliospheric Observatory, SOHO, has been watching it continuously since 1995.

... and underground!
Sudbury Observatory in Canada lies 2,073 m (6,800 ft) underground. From it, scientists detect particles from the centre of the Sun that are travelling through Earth.

WEIRD OR WHAT?

The Sun's gravity pulls gas inwards, but the pressure of the gas at the centre pushes outwards. The two forces balance to give the Sun its ball shape.

Night lights

01: Material streams from the Sun's corona (outer layer) and is known as **solar wind**.

02: Solar wind travels towards Earth at about **450 km/sec** (280 miles/sec).

03: The wind causes gas particles above Earth's polar regions to glow and give colourful light displays called **auroras**.

Tell me more: the Sun

About 75 per cent of the Sun is hydrogen, most of the rest is helium.

The Sun is about 4.28 light years from its nearest starry neighbour, Proxima Centauri.

The Sun is about 5 billion years old. That's a lot of candles!

It is about 1.4 million km (870,000 miles) across.

Eight planets orbit around the Sun – only about 4 per cent of the stars in the sky have planets.

Blasts from the past

434 BCE
Greek philosopher Anaxagoras suggests the Sun is a fiery stone about a quarter the size of Greece

270 BCE
The first attempt to measure the Sun's distance is made by Greek astronomer Aristarchus of Samos. He thinks it is 31 times closer than it actually is

1609
Italian astronomer Galileo Galilei realizes that the Sun takes about a month to rotate

1842
French photographer Noël Paymal Lerebours takes the first photograph of the Sun

1869
Englishman Norman Lockyer observes the Sun and discovers a chemical element he calls helium after Helios – the Greek Sun god

How to: watch a total solar eclipse

01. Using an eclipse viewer, observe the Moon passing directly in front of the Sun – a rare occurrence not to be missed!

02. Observe the Moon looking like a dark disc, covering more and more of the Sun's face and slowly day seems to turn to night.

03. "Totality" occurs when the Moon covers the Sun's face completely, revealing its corona, and lasts 3–4 minutes.

04. As the Moon continues on its path, watch the Sun come back into view. The sky brightens and distant stars become invisible again.

05. The eclipse is almost over; only a fraction of the Sun remains covered, and the shadow cast on Earth by the Moon has all but gone.

Six layers of the Sun

01. Corona: The outer atmosphere, seen during an eclipse

02. Chromosphere: The inner atmosphere

03. Photosphere: The visible surface of the Sun from which energy is released in a blaze of light

04. Convective zone: The layer through which the Sun's energy travels outwards through the Sun by "convection"

05. Radiative zone: The layer through which energy travels outwards from the core as radiation

06. Core: The centre of the Sun where nuclear reactions convert hydrogen to helium, producing energy

What about me?

You should never, ever, look directly at the Sun. It emits dangerous radiation that can damage cells at the back of your eyes and cause blindness.

Hot, hot, hot

How hot is the Sun?
It depends where you put your thermometer…
Corona: 2 million°C (3.6 million°F)
Transition region (between chromosphere and corona):
20,000°C (36,000°F) to 1 million°C (1.8 million°F)
Chromosphere: from bottom to top, 4,500°C (8,100°F)
to 20,000°C (36,000°F)
Photosphere: 5,500°C (9,900°F)
Core: 15 million°C (27 million°F)

Why does the Moon change shape?

The Moon is a large ball of rock that doesn't change shape – it just looks as though it does. The shape we see in the sky today depends on how much of the Moon's face is lit up. Sometimes we observe a thin crescent, and at other times we see half or three quarters of the Moon, and then a fully lit face – a Full Moon.

Lunar cycle

The view we have of the Moon changes according to the relative positions of the Sun, Earth, and Moon. A complete cycle of shapes, known as phases, takes 29.5 days.

New Moon   Crescent   First quarter   Waxing gibbous   Full Moon   Waning gibbous   Last quarter   Crescent

Blasts from the past

1546
John Heywood suggests the Moon is made of "green cheese". But not the colour green – by "green" he means fresh and un-matured

1609
Englishman Thomas Harriot is the first to look at the Moon through a telescope. A few months later Galileo sees lunar mountains, and he estimates their heights by the length of the shadows they cast

1969
On 20 July, Neil Armstrong is the first person to walk on the Moon. Buzz Aldrin (pictured below) follows 19 minutes later

Tell me more: how the Moon was formed

Most astronomers think that the Moon was formed out of Earth about 4.5 billion years ago. It is known as the giant-impact theory.

01: A Mars-sized asteroid collides into Earth at a speed of 20 km per sec (12 miles per sec).

02: Smashed asteroid pieces and material gouged out of Earth's rocky mantle form a ring around Earth.

03: Over several million years, the pieces of orbiting material bump into each other and join together.

04: They form one large body – the Moon. About a quarter the size of Earth, it slowly moves out to its present orbit.

WHAT'S IN A NAME?

A new mineral discovered on the lunar surface by the *Apollo 11* crew in 1969 was named in their honour. **Armalcolite** takes letters from their names: Armstrong, Aldrin, and Collins.

I don't believe it!

In 1835, six articles in the *New York Sun* newspaper described bat-winged human-like creatures seen on the Moon through a telescope. Amazingly, the stories were believed for several weeks.

There's so little gas in the Moon's atmosphere that the amount was doubled when the *Apollo* craft used its rocket motors to land on the surface.

01: The pull of Earth's gravity keeps the Moon in orbit.

02: The Moon's surface gravity is about one-sixth of Earth's.

03: The Moon's gravity pulls on Earth's oceans to produce tides.

04: The "far side" of the Moon we don't see was first imaged in 1959 by the Soviet spacecraft, *Luna 3*.

05: The Moon reflects light like a very dirty mirror. Although the Full Moon looks bright, it is 400,000 times dimmer than the Sun.

06: The Moon is 400 times smaller than the Sun, but as it is 400 times closer they look the same size.

07: The Moon's surface temperature changes every Moon-day from hotter than boiling water to colder than liquid air.

Astronauts' footprints will stay visible for about a million years. They are slowly being worn away by dust particles, mainly from decaying comets that hit the Moon and produce tiny craters. This process is called "lunar gardening" as gradually the lunar soil is turned over.

Top eight places to visit on the Moon

01: *Apollo 12 landing site* A short walk away from the spacecraft, *Surveyor 3*.

02: **Mare Orientale Crater** A huge crater surrounded by mountains.

03: **Crater Linné** Changes in this area have lead it, at one time, to disappear from view.

04: *Apollo 15 landing site* Hadley Rill, the first Lunar Rover, is still parked there.

05: **Highland, Tycho Crater** The oldest part of the Moon – who knows what is buried deep below!

06: *Apollo 11 landing site* Look out for Neil Armstrong's footprints, the first made on the Moon.

07: **Lunar domes, Hortensius Crater** Volcano domes that in the distant past sent lava over the Moon's surface.

08: **Mons Piton** A strange, isolated mountain, rising 2.3 km (1.4 miles).

In numbers

384,400 km
(238,855 miles) The distance between the Moon and Earth

60
How many hours it takes a spacecraft from Earth to reach the Moon

27.32
The number of days it takes the Moon to spin once on its axis, and also to orbit the Earth. This means the same side of the Moon always points towards Earth

3.82 cm
(1.5 in) The annual increase in distance between Earth and the Moon

0.18
How many milliseconds longer a day on Earth becomes every century as the distance between Earth and the Moon grows

Moon rock

○ More than 2,000 samples of rock, sand, and dust were brought back by the six *Apollo* crews that walked on the Moon between 1969 and 1972.

◉ Samples were also collected and brought to Earth by three robotic craft sent by the Soviet Union (1970–1976).

● More than 50 pieces of Moon rock have blasted off the Moon's surface by asteroid impact, and then landed on Earth as meteorites.

Are there other planets like Earth?

No, we don't know of any other planets exactly like Earth, with its unique life forms. But Earth has similarities to three other planets orbiting the Sun – Mercury, Venus, and Mars. All four are made of rock and metal, orbit close to the Sun, and have relatively hot surfaces. They are known as the terrestrial or rocky planets.

Swift Mercury

- Mercury is named after the Roman messenger to the gods because of its speedy movement.

- It is the smallest planet – Earth is 2.5 times bigger.

- It is also the densest planet, with a huge iron core.

- The temperature on Mercury ranges from 430°C (800°F) in the day to -180°C (-290°F) at night.

- The planet has a dark, dusty, surface, covered with craters and unchanged for a billion years.

Lost in space?

If you could be zapped onto any of the rocky planets, which should you choose?

Mercury: If you arrive at night, you will freeze to death, if you arrive during the day, you will be toast.

Venus: Difficult to know if you will dissolve in the sulphuric acid clouds before you are cooked by the heat.

Earth: Be prepared to swim in case you land in water. If you come across other living things, check if they look friendly or hungry and either smile or run.

Mars: If you have your own oxygen supply, and land in the warmest regions, you might be fine for a while, but the violent winds and dust storms are unbearable.

Rocky planets

01: The rocky planets were formed about 4.56 billion years ago from a vast cloud of gas and dust that produced the Sun and other bodies in the Solar System.

02: Material close to the Sun clumped together, eventually producing four large balls – the rocky planets.

03: The metal sank to the planets' cores and the lighter rock moved to the surface.

04: Over time, the planets cooled and their different surfaces were formed by meteorite bombardment, volcanic activity, water, and movements in their crusts.

FAST FACTS

Vital statistics

Mercury
Diameter: 4,875 km (3,029 miles)
Distance from Sun: 57.9 million km (36 million miles)
Rotation: 59 days
Orbit of the Sun: 88 days

Venus
Diameter: 12,104 km (7,521 miles)
Distance from Sun: 108.2 million km (67.2 million miles)
Rotation: 243 days
Orbit of the Sun: 224.7 days

Earth
Diameter: 12,756 km (7,926 miles)
Distance from Sun: 149.6 million km (93 million miles)
Rotation: 23.93 hours
Orbit of the Sun: 365.26 days

Mars
Diameter: 6,780 km (4,213 miles)
Distance from Sun: 227.9 million km (141.6 million miles)
Rotation: 24.63 hours
Orbit of the Sun: 687 days

Life on Earth

 Earth is the only place in the Universe where life is known.

It is home to 1.5 million distinct forms of life and more are being discovered all the time.

Earth is just far enough away from the Sun for liquid water and life to exist. If it were any closer, Earth would be too hot, any further away, and it would be too cold.

More than 70 per cent of Earth is covered in water. If the planet was perfectly smooth its surface would be covered with a layer 2.8 km (1.7 miles) deep.

Earth has just the right temperature for its water to be liquid. Mercury and Venus are too hot, and their water has evaporated. Most of Mars' water is frozen beneath its surface.

What about me?

Venus is the easiest planet to see in Earth's sky. Look out for it in the east just before sunrise and in the west just after sunset. It looks like a brilliant star, and is nicknamed the "morning star" and "evening star".

I don't believe it!

A Venusian day is longer than a Venusian year. Venus is the slowest spinner of all the planets, taking 243 days to spin once. But as it spins it travels on its orbit around the Sun once every 224.7 days. The time between one sunrise and the next is 117 Earth days.

Venusian volcanoes

Venus has hundreds of volcanoes and about 85 per cent of the planet is covered in volcanic lava. The biggest are shallow shield volcanoes, like those in Hawaii on Earth.

name	height	diameter
Maat Mons	8 km (5 miles)	395 km (245 miles)
Gula Mons	3 km (2 miles)	276 km (171 miles)
Sif Mons	2 km (1.2 miles)	200 km (124 miles)
Sapas Mons	1.5 km (1 mile)	217 km (135 miles)

Cloudy Venus

01: Venus is named after the Roman goddess of love and beauty.

02: It is surrounded by dense clouds stretching up to 80 km (50 miles) above the surface.

03: The clouds are made of dilute sulphuric acid droplets and reflect 80 per cent of the sunlight, making Venus overcast.

04: Heat is trapped by the clouds in the same way glass traps heat in a greenhouse.

Martian myths

In the 1870s, an Italian astronomer was mistranslated, which led people to believe he had seen canals on Mars built by Martians.

When a radio version of the H G Wells book *War of the Worlds* was broadcast in 1938, listeners panicked because they thought they had tuned into a news alert and that Martians had landed on Earth.

Photographs taken by spacecraft in 1976 seemed to show a 3.2-km- (2-mile-) long human face on Mars' surface. It later proved to be a huge rock formation.

About 50 years ago, astronomers studying Mars' moon Phobos concluded it was artificial – a metal hollow sphere made by Martians.

Red surface: Mars is named after the Roman god of war because of its blood-like colour

Ascraeus Mons: A giant shield volcano

Atmosphere: This is 95 per cent carbon dioxide

Valles Marineris: This is a complex system of canyons more than 4,000 km (2,500 miles) long and on average 8 km (5 miles) deep

Olympus Mons is the **largest volcano** on Mars, and in the Solar System. It is 24 km (15 miles) high and 648 km (403 miles) across.

I don't believe it!

Just over 100 years ago, a large money prize was offered for the first person to communicate with an extraterrestrial. Mars was excluded from the competition, because it was thought that getting in touch with Martians would be too easy.

Which planet is the biggest?

Jupiter is the biggest and is truly giant. It is large enough for 11 Earths to fit across its face and 1,300 to fit inside it. There are four giant planets in our Solar System. The next biggest is Saturn, followed by Uranus, and Neptune. They are also known as "gas giants" because of their colourful, ice-cold gas atmospheres.

I don't believe it!

Jupiter is shrinking. When it was young it was five times its present size. It is cooling and getting smaller by about 2 cm (0.8 in) a year.

Giant planet structure

01: Temperature and density increase towards the centre of the giant planets. This affects the physical state of the material the planets are made up of.

02: In Jupiter and Saturn, squashed gases become fluid and more like liquids. Deeper still, the gases are like molten metal.

03: In the heart of all four giants are round cores of rocky and metallic material.

04: All four giant planets have rings. They look solid from a distance but are made of individual pieces that follow their own orbits around their planet.

Jupiter

Diameter: 142,984 km (88,846 miles)
Distance from Sun: 778.3 million km (483.6 million miles)
Rotation: 9.9 hours
Orbit of the Sun: 11.9 years

Saturn

Diameter: 120,536 km (74,898 miles)
Distance from Sun: 1.43 billion km (888 million miles)
Rotation: 10.7 hours
Orbit of the Sun: 29.5 years

Uranus

Diameter: 51,118 km (31,763 miles)
Distance from Sun: 2.87 billion km (1.78 billion miles)
Rotation: 17.3 hours
Orbit of the Sun: 84.0 years

Neptune

Diameter: 49,532 km (30,760 miles)
Distance from Sun: 4.5 billion km (2.8 billion miles)
Rotation: 16.1 hours
Orbit of the Sun: 164.8 years

Jupiter is named after the king of the Roman gods and ruler of the heavens.

Tell me more: Jupiter

Clouds: Jupiter's stripes are clouds in its violent atmosphere. They are pulled into bands parallel to the equator by the planet's fast spin

Zones: White bands of cool rising air

WEIRD OR WHAT?

Jupiter has a powerful **magnetic field** – it is as if there is a large bar magnet inside the planet. It's the strongest field of any planet – about 20,000 times more forceful than Earth's.

Belts: Red-brown bands of warmer, falling air

Ringed world

● As Saturn orbits the Sun, its rings can be seen from different angles.

● The rings are made of particles and chunks of dirty ice in orbit around the planet.

● The pieces range in size from dust grains to large boulders several metres across.

● The pieces are also very reflective. The rings shine brightly and are easy to see.

Tell me more: Saturn

○ Saturn is named after the father of the Roman god Jupiter.

○ The first to see Saturn's rings was Italian astronomer Galileo Galilei in 1610. He thought they were handle-like ears fixed to the sides of the planet.

○ None of the gas giants are perfect spheres. They are all oblate (squashed balls). Saturn's diameter is almost one-tenth bigger at its equator than at its poles.

Rings: Saturn has seven main rings and hundreds of smaller ringlets

I don't believe it!

Saturn is the least dense of all the planets – if you could put it in a bath of water, it would float.

Spots: Giant weather storms

Uranus

● Uranus is named after the father of the Roman god Saturn.

● Uranus became the seventh planet in the Solar System, and the first to be discovered by telescope when it was unexpectedly spotted by astronomer William Herschel on 13 March 1781.

● Uranus rolls around its orbit on its side. The planet is tilted over by 98 degrees, possibly as a result of a collision with a large asteroid when it was young.

● Like the other three gas giants, Uranus's atmosphere is mostly hydrogen. It also contains methane, which absorbs red light and makes the planet blue.

Neptune

● Neptune is named after the Roman god of the sea.

● It's the fourth largest of the gas giants.

● Neptune is about 30 times further from the Sun than Earth.

● It is the coldest giant, -200°C (-320°F) at its cloud tops, and has the fastest winds of any planet, reaching speeds up to 2,160 kph (1,340 mph) near its equator.

I don't believe it!

Neptune was only discovered on 23 September 1846. Although it had been noticed many times before, astronomers thought it was a star.

Great Red Spot: This weather storm is bigger than Earth. It rotates anticlockwise every 6–7 days, and has been raging for more than 300 years

What is a dwarf planet?

Astronomers are constantly discovering new objects that they need to describe. In 2006, they decided on a new class – dwarf planets. These are small, almost round bodies that orbit the Sun in a belt of other objects. The Solar System is also full of other small bodies, including moons that orbit planets, asteroids, Kuiper Belt Objects that form a flattened belt beyond Neptune, and comets.

STREAKERS

Meteors occur in the sky every night. They are fleeting streaks of light caused by **comet dust particles** travelling through Earth's atmosphere. They are best spotted during one of the 20 or so annual meteor showers.

Dwarf planets

At present we know of five dwarf planets – four in the Kuiper Belt, and Ceres in the Main Belt of asteroids between Mars and Jupiter.

dwarf planet	discovery date	moons
Eris	2005	1
Pluto	**1930**	**3**
Haumea	2005	2
Makemake	**2005**	**0**
Ceres	1801	0

Impact craters

Most extraterrestrial bodies heading for Earth are broken up as they pass through the atmosphere, but sometimes big objects, or parts of them, survive and crash onto the surface as meteorites, gouging out vast craters. The five largest impact craters include the Manicouagan Crater, seen here from space.

I don't believe it!

Jupiter's biggest moon, Ganymede, and Saturn's biggest moon, Titan, are both larger than the planet Mercury.

name	location	diameter	age (years)
Vredefort	South Africa	300 km (185 miles)	more than 2 billion
Sudbury	Canada	250 km (155 miles)	1.85 billion
Chicxulub	Mexico	170 km (105 miles)	65 million
Popigai	Russia	100 km (60 miles)	35.7 million
Manicouagan	Canada	100 km (60 miles)	214 million

From out of the sky

- Rocks from space sometimes make it to Earth and are known as meteorites.
- Most come from asteroids but some originate from the Moon and Mars.
- About 3,000 meteorites weighing more than 1 kg (2 lb) land on Earth every year – most fall into the oceans.
- More than 22,500 meteorites have been collected and catalogued.
- The largest meteorite ever found landed in Hoba West, Namibia in 1920. It weighed 66 tonnes.
- There are three main types of meteorite:

stony   **iron**   **stony-iron**

Mysterious moons

Miranda
This is the smallest of Uranus's five major moons. Its rugged surface is covered with huge canyons.

Io
This moon of Jupiter is covered in active volcanoes that are constantly renewing its surface.

Titan
The largest of Saturn's moons, it is the only planetary moon to have a thick atmosphere.

Phobos
Mars has two tiny moons. Phobos, the largest, which is 27 km (17 miles) across, and Deimos.

Planets and their moons

planet	number of moons
Mercury	0
Venus	0
Earth	1
Mars	2
Jupiter	at least 63
Saturn	at least 60
Uranus	27
Neptune	13

Top 10 biggest moons

	name	diameter	parent planet
01:	Ganymede	5,260 km (3,270 miles)	Jupiter
02:	Titan	5,150 km (3,200 miles)	Saturn
03:	Callisto	4,820 km (3,000 miles)	Jupiter
04:	Io	3,640 km (2,260 miles)	Jupiter
05:	Moon	3,480 km (2,160 miles)	Earth
06:	Europa	3,120 km (1,940 miles)	Jupiter
07:	Triton	2,710 km (1,680 miles)	Neptune
08:	Titania	1,580 km (980 miles)	Uranus
09:	Rhea	1,530 km (950 miles)	Saturn
10:	Oberon	1,520 km (945 miles)	Uranus

Asteroids

01: Asteroids are remains of a rocky planet that failed to form between Mars and Jupiter 4.5 billion years ago.

02: The remains did not stick together but smashed into each other.

03: These rocky and metallic objects were scattered throughout the Solar System crashing into planets.

04: Eventually, a belt of rocky bits, known as the Main Belt, settled between Mars and Jupiter, plus a small number of asteroids on other orbits around the Sun.

05: Some asteroids, known as near-Earth asteroids, travel close to the Earth and have the potential to hit it.

Tell me more: comet anatomy

Cool comets

Comets are huge dirty snowballs left over from when the giant planets formed.

Their paths take them in all directions as they orbit around the Sun.

There are trillions of comets. They make a vast sphere, called the Oort Cloud, which surrounds the planetary part of the Solar System.

Some comets have left the Oort Cloud and now orbit in the inner Solar System returning again and again to the Earth's sky.

1 Nucleus: The heart of the comet is an irregular-shaped ball of snow and dust covered in a thin crust of dust.

2 Coma: As the comet moves close to the Sun it forms a huge head of gas and dust.

3 Gas tail: The Sun's heat turns the nucleus snow to gas, which flows out as a blue tail.

4 Dust tail: Dust released from the nucleus trails away from the coma as a white tail.

Kuiper Belt

★ The Kuiper Belt is a flat belt of comet-like bodies beyond Neptune, which stretches from 6 to 12 billion km (3.7 to 7.4 billion miles) from the Sun.

★ More than 1,000 Kuiper Belt Objects are known and it is suspected at least 70,000 more than 100 km (60 miles) across are awaiting discovery.

★ Four known dwarf planets exist in the belt, and at least 200 more are expected to be found.

★ Most objects in the Kuiper Belt take more than 250 years to orbit the Sun.

How many constellations are there?

There are 88 constellations in the night sky. Each one is a straight-edged area of sky that includes a pattern made from bright stars, and they all fit together like pieces of a jigsaw to make up the entire sky around Earth.

celestial equator   Earth   ecliptic (the Sun's path)

Tell me more: **the celestial sphere**

★ Ancient astronomers imagined the night sky as a giant sphere of stars rotating around the Earth.

★ The idea of a celestial sphere is still used to describe a star's position.

★ The sphere is divided into the 88 constellations.

★ The outline of the Orion constellation (left) is shown in orange.

Who's who in the sky

The Compass

PYXIS

θ κ
λ δ γ
ζ
τ○ α
β

🗣 Thirteen constellations feature humans. Twelve come from Greek mythology, and the thirteenth is Native American.

🐇 **The 15 animal constellations include a bull and a wolf.**

🐦 The eight birds include a peacock and a toucan.

🦀 **A crab, a dolphin, and a sea monster are amongst nine water-based constellations.**

🕐 Twenty-eight objects include a harp, a compass, a cross, a clock, and a microscope.

🪰 **The remaining 15 are a miscellany, from a fly to mythical creatures.**

Far, far away

The stars in a particular pattern only appear close together in space. In fact, the stars are totally unrelated and at vastly differing distances from Earth.

How to: **spot Orion**

01. Face the horizon. Hold out your arm with hand outstretched. Orion is a little bigger than your hand. If you are in the southern hemisphere, Orion appears upside down.

02. Look for a row of three bright stars very close together in the sky. This is his belt.

03. At equal distance, one above and one below the belt, are two bright stars. The brightest, with a warm red glow, is Betelgeuse. The whiter star is Rigel.

Orion

21 75
69
ξ ν
μ α
Betelgeuse
Orion

2 χ
χ
λ φ¹
φ²
γ
32
Bellatrix
ω ν 23
ψ ρ
56 π⁶ π⁵
51 δ
M78 ε 22
NGC 2024 31
IC 434 σ η
M 42
κ 29 τ β
Rigel

15 11
o¹
o²
π¹
π²
ORION
π³
π⁴

Large Dog

CANIS MAJOR
θ
μ
NGC γ
2360 α
ι Sirius
ν³
π ν²
15
M41
UW NGC o² o¹ ξ¹
2362 ξ
27 ω δ
σ Adhara
η ε
ζ
κ λ

Blasts from the past

2000 BCE The first constellations are devised by Sumerians and Babylonians

150 CE Greek astronomer Ptolemy lists 48 constellations

1596–1603 Twelve constellations are introduced by Dutch navigators Peter Keyser and Frederick de Houtman

1690 Seven new constellations complete the northern sky

1754 Fourteen constellations are introduced by French astronomer Nicolaus de Lacaille to complete the southern sky

1922 The 88 constellation patterns are sanctioned by the International Astronomical Union

1930 The constellations' straight-edge official boundaries are agreed

I don't believe it!

The star patterns aren't going to last for ever, but neither are they going to change any time soon. All stars are moving at about 50–100 km (30–60 miles) a second, but we can hardly tell because they are so far away. Constellation stars are typically 100 light years away, and so it takes us about 10,000 years before we start to notice a star's changing position.

The biggest constellation is **Hydra**, a water snake that meanders its way across 3.16 per cent of the whole sky. The smallest constellation is **Crux**, the southern cross, which is also the brightest constellation.

WEIRD OR WHAT?

The strangest constellation has got to be a **head of hair**. Its official name is **Coma Berenices**, because it is named for the hair of Berenice, the Queen of Egypt.

Great Bear

Bear necessities

01 There are **two bears** in the sky, **Ursa Major** (Great Bear) and **Ursa Minor** (Little Bear). They are both found in northern hemisphere skies.

02 One of the most famous stars of all is **Polaris**, the **Pole Star**, at the tip of Ursa Minor's tail. It lies above Earth's North Pole.

03 No one knows why both bears are given long tails, as real bears have short stubby tails.

The Zodiac

🌀 Twelve constellations form the backdrop to the Sun's path across the stars. Together they are known as the Zodiac.

☀ The Sun completes one circuit of the Zodiac in a year, taking about a month to pass through each constellation.

⚖ The word "Zodiac" comes from the Greek for animal and, with one exception, is a circle of creatures. Libra, the scales, was introduced long after the others.

Aries — Taurus — Gemini — Cancer — Leo — Virgo — Libra — Scorpio — Sagittarius — Capricorn — Aquarius — Pisces

CANIS MINOR
Procyon α γ ε β 6

Small Dog

Starry dogs

🐕 There are four dogs in the sky. Two make the constellation **Canes Venatici**, the hunting dogs. The other two are Orion's hunting dogs, **Canis Major** (Large Dog) and **Canis Minor** (Small Dog).

🐕 The star **Sirius**, in **Canis Major**, is the brightest star in the sky. It is sometimes called the **Dog Star**.

🐕 The ancient Greeks and Romans called the hottest days of summer "the dog days" because these were the days when Sirius rose in the sky as the Sun set.

🐕 Sirius is, in fact, a double star. Its companion, Sirius B, is fondly known as "the pup".

Dutch artist Vincent van Gogh shows the Plough in his painting *Starry Night Over the Rhône.*

URSA MAJOR
THE PLOUGH
M82 24 ρ σ π² τ 23 ο υ α Dubhe φ 18 θ 15 26 ι κ
M81
M108 Merak 36 β
M109 Phad M97 γ χ ψ 56 λ ω μ 55 ν ξ
M101 Alcor 78 δ Alioth
83 ζ Mizar ε
Alkaid η

One of the best-known patterns in the night sky, **the Plough**, is not a constellation but a star pattern known as an **asterism**. The seven stars are part of **Ursa Major**, the Great Bear.

How does a telescope "see" in the dark?

A telescope is a light bucket. It collects light from the objects in space using either a lens or, more usually, a mirror. A main mirror reflects the light to a smaller one, which brings the light to a focus where an image of the object is formed.

Types of telescopes

Refracting telescope
Uses a large lens to refract, or bend, the light to form an image of a distant object

Reflecting telescope
Uses a large curved mirror to pick up the faint light from distant stars

Radio telescope
Captures invisible radio waves given out by stars and other objects in space

Space telescope
Controlled by engineers on the ground, orbits Earth and works 24 hours a day

Tell me more:
inside an observatory

Prime focus: The astronomer originally sat here but today the view is recorded on to a computer

Mount: Horseshoe-shaped mount supports telescope and turns it to point to a particular part of the sky

Dome: The aluminium and steel dome rotates and opens so the telescope can look at different parts of the sky

Torch light: In this time-lapse image, the light is somebody walking around with a torch

Base: Telescope is mounted on a crushed granite base in case of an earthquake

In numbers

34
The number of telescopes at The Kitt Peak National Observatory, Arizona, USA, and the Mauna Kea Observatory in Hawaii

24.5 m
(80 ft) The diameter of the mirror in the Giant Magellan Telescope, in Las Campanas, Chile, scheduled for completion in 2017. It will be the biggest telescope ever

36
The number of separate hexagonal pieces, each 1.8 m (6 ft) across, which make up the mirror in each of the twin Keck telescopes at Mauna Kea, Hawaii, USA

Top five telescopes

name and location	main mirror diameter
Gran Telescopio Canarias La Palma Island, Spain	10.4 m (34.1 ft)
Keck I and Keck II Mauna Kea, Hawaii	10 m (32.8 ft)
Southern African Large Telescope South Africa	10 m (32.8 ft)
Hobby-Eberly Mount Fowlkes, Texas, USA	9.2 m (30.2 ft)
Large Binocular Telescope Mount Graham, Arizona, USA	8.4 m (27.6 ft)

WEIRD OR WHAT?

A batch of radio telescopes known as the Allen Telescope Array **listen out for signs of alien life**. Together they will survey a million stars for radio signals generated by extra-terrestrial intelligence.

Beyond vision

Stars don't just emit light but give off energy in a range of wavelengths. Different types of telescope detect different types of energy, which reveal a whole range of activity in the Universe.

Looking back

 Light travels at 300,000 km (186,000 miles) per second, so light from very distant objects takes a long time to reach us.

Light from the Sun takes 8.3 minutes to reach us.

Light from the nearest star after the Sun takes 4.28 years, so we say this star, Proxima Centauri, is 4.28 light years away.

The Andromeda Galaxy is 2.5 million light years away from Earth. This means we see the galaxy as it was 2.5 million years ago. We are looking back in time.

gamma ray image
gamma-ray burst

X-ray image
Bullet galaxy cluster

ultraviolet image
the Sun

visible light
Flame nebula

infrared image
Pinwheel galaxy

radio wave image
Whirlpool galaxy

1608
Flemish spectacle maker Hans Lippershey applies for a patent for his newly invented telescope

1609
Italian scientist Galileo Galilei makes a telescope out of a couple of spectacle lenses

1668
English scientist Isaac Newton invents a reflecting telescope that uses two mirrors instead of lenses

1838
German astronomer Friedrich Bessel uses a telescope to measure the distance to the star 61 Cygni – the first star distance measured after the Sun

1887
Lick Observatory, Mount Hamilton, California, becomes the first permanent mountaintop observatory

1919
The 2.5-m (8-ft) Hooker Telescope on Mount Wilson, California, shows that most nebulae are distant galaxies, and that the Universe is expanding

1962
Ariel 1 is launched. It is the first telescope put into orbit around Earth

What about me?

With the naked eye you can just about make out something 130 km (81 miles) across on the Moon's surface. The best Earth-based telescope can detect objects 1 km (0.6 miles) across.

The **largest single radio telescope** is the 305-m (1,000-ft) dish at Arecibo, Puerto Rico. Built in a hollow in the island's hills, it faces different parts of the sky as the Earth turns.

Working together

Some telescopes work together to produce a more detailed image. The Very Large Array in New Mexico, USA, consists of 27 radio dishes, each 25 m (82 ft) across.

● **The Hubble Space Telescope was launched into space on 24 April 1990, costing US$1.5 billion.**

● The 13.2-m- (43.5-ft-) long telescope orbits Earth every 97 minutes at an altitude of 569 km (353 miles), travelling at 8 km/sec (5 miles/sec).

● **Its main mirror collects light, which is directed to cameras and instruments. The data they record is sent to Earth about twice a day.**

● Hubble's replacement, the James Webb Space Telescope, will launch in 2013. It will be located 1.5 million km (930,000 miles) from Earth.

Observatories

01: The best observatory sites are high altitude desert regions close to the Equator.

02: They are usually about 80 km (50 miles) from a small town – near enough for supplies, but far enough away from light pollution.

03: They are in mountain locations, so clouds won't obscure the view.

04: Telescopes are placed high on the observatory building so they are not affected by the Earth's heat.

What is a space probe?

A space probe is the everyday name given to an unmanned spacecraft, and there are several types. Fly-by crafts travel past their target, orbiters fly around it, and landers touch-down on it, either standing still or releasing a rover to travel across its surface.

Sun watchers
The spacecrafts *Ulysses*, *SOHO*, and *Hinode* are all monitoring the activity of the Sun.

Planetary orbiters

Planet: Mercury
First orbiter: *Messenger*
Date into orbit: March 2011

Planet: Venus
First orbiter: *Venera 9*
Date into orbit: October 1975

Planet: Mars
First orbiter: *Mariner 9*
Date into orbit: November 1971

Planet: Jupiter
First orbiter: *Galileo*
Date into orbit: December 1995

Planet: Saturn
First orbiter: *Cassini*
Date into orbit: July 2004

Tell me more: spacecraft anatomy

A probe is a car- or bus-sized robot that is individually designed for a specific purpose. This is *Rosetta*, which will orbit a comet and travel with it as it journeys around the Sun.

Solar panels: Convert the Sun's energy into electrical energy to power the craft. The total wingspan is 32 m (105 ft)

Instruments: *Rosetta* carries 11 instruments. This one tests the comet's environment

Radiator: One in a series of radiators that prevent the craft from overheating

Antenna: The 2.2-m- (7 ft-) wide steerable antenna will send collected data to Earth

MIRO: The name of the microwave instrument that senses the sub-surface temperature of the comet's nucleus

Philae: Released by *Rosetta* to land on the comet's nucleus and drill into it for samples

Insulation: *Rosetta*'s body is covered with dark thermal insulation to keep its warmth when in the cold outer Solar System

RECORD BREAKER

The spacecraft *Helios 2* is the **fastest artificial object**. It studied the Sun in the late 1970s, whizzing around it at a staggering 68.75 km/sec (42.72 miles/sec).

I don't believe it!

In 1999, *Mars Climate Orbiter* moved into the wrong orbit around Mars and it was destroyed. The robot wasn't to blame; humans back on Earth had directed it using imperial measures rather than the metric units it was expecting.

Cassini-Huygens

01: After a seven-year voyage, *Cassini-Huygens* – the most expensive and one of the most sophisticated missions to date – arrived at Saturn in July 2004.

02: It used its 12 instruments to study Saturn and its moons.

03: Smaller *Huygens*, hitching a ride with *Cassini*, parachuted to the surface of Titan, which is Saturn's largest moon.

04: The whole mission cost US$3.26 billion. The United States contributed US$2.6 billion, the European Space Agency US$500 million, and Italy gave US$160 million.

05: A DVD on *Cassini* contains signatures from 616,420 people from 81 nations.

06: The signatures of the astronomers Jean Cassini and Christiaan Huygens, whose names the craft bear, were taken from manuscripts and included in the DVD.

Fly-by tour

The twin *Voyager* craft, which between 1979 and 1989 investigated all four giant planets and 48 of their moons, are together the two most outstanding fly-by missions. They both flew by Jupiter and Saturn; *Voyager 2* continued on past Uranus, then Neptune, and remains the only craft to visit these two planets.

Space debris

An enormous amount of spacecraft debris is orbiting Earth, from whole derelict crafts and pieces of rocket, to flecks of paint.

There are 17,000 or so chunks floating around larger than 10 cm (4 in).

More than 200,000 pieces are between 1 and 10 cm (0.4 in and 4 in).

Millions of pieces are smaller than 1 cm (0.5 in).

Most debris is within 2,000 km (1,243 miles) of the Earth's surface.

Where are they now?

Unlike astronauts, robotic craft do not have to return home once their work is done. Many "dead" probes still orbit targets or remain where they landed.

After eight years studying Jupiter and its moons, *Galileo* was deliberately put on a collision course with Jupiter. In September 2003, the craft disintegrated in the planet's atmosphere.

Surveyor 3 (*pictured*) landed on the Moon in 1967. Two years later Charles Conrad and Alan Bean walked from their *Apollo 12* module to *Surveyor 3* and took away a camera, soil scoop, and other bits of the craft for return to Earth.

NEAR-Shoemaker, the first craft to land on an asteroid, is still there. It was not originally meant to be there, as it was built only to orbit the asteroid.

RECORD BREAKER

Voyager I is more than 16 billion km (10 billion miles) away – **further from Earth than any other spacecraft**. What's more, it is more than 100 times further from the Sun than Earth.

First landers

Roving robots

Moving landers – commonly called rovers – have worked on the Moon and Mars.

Lunokhod 1
The first rover to any Solar System body, from 17 November 1970 it explored the Moon for about 10 months. Cameras allowed scientists on Earth to direct it.

Sojourner
The first rover to a planet was a microwave-oven sized buggy. It was carried to Mars by the landing craft *Pathfinder* and worked for almost three months in 1997.

Spirit and Opportunity
Identical crafts that arrived on opposite sides of Mars in January 2004. Five years later, these robot geologists continue to roll across Mars at a speed of 5 cm/sec (2 in/sec).

Sample return

Occasionally, a robotic mission returns from space with a sample of a celestial body, such as:

 moon soil and rock

 solar wind particles

 comet particles

How many humans have been into space?

About 500 people from nearly 40 nations have travelled into space. However, only three countries have launched astronauts into space – Russia, the United States, and China. The Moon is the farthest destination that any human has been in space.

Where did they go?

- Most astronauts have travelled only as far as a few hundred kilometres above Earth.

- The first astronauts were launched inside a capsule. They sat in the nose part of a rocket. Once above the ground, the rocket fell away, and the astronauts inside the capsule began their orbit of Earth.

- Today, astronauts are launched by rocket or space shuttle, and the majority are delivered to the International Space Station (ISS).

- Twenty-six astronauts have travelled to the Moon and back, and 12 of these have walked on the surface of the Moon.

Like father, like son

Russian **Alexander Volkov** first flew into space in 1985. His son, **Sergei Volkov**, followed in his footsteps when he flew to the International Space Station in April 2008.

RECORD BREAKER

On 11 March 2001, US astronauts Susan Helms and Jim Voss spent 8 hours 56 minutes working outside the International Space Station, the **longest period of extra vehicular activity** to date.

How to: fix the Hubble Space Telescope

01. Get suited up, then pick up the new telescope part and your tools for fixing it in place.

02. With your feet and back attached to the space shuttle's robotic arm, move yourself into position.

03. A second astronaut attached to a tether uses a screwdriver to remove an old part.

04. Use your helmet light to see as you install the new part. Helmet cameras record every move.

05. Job done. Once you are both back inside the space shuttle, release the telescope into its orbit.

Five space firsts

Yuri Gagarin
The Russian astronaut was the first human in space. He travelled once around Earth in *Vostok 1* on 12 April 1961 in 108 minutes.

Valentina Tereshkova
On 16 June 1963, the Russian became the first woman in space. She made 48 orbits of Earth in 71 hours.

Neil Armstrong
The first person to walk on the Moon, on 21 July 1969, said "That's one small step for man, one giant leap for mankind."

Alexei Leonov
On 18 March 1965, Leonov became the first person to spacewalk. Attached to a tether, he walked in space for a total of 10 minutes.

Dennis Tito
American Dennis Tito paid US$20 million to become the first space tourist on 28 April 2001. In seven days he orbited Earth 128 times.

The planetary geologist Eugene Shoemaker's dream of going to the Moon finally came true after he died, when his **ashes travelled to space** inside the *Lunar Prospector* spacecraft.

Astronaut wanted

The European Space Agency enrols candidates with the following attributes. When they last advertised, in June 2008, 8,413 people applied.

- **Age range:** 27 to 37
- **Height:** 153–190 cm (5ft 1in–6 ft 2 in)
- **Language:** Speak and read English
- **Education:** University degree or equivalent in science-based subject
- **Health:** Good, of normal weight, mentally sound
- **Personal qualities:** Good reasoning capability and memory, high motivation, flexibility, emotional stability, manual dexterity
- **Extra assets:** Flying experience, speak Russian

What about me?

Do you want to go into space? For US$200,000 you can book a seat on *SpaceShipOne* for a 100-km (62-mile) altitude, edge-of-space trip in 2010, to experience about six minutes of weightlessness.

Astronauts don't wash up after a meal but **clean up** with **wet and dry wipes**.

Fun and games

☞ Alan Shepard hit two golf balls on the Moon in 1971 using a club fashioned from lunar tools. His best shot sent the ball 366 m (1,200 ft).

☞ Greg Chamitoff (above) took a chess board to the ISS in 2008 and played long distance against the ground-based control centres. The centres in Russia, the United States, Japan, and Germany took it in turns to make a move.

☞ Since 1985, 50 different toys, including a skipping rope, yo-yo, marbles, and a boomerang have been used in space. They are part of a programme to educate children about weightlessness.

How space affects the human body

01: Nearly all astronauts experience space sickness soon after entering space. The symptoms, such as headaches, nausea, and vomiting, last for only a day or two.

02: Body fluids rise to your head and give you a head cold, stuffy nose, and puffy face.

03: Less fluid in the lower body results in a smaller leg circumference called "bird legs".

04: Calcium is lost from the bones and excreted in toilet waste. Decreased bone density can lead to fractures, but exercise on the treadmill helps to prevent this.

05: The heart shrinks because it does not have to work so hard in space.

06: Dust doesn't settle in space and hangs around in the air. It gets up astronauts' noses and they can sneeze more than 100 times a day!

WHAT'S IN A NAME?

The word **astronaut** comes from the Greek for "star" and "sailor", and it's used to describe all space travellers. Russian space travellers are called **cosmonauts**, and Chinese **taikonauts**.

Tell me more: space missions

Every space mission has an emblem, and these are often produced as embroidered patches. On manned missions the astronauts wear them on their suits. Here are the mission patches from some of the highlights in the story of space exploration. The many space shuttle flights are given STS (Space Transportation System) numbers.

1961 Mercury 3
First American astronaut in space

1965 Gemini 4
First American space walk

1975 Viking Mission
Two landers are launched to Mars

1978 Soyuz 31
The crew on this Russian mission includes the first German astronaut

1981 STS-1
First ever American shuttle mission

1982 Salyut 7
First French astronaut visits the Russian space station

1988 Buran
Only flight of the Russian space shuttle program

1989 STS-34
Launch of Galileo probe to Jupiter

1990 STS-31
Launch of Hubble Space Telescope

1990 STS-41
Launch of Ulysses probe to explore the polar regions of the Sun

1996 Mars Pathfinder
Launch of robotic rover to Mars

1998 STS-95
American John Glenn becomes the oldest astronaut in space at the age of 77

1999 STS-93
Launch of Chandra X-ray space telescope

2000 ISS Expedition 1
Launch of first crew to the International Space Station (ISS)

Space agencies
Astronauts and spacecraft also carry the emblem of their country's space agency.

NASDA: Japanese space agency

ESA: European space agency

MOA: Chinese space agency

1968 Apollo 8
The first manned mission
to orbit the Moon

1969 Apollo 11
First mission to land humans
on the Moon

1972 Apollo 17
Last mission to land humans
on the Moon

1975 Apollo-Soyuz
American and Russian
craft dock for the first time

1983 STS-8
Launch of an Indian satellite
into space

1984 Salyut 7
First Indian astronaut to the
Russian space station

1984 STS 41-B
First untethered space walk

1985 Spacelab 2
A European Space laboratory travels
on board the space shuttle

1991 STS-40
First laboratory dedicated to life
sciences taken into space

1991 STS-48
Launch of Upper Atmosphere
Research Satellite

1993 STS-61
First mission to repair the
Hubble Space Telescope

1995 Shuttle–Mir Program
Shuttle docks with the Russian
space station

2001 STS-100
Delivery of a Canadian
robotic arm to the ISS

2006 STS-115
Installation of solar panels
on the ISS

2008 STS-122
Delivery of European Columbus
Laboratory to the ISS

2008 STS-123
Delivery of the Japanese Kibo
Laboratory to the ISS

CNES: French space agency

PKA: Russian space agency

NASA: United States' space agency

astronauts do on a space station?

Astronauts stay for weeks or months at a time and spend their days carrying out scientific investigations, such as the effect of space on the human body and growing plants. They also maintain the station.

Blasts from the past

1971
Launch of the first space station, the Russian Salyut 1. Six more Salyuts follow, with Salyut 7 in orbit until 1991

Salyut 1

1973
America's first space station, Skylab, is launched

Skylab

1986
The construction in space of Russian space station Mir begins

Mir

1998
The first part of the International Space Station (ISS) is launched

FAST FACTS

International Space Station (ISS)

01: On 2 November 2000, the first crew moved into the ISS and stayed 138 days.

02: There has been a crew on board ever since – most stay for about six months.

03: There is a crew of three, but this will increase to six as the station grows.

04: The ISS is 108.5 m (356 ft) by 72.8 m (239 ft) – about the size of a football pitch.

05: The station orbits Earth at 28,000 kph (17,500 mph).

How to: **build a space station**

Robotic arm: Moves equipment and astronauts around outside the ISS

01. Get space scientists from across the world to design the station, then plan and build its different parts.

solar panels

Zarya module: Equipment is stored in this section

02. Launch the first module – a unit for astronauts to live in. Parts can be transported by Russian rocket or American space shuttle.

03. Take up more and more parts, one at a time, and assemble them in space.

In numbers

16
The number of countries collaborating on the ISS: 11 European Space Agency countries, USA, Russia, Canada, Japan, and Brazil

18
The number of major ISS components joined together in space to date

18,000
The number of meals that have been eaten on board the space station

WEIRD OR WHAT?

Astronauts aboard the space station witness sunrise about every 90 minutes as the craft orbits Earth, moving between the sunny and dark sides of the planet.

Day in the life of an astronaut

- Eat breakfast and do housekeeping tasks
- **Take blood sample for analysis and check day's schedule with Mission Control**
- Do air quality check and start work on allotted experiment
- **Exercise for two hours followed by lunch**
- Break, then maintenance and experiment work
- **Another hour of exercise**
- Finish work tasks, clean up experiments, and check the station's systems
- **Evening meal and conference to plan the next day**

Tell me more: staying in orbit

- A space station is kept in orbit by boosts from visiting craft.
- **Without boosts, the ISS loses about 90 m (300 ft) in altitude each day.**
- If abandoned, initially the station would continue to orbit, though its altitude would decrease.
- **Eventually, it would tumble to Earth, but most of it would break up and burn in the atmosphere.**
- Mir's descent was controlled so that in March 2001, several tonnes of material plunged into the Pacific Ocean.

04. Send out astronauts, secured to the robotic arm, to attach framework and other parts to the ISS.

Radiators:
These panels help control the temperature inside the space station

Zvezda module:
Here the crew eat and sleep

06. Once the station is complete you'll need to service it regularly to keep things working smoothly.

05. Add laboratory modules, where the astronauts can work, and solar panels to power the station.

The smallest room

For the first ten years there was only one toilet on the ISS, in the Russian-built Zvezda module. Hang on in there!

In May 2008 the toilet broke and a new pump had to be rushed from Russia to America, then delivered by space shuttle. This took two long weeks! While the toilet was out of action the crew used facilities in the Soyuz transport capsule.

A second toilet, costing US$19 million, was installed in the American side of the ISS in November 2008. Is this the most expensive toilet in the Universe?

Leg and thigh restraints keep the astronaut in position as fans suck waste away. Urine is collected through hoses attached to personalized funnels.

Russian cosmonaut **Valeri Poliakov** lived aboard Mir for a record breaking 437.7 days between January 1994 and March 1995.

What about me?
The ISS orbits Earth more than 15 times a day, and so regularly passes over where you live at a height of about 390 km (240 miles).

Earth

Do the continents really move?

Yes, the continents and oceans are constantly moving on the Earth's crust. More than 200 million years ago, the continents were joined in one huge land mass, but over millions of years this drifted and separated into the seven main continents we know today: Asia, Africa, Europe, Australia, Antarctica, North America, and South America.

How to: assemble the Earth

01. Take a large rocky ball as the base. Watch out as the surface is slowly moving, so when you place the pieces on it they won't stay still.

02. Sort out your crust. There are seven big pieces, and lots and lots of really fiddly small pieces. It will help if you know your geography!

Cocos plate

Scotia plate

Indian plate

Philippine plate

Caribbean plate

Nazca plate

North American plate

Antarctic plate

Pacific plate

South American plate

Arabian plate

Australian plate

Eurasian plate

In numbers

11%
The percentage of the Southern Hemisphere above water

65%
The percentage of land area that lies in the Northern Hemisphere

70 km
(43 miles) The maximum thickness of the continental (land) plates

99%
The percentage of Antarctica permanently under ice

Plates move between 2–20 cm (0.75–7.75 in) per year – the rate at which fingernails grow.

Land mass

The proportion of land per continent is:

- Asia 30 per cent
- Africa 20 per cent
- North America 16 per cent
- South America 12 per cent
- Antarctica 9 per cent
- Europe 7 per cent
- Australia 6 per cent

Tell me more: inside the Earth

Crust: There are two types – continental crust (land) and the thinner oceanic crust (sea floor)

Mantle: A thick layer of rock that begins between 5–70 km (3–45 miles) below the surface. Heat rising from the core keeps the mantle moving slowly

Outer core: At a depth of 5,150 km (3,200 miles), it is made of molten iron with a temperature in excess of 3,980°C (7,200°F)

Inner core: In the solid iron core the temperature reaches 4,700°C (8,500°F)

What's in a name?

Africa comes from the Latin name of the ancient Roman colony in northern Africa.

Australia comes from the Latin meaning "southern", as 18th-century explorers hoped to find a giant landmass in the southern oceans.

Europe may be named after princess Europa who appears in Ancient Greek mythology.

Antarctica comes from the Ancient Greek word *antarktikos*, which means "opposite of the north".

Asia is first mentioned by the Greek historian Herodotus writing about 440 BCE, who said it was named after the Lydian prince Asias. The word may have originally meant "land of the sunrise".

Blasts from the past

200 million years ago
Many of the continents are locked together in a landmass named Pangaea.

100 million years ago
Divergent plates begin to open up the Atlantic Ocean. South America drifts west, Antarctica heads for the South Pole, and India creeps towards Asia.

Today
India is in place after colliding with the Eurasian mainland. Greenland separates from North America, which has a land bridge with South America. Australia drifts in the Pacific Ocean.

I don't believe it!
The deeper down inside the Earth a tunnel goes, the hotter it becomes. The deepest gold mines in South Africa have to be cooled down artificially so that people are able to work in them.

Converge
At a convergent boundary two plates move together, forming mountain ranges.

Europe is only a continent for political reasons – geographically it should be part of Asia.

Diverge
You get a divergent boundary when two plates move apart. The huge gaps form the world's oceans.

Slide past
Where plates slide past one another, you get what is called a transform fault. They don't slide past smoothly and so you get earthquakes.

03.
Assemble the pieces around the ball. Be careful to fit the edges of the plates correctly – there are three main types of boundary.

African plate

Violent Earth

Exciting new imaging techniques mean that we can see where the continents are crashing into each other, ripping apart, and where new land is forming.

Pulling the ocean apart
Magma rising up into the gap created as the African plate moves east has formed a ridge of undersea mountains down the middle of the Atlantic Ocean.

Splitting from Africa
The Red Sea marks the split where Arabia is breaking away from Africa, and is growing wider all the time.

Crashing into Asia
The mountains of the Himalayas are the youngest mountains on Earth and are still rising as India crashes into the Eurasian plate.

Volcanic hotspot
The islands of Hawaii formed over a "hotspot" in the mantle. Unlike many volcanoes, those over hotspots form chains and are not on plate margins.

Looking through the **Earth's crust**

This cross-section through the crust along the Equator shows how the continents fit together, and the rises and falls of Earth's surface.

Sao Tome Principe | Mount Kenya | Sumatra | Java trench | Borneo | Indian plate | Caroline plate | Andes mountains | Amazon Basin | Mid-Atlantic Ridge

African Rift Valley

African plate | Indian plate | Eurasian plate | Pacific plate | Nazca plate | American plate | African plate

no land rise above the Pacific Ocean for thousands of kilometres

The five oceans

Pacific: 155.6 million sq km (96.6 million sq miles)

Atlantic: 82.4 million sq km (51.2 million sq miles)

Indian: 73.6 million sq km (45.7 million sq miles)

Southern: 20.3 million sq km (12.6 million sq miles)

Arctic: 14.1 million sq km (8.7 million sq miles)

How many oceans are there?

Earth is not nicknamed the "Blue Planet" for nothing – no other known planet is as watery. We divide this huge body of water into the Pacific, Atlantic, Indian, Arctic, and Southern oceans, but in reality, they are all connected as one vast ocean.

Tell me more: ocean water

≈ Salt
On average, each litre (2 pints) of water contains about 35 g (1.2 oz) of salt, although shallow, warmer seas are usually saltier.

≈ Light
Sunlight allows plants to grow underwater to a depth of about 200 m (655 ft). Below this, the waters get darker the deeper you get and plants cannot grow.

≈ Pressure
The deeper you go in the sea, the more pressure, or squeezing force, there is. The polystyrene cup on the right was the same size as the one on the left until attached to the outside of a deep-sea submersible and crushed by pressure.

≈ Temperature
The surface temperature of tropical seas is about 25°C (77°F), and in most other seas about 17°C (62°F) in summer and 10°C (50°F) in winter. The temperature at the bottom of the ocean is 2°C (36°F).

≈ Sound
Sound travels at a speed of 1,531 m (5,022 ft) per second under water – four times faster than it does in the air.

Five largest seas

01: **South China Sea**
2,974,600 sq km (1,848,300 sq miles)

02: **Caribbean Sea**
2,515,900 sq km (1,563,300 sq miles)

03: **Mediterranean Sea**
2,510,000 sq km (1,559,600 sq miles)

04: **Bering Sea**
2,261,100 sq km (1,404,900 sq miles)

05: **Gulf of Mexico**
1,507,600 sq km (936,700 sq miles)

The **oceans affect climate** as water warms more slowly than land, and cools more slowly than land, so islands and the coasts of continents have cooler summers and warmer winters than inland areas.

I don't believe it!

An underwater mailbox, where divers can post special waterproof postcards, lies 10 m (33 ft) below the waves in Susami Bay, Japan. It's an official mailbox and is emptied every day.

How to: **find lunch in the ocean**

01. If you're feeling hungry, head for where currents lift nutrients from the ocean floor towards the surface.

02. Where there are nutrients you'll find tiny organisms called plankton, the first link in the food chain.

03. Wherever you find plankton, small fish such as sardines swarm to feed off them. Enjoy the feast!

04. A word of warning – large predators will be attracted by the fish, so make sure you don't end up as their lunch!

Ocean zones

Our oceans are divided into different zones, depending on their depth. From the sunlit zone to the deepest depths, a variety of marine life can be found.

Sunlit zone
Most sea animals live near the surface where there is lots of light. Fish live off plankton (microscopic plants and animals) and in turn they are eaten by larger predators.

Twilight zone
From 150 m (492 ft) to 1000 m (3,280 ft) is known as the twilight zone. Many creatures living here produce their own light and glow, either to attract prey or scare predators.

Deep ocean
Even at the greatest depths, 10 km (6 miles) below the surface, strange animals lurk on the dark sea floor waiting for dead things to fall from the waters above.

FAST FACTS

Seas
01: Seas have specific features and form part of a larger ocean.

02: They are shallower than oceans, with no major currents flowing through them.

03: Seas have salt water, but names can be confusing. One of the world's saltiest seas, the Dead Sea in Israel, is actually a lake because it is not connected to an ocean.

Extreme ocean

The tallest mountain on Earth is Mauna Kea, a volcano in Hawaii. At 10,205 m (33,480 ft), it is much taller than Mount Everest but most of it is underwater.

The ocean's deepest point is the Challenger Deep in the Mariana Trench, in the Pacific, at a depth of 11,034 m (36,200 ft).

In the deepest ocean trenches, springs of hot water, called black smokers (pictured), gush clouds of chemicals up to 400ºC (750ºF) from the seabed.

WHAT'S IN A NAME?
The word **ocean** comes from Oceanus, who in Greek mythology was the son of Uranus, god of the sky, and Gaea, goddess of the Earth. Oceanus was also the river they believed surrounded the flat Earth.

In numbers

-40°C
(-40°F) The average winter temperature of the Arctic Ocean

70%
The percentage of the Earth's surface covered by oceans and seas

97%
The percentage of the world's water in the oceans – 2 per cent is ice and 1 per cent is fresh water or water vapour in the atmosphere

30,000
The number of islands in the Pacific Ocean. Some are the peaks of underwater volcanoes

How do mountains grow?

Where the plates of Earth's crust crash into each other, land is pushed upwards, forming mountains. The Himalayas are the tallest mountains on Earth, and the youngest. They formed over the last 145 million years, as India crashed into Asia. Mountains are also formed when volcanoes erupt and molten rock builds up into steep mounds.

Four famous peaks

Kilimanjaro, Tanzania
At 5,895 m (19,340 ft), this extinct volcano is the tallest mountain that is not part of a mountain range.

Mount Fuji, Japan
Each year, more than 200,000 people climb 3,776 m (12,388 ft) to the top of the tallest mountain in Japan, also a sacred site.

Matterhorn, Switzerland
At 4,478 m (14,692 ft) high, it's not the tallest mountain in the Alps, but has a classic pyramid-shaped peak.

K2, Pakistan and China
The world's second highest mountain, at 8,611 m (28,253 ft), is said to be the trickiest mountain to climb.

The tallest mountains in every continent

Asia
▲ Mount Everest, Nepal and China
8,848 m (29,028 ft)

South America
▲ Aconcagua, Argentina
6,960 m (22,834 ft)

North America
▲ Mount McKinley, USA
6,194 m (20,320 ft)

Africa
▲ Mount Kilimanjaro, Tanzania
5,895 m (19,340 ft)

Europe
▲ Mount El'brus, Russia
5,642 m (18,510 ft)

Antarctica
▲ Vinson Massif
4,897 m (16,066 ft)

Australasia
▲ Puncak Jaya, New Guinea
5,040 m (16,535 ft)

WHAT'S IN A NAME?

There's no official **definition of a mountain**, though in most places mountains are more than 600 m (1,970 ft) high. Some so-called mountains may just be hills, but a mountain should be steep and have an obvious summit.

I don't believe it!

From the ground, mountains make the Earth's surface look very bumpy, but if the Earth was reduced to the size of a 1 m (3 ft) diameter ball, Mount Everest would be a pimple no more than 0.69 mm (0.03 in) high!

FAST FACTS

Avalanches

01: You rarely get avalanches (masses of snow rushing down mountains) where the slope is less than 25 degrees.

02: Slab avalanches are the most deadly and occur when a frozen slab of ice on the surface of the snow breaks off

03: When snow gets heavy because it's saturated with water you get what's known as an isothermal avalanche.

04: As an avalanche shoots down the slope it collects more snow. If it picks up lots of air with the snow it becomes what's called a powder snow avalanche. These are the largest avalanches and can reach speeds of 300 kph (190 mph).

Major mountain ranges

The world's longest mountain ranges usually follow the edges of the Earth's plates.

Aleutian Range
2,650 km (1,650 miles)

Himalayas
3,800 km (2,400 miles)

Tien Shan
2,250 km (1,400 miles)

Rocky Mountains
4,800 km (3,000 miles)

Central New Guinea Range
2,000 km (1,240 miles)

Andes
7,200 km (4,500 miles)

Brazilian Atlantic Coast Range
3,000 km (1,900 miles)

West Sumatran-Javan Range
2,900 km (1,800 miles)

Great Dividing Range
3,600 km (2,240 miles)

RECORD BREAKER

The **tallest mountain** on Earth is Mauna Kea in Hawaii, which rises 10,205 m (33,480 ft) from its base on the seabed to its summit.

The **longest mountain range** on Earth is the mid-Atlantic ridge, which runs for nearly 16,000 km (10,000 miles) below the Atlantic Ocean.

Tell me more: mountain zones

As you climb up a mountain the average air temperature drops by about 1°C (1.8°F) for every 200 m (650 ft). There is also less oxygen in the air the higher you go. As a result, mountains can be divided into distinct habitat zones.

The top: High mountain peaks are harsh environments, of either bare rock or snow, where little if anything will grow.

High altitude: Above the tree line only specially adapted mountain species, such as Alpine ibex, can survive.

Mid altitude: Foothills are often covered by forests, but these end at a "tree line", beyond which it is too cold and dry for trees to grow.

Five crazy mountain sports

Paragliding
Leap off a mountain harnessed to a fabric wing and soar down on the wind – it's probably the nearest you can get to flying.

Heliskiing
For the ultimate off-trail skiing, take a helicopter to the top of an isolated peak, jump off, and head downhill.

Canyoning
To scramble down a mountain along the path of a river you need to be a confident climber and swimmer.

Ice climbing
This is the sport of hacking your way up a steep wall of ice, such as a mountain icefall or frozen waterfall, using ice axes.

Climbing
There are many ways up a mountain, and some people choose the route up vertical faces and overhanging rocks.

Ten questions **you need to ask before you climb Everest**

01: Will I make the top?
Of the hundreds of people that attempt to climb Everest each year, only about 30 per cent succeed. The biggest problem is bad weather, which can trap climbers at Base Camp or force them to turn back.

02: Do I need to be fit?
Yes, the route to the summit at 8,848 m (29,028 ft) is over rock, snow, and ice. However, age is no barrier. The youngest to make it was Temba Tsheri, 15, the oldest was Bahadur Sherchan, 76, both from Nepal.

03: How long will it take?
It's impossible to predict, but, from Base Camp, four days up and four days down is reasonable. The fastest ascent was by Italian Hans Kammerlander, who got to the top in 16 hours and 45 minutes in 1996.

04: What should I take?
What you take up, you must bring down, so take only the bare essentials. There's an estimated 50 tonnes of rubbish on Mount Everest, made up of equipment and supplies left behind – much of it at Base Camp.

05: Will it be cold?
The temperature at the summit averages -36°C (-33°F), but can drop as low as -60°C (-76°F). This can freeze the skin, causing frostbite. Toes are the first to suffer, so warm socks are essential.

06: What is snow blindness?

This is when snow reflects the Sun's rays and it burns the back of the eyes so you can't see. Sun goggles are essential. They absorb the harmful UV rays.

07: What is altitude sickness?

Above 3,660 m (12,000 ft), oxygen levels drop by 40 per cent and most climbers gasp for breath. To avoid serious symptoms they need to breathe oxygen from cylinders.

08: Is the climb risky?

Yes, to date, the mountain has claimed 210 lives. Photographer and climber Bruce Herrod fell and died on Everest in 1996. The picture of him above, was developed from his camera, found a year later.

09: What's the Death Zone?

This is the region above 8,000 m (26,246 ft), where there is only half the normal level of oxygen. Even with an oxygen supply, the body starts to shut down and the slightest exertion takes tremendous effort.

10: What's at the top?

From the top of the world you get a unique view over the Himalayas of Tibet, India, and Nepal. You can see for more than 160 km (100 miles) and even make out the curvature of the Earth's surface.

What happens when a volcano erupts?

A volcano erupts when hot molten rock from deep inside the Earth bursts out of the ground. Rivers of liquid rock, called lava, flow down the side of the volcano burning trees, houses, and anything else in their paths. An exploding volcano may also fling out ash, mud, and poisonous gases. Volcanoes are not just destructive, however, and often create new mountains and islands.

Inside a volcano

Beneath an active volcano lies a chamber of hot molten rock, called magma. The magma is less dense than the solid rock around it, so rises to the surface through cracks or fissures and a main outlet, called a vent. Magma that contains a lot of dissolved gases will explode at the surface, throwing ash and rocks, known as bombs, into the air. Sometimes, burning gas and ash, known as a pyroclastic flow, pour down the sides. Magma that contains very little gas flows more slowly.

spreading ash cloud

erupting volcanic vent

volcanic bombs

pyroclastic flow

In numbers

1200°C
(2192°F) The top temperature of the rivers of basalt lava that flow from Hawaiian volcanoes – 12 times hotter than a boiling kettle

200
The number of megatons of energy released when Krakatoa erupted in 1883 – the same as 15,000 nuclear bombs

550
The number of volcanoes that have erupted on Earth's surface since records began – about 60 are active each year

90%
The percentage of volcanoes that lie along the Ring of Fire, a circle of volcanic activity around the edge of the Pacific Ocean, at the boundaries of the Earth's plates

Tell me more:
Kilauea volcano, Hawaii

Clouds of gas: Water vapour, carbon dioxide, and sulphur dioxide form clouds above the vent

Magma: Some of the molten rock hurled into the air forms "bombs"

Crater: Lava, cinders, and volcanic ash build a rocky but fragile ridge around the vent

Burning river: Lava flows downhill at speeds of up to 100 kph (60 mph)

Red hot: Flowing lava has a temperature of about 1,000°C (1,832°F)

Cooling surface: A wrinkled or rough skin forms as lava cools

WHAT'S IN A NAME?

Volcanoes are named after **Vulcan**, the Roman god of fire and metalwork who was said to have had his workshop under Mount Vulcano, an island off the north coast of Sicily.

Types of volcano

Cinder cone
These are the smallest but most common type of volcano, such as Parícutin, Mexico, and are made up of loose volcanic rock from repeated eruptions.

Shield volcano
Runny lava spreads out as it flows from the volcano and, over time, layers of lava build to form a vast low mound, seen here at Puu Oo in Hawaii.

Stratovolcano
Large steep mountains, like Mount Fuji in Japan, are formed from layers of ash and lava from repeated eruptions.

Supervolcano
These vast volcanoes can cause a long-lasting change to weather, threaten the extinction of species, and cover huge areas with lava and ash.

Submarine volcano
Where volcanoes erupt beneath the seabed, the weight of water prevents big explosions, and pillow lava may form, seen here off the coast of Hawaii.

Four reasons to like volcanoes

01: Hot springs occur naturally around volcanoes. Known for their healing properties, these are enjoyed by people (and Japanese macaque monkeys)!

02: Geothermal power stations tap the energy from hot magma under the ground.

03: The mineral-rich ash that falls on the soil around volcanoes is ideal for growing crops.

04: Some volcanoes, such as Mount Fuji in Japan and Mount Kilimanjaro in Tanzania, have become sacred sites.

How to: live with an active volcano

01. Wear hard hats. Children living near Sakurajima volcano in Japan, must wear them to school to protect against flying debris.

02. Don't get too settled. If you live next to Mount Etna in Sicily, you need to be ready to evacuate.

03. Drive carefully. Lava flows on Hawaii don't obey road signs, and might appear around any corner.

04. Wear a mask. After the eruption of Merapi in Indonesia the air was filled with ash for days.

Six types of eruption

Hawaiian In this quiet, slow type of eruption, lava streams out of the vent and sometimes collects in great lakes.

Strombolian An eruption with frequent but small explosions releasing gas and sending lumps of lava whirling through the air.

Vulcanian A violent explosion where gas escapes from beneath a crust of lava, and forms a dense white cloud.

Vesuvian A huge cloud, thick with ash and gas shoots violently into the air and rises high over the volcano.

Plinian The most powerful type of eruption, as sticky lava explodes violently. Large Plinian eruptions, like that at Mount St Helens, USA, in 1980 (pictured) often have pyroclastic flows.

Peléan Highly destructive eruptions where a high-speed avalanche of gas, dust, ash, and burning lava fragments sweeps down the sides of the volcano.

magma chamber

magma filled cracks and fissures

Blasts from the past

c 1630 BCE
An eruption blows apart the island of Santorini, Greece, creating a tsunami (giant wave) that may be the origin of the legend of the submerged city of Atlantis

79 BCE
When Mount Vesuvius in Italy erupts, inhabitants of Pompeii are buried by a cloud of cinder and ash (pictured)

1783 CE
Deadly gases at the eruption of Laki, Iceland, poison 200,000 animals, and cause a famine that kills 9,000 people

1792
When part of Mount Unzen in Japan collapses, it causes a tsunami that kills more than 14,300

1815
The eruption of Tambora, Indonesia, is the biggest for 1,000 years and kills more than 90,000 people

1883
Krakatoa island, Indonesia, explodes, unleashing a tsunami that kills 36,000 and a cloud of dust that lowers the world's temperature by 1°C (1.8°F)

1985
Some 23,000 people die in Colombia when the eruption of the Ruiz volcano causes massive mudflows, which swamp the town of Armero, 70 km (44 miles) away

Why does the Earth quake?

The surface of the Earth is like a massive jigsaw puzzle made up of huge rocky pieces called tectonic plates. The pieces of this puzzle are constantly moving about very slowly, but with immense force. If they slide past or crash into each other the Earth shakes and quakes.

How to: **survive an earthquake**

In earthquake zones, such as California, USA, and Japan, school children regularly practise an earthquake drill. In California, children are taught to "Duck, Cover, and Hold".

01. As soon as you feel the earth shaking, duck or drop down to the floor.

02. Take cover under a desk or table and protect your head and neck with your arms.

03. Hold onto the desk, table, or furniture and move with it, if necessary. Remember to stay put until the shaking stops.

Warning signs?

Some people claim that you can predict an earthquake by spotting changes in some animals' behaviour in the days before an earthquake.

 Hens stop laying eggs

 Bees leave their hives

 Rats, weasels, and centipedes leave their homes in large numbers

Dogs bark or whine excessively

Flamingos abandon their low-lying breeding grounds

Mass migration of toads to safer ground

Most earthquakes occur at **depths of less than 80 km** (50 miles) below the Earth's surface.

Moonquake

It's not only the Earth that's shaking – there are quakes on the Moon, too. These "**moonquakes**" happen less often and are of smaller magnitude than those on Earth.

Cracks in the Earth

In some places you can clearly see the cracks, called faults, at the edges of the Earth's plates.

Thingvellir Rift, Iceland
These exposed fault lines show the rift that lies on the boundary separating the American and Eurasian plates.

San Andreas Fault, California, USA
This is a strike-slip fault, which indicates that the rocks move sideways and in opposite directions.

Great Alpine Fault, New Zealand
This fault line runs almost the entire length of New Zealand's South Island and is visible from space.

1755 Lisbon, Portugal
One of the worst earthquakes in history was followed by a tsunami and many fires.

1906 San Francisco, USA
Fires following this massive quake left 3,000 dead and 20,000 homeless.

1964 Alaska, USA
This powerful quake lasted nearly five minutes and was followed by a tsunami.

1995 Kobe, Japan
Lasting barely 20 seconds, this quake killed 6,400 people and caused US$200 billion in damage.

2003 Bam, Iran
The city's many mud-brick buildings were destroyed by this massive earthquake.

I don't believe it!

According to the United States Geological Survey, there are more than 3 million earthquakes every year. That's about 8,000 a day, or one every 11 seconds! Most of these are too weak to be noticed.

Tsunami
If an earthquake happens under water it can cause a tsunami – a series of **powerful and destructive ocean waves**. An earthquake in the Indian Ocean on **24 December 2004** triggered a series of tsunamis that **killed more than 225,000 people** in 11 countries.

Part of Indonesia's coastline before and after the 2004 tsunami

Most powerful earthquakes

- **Chile**
Date: **22 May 1960**
Richter measure: **9.5**
- **Prince William Sound, Alaska**
Date: **28 March 1964**
Richter measure: **9.2**
- **Indian Ocean**
Date: **26 December 2004**
Richter measure: **9.1**
- **Andreanof Islands, Aleutian Islands**
Date: **9 March 1957**
Richter measure: **9.1**
- **Kamchtka, Russia**
Date: **4 November 1952**
Richter measure: **9.0**

High rise buildings in California and Japan must be able to **withstand severe earthquakes**. Foundations are fitted with mechanical dampers, which act like the shock-absorbers used in cars.

Quake measures
Scientists measure earthquakes in two different ways – by its **magnitude** or its **intensity**. Magnitude means the power of the shock waves, and it's usually measured on the **Richter scale**. The **Modifed Mercalli Intensity scale** measures the effects of an earthquake.

The Richter scale

magnitude	description	effects
less than 2	micro	not felt
2–2.9	minor	generally not felt, but recorded
3–3.9	minor	often felt but damage rare
4–4.9	light	noticeable shaking of indoor items, rattling noises
5–5.9	moderate	can cause damage to poorly constructed buildings over small areas. At most, slight damage to well-designed buildings
6–6.9	strong	can be destructive in areas up to 160 km (100 miles) across
7–7.9	major	can cause damage over larger areas
8–8.9	great	can cause serious damage in areas several kilometres across
9–9.9	great	devastating in areas several thousand kilometres across
10+	epic	never recorded

Could the River Amazon ever run dry?

River Amazon

01: The water flows at an average speed of 2.4 kph (1.5 mph).

02: The mouth of the river is more than 320 km (200 miles) long.

03: Where the river meets the sea, it discharges 770 billion litres (170 billion gallons) of water an hour. This is enough to fill almost two million baths every second.

04: If you were 100 km (60 miles) from the mouth of the Amazon, way out in the Atlantic Ocean, you could still scoop a pan of fresh Amazon water.

05: There are about 2,500 species of fish in the Amazon – that's more than there are in the Atlantic Ocean.

06: There are no bridges over the Amazon.

No. The water that flows down the River Amazon in South America fell as snow or rain in a vast area known as a drainage basin. This drainage basin is the largest in the world and includes eight countries, covering an area three-quarters the size of the USA.

Nile knowledge

▲ The River Nile in north Africa has two sources. The longer White Nile flows from Lake Victoria in east Africa. It is joined at Khartoum, Egypt, by the Blue Nile, which has its source in the highlands of Ethiopia.

▲ Downstream, beyond Khartoum, the White Nile contributes just 16 per cent of the volume of the river's water, and the Blue Nile contributes the rest.

▲ The River Nile floods every year, when heavy summer rain and melting snow in the mountains of Ethiopia swell the river.

▲ Only 22 per cent of the Nile is in Egypt.

I don't believe it!

In winter, all 1,705 km (1,060 miles) of the MacKenzie River – Canada's longest – freezes.

RECORD BREAKER

The **world's shortest river** is the Rose River in Montana, USA. It is just 61 m (201 ft) long.

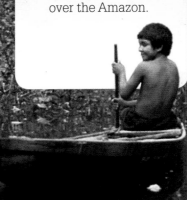

Top five longest rivers in the world

Nile (Africa)
6,695 km (4,160 miles)

Amazon (South America)
6,448 km (4,007 miles)

Yangtze (Asia)
6,378 km (3,964 miles)

Mississippi/Missouri (North America) 6,228 km (3,870 miles)

Ob (Asia)
5,570 km (3,460 miles)

Gorge

The Colorado River, USA, carved the steep-sided Grand Canyon. This gorge stretches more than 350 km (220 miles), and measures 29 km (18 miles) at it widest point.

Waterfall

The waterfall with the longest single drop is Angel Falls on the Carrao River, Venezuela. The water plunges 979 m (3,212 ft), with much of the water turning into mist as it falls.

Meander

The snaking pattern of a river forms when the moving water erodes on the outer of bends and deposits on the inner. This widens the valley, creating a looping, S-shaped curve in the river.

Delta

This is a flat plain where a river meets the sea. The world's largest is where the Ganges, Brahmaputra, and Meghna rivers of India and Bangladesh empty into the Bay of Bengal.

Top five largest lakes

01: Caspian Sea
central Asia
371,000 sq km
(143,000 sq miles)

02: Michigan/Huron
Canada/USA
117,436 sq km
(45,342 sq miles)

03: Superior
Canada/USA
82,103 sq km
(31,700 sq miles)

04: Victoria
east Africa
69,485 sq km
(26,828 sq miles)

05: Tanganyika
central-east Africa
32,893 sq km
(12,700 sq miles)

The **Caspian Sea** lake in central Asia was **once a sea**. It was cut off from the Mediterranean Sea when sea levels dropped during the last Ice Age, and is now **landlocked**. Unlike most lakes, it contains salty sea water.

FAST FACTS

Dams

01: About 15 per cent of the world's river water is held back by dams built to control flooding and generate hydroelectric power.

02: Almost one-fifth of the world's electricity is supplied by dams.

03: The Rogun Dam in Tajikistan is the highest in the world. At 335 m (1,099 ft) it is taller than the Statue of Liberty.

04: The largest dam in the world will be the Three Gorges Dam across the Yangtze River, China. It should be fully operational in 2011 and will be 2,335 m (7,661 ft) long and 101 m (331 ft) high.

Great lakes

Lake Titicaca (Peru and Bolivia)
Sitting on the edge of the Andes, Titicaca is 195 km (120 miles) long and about 80 km (50 miles) wide. Reeds that grow in its marshes are used to make boats.

Great Salt Lake (USA)
The water in this vast salt lake is about five times saltier than sea water. It has three major tributaries that fill the lake with minerals, and the rocky shores are covered with salt crystals.

Lake Manyara (Tanzania)
The water is inhabited by hippopotamuses, and the surrounding national park protects elephants and is famous for tree-climbing lions. The groundwater in the lake is saturated with minerals derived from volcanic rock.

Lake Eyre (Australia)
This salt lake is the lowest point on the Australian continent. It receives water from streams and is fed by erratic rainfall. It is thought to have once dried out completely, but has reached its present size following exceptionally heavy rain at the end of the 20th century.

River cities

Many great cities lie on rivers. Can you match the rivers with the right city? Watch out, one river passes through two major cities. You'll find the answers below.

CITY	RIVER
St Petersburg, Russia	Nile
Montreal, Canada	Tigris
Rome, Italy	Danube
Paris, France	River Plate
Shanghai, China	St Lawrence
Vienna, Austria	Tiber
New York City, USA	Neva
Ho Chi Minh City, Vietnam	Huangpu
Baghdad, Iraq	Vistula
Alexandria, Egypt	Seine
Warsaw, Poland	Saigon
Budapest, Hungary	Hudson
Buenos Aires, Argentina	

Lake Baikal in Russia is the **deepest lake in the world**, and dips to 1,741 m (5,712 ft) in parts. It is deep enough to **stack five Eiffel Towers** and still not break the surface.

ANSWERS: Nile – Alexandria, Tigris – Baghdad, Danube – Budapest and Vienna, River Plate – Buenos Aires, St Lawrence – Montreal, Tiber – Rome, Neva – St Petersburg, Huangpu – Shanghai, Vistula – Warsaw, Seine – Paris, Saigon – Ho Chi Minh City, Hudson – New York City

Rivers and lakes 050|051

How much ice is there on Earth?

About one-tenth of Earth's land surface is covered in ice. Built up over thousands of years, most ice occurs in thick ice sheets that cap the land at the North and South Poles. Ice also tops the peaks of high mountains, and rivers of ice called glaciers gouge deep valleys in polar and mountain regions.

Iceberg shapes

Blocky
Box-shaped with steep vertical sides

Tabular
Steep sides with a flat top, like a huge tablet

Dome
A very rounded and smooth top

Wedge
The top narrows to a pyramid-like point

Drydock
A U-shaped opening in the middle due to erosion

Pinnacle
One or more spires rise very high

Tell me more: icebergs

✳ Icebergs form, or "calve", when huge chunks of ice from glaciers and ice caps break off and fall into the ocean.

✳ Seven-eighths of an iceberg's mass is below water. The one-eighth you see is just the "tip of the iceberg".

❂ Just like ice cubes in your drink, icebergs float because the density of ice is less than water.

I don't believe it!

Sometimes when moving icebergs scrape past each other they produce a sound like barking dogs or screeching monkeys – but a lot louder! Some of these "icequakes" are as deafening as the tremors caused by a large earthquake.

Top 10 coldest places in the world

01: **Vostok, Antarctica:** -89°C (-129°F)

02: **Plateau, Antarctica:** -84°C (-119°F)

03: **Oymyakon, Russia:** -71°C (-96°F)

04: **Verkhoyank, Russia:** -68°C (-90°F)

05: **Northice, Greenland:** -66°C (-87°F)

06: **Eismitte, Greenland:** -65°C (-85°F)

07: **Snag Yukon, Canada:** -63°C (-81°F)

08: **Prospect Creek, Alaska, United States:** -62°C (-80°F)

09: **Fort Selkirk, Yukon, Canada:** -59°C (-74°F)

10: **Rogers Pass, Montana, United States:** -57°C (-70°F)

Oymyakon, **Russia**

airborne snow

snow (85–90% air)

Snow to ice

Snow falls to the ground and compresses into small, round ice particles called granular ice. As the ice compacts it contains less air and forms larger granules, known as "firn". With the pressure of further snow, the firn welds into solid, glacial ice, called "blue ice".

granular ice
(30–85% air)

firn
(20–30% air)

blue ice (less than 20% air)

In numbers

30 million cubic km

(7.2 million cubic miles) The volume of the largest piece of ice on Earth – the Antarctic ice sheet

70%

The percentage of fresh water frozen in the Antarctic ice sheet

4 km

(2.5 miles) The depth of the ice cap covering the South Pole

RECORD BREAKER

In 1953, the Kutiah Glacier in Pakistan set the record for the **fastest glacial surge**, covering more than 12 km (7 miles) in three months, and averaging a distance of 112 m (368 ft) per day.

Greenland

Despite its name, Greenland is mostly covered in a layer of ice averaging 1,790 m (5,900 ft) thick. A single glacier makes up most of this ice.

Five glacial features

Ice pinnacle
Large piece of ice that juts out from a glacier

Retreating glacier
Thinning of snow and ice on a glacier

Iceberg
Floating ice that has broken away

Crevasse
Vertical crack in the ice as a glacier moves

Meltwater cave
Cave formed by melted snow or ice

Tell me more: glacier anatomy

❋ A glacier is a huge, slow-moving river of ice.

❋ As a glacier moves downhill it carves steep-sided, U-shaped valleys.

❋ There are two main types of glaciers. Valley glaciers are streams of flowing ice that are confined within steep-walled valleys. Continental glaciers resemble huge chunks of ice and can cover a large part of a continent, like Antarctica.

Terminal moraine: Rock debris that forms at the end of a glacier

Glacial lake: Lake formed by a melting glacier

Outwash plain: Sand, gravel, and mud that has washed out from a glacier

Lateral moraine: Pile of rocks that forms alongside the glacier

Rock avalanche: Ground movement causes rocks to fall

Ice-fall: Glacier flows over a steep slope

Rock-fall: Fragments of loosened rock fall from the face of cliff

Cirque: Deep recess in a mountain with steep walls

Crevasse: Deep crack in a glacier caused by motion

Englacial debris: Rocks that were once carried along with a glacier

Medial moraine: Created when two glaciers meet

How dry is a **desert?**

The dry conditions in deserts occur due to the lack of rain and snow, which is usually less than 25 cm (9.8 in) in a year. The driest desert on Earth is the Atacama, Chile, where in many parts there has not been any rainfall in living memory.

Five things to do in deserts

Store planes
The Sonoran Desert in the United States is a graveyard for thousands of disused planes.

Run a race
In Alice Springs, Australia, people race in bottomless boats down a dry river-bed.

Harvest salt
A vast amount of salt is harvested in the Salar de Uyini desert in Bolivia, South America.

Test probes
NASA tested the *Viking* lander space probes in the Atacama desert, Chile.

Grow things
Large scale desert irrigation makes it possible to grow fruits and vegetables.

Tell me more: hot and cold places

■ **Hot deserts** are found close to the tropics, where the Sun's rays are strongest.

■ Hot deserts are **freezing at night** because there are no clouds to trap the Earth's heat.

■ **Cold deserts** have hot summers but extremely cold winters – in the Gobi desert, in Central Asia, temperatures can drop to -40°C (-40°F).

Top five largest deserts

01: **Sahara**
Northern Africa, 9,100,000 sq km (3,514,000 sq miles)

02: **Australian**
Australia, 3,400,000 sq km (1,313,000 sq miles)

03: **Arabian Peninusula**
Southwest Asia, 2,600,000 sq km (1,004,000 sq miles)

04: **Turkestan**
Central Asia, 1,900,000 sq km (734,000 sq miles)

05: **Gobi**
Central Asia, 1,300,000 sq km (502,000 sq miles)

How to: identify a desert

01. Check the rock features around you. They should be eroded by very strong winds and extreme temperatures.

02. Examine the terrain. It should be bleak – sand, rocks, and stones and, in polar deserts, snow.

03. Try to find surface water. No luck? That's a good sign you are in a desert.

Striking landmarks

Erg
Arabic word for an extensive area of sand dunes, such as those found in the Sahara.

Playa
An almost flat area in the centre of a basin in which lakes form periodically.

The mighty Sahara

The world's largest hot desert is the size of the USA and covers 11 North African countries.

- Algeria
- Chad
- **Egypt**
- Libya
- **Morocco**
- Mauritania
- **Mali**
- Niger
- **Sudan**
- Tunisia
- and **Western Sahara**

05. Look up. You should see clear blue skies with not a rain cloud in sight.

04. Make sure there is little or no vegetation – just tough desert plants.

Not everyone agrees that **Antarctica is a desert**, but it's certainly dry – some valleys here have **not had rain for 4 million years**. It is bigger than the Sahara, with an area of 13.7 million sq km (5.3 million sq miles).

Spooky desert names

- **Death Valley, USA**
  The country's hottest landscape is breathtaking

- **Takla Makan, China**
  Means "you can get in, but you'll never get out", also nicknamed "Sea of Death".

- **Skeleton Coast, Namibia**
  Named after the wrecks of ships, not people, that line the dunes where desert meets the sea.

- **The Empty Quarter, Saudi Arabia** An area of sand the size of France.

I don't believe it!

More people drown in deserts than die of thirst! When rain falls in a desert, it comes suddenly, and dried up river-beds can turn into surging rivers in just a few minutes.

Survival tips

Cover up
Wear light clothes and a hat to protect you from the Sun and insects, and to reduce evaporation of sweat.

Keep drinking
Dehydration (loss of water) and overheating are the greatest dangers.

Find some shade
Don't shelter inside a hot, stuffy vehicle, but in its cooler shadow.

Do not travel
Stay put in the heat of the day, and only travel at dusk or dawn.

Keep off the ground
Try not to sit or lie on the ground where it's hot, and where scorpions, spiders, and snakes may lurk.

Butte
A flat-topped hill with steep sides capped with a layer of resistant rocks.

Inselberg
An isolated hill with steep sides that stands out above the plains of the desert.

Arch
Stunning creation formed by whirling winds blasting at rock, and wearing it away.

Wadi
A steep-sided valley formed by a river in a semi-arid or arid desert region.

How many trees make a forest?

The definition of a forest varies around the world, but the main characteristics are the same – it is an region that is densely planted with tall trees, and covers a large area. More than 50 per cent of Earth's animal and plant species can be found here.

About 300 million people are born, live, and die in the world's forests, and 60 million of them are almost totally dependent on the forests to maintain their lifestyle.

The trees of the Amazon rainforest have their roots in nine different countries:

Brazil
Peru
Colombia
Venezuela
Ecuador
Bolivia
Guyana
Suriname
French Guiana

Tell me more: deforestation

The clearing away of trees, known as deforestation, affects our planet in a variety of ways.

🍁 It destroys forest habitats and kills the animals living there. Two-thirds of all species on Earth need forests for shelter or food.

🍁 The lower number of trees to convert carbon dioxide into oxygen contributes to global warming.

🍁 Trees give off water vapour, so the fewer trees there are, the less water there is in the atmosphere.

🍁 Without tree roots to hold the soil together, there is an increased chance of soil erosion, flooding, and landslides.

How to: reach the top of a rainforest

04. Arrive at the top, known as the emergent layer. Here the very tallest trees reach the sky, sometimes at a height of 70–80 m (230–262 ft) above ground.

03. Stop off at the canopy, where the tops of taller trees spread out to form a dense canopy that traps sunlight.

Types of forest

Rainforest
Lush tropical forests are found in hot regions with high rainfall, usually around the tropics of Cancer and Capricorn.

Tropical dry forest
Vegetation that can survive the long, parched months of a dry season grow in these forests.

Coniferous forest
Vast areas of coniferous forest stretch across the cold regions of North America, northern Europe, and Asia.

Temperate forest
In areas with distinct cool and warm seasons grow broadleaved trees that lose their leaves in the winter months.

In numbers

The Amazon rainforest contains an amazing variety of flora and fauna.

1 million
insect species

40,000
plant species

3,000
fish species

428
amphibian species

427
mammal species

378
reptile species

1,294
bird species

More than five million native Indians once lived in the Amazon rainforest, but now only about 200,000 remain.

01. Start in the damp, shady forest floor. In some forests, only two per cent of light reaches this area, which is covered in leaves and roots.

02. Climb up to about 15 m (50 ft) from the floor. You're now in the understory where small trees can branch out.

About 30 per cent of Earth's total land area is forested.

Forest fires

Fires can sweep through forests causing huge devastation to trees, plants, and animal life. However they can also help regenerate a habitat by clearing the area for new growth and leaving a layer of rich ash where new seeds will flourish. The main causes of forest fires are these:

⚡ **human activity or deliberate fire-starting (arson)**

⚡ **lightning**

⚡ **excessively hot and dry conditions help the fire spread**

Forested regions

USA: Many of the USA's forested areas are protected as national parks

Canada: Almost one million Canadians are involved in the country's forest industry

Russia: About 20 per cent of the world's forests can be found in the largest country on Earth

China: Forests in China grew by 1.2 per cent every year between 1990 and 2000, the highest growth rate in the world

Central Africa: This tropical rainforest is home to 11,000 plant species and more than 400 species of mammal

Brazil: The Amazon rainforest covers more than half of Brazil and is the largest remaining tropical rainforest on Earth

I don't believe it!

Stretching 112 m (367 ft) into the skies, a redwood sequoia tree in Montgomery State Reserve near Ukiah, California, USA, can claim to be the tallest tree. However, it is not the tallest tree in history. Two trees in Australia measured 143 m (470 ft) and 150 m (492 ft) before they died.

Not all rainforests are hot and steamy. The cool west coast of North America can get up to 350 cm (132 in) of rain each year, and here you find dense rainforests of giant conifers, such as redwoods covered with thick mosses.

Is a coral reef animal, vegetable, or mineral?

It's animal, vegetable, and mineral! A coral reef is a colony of millions of tiny animals called polyps. As they grow, each polyp produces a hard, limestone skeleton, on which the next generation of polyps grow. Corals also contain an algae, which is essential for their survival.

How to: grow a tropical coral reef

01. Choose a sea that is clear, well lit, and free of any pollutants.

02. Check the depth – a reef won't grow below 30 m (98 ft), because there's not enough sunlight.

03. The water must be just the right temperature – no colder than 21°C (70°F) and no warmer than 30°C (86°F).

04. The sea should be low in nutrients, otherwise algae thrive and the coral suffocates.

Scientists have discovered a **freaky stony coral** at depths of nearly 6,000 m (19,685 ft). Little is known about it but, unlike tropical coral, they live in total darkness.

Tell me more: inside a polyp

Tentacles: These catch food and push it into the cup-like mouth

mouth

Gut cavity: Tissue around the gut cavity lays down limestone on the rock below

Limestone skeleton: A hard coral skeleton builds up

Living coral looks like an upside-down jellyfish, with a tubular body and tentacles around its mouth. Tropical reef-building corals use their tentacles to catch plankton from the water.

Name the coral

There are two main types of coral – hard, stony corals that build reefs, and soft corals that don't. They often have very descriptive names – what do you think?

Brain coral
The wrinkled ridges of this hard coral make it look like a giant brain.

Fan coral
The polyps of fan coral link together to form a large lacy skeleton.

Dead-man's-fingers
The tentacles of these polyps look like decomposing fingers.

Staghorn coral
This antler-like coral is one of the speediest growers on the reef.

Why we need reefs

Although coral reefs cover less than 1 per cent of the Earth's surface, they are home to 25 per cent of all marine fish species.

Reef fish and molluscs feed between 30 and 40 million people every year. An estimated 500 million people rely on coral reefs for their food or livelihoods.

Chemical compounds found in reefs are used to make several important medicines.

Coral polyps turn the carbon dioxide in water into limestone. Without coral, the amount of carbon dioxide in the water would rise, destroying precious habitats.

Coral reefs form natural barriers that protect nearby shorelines from strong waves or currents.

Australia's Great Barrier Reef is home to...
500 species of coral
400 species of seaweed
1,000 species of sea sponge

175 species of bird

30 species of mammal

1,500 species of fish

Fringing reefs
These reefs follow the shorelines of continents and islands in tropical seas, and are found close to shore.

Barrier reefs
Lying further offshore, barrier reefs are separated from land by a deep lagoon.

Atoll reefs
A ring of coral that grows on top of a sunken volcano, forming a lagoon, is called an atoll.

Patch reefs
Patches of young coral commonly grow at the bottom of the sea in the lagoon behind a barrier or atoll reef.

Platform reefs
When coral reaches the surface of the sea and branches out, growing horizontally, a platform reef is formed.

I don't believe it!

Many corals on the Great Barrier Reef spawn (produce eggs) once a year. They all do it at exactly the same time – four to five days after the Full Moon in October or November – to create a spectacular "underwater snowstorm" as the sea is filled with eggs.

Great reefs of the world

01: The Great Barrier Reef, Australia
About 3,000 reefs combine to form the largest living structure on Earth, more than 2,010 km (1,250 miles) long.

02: Kwajalein, Marshall Islands
The world's largest atoll surrounds a lagoon 97 km (60 miles) long.

03: Bikini Island, South Pacific
In 1946, the bikini swimsuit was named after this atoll.

04: Lighthouse Reef, Belize
At the centre of this Caribbean atoll lies the Great Blue Hole, 145 m (480 ft) deep.

Threats to coral reefs

Global warming
If the temperature of the ocean rises, the algae in coral dies. This kills the coral, which is dependent on it.

Rising seas
Global warming is also causing sea levels to rise, which will have a dramatic effect on coral reefs.

Pollution
Reefs are damaged by pollution from untreated sewage, mining, fertilizers, pesticides, and oil spills.

Aquarium trade
Some fishermen in Indonesia and the Philippines use cyanide poison to stun fish. They then use crowbars to rip apart the coral to get at the fish.

Overfishing
The overfishing of sea urchins – the spiny predators of coral-eating starfish – leaves coral vulnerable.

Blasts from the past

500 million years ago
The world's first coral reefs appear

230 mya
Modern corals first develop in the Early Triassic era

199 mya
Mass extinction – two thirds of coral types are wiped out by climate change, at the end of the Triassic era

18 mya
The formation of Australia's Great Barrier Reef begins. Its growth will stop and start several times

18,000 years ago
Temperatures on the Earth fall and sea water becomes trapped as ice in enormous glaciers, causing sea levels to fall to their lowest levels ever. Any coral reefs exposed during this period die

10,000–8,000 years ago
The reefs we can see today begin to develop at the end of the last great Ice Age. Glaciers melt and sea levels rise to the position they are still at today

Why does the wind blow?

The Earth's weather is caused by the Sun heating the atmosphere, oceans, and Earth's surface. The hot air rises, and the cool air sinks and all this activity gets air moving across the globe. The Sun also evaporates water in lakes, rivers, and seas to make clouds and rain.

It takes about a million cloud droplets to make one raindrop.

Global warming

☼ Earth's climate is heating up faster than ever before.

☼ Most scientists believe this is due to a build-up of greenhouse gases in the atmosphere. These are gases produced by power stations, factories, and cars that trap heat around the Earth.

☼ If the polar ice caps melt on a large scale, sea levels will rise, putting at risk islands such as the Maldives, which lie only 1 m (3.2 ft) above sea level.

☼ Global warming may also cause more extreme weather, such as storms, droughts, and hurricanes.

WHAT'S IN A NAME?

Monsoon means "season" in Arabic, because the monsoon winds always bring **heavy rainfall** to southern Asia in the summer.

Stormy weather

Tropical storm
Cyclones, also known as hurricanes or typhoons, start at sea.

Sandstorm
In desert regions, winds often whip up sand and dust into thick clouds.

Ice storm
This occurs when half-frozen rain freezes in a thick layer on and around the ground.

Thunderstorm
Electricity in thunderclouds causes flashes of lightning and loud booms.

The water on our planet gets **used over and over** again. When your sweat evaporates, it comes back as rain about 10 days later! The raindrops falling on your head contain the same water that fell on the dinosaurs more than 65 million years ago.

I don't believe it!

In 1930, a German glider pilot got caught in a hailstorm and had to bail out. Tragically, he was sucked up into the storm and covered with heavy layers of ice to become a human hailstone, and fell 11 km (7 miles) to his death.

Weather black spots

Coldest
The coldest temperature ever was a brain-numbing -89.6°C (-123.8°F) recorded at Vostok Research Station, Antarctica on 21 July 1983.

Wettest
Cherrapunji in northeastern India receives an annual rainfall of 1,270 cm (500 in).

Windiest
Port Martin in Antarctica has an average wind speed of 174 kph (108 mph), but gusts can blow at speeds up to 320 kph (200 mph).

Most snow
Between 19 February 1971 and 18 February 1972, 31.1 m (102 ft) of snow fell on Mount Rainier, USA.

Four snowflake facts

01: All snowflakes have six sides, but each snowflake is unique.

02: In cold air, snowflakes tend to be needle-shaped, while in warmer air, they are star- or plate-shaped.

03: The largest snowflakes can be 5 cm (2 in) across.

04: The average snowflake falls at a speed of 5 kph (3 mph).

Tell me more: **tornadoes**

Dark skies: A tornado begins when air inside a thundercloud starts to spin

Funnel-shaped cloud: When the funnel of wind hits the ground, the tornado moves off across the countryside – it can reach speeds of up to 115 kph (70 mph)

Rising air: The whirling air spins faster and faster, sucking dust and objects as big as cars from the ground, and destroying everything in its path

Base of tornado: This usually measures less than 1 km (0.6 miles) across

Five ways to predict the weather

In the past, farmers and sailors used natural signs to predict the weather.

Hang a piece of dry seaweed up – when rain is on the way it will feel sticky.

Your hair is longer on a damp day because it takes in water from the air and expands!

Look out for the storm petrel, a sea bird that flies inshore when a storm is on its way.

Oak and maple trees have leaves that curl when the humidity is very high and the wind is blowing strongly, both signs that a storm is coming.

There's a saying that "when chairs squeak, it's about rain they speak," because wooden chairs absorb moisture from the air, causing them to squeak.

In numbers

6,000
The number of lightning flashes around the world each minute

21
The number of people killed by the same lightning bolt when it struck a hut in Zimbabwe in 1975

730
The average number of tornadoes each year in the USA, causing more than 100 deaths annually

44,000
The number of storms that can rumble over the Earth each day

190 km
(120 miles) The length of the longest lightning bolt ever recorded

Clouds

01: Clouds form when warm air rises.

02: High in the sky, invisible water vapour in the warm air cools and turns into water droplets.

03: High-level clouds float at 12,000 m (40,000 ft), while clouds that touch the ground create fog and mist.

04: An average cloud weighs as much as a jumbo jet, but luckily this weight is spread out over a large area!

Beaufort scale

Wind speeds are based on the Beaufort scale, which ranges from 0–12.

0 Calm Smoke rises vertically, the surface of the sea is like a mirror

1 Light air Smoke drifts in the wind, ripples are seen on the surface of water

2 Light breeze Wind is felt on face, leaves rustle, small wavelets produced

3 Gentle breeze Small twigs move, flags flutter, waves break

4 Moderate breeze Dust is raised, small branches move, small waves form

5 Fresh breeze Small trees begin to sway, waves form "white horses"

6 Strong Breeze Large branches move, large waves form

7 Near gale Whole trees move, sea whipped up to form white foam

8 Gale Twigs broken off trees, difficult to walk against the wind, waves are high

9 Severe gale Chimney-pots and slates fall, crests of waves topple

10 Storm Trees uprooted, damage to houses, sea white with foam

11 Violent storm Widespread damage, small ships hidden by waves

12 Hurricane Extensive damage, huge waves, air filled with foam and spray

What are rocks made of?

Every type of rock has its own "recipe" of one or more minerals. There are about 4,000 minerals found on Earth, each with its own unique shape and colour. Earth's rocks are like buried treasure – they are full of valuable minerals and contain metals, gemstones, fossils, and fuels, such as coal and gas.

Rocks

01: Earth started as a fiery mass of molten rock, but about 4 billion years ago the outer layer began to cool and form a hard crust.

02: There are many types of rocks, formed in three main ways.

03: Most igneous rocks appear on the surface as melted rock (magma) brought to the Earth's surface by volcanoes. When this cools, it crystallizes into solid rock.

04: Sedimentary rocks are made from loose rocks, and the ancient remains of animals and plants. Carried by wind and water, they compact and harden into solid rock over millions of years.

05: Metamorphic rocks are rocks that change when they are baked and crushed by the heat and pressure deep below the Earth's surface.

Tell me more: the rock cycle

Mountain top: Ice and snow in mountains create sediments

Erosion: Rivers create valleys and make sediments

Rivers: Carry sediment down to the sea

Igneous rocks: Formed by lava cooling at the surface

Sediment: Layers build up on the seabed

Sedimentary rock: Forms from compressed sediments

Magma: Heats and changes surrounding rocks into metamorphic rock

Metamorphic rock: Forms when sedimentary rocks are heated and crushed

Mineral ID

To identify a mineral you need to test for:

01 **Colour, lustre, and habit** The colour of a mineral's crystal, its surface shine (lustre), and the form (habit) of its crystals

02 **Streak** The colour of a streak left by the mineral when rubbed across a tile

03 **Cleavage** How the mineral breaks when hit with a hammer

04 **Hardness** Measured on the Mohs scale, from 1 (very soft) to 10 (very hard)

05 **Crystal system** The basic geometrical shape of the mineral's crystals

WHAT'S IN A NAME?

Scientists in the 19th century came up with the **Wrinkled Apple Theory** when they saw the folded rocks in some mountains. They thought the Earth's crust was wrinkling, like an old apple skin!

Crystal clear

Crystals are minerals that grow into regular shapes with smooth, flat faces and sharp edges.

A crystal's shape is known as its habit. Salt crystals are like tiny cubes, zircon crystals (used in jewellery) are like pyramids, while asbestos grows in long strands.

Millions of tiny crystals can cluster together to make a chunk of rock.

Given enough room, crystals can grow underground to an incredible length of 11 m (36 ft).

Five famous **rocks**

Uluru
In central Australia lies one of the world's largest single pieces of rock, 383 m (1,256 ft) high and 2 km (1.2 miles) long.

Ship Rock
The Ship Rock in New Mexico, USA, is a giant pillar of stone that rises 500 m (1,640 ft) out of the plain.

Mount Rushmore
Four American presidents' faces were carved out of a rock in South Dakota.

Sugar Loaf Mountain
The majestic Sugar Loaf Mountain in Rio de Janeiro, Brazil, rises to 396 m (1299 ft).

Delicate Arch
This 16-m- (53-ft-) high sandstone arch has worn away over time by weathering and erosion.

The size of a gem is given by weight units called **carats**. One carat is the same as 200 mg (0.007 oz).

Five famous **diamonds**

 Star of Africa (530.2 carats)
In 1908 this diamond was mounted in the Royal Sceptre, part of the British crown jewels.

 Millennium Star (203 carats)
Discovered in 1990, it took three years for lasers to cut and shape this pear-shaped diamond.

 Regent (140.5 carats)
Found in 1698 by an Indian slave who hid it in a wound in his leg, it was stolen by an English sea captain. In 1812, it was used to decorate Napoleon's sword.

 Koh-i-noor (105.6 carats)
Since 1304, it has belonged to various Indian and Persian rulers, but became part of the British crown jewels after Queen Victoria became Empress of India in 1877.

 Blue Hope (45.5 carats)
One of the most famous owners of this cursed diamond (pictured), Marie Antoinette, wife of King Louis XVI of France, was beheaded in 1793, during the French Revolution.

I don't believe it!

About 100,000 tonnes of uranium ore produces 25 tonnes of radioactive uranium, the annual amount used by a nuclear power station.

RECORD BREAKER

The **largest gold nugget** ever found weighed 72 kg (158 lb). Discovered in Moliagul, Australia, in the 1869 gold rush, it was named the "Welcome Stranger".

Weird or what?

Although both are forms of the element carbon, graphite is dark grey and one of the softest minerals, while diamond is clear and the world's hardest natural substance.

Rocks with strange powers

Magnetic
Minerals, such as magnetite, are naturally magnetic.

Radioactive
Uraninite is a radioactive mineral from which uranium is extracted.

Luminous
Some minerals, such as sodalite, glow when ultraviolet light is shone over them.

Tell me more: **minerals and rocks**

The Earth's landscape is made up of rocks and minerals, some precious and rare, others plentiful. Many are useful in our day-to-day lives.

barite

wavellite

brochantite

daisy gypsum

flourite

lazurite

rhodochrosite

halite

crystalline adamite

carnallite

turquoise

quartz

calcite

cuprite

azurite

tourmaline

botryoidal hemimorphite

pyrite crystal (fool's gold)

chalcopyrite

diaspore

artinite

olivine

jadeite

marcasite

sulphur

wulfenite

magnetite

malachite

hematite

cinnabar

sphalerite

agate

augite

garnet

cassiterite

graphite

galena

gneiss

marble

schist

slate

clay

conglomerate

sandstone

limestone

flint

obsidian

dolerite

tuff

pumice

basalt

granite

gabbro

aquamarine

emerald

diamond

topaz

sapphire

ruby

opal

amber

coral

pearl

jet

aluminium

copper

titanium

gold

iron

mercury

bismuth

nickel iron

platinum

silver

cobaltite

zinc

Key

Minerals: Solid mixtures of naturally occurring chemicals

Rocks: A combination of mineral grains found in the Earth's crust

Metamorphic: Created by Earth's heat and pressure

Sedimentary: Composed of sand, pebbles, and even fossils

Igneous: Cooled down volcanic material

Precious stones: Each gem is a highly prized, often rare, mineral

Living stones: Gemstones not produced from rocks

Metals: Specific types of minerals, often easy to bend and shape, and usually shiny

Where does the **world's energy** come from?

Solar power converts sunlight to electricity. We also release energy when we burn fuels such as oil, gas, and coal. Wind and water are examples of renewable resources, as they never run out.

FAST FACTS

Energy resources

01: **Coal** makes up 24 per cent of the world's energy

02: **Gas** supplies 21 per cent of the world's energy

03: **Oil** is used more than any other fuel, supplying 35 per cent of the world's energy

04: **Solar power** can be harnessed directly using special solar-electric cells

05: **Wind** can turn into electricity using machines called turbines

06: **Tide movement** and the waves in oceans can be used to make electricity

07: **Nuclear energy** involves splitting atoms, which causes a nuclear explosion that generates huge amounts of power

08: **Hydroelectric power** is the energy generated by rushing water harnessed by special dams

09: **Geothermal** means "hot rock", and its energy can be tapped where heat from deep inside the Earth rises to the surface

10: **Biomass** is the use of natural materials and waste to make energy

In numbers

70 million
The number of barrels of oil that are pumped from the ground each day

1.3 million
The number of people who receive electric power from the Hoover Dam, on the Colorado River, USA

2050
The year that oil is expected to run out. Gas is expected to run out in 2100, and coal by 2250

75%
The percentage of fuel wasted by cars in generating unnecessary heat and noise

Top 10 users of electricity (2007)

01: United States
3,717,000,000,000 kWh

02: China
2,494,000,000,000 kWh

03: Japan
946,300,000,000 kWh

04: Russia
940,000,000,000 kWh

05: India
587,900,000,000 kWh

06: Germany
3524,600,000,000 kWh

07: Canada
522,400,000,000 kWh

08: France
482,400,000,000 kWh

09: Brazil
415,900,000,000 kWh

10: United Kingdom
345,200,000,000 kWh

kWh stands for kilo Watt hour, and is a unit of energy measuring the amount of power used in one hour.

Canada: Produces 52% more than it uses

USA: Uses one-third more than it produces

South America: Produces 42% more than it uses

WHAT'S IN A NAME

Coal, oil, and gas are known as "**fossil fuels**" because they are formed from plants and plankton that lived up to 300 million years ago.

Odd one out

Oil is an important resource. Not only does it produce energy, but it contains chemicals that are used to make all sorts of things. It's used in all the objects below except one. Can you spot the odd one out? (answer opposite page)

a) umbrella

b) metal nails

c) soap

d) dice

e) CD

f) balloon

g) non-stick pan

h) lipstick

What is biomass?

Biofuels, such as ethanol, are liquid fuels made from biomass. This includes organic materials than can be burned to provide heat and produce steam.

crops, such as sugar, hemp, or rapeseed

rubbish, such as cardboard

animal manure

corn stalks

woodchips or pellets

seaweed

Six ways **to save energy**

Walk or cycle instead – it costs nothing and is good for you.

Use energy efficient light bulbs instead of traditional bulbs, as they use one-fifth of the energy and last up to 10 times longer.

Turn your heat down by reducing the thermostat in your home by just 1°C (1.8°F) – this will knock 10 per cent off the heating bill.

Insulate your home, especially your attic. Windows should be double-glazed.

Don't overfill your kettle, and only boil the water you need.

Reusing products saves the energy used to make replacements.

Blasts from the past

Tell me more: **world energy producers and consumers**

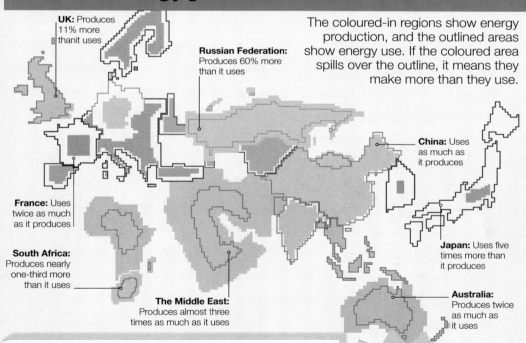

The coloured-in regions show energy production, and the outlined areas show energy use. If the coloured area spills over the outline, it means they make more than they use.

UK: Produces 11% more than it uses

Russian Federation: Produces 60% more than it uses

China: Uses as much as it produces

France: Uses twice as much as it produces

South Africa: Produces nearly one-third more than it uses

The Middle East: Produces almost three times as much as it uses

Japan: Uses five times more than it produces

Australia: Produces twice as much as it uses

Three ways to cook an egg

1. Sunny side up
The energy given off from the Sun in a scorching desert can heat rocks high enough to fry an egg.

2. Boiling hot
Water erupting from an overheated geyser can reach a scalding 95°C (204°F) – anyone for boiled eggs?

3. Light a fire
The heat energy from burning wood will ensure a tasty treat.

The population of China is **four times bigger** than the USA, but they use **less than half** the amount of energy.

I don't believe it!

In August 2003, around 50 million people in cities from New York, USA, to Toronto, Canada, were affected by a mass power cut. People were trapped in lifts and subway trains, and the loss of power in pumping stations led to sewage spills.

Dinosaurs

Why were some dinos so huge?

With necks as long as 11 m (36 ft) and bodies the size of buses, sauropods were the most distinctive dinosaurs to roam throughout the Jurassic and Cretaceous Periods, 200 to 65 million years ago. These giant vegetarians were able to browse leaves high up in trees and their huge size deterred predators.

Sauropod myths

MYTH: *It was once believed that sauropods lived in water because they were so heavy they would not have been able to support their weight on land.*
TRUTH: Scientists can tell now from their footprints that they did not live in water, but were land-living animals.

MYTH: *It was once thought that their necks could have been used as snorkels, so they could breathe while submerged under water.*
TRUTH: The long neck as snorkel idea would never have worked, as water pressure would not have allowed the lungs of the submerged animal to expand, leading to breathing problems.

SAUROPOD SALAD

(crunchy) **conifers**
(low-calorie) **cycads**
(glorious) **gingko**
(sumptuous) **seed ferns**
(mushy) **moss**

How to: survive as a Jurassic plant-eater

Dinosaur skulls are made up of delicate bones which do not often fossilize. Scientists did not find a skull of the most famous sauropod, *Apatosaurus* (or *Brontosaurus* as it was known then) until a hundred years after the first skeletons had been found.

01. Grow thick skin like *Barosaurus* – it will help protect you from predators.

02. You will need a long, muscular, whip-like tail for balance and protection.

03. Large, elephant-like feet will help support your heavy body.

04. Your intestinal system needs to be extensive enough to digest large amounts of low-quality leaves. Swallow stones to help mash up the food inside the stomach.

In numbers

53 The number of bones in the tail of the sauropod *Camarasaurus*

2.45 m (8 ft) The length of the largest shoulder blade fossil found. It belonged to the sauropod *Brachiosaurus*

1.8 m (6 ft) The length of the largest neck vertebra found. It came from a *Diplodocus*

1 m (3 ft) The size of the first sauropod embryo fossil ever discovered

RECORD BREAKER

Mamenchisaurus had the **longest neck** of any of the Jurassic sauropods. It measured 11 m (36 ft), and consisted of 19 vertebrae bones.

05. Use your long neck and lightweight head to browse very high parts of trees for food.

06. You need peg-like teeth. You won't be able to chew, but they are perfect for raking leaves from branches.

I don't believe it!

The sauropod *Diplodocus* used a long whip-like tail for defence. When thrashed, the tip of the tail could break the sound barrier, producing a thunderous crack to signal to other dinosaurs.

Mind your step

As the smallest Jurassic dinosaur, the tiny *Compsognathus* had to be careful it was not squashed in the land of giants. It was about the size of a chicken and may have travelled in groups to scavenge the kills of larger animals.

Sauropod enemies

Allosaurus was a fearsome 12-m- (38-ft-) long predator. It walked on two legs, had a massive tail, and a bulky body. It had sharp claws up to 15 cm (6 in) in length.

Ceratosaurus could grow up to 6 m (20 ft) long. It had large, powerful jaws and sharp teeth.

Megalosaurus grew up to 9 m (30 ft) long. As well as hunting sauropods, it is likely that it also scavenged already dead animals.

Camarasaurus 18 m (59 ft)
Probably fed by swinging its strong neck stiffly sideways and down to strip tough leaves from shrubby trees

Brachiosaurus 30 m (98 ft)
Long, spoon-shaped teeth capable of pulling twigs and needles from the highest conifer trees

Paralititan 27 m (89 ft)
Its neck accounted for one-third of its entire body length; estimated to have weighed 80 tonnes

Saltasaurus 27 m (89 ft)
Like many of the later sauropods, *Saltasaurus* had thick, armour-like skin along its back

Super **sauropods**

Why did some **dinos have crests?**

Hadrosaurs are a group of dinos famous for their flat beaks. Not all of them had head crests, but those that did could have been a real hoot. Some scientists believe that when the dino blew air through its crest, it made a noise like a trombone. Other theories are that crests made it easier to recognize one another, or perhaps worked as a cooling system.

Craziest crests

Hadrosaur crests came in a wide range of shapes and sizes. *Parasaurolophus*'s stick-like crest was up to 1.8 m (6 ft) long.

Tsintaosaurus

Saurolophus

Parasaurolophus

Corythosaurus

Three good reasons to make a noise

01 Warn the herd of predators.

02 Keep the herd grouped together.

03 Attract a mate. (Who could resist a booming trombone?)

How to: **qualify as a hadrosaur**

01. Check out how you look. As an *Edmontosaurus* you should have a long face and a broad, flat snout.

02. Grind any rough vegetation and digest your food using the teeth along the inside of your cheek.

03. Your large eyes, excellent hearing, and a good sense of smell help you to avoid predators.

04. Support your weight and forage for food using your forelimbs.

05. Walk comfortably using your hoof-like nails.

06. Use your hind legs to run, and all four legs to walk slowly or graze.

07. Keep warm and protect yourself with your tough skin.

08. Your bulky body will come in handy against any predators, like *T rex*.

09. Balance and support yourself using your long, stiff tail.

10. Run faster with the help of your large and powerful hind legs.

Eight amazing *Maiasaura* facts

01: *Maiasaura*'s name means "good mother lizard".

02: They grew up to 9 m (30 ft) long, and weighed about 3 tonnes.

03: *Maiasaura* lived in the late Cretaceous Period, about 80–65 million years ago.

04: They lived in herds with possibly up to 10,000 individuals.

05: A colony of *Maiasaura* nests was discovered in Montana, USA.

06: Their nests were made of scooped out earth, containing eggs the size of grapefruits.

07: The mother did not sit on her eggs, but probably covered them in rotting vegetation to keep them warm.

08: Newborn hatchlings were about 30 cm (1 ft) long.

Survival tips
(for hadrosaurs)

01 Hang out in a herd. There is safety in numbers.

02 If you spot a predatory carnivore, like a *Tyrannosaurus rex*, hoot loudly to alert the herd and leg it.

03 Keep an eye on any old or sick herd members in case the *T rex* tries to isolate them from the herd.

04 Run as quickly as possible until you are a safe distance from the predator.

05 Continue to graze vegetation – you need to keep your energy levels boosted!

Daily grind

Hadrosaurs had hundreds of teeth in their cheeks, which ground and chopped their vegetarian food before they swallowed it. The teeth wore out because of the constant grinding action, but there were always new teeth growing to replace the old.

Hadrosaur cuisine

Breakfast
Lip-smacking leaves with fragrant flowers

Lunch
Tasty twigs with a side of sumptuous seeds

Dinner
Prickly pine needles washed down with fresh water from the lake

RECORD BREAKER

Bigger than a bus at 15.5 m (50 ft), the *Shantungosaurus* was the **largest hadrosaur**. It weighed around 18 tonnes – about ten times heavier than an elephant.

WHAT'S IN A NAME?

Hadrosaur means "duck-billed" because they had broad and flat beaks, a bit like that of a duck. But while a duck's bill is soft and sensitive, hadrosaurs had tough, horny beaks.

I don't believe it!

In 1999, a teenage palaeontologist found the remains of the most intact hadrosaur ever in North Dakota, USA. The dinosaur had been mummified before it was fossilized and so soft tissue, such as skin and muscle, were preserved. The rare fossil was analyzed by a huge scanner usually used to examine aircraft.

Meet (some of) the family

Corythosaurus
Lived: 80–65 million years ago
Where: Alberta, Canada
Length: 10 m (35 ft)
How to spot: Hollow crest like half a dinner plate

Saurolophus
Lived: 72–68 million years ago
Where: Canada and Mongolia
Length: 10 m (35 ft)
How to spot: Long, pointy tail and bony head spike

Maiasaura
Lived: 80–65 million years ago
Where: Montana, USA
Length: 9 m (30 ft)
How to spot: Flat skull with small crest in front of eyes

Lambeosaurus
Lived: 83–65 million years ago
Where: Alberta, Canada
Length: 15 m (50 ft)
How to spot: Two-part crest with spike behind

Brachylophosaurus
Lived: 83–75 million years ago
Where: Alberta, Canada
Length: 9 m (30 ft)
How to spot: Flat, plate-like crest and long forearms

Was *T rex* really "king of the reptiles"?

The name literally means the "king of the tyrant reptiles". *Tyrannosaurus rex* was the most ferocious meat-eating predator of the tyrannosaur family of dinosaurs. Tyrannosaurs lived between 80 to 65 million years ago. They could grow longer than a bus, were as heavy as an elephant, and tall enough to look into an upstairs window.

T rex

01: At full stretch, *T rex* stood at a massive 12 m (40 ft) long and 6 m (20 ft) tall.

02: It had an enormous head – a whopping 1.5 m (5 ft) long – and a short, flexible neck.

03: *T rex*'s jaws were up to 1.2 m (4 ft) long, with 60 bone-crunching teeth.

04: It had excellent sight and a powerful sense of smell.

05: *T rex* had two-fingered hands equipped with sharp claws.

06: Its stiff, pointed tail allowed it to make quick turns.

07: It walked on its toes and could probably run at 15–30 kph (10–20 mph).

How to: hunt like a *T rex*

01. Walk around heavily on your great hind limbs, head jutting forwards, and with a level back and tail.

02. Trail after small horned or duck-billed dinosaurs.

03. Once you have a target in your sights, move in for the kill with gaping jaws. Bite a large part of its flesh, hooking your finger claws into the prey to hold it still.

04. When your prey dies from loss of blood, step on the creature, and tear out huge chunks of meat. Enjoy your feast, but keep an eye out for rival *T rexes*!

Tyrannosaurus rex's eyes were angled forwards, so the field of view overlapped at the front. This gave the dinosaur **stereoscopic vision** – it could have judged distances and seen things in three dimensions, just like humans do.

Meet the family

Although *Tyrannosaurus rex* was the biggest meat-eater, there were other equally scary members in the Tyrannosaur family.

Tarbosaurus
Lived: 70–65 million years ago
Where: Mongolia and China
Length: 12 m (40 ft)

Albertosaurus
Lived: 76–74 million years ago
Where: Canada
Length: 10 m (33 ft)

Gorgosaurus
Lived: 76–68 million years ago
Where: North America
Length: 9 m (30 ft)

Alioramus
Lived: 70–65 million years ago
Where: Mongolia
Length: 6 m (20 ft)

Superstar Sue

The most complete *T rex* fossil ever found is on display at the Field Museum, Chicago, USA, and she's known as Sue.

- The fossil was discovered on 12 August 1990 by the Cheyenne River, South Dakota, USA.
- We don't know if Sue is male or female, the fossil is named after Sue Hendrickson, the fossil hunter who discovered it.
- The fossil was bought by the museum for nearly US$8.4 million.
- Sue died 67 million years ago.
- When she was alive, she would probably have weighed 7 tonnes.
- She was 12.8 m (42 ft) long from snout to tail.
- Her skeleton is made up of more than 200 bones.
- She had 58 teeth in her awesome jaws.
- The skull in the display is a replica – the real skull is just too heavy to hold in place.
- Her brain is just big enough to hold a litre (quart) of milk.

Fright bite

T rex had a mouth full of teeth of different sizes. Some teeth have been found as long as 33 cm (13 in).

Five good reasons NOT to invite a T rex to dinner

01: You'll need an awful lot of meat to keep your guest happy as *T rex* can tear off 230 kg (500 lbs) of meat in one bite.

02: Expect bad table manners. With such tiny short arms, *T rex* would guzzle straight from the plate.

03: It won't be a pretty sight. *T rex* eats with its mouth open, chopping up food with teeth like giant spikes.

04: Your other guests might be a tad nervous – and some may end up as an extra course if your meat supplies aren't sufficient.

05: With rows of teeth where meat can get caught and rot, and no sign of a Cretaceous toothbrush, you can guarantee that this guest would have fearsome breath.

What about me?

One of the largest parts of the *T rex*'s brain was the area that identified odours – so it would have no trouble sniffing you out. You would, however, be just a light snack!

I don't believe it!

A coprolite (fossilized dropping) belonging to *Tyrannosaurus rex* has given scientists clues about the diet of these feared predators. Nearly as long as a man's arm and weighing as much as a six-month-old baby, this dropping contained chewed bits of bone from a plant-eating dinosaur as big as a cow.

Movie star

T rex has appeared many times on the silver screen, though sadly he only gets to play the villain. Here are just a few of his most recent films.

- **Jurassic Park** (1993) and II (1997), and III (2001)
- **King Kong** (2005)
- **Night at the Museum** (2006)
- **Journey to the Centre of the Earth** (2008)

How did dinosaurs defend themselves?

Different dinosaurs reacted in different ways when they came across predators. *Iguanodon* would blend into its surroundings – its skin patterns and colour camouflaging it. *Gallimimus* used its speed to escape predators such as *Tyrannosaurus rex*, reaching speeds of 56 kph (35 mph). Others relied on sturdy body armour.

How to: be indestructible

01. As a *Protoceratops* you have nothing to fear, swing round to face the danger. Your shield will protect your neck.

02. Stand and face your enemy so that the bright colours of your neck shield can be seen.

03. Have your sharp beak ready to snap at limbs or soft underbellies if your enemy comes too close.

04. It is best to go about in a herd, so that you are less likely to be picked upon.

Tail tales

■ **Scelidosaurus** may have used its tail for balance while it reared itself up on its hind legs to flee predators.

■ **Euoplocephalus** had tail bones that were fused together to make it straight, so it could swing its tail club from side to side like a mace.

■ **Gastonia** had big spines all over its tail, which made it a formidable weapon. The rest of its body was also studded with sharp defensive spines.

WEIRD OR WHAT?
Euoplocephalus may have used its club-like tail as a decoy head.

Sticking together

Growing family In a big group with lots of females, the dominant *Pachycephalosaurus* male was able to find many mates, increasing the herd.

Child-minding *Hypacrosaurus* raised young in large groups – greater numbers meant better defence against predators.

Protection Big dinosaurs that couldn't run fast, like *Centrosaurus*, found safety in numbers.

Hunting in herds Small, fierce dinosaurs, like *Deinonychus*, made up for their size by hunting in packs, like lions.

Killer claws

Deinonychus grabbed its prey with its jaws and hands. It then balanced on one leg and slashed the claws of the other foot back and forth, to disembowel its victim.

Claws: Rose up and flicked forwards with brutal force

What to do if you meet a...

Triceratops
Keep behind the frill where it can't see you. But beware, *Triceratops* move about in herds, so there may be another one creeping up behind you!

Euoplocephalus
Vulnerable parts lie underneath, so hide on the ground until it walks over you, and strike from below.

Stegosaurus
Keep clear of the tail and watch out. Even after a fatal blow to the head, *Stegosaurus* (pictured) could still be active as nerves in the hip keep the hind legs and tail working for a while.

Skin deep
The **armour-plated skin** of some dinosaurs provided extra protection. Predators would find slashing or biting the tough skin hard going.

Scary horns

Horns on dinosaurs may have been used for defence against meat-eaters, fighting for leadership of a herd, and for showing off.

Triceratops
Three horns, one on the nose and two above the eyes

Styracosaurus
One horn on the nose, and six around the rim of the neck

Centrosaurus
One crooked horn on the nose

Three ways to catch your prey

01: Sudden ambush
Hiding in trees, the massive *Giganotosaurus* (pictured) probably waited patiently until a slow-moving herbivore passed by, then grabbed it in its jaws.

02: Chasing down prey
Compsognathus was a fast sprinter, and used its speed and agility to pursue its prey.

03: Snatch and grab
Baryonyx snatched unsuspecting fish in its narrow jaws and hooked thumb claw, piercing the prey with its teeth.

Most plant-eating dinosaurs had **eyes on the sides of their heads**. This gave them a wide field of vision, allowing them to scan the landscape for predators.

Tell me more: *Gorgosaurus* teeth

Front teeth: Short, and stout for clamping on to struggling prey

sharp serrated edge

Back teeth: Blade-like and serrated to slice the flesh

Jaw: Hinged to open wide and engulf prey

Were dinosaurs able to fly?

Dinosaurs could not fly, but their reptile relatives, pterosaurs, soared high above them. Pterosaurs ruled the skies, flying over land and sea while the dinosaurs stalked the Earth. These majestic winged reptiles died out at the same time as the dinosaurs, 65 million years ago.

How to: **fly like a *Dimorphodon***

01. Keep your head warm with just a few short, fine threads of hair.

02. Spot prey far away using your large, probing eyes.

03. Dive towards the sea and use your sharp teeth to spear fish.

04. Stretch out your neck while flying to reduce drag from air resistance.

05. Support your wing with your long fourth finger. Use the other three sharp, hook-like fingers for defence.

06. To keep airborne, flap your leathery wings, which are made of skin and muscle. When not flying, fold your wings against your body.

07. Steer yourself through the air using the flap of skin at the end of your tail as a rudder.

RECORD BREAKER

The **biggest flying creature** ever to soar the skies was the pterosaur *Quetzalcoatlus*. Its wingspan was 12 m (40 ft) – as big as a small aircraft.

I don't believe it!

In 1856, builders constructing a railway tunnel claimed to see a large creature resembling a *Pteradactyl*. It apparently fluttered its wings before dropping down dead and turning to dust. Hmm. With no evidence to corroborate the story, was it really a flying reptile or just a flight of fancy?

High flyers

Winging it through the skies with the pterosaurs was a collection of animals that had evolved from therapod dinosaurs. These animals, not pterosaurs, are considered to be the first birds.

Peteinosaurus

Lived: 220 million years ago
Habitat: Swamps and river valleys
Where: Southern Europe
Length: 60 cm (24 in)
Diet: Flying insects

Pterodactylus

Lived: 150 million years ago
Habitat: Lake shores
Where: Europe
Length: 1 m (3 ft)
Diet: Fish

Pteranodon

Lived: 88 million years ago
Habitat: Oceans, shores
Where: North America
Length: 1.8 m (6 ft)
Diet: Fish

Pterodactylus

Walking on wings

The biggest pterosaurs, the azhdarchids, liked to walk as well as fly. They had strong back legs, and at the front they used their wing "hands" as front legs.

Like pelicans, pterosaurs had long, narrow heads and **throat pouches**. They plunged their beaks beneath the water to grab fish, which they stored in their pouches.

Dimorphodon

What's the difference?

pterosaurs
furry body
most had teeth
claws on the wings
membrane-type, bat-like wings

birds
feathered body
most are toothless
no claws on the wings
feathered wings

goshawk

Giant jaws

- Birds have beaks, but pterosaurs mostly had toothy jaws.
- A few had crests, possibly for cleaving (passing through) the water as they dipped for fish.
- Sharp, pointed, widely spaced teeth were good for seizing fish or other slippery prey.
- Some crests were brightly coloured.
- Some pterosaurs were toothless.

Dinobirds

It is believed that today's birds are not the descendants of pterosaurs, but of dinosaurs that took to the air. The reason is the discovery over the last 150 years of fossils of animals that were half-bird and half-dino, such as *Caudipteryx*.

Pterosaurs

01: The first pterosaurs were small flappers, but over millions of years they evolved into giant gliders.

02: Slim, hollow bones made pterosaurs **very light for flying.**

03: Pterosaur skulls contained air sacs to make them lighter.

04: Some pterosaurs had curious head crests, possibly for courtship displays.

05: Some pterosaurs gathered together in huge colonies to mate and breed.

06: A fossil pterosaur egg contained an unhatched baby inside a soft eggshell, like that of a modern reptile.

Marine reptiles

01: The marine reptiles were completely unrelated to dinosaurs.

02: They became extinct at the same time as the dinosaurs.

03: Many were giants with huge jaws, some wide enough to swallow large prey whole.

04: They could be found in deep oceans, shallow seas, and coastal regions.

05: Since they lived in the sea, where fossilization is more likely, many fossils of marine reptiles are well preserved.

Could dinosaurs swim?

No, but while dinosaurs ruled the land, marine reptiles ruled the sea. These ichthyosaurs, pliosaurs, plesiosaurs, placodonts, and mosasaurs were carnivores – preying on other sea creatures as well as each other. They needed air to breathe, so they had to swim to the surface to refill their lungs, before disappearing back into their underwater world.

WEIRD OR WHAT?

Some scientists think that small plesiosaurs crawled onto sandy beaches to lay their eggs, just like turtles.

How to: live like an *Elasmosaurus*

02. Slide slowly through the water. It takes a lot of energy to move a body that weighs up to 3 tonnes.

01. Use your four paddle-shaped flippers to help you swim.

03. Use your tail to stabilize and steer your body.

04. Keep afloat using the small stones in your stomach as a ballast (a weight to keep your body stable).

05. Protect your chest and support your powerful paddle muscles using your large plate-like shoulder bones.

I don't believe it!

In 1997, the skeleton of a giant ichthyosaur *Shonisaurus* was found in a mountain stream in British Columbia. It was 21 m (69 ft) long, but the only way palaeontologists could get a proper look at the whole thing was through aerial photography!

In numbers

26 cm (10 in) The width of each eye of some ichthyosaurs

14 m (46 ft) The length of *Elasmosaurus*, which lived in oceans 66 million years ago

72 The number of vertebrae bones in an *Elasmosaurus*'s neck. This is more than any other animal

1.8 m (6 ft) The length of the skull of *Deinosuchus* – a giant distant cousin of modern crocodiles

5 tonnes The weight of *Deinosuchus*

Tell me more: **pliosaur anatomy**

Pliosaur fossils, like this *Liopleurodon* skeleton, suggest that these vast creatures glided through the waters like a sealion. But at around 25 m (82 ft) long, and weighing around 150 tonnes, it was 10 times bigger.

enormous head

Dagger-like teeth:
Fish were impaled on the sharp points

Bony plates:
The underneath of the reptile is protected by broad chest bones and hip bones

Backbone: Long, arched back

Back flippers:
Enabled them to swim at speed

Huge front flippers:
Measuring up to 3 m (10 ft), they propelled the reptile underwater

---

Like divers, marine reptiles sometimes suffered from a disease called "the bends", which occurs when **bubbles of nitrogen** appear in the blood stream after surfacing too quickly.

Fossil finds

01 Fossils of marine reptiles were found before anything was known about the dinosaurs.

02 The first complete ichthyosaur skeleton was discovered in 1791.

03 At first, scientists thought ichthyosaurs were a type of extinct dolphin or crocodiles – or even a sea dragon!

Seafood (and eat it)!

There was a wide and tantalizing menu for marine reptiles to feed on.

Ammonites: Coiled shell-bearing squid relatives, eaten by ichthyosaurs and mososaurs

Fish: A wide variety eaten by sharp-toothed plesiosaurs and ichthyosaurs

Squid: Soft-bodied animals were a lip-smacking favourite of toothless ichthyosaurs

Shellfish: Eaten by broad-toothed, strong-jawed ichthyosaurs, mososaurs, and early walrus-like placodonts.

Sea monsters

Tylosaurus
This 11-m (36-ft) mosasaur predator hunted fish, squid, and turtles.

Ichthyosaurus
Females gave birth to live young, tail first. Adults grew to 2 m (6.5 ft) and weighed up to 90 kg (200 lb).

Kronosaurus
This 10-m (33-ft) long, 7-tonne giant pliosaur had wing-like flippers and huge, powerful jaws.

Nothosaurus
This slender, 14-m (46-ft) long reptile fed mainly on fish.

---

08. Use your excellent vision to spot prey.

06. Use your long, snaking neck to give you strength and flexibility.

07. Use your sharp teeth and strong jaws to catch slippery prey, like fish and squid.

What on Earth can digging unearth?

WHAT'S IN A NAME?

A **palaeontologist** is a scientist who studies rocks and fossils. Palaeontology literally means **"the study of prehistory"**, which is life before humans began recording events.

If you know where to look, you might find a fossil – the word fossil even comes from the Greek for "dug up". Fossils are the ancient remains of organisms that have been preserved in rocks. From them, scientists are able to find out about the different life forms that existed millions of years ago.

LIFE ON EARTH

Earth's history is divided up into four main periods:

- **EARLY PALAEOZOIC 545–417 million years ago**
  Living things that have been living in the seas for 3,000 million years develop hard shells. Plants begin to colonize the land.

- **LATE PALAEOZOIC 417–248 million years ago**
  More life forms evolve. Amphibians, reptiles, and insects inhabit the land, living on the plants. Many species die out in a mass extinction at the end of this period.

- **MESOZOIC 248–65 million years ago**
  Dinosaurs stalk the land, pterosaurs rule the skies, and marine reptiles lurk in the waters. The first flowering plants and small mammals appear. Another mass extinction wipes out many species, including all dinosaurs.

- **CENOZOIC 65 million years ago to present day**
  Mammals and flowering plants become more varied and dominate the land, while bony fish thrive in the seas. Humans evolve.

Fossil finds

Sometimes insects get engulfed in sticky pine tree resin and become fossilized as it hardens into **amber**.

In some rare instances **dinosaur skeletons** may be found intact, with the bones still joined up.

A **jigsaw of bones**, all jumbled up, gives scientists freedom to cut up the skeleton for further investigation.

An **isolated bone** is the most common find and must be examined for clues about what it is and where it's from.

Tell me more: **becoming a fossil**

01: For a dead animal to become a fossil it needs to be buried quickly before it is eaten or decomposes, by falling into a muddy river bed, or by a sandstorm, for example.

02: Soft tissue rots away, but the skeleton remains to be replaced by minerals and turned to rock over millions of years.

03: Over time, mud and river sediments build up over the fossil, forming layer upon layer of sedimentary rocks.

04: Over more millions of years, erosion and movements in the Earth's crust can expose the fossil, and, with luck, a palaeontologist may find it.

PLANT LIFE

Plant fossils help to draw a picture of the lands through which animals like the dinosaurs roamed.

Ferns and club mosses: The first plant types

Cycads: Palm-like plants related to conifers

Conifers: Trees such as the giant redwood and monkey puzzle

Broad-leaved trees: First appear at the end of the Age of the Dinosaurs

How to: excavate a dinosaur

01. Remove the soil and rock from above the dinosaur skeleton, until you are just above the level of the fossil.

02. Delicately remove the last layer with knives, needles, and brushes, until the skeleton is exposed.

03. Place a grid over the exposed skeleton, and draw a map of the bones. This will help to work out how the dinosaur died.

04. Protect the bones with varnish, then wrap in plaster, like a broken leg, to keep them whole until they get to the laboratory.

The **world's oldest fossils** are of minute bacteria-like cells **3,500 million years old**.

Fossilized poo, called a coprolite, is a trace fossil. These reveal how the animal lived and what it ate.

Some very detailed **fossil casts** can reveal an animal's skin texture, as well as its bones.

Fossilized dinosaur **footprints** can help work out an animal's height and how fast it moved.

Dinosaur **eggs** and nests are also fossilized. At a site in Spain, 300,000 eggs have been found.

Four famous fossil hunters

William Buckland In 1824, Buckland became the first to describe a dinosaur as a "big reptile" or *Megalosaurus*.

Sir Richard Owen In 1841, this British scientist first came up with the name "dinosaur", meaning "terrible lizard".

Mary Anning A professional fossil hunter, Anning excavated marine reptiles for scientists in the early 19th century.

Roy Chapman Andrews This scientist and explorer made the first dinosaur discoveries in Asia.

Top five fossil sites

01: **Dinosaur National Monument, Utah, USA** Hundreds of dinosaurs have been found in an ancient floodplain.

02: **Liaoning, China** Fine lake sediments have preserved tiny dinosaurs and early birds in detail.

03: **Mt Kirkpatrick, Antarctica** The first site to reveal evidence that dinosaurs lived in Antarctica.

04: **Egg Mountain, Montana, USA** The site of a dinosaur nesting colony.

05: **Patagonia, Argentina** The biggest dinosaurs ever, both meat-eaters and plant-eaters, have been found here.

sea fossils

Marine fossils are the most common because dead sea creatures are quickly covered by silt and sand when they fall to the sea floor.

Ammonite: An octopus-like animal in a coiled shell, now extinct

Belemnite: An animal like a squid, but with a pencil-shaped internal shell

Trilobite: An ancient jointed animal that crawled on the sea floor

Shark's teeth: Commonly preserved as fossils because they are so hard

Fish: Primitive vertebrates that first appeared about 500 million years ago

Who ruled the world **after the dinos died out?**

Sixty-five million years ago, a mass extinction wiped out the dinosaurs. Mammals had been around since the Jurassic Period. Living alongside the dominant dinosaurs, they were just a small group of tiny, rodent-like creatures. When the dinos died out, so did many of the mammals, but the survivors evolved to become the most successful type of animal around.

What about me?
Modern humans evolved 200,000 years ago, when woolly mammoths still stalked the icy plains.

Newcomers
New groups of animals that soon appeared on the scene included big plant-eaters like elephants, hoofed mammals like pigs and tapirs, sea mammals like whales and dolphins, and the first bats.

Scary beasts

Andrewsarchus
A wolf-like hoofed animal, the largest known carnivorous land mammal ever

Canis dirus
Wolf-like creature with a wide head, strong jaws, and large teeth – perfect for breaking and eating bones

Smilodon
Far-from-friendly feline with enormous gnashers

Daeodon
"Killer buffalo pig" – the name says it all, really

How to: **be a prehistoric mammal**

01. You will need your wits about you, so a large brain is a must-have.

02. Use your sensory whiskers to aid navigation.

03. A covering of fur will help keep you warm.

04. Catch and eat prey using your specialized teeth.

05. Your warm-blooded metabolism will keep you alert and active.

06. Make sure your limbs are tucked beneath your body instead of sprawling like a lizard's legs.

Five strange new species

Moetherium
A primitive elephant with a massive body, short legs, and a long thick neck.

Arsinotherium
A heavy, rhino-like plant-eater with massive horns, which were covered in skin.

Macrauchenia
This animal had a body like a horse, a neck like a camel, and a short trunk like a tapir.

Phenacodus
Like a wild boar, it had a skeleton suited to a lifestyle of running in open woodlands.

FAST FACTS

Mammoths

01: Mammoths lived from around 4.8 million years ago until most died out in the last Ice Age, 10,000 years ago.

02: One group of pygmy woolly mammoths still existed in the Arctic until 1650 BCE.

03: Several woolly mammoths have been found preserved in the frozen ground of Siberia, with bits of fur, skin, and even stomach contents intact.

04: The woolly mammoth could grow to 3.3 m (11 ft) tall and was covered in hair up to 90 cm (3 ft) long.

I don't believe it!

Modern-day bowhead whales are thought to be the exact same species as certain fossilized whales that have been found to date back to between 1.8 and 10 million years ago. That's some staying power!

Meteorite strike!

When dinosaurs were wiped out, so were around 70 per cent of all animal and plant species. Many scientists believe this mass extinction was caused by a meteorite crashing into Earth.

1 The shock wave destroyed every living thing in the immediate area.

2 Heat of the impact produced extensive forest fires.

3 Tsunamis swept across low-lying lands.

4 Smoke and ash cut out sunlight and killed plants.

5 Acid rain from the clouds also destroyed many plants.

Extinction winners and losers

Reptiles
All species of dinosaur, pterosaur, and plesiosaur were wiped out, along with 36 per cent of crocodilians, 27 per cent of turtles and tortoises, and 6 per cent of lizard and snake species.

Mammals
All types of mammals lost species, but the marsupials were hit the hardest, with 75 per cent of species wiped out.

Birds
Seventy-five per cent of bird species disappeared.

Fish
Fish got off lightly, with only 15 per cent of species lost for ever.

Amphibians
The amphibians hopped off the winners – no species were lost.

WHAT'S IN A NAME?

Basilosaurus sounds like a dinosaur, but was actually a kind of whale. The scientist who first studied it thought it was a reptile, and the rules of scientific naming meant that the name he gave to it had to stick.

Top of the tusks

Phiomia
Resembling an overgrown warthog, it had lower tusks like shovels, for digging.

Dienotherium
Its tusks curved downwards from the lower jaw and were used as picks.

Gomphotherium
Four tusks, two at the top and two at the bottom, were used for all sorts of tasks, such as digging and scraping.

Mammoth
This woolly creature's long, curving tusks were used as snowploughs.

Plants

Why don't some plants have flowers?

Although many plants use flowers to reproduce, some do not. There are more than 30,000 types of these non-flowering plants. Mosses, for example, release tiny spores that are spread by the wind. Conifers make seeds inside scaly cones. Both spores and seeds grow into new plants.

Spore producers

8,000 species

Liverworts
These simple plants live in damp or wet places, and lack proper stems, roots, or leaves.

100 species

Hornworts
Resemble liverworts, and live in damp places; they can grow on the bark of trees.

9,500 species

Mosses
Small, leafy upright plants, they can usually be found in bogs and damp woodlands.

6 species

Whisk ferns
The ferns are the simplest plants to have internal plumbing. Tiny tubes carry food and water.

1,000 species

Club mosses
These plants are notable for their flat or upright stems with spiralling leaves.

15 species

Horsetails
This plant's cylindrical stems and rings of narrow leaves look like brushes.

11,000 species

Ferns
A familiar spore producer, armed with tough stems and complex leaves.

Seed producers

70 species

Gnetophytes
Pronounced "neat-o-fights", they include shrubs, trees, and the desert welwitschia.

1 species

Ginkgo
Also known as the Maidenhair tree, it has fan-shaped leaves that fall in autumn.

140 species

Cycads
They resemble palm trees, live in warm places, and can be male or female.

550 species

Conifers
They are mostly trees, and include pines, cedars, spruces, larches, and firs.

I don't believe it!

If wet sphagnum moss is dried out, it becomes very absorbent. In the past it was used in babies' nappies to soak up urine and in hospitals to dress wounds in order to soak up blood.

RECORD BREAKER

Bristlecone pines are the **oldest trees** on the planet. Growing slowly on cold, windswept mountainsides in western USA, they can live for thousands of years. The oldest specimen is known as Methuselah, and is about 4,800 years old.

Can a cone predict rain?

01: Find a pine tree and collect a fallen cone.

02: Put the cone somewhere convenient at home.

03: Look at your cone when you get up in the morning.

04: If the cone's scales have opened up, it's likely to be a dry day.

05: If the cone's scales have closed, it will probably be drizzly or rainy.

Which of these are *not* plants? (answers at bottom of page)

a) Green seaweed

b) Green stain mushroom

c) Reindeer moss

d) Brown seaweed

e) Staghorn coral

How to: **make food if you're a plant**

04. Take the gas carbon dioxide from the air into your leaves.

01. Make sure the Sun is shining.

05. Use sunlight to combine with carbon dioxide and water to make energy-rich glucose (sugars). Yum!

06. Release the waste gas oxygen from your leaves into the air.

02. Take plenty of water in from the soil using your roots.

03. Transport the water up the stem and to your leaves.

FOUR USES FOR NON-FLOWERING PLANTS

01: Horsetails were used – and still are in some places – as pan scourers. Hard silica (from sand grains) in their stems makes them abrasive.

02: Some people believe that an extract made from gingko tree leaves helps memory.

03: If lycopodium powder – from the spores of club mosses – is thrown into the air and ignited it creates an amazing fireball. Don't try at home!

04: Edible pine nuts (the seeds produced by certain pine trees) have been eaten for thousands of years, and are a key ingredient of Italian pesto.

KEY

➤ glucose
➤ carbon dioxide
➤ water
➤ oxygen

Why welwitschia is weird

- It lives in the arid Namib Desert, Africa, and gets water from morning dew.
- It can live for more than 1,000 years.
- It has just two long, curly, and hard leaves that split as they grow.
- Older specimens look more like a pile of rubbish than plants.

Sunlight to sugars

All plants make their own food by a process called photosynthesis. Whether they have flowers or not, all plants make their own food. Plant leaves contain **chlorophyll**, which makes them green. Chlorophyll "captures" energy in sunlight and uses it to make energy-rich sugars, like glucose, from simple raw materials.

ANSWERS: None of them are plants. a) and d) are algae; b) is a fungus; c) is a lichen (partnership between an alga and a fungus); e) is an animal colony.

Non-flowering plants 088|089

Why do some plants **have flowers?**

Flowering plants are the most successful and numerous plants on the planet, and grow just about everywhere. Whether it's a cactus, daisy, maple tree, or rice plant, every flowering plant produces flowers. At the centre of each flower are ovaries that make the seeds that will grow into that plant's offspring.

Five ways to get **pollinated**

Wind
Willow catkins blowing in the wind release lightweight pollen.

Butterflies
By feeding on flowers, butterflies pick up pollen.

Flies
Flowers that smell of dead meat will attract flies.

Hummingbirds
Hovering in front of flowers, hummingbirds feed on nectar and pick up pollen.

Bats
They feed on nectar and pick up pollen.

How to: **pollinate a flower**

01. Find a suitable flower, land on the petals, and locate the nectary. Petal patterns will guide you in the right direction.

02. Stick out your proboscis (tongue) and use it to suck up sweet nectar from the nectary.

03. While feeding, you will accidentally pick up pollen grains on your hairy back from the flower's anthers.

05. Land on the new flower, look for nectar, and unknowingly transfer pollen to the flower's sticky stigma. Job done!

04. Leave that flower and buzz through the air carrying pollen grains until you find another flower.

Life cycle of a flowering plant

1. Flower opens up and attracts insects that carry pollen from the same type of flower

2. Fertilization happens, seeds grow inside the ovaries, and the petals fall off. The seeds scatter and fall to the ground

3. Seeds germinate and grow if the soil is warm and moist

4. Young plant grows out of the soil, and its leaves use sunlight energy to make food

5. Plant matures and produces one or more flower heads

I don't believe it!

Some species of bamboo grow so fast you can almost watch it happening. Bamboo belongs to the grass family, and the fastest growing specimens can add more than 1 m (3 ft) in height every day.

Most of our plant food comes from flowering plants. We eat many different parts, including roots, stems, leaves, fruits, and seeds.

Tell me more: parts of a flower

Flowers vary enormously in shape and size, but all have the same basic parts.

Sticky stigma: Collects pollen from visiting insects

Petal: Attracts and guides insects towards the flower

Anther: Makes pollen containing male cells and dusts it onto visiting insects

Ovary: Contains female cells that will develop into seeds once they are fertilized by male cells

Flower stalk: Holds up the flower

Types of flowering plants

There are more than 250,000 species of flowering plants, which are divided into two groups – monocots and dicots.

Monocots usually have narrow leaves with parallel veins, and three (or multiples of three) petals.

grass

lily

orchid

palm

Dicots have broad leaves with a central midrib that connects to a smaller network of veins. They have four or five (or multiples of four or five) petals, and also include trees, such as oaks and maples.

magnolia

poppy

lupin

buttercup

In numbers

130–140 million How many years ago the world's first flowers began to bloom. They would have been similar in appearance to today's magnolia

6,400 m (21,000 ft) The altitude of the highest living flowering plant, *Ranunculus lobatus*, which is found in the Himalayan mountain range

150 How many years it takes the slowest flowering plant, *Puya raimondii*, to flower. It is found high up in the Andes mountain range of Bolivia and Peru

93 m (305 ft) The height of the tallest flowering plant – the Australian majestic mountain ash tree

2 m (6.5 ft) The size of the largest floating leaves, which belong to the Amazon water lily, and are able to support the weight of a child

RECORD BREAKER

The **world's tallest flower** is the *titan arum*, which rises to 3 m (10 ft). Smelling of rotting meat to attract the tiny bees that pollinate it, it is short-lived and rarely seen.

What are fruits?

To reproduce, a flowering plant makes seeds inside each flower's ovary. Around a seed or seeds, the ovary grows into a fruit. Fruits come in all shapes and sizes, and can be juicy and succulent, or dry and hard. They protect the seeds, and help them disperse far away from the parent plant so new plants don't compete for water and light.

What about me?

If you eat fruits such as oranges, apples, or peaches, you not only get a juicy treat, but also a supply of essential vitamins and minerals.

Foul fruit

The durian is a large fruit that grows on trees in southeast Asia. Although it is prized for its sweet flesh, it gives off a **disgusting smell**. In Singapore, it is forbidden to take durians on public transport because of the unbearable stink.

Fruit fight!

● The Battle of the Oranges takes place in the Italian town of Ivrea. Every February, thousands of locals, divided into teams, throw oranges at each other – although nobody is really sure why.

● La Tomatina (pictured) is the world's biggest food fight. For just one hour every August in the small Spanish town of Buñol, tens of thousands of people throw tonnes of ripe, squashy tomatoes at each other.

I don't believe it!

The oldest seeds that have been germinated belong to the Judean date palm and are approximately 2,000 years old.

How to: turn a flower into fruit

01. Attract insects to your flower's brightly coloured petals.

02. Allow an insect to pollinate your flower. After pollination, seeds form inside your flower's ovary.

03. No longer required, your petals should fall off and the ovary begin to swell.

How to: **grow a bean seed**

true leaf

01. Begin to sprout. You need fertile soil, ample water, and for it to be warm.

02. Begin to expand. Your outer covering splits, and your radicle (root) grows outwards and down into the soil.

03. Grow upwards. After three days, a plumule (young stem) should sprout up, using energy from the cotyledons (seed leaves).

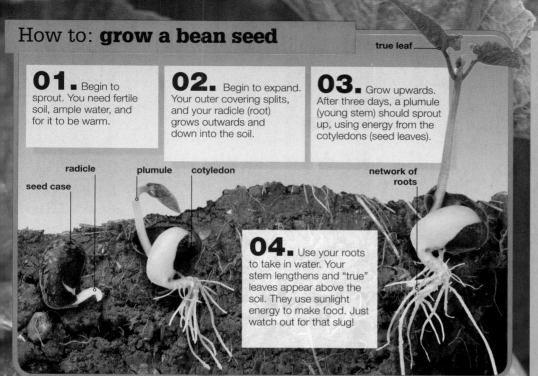

radicle

plumule   cotyledon

seed case

network of roots

04. Use your roots to take in water. Your stem lengthens and "true" leaves appear above the soil. They use sunlight energy to make food. Just watch out for that slug!

04. Congratulations! You've grown a bright orange pumpkin. Who's for soup?

RECORD BREAKER
The **heaviest cultivated fruit** is the pumpkin. It can reach an astonishing 600 kg (1,322 lb) – the same as the combined weight of eight adult men.

Fruit or not?

Do you know your fruits from your vegetables? Look at the list below, and see if you can pick out which are the fruits.

a. banana
b. sweet potato
c. cucumber
d. chilli pepper
e. aubergine
f. asparagus
g. strawberry

(answer below)

Smallest seed
The world's smallest seed-bearing plant, the watermeal, is 0.1 cm (0.039 in) wide. It produces fruits that are tinier than salt grains.

Biggest seed
The biggest seed is produced by the coco de mer, or double coconut palm. It weighs 20 kg (44 lb), and grows in the Seychelles Islands in the Indian Ocean.

How seeds spread

Raspberries
Eaten by animals, the seeds come out in droppings

Burrs
Their spines or hooks stick to animal fur

Pea pods
Pods dry out and explode, launching seeds into the wind

Poppy seeds
The head of a poppy acts like a pepper pot to release seeds

Sycamore seeds
These have "wings" that spin through the air like a helicopter

Coconuts
Fall into the sea and are carried by the currents

Brazil nuts
Seeds are buried by animals, such as agoutis (a type of rodent)

Squirting cucumber
Explode under high pressure, showering seeds

ANSWER: a, c, d, e, and g are fruits; b is a root vegetable; f is a plant stem

How long do **trees** live?

Trees can live for an extremely long time – tens, hundreds, even thousands of years. Most trees have a single woody stem called a trunk that supports a mass of branches carrying leaves. There are an estimated 100,000 tree species worldwide.

Leaf **types**

Simple
Like most trees, the sweet chestnut has simple leaves with single blades (the "leafy" bit).

Compound
The false acacia tree has compound leaves made up of many leaflets sprouting from a long stalk.

Needle
Pine trees have thick, tough needles that thrive in the extreme cold climates that would damage other leaves.

How to: **be a tree**

01. Trap sunlight and make food using thousands of leaves.

02. Support leaves, flowers, and fruits with a mass of twigs growing from branches.

03. Spread out branches from your trunk to form a "crown".

04. Use your strong trunk to support the weight of the branches so you can sway in the wind.

05. Protect inner tissues from bugs and cold with hard bark covering.

My Year, by A. Tree

In northern Europe and North America, deciduous (leaf-shedding) broadleaved trees follow the seasons.

Spring
As days lengthen and temperatures increase, buds burst open to produce new growth, leaves, and flowers.

Summer
Trees are in full leaf, and a variety of fruits develop from flowers pollinated by insects, or by the wind.

Autumn
Fruits fall or are eaten, leaves change colour and drop from trees, and tiny buds remain dormant until spring.

Winter
During the short days of cold winter months, the trees "rest", and the branches are bare of leaves.

Five top tree careers

01: Tree surgeon
Treats old trees to preserve them

02: Lumberjack
Fells trees for timber

03: Dendrochronologist
Dates events by counting tree growth rings

04: Forester
Manages and maintains forest areas

05: Topiarist
Clips trees or shrubs into interesting shapes

RECORD BREAKER

Growing in California, USA, the **world's tallest tree** is a coast redwood, rising to the dizzying height of 112 m (368 ft) – taller than the Statue of Liberty.

I don't believe it!

If African acacia trees are chewed by a giraffe or other hungry plant-eater, they immediately boost levels of nasty-tasting chemicals inside their leaves to deter the diners. What's more, they release a gas that tells neighbouring acacia trees to do the same thing.

Bonsai is the ancient Japanese art of growing miniaturized trees in pots. These are normal trees, but their branches and roots are pruned in a specific way to resemble fully grown trees.

Tell me more: inside the trunk

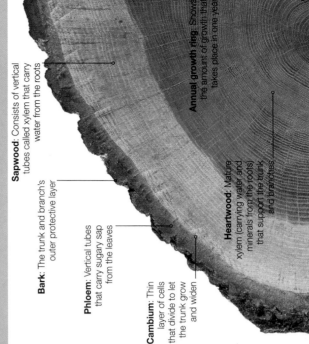

Annual growth ring: Shows the amount of growth that takes place in one year

Sapwood: Consists of vertical tubes called xylem that carry water from the roots

Bark: The trunk and branch's outer protective layer

Phloem: Vertical tubes that carry sugary sap from the leaves

Heartwood: Mature xylem (carrying water and minerals from the roots) that support the trunk and branches

Cambium: Thin layer of cells that divide to let the trunk grow and widen

In numbers

4,600 m
(15,000 ft) The altitude at which the Silver fir grows, in southwest China – higher than any other tree.

2,500 tonnes
The weight of the heaviest tree, the giant sequoia, which grows in California, USA.

120 m
(400 ft) The depth of the roots of the Himalayan wild fig tree.

24 m
(79 ft) The size of the world's largest leaves, which are found on the African raffia palm.

5 cm
(2 in) The size of the dwarf willow, the world's smallest tree, which grows in the Arctic tundra region.

-65°C
(-85°F) The lowest temperature at which the most cold-tolerant tree, Tamarack larch (found in northern North America), continues to grow.

Three types of trees

Broadleaved
There are about 25,000 species of broadleaved trees, including birch, oak, and maple. They are flowering plants and have broad, veined leaves. Many are deciduous, losing their leaves in winter.

Palm
The 3,000 species of palm trees are flowering plants. They include coconut and oil palms, and most grow in warm places. The trunks are fibrous not woody, and are topped with tufts of large leaves.

Conifer
The 550 species of conifers include pines, firs, and spruces. They are non-flowering plants that produce seeds inside cones. They have slender trunks and tough evergreen leaves.

Six good reasons not to cut down trees

01 Trees release oxygen into the air. Every year, one hectare (2.5 acres) of mature trees release the oxygen needed by 45 people.

02 Trees store the carbon dioxide breathed out by all living things and released by burning fossil fuels. Since carbon dioxide is a greenhouse gas (a gas that contributes to climate change) without trees global warming would be far worse.

03 Trees clean the air by removing tiny airborne particles and polluting gases.

04 Trees provide shade from the Sun, and act as natural "air conditioners" to reduce summer temperatures.

05 Tree roots stabilize the soil and prevent it from being eroded (blown away) by wind, or washed away by heavy rain.

06 Trees provide homes for thousands of animals, including insects, birds, frogs, and monkeys.

06. Fix yourself in the ground by strong roots that also take in vital water and minerals.

How do plants survive?

Survival means different things to different plants. Parasitic plants survive by stealing water and nutrients from other plants. Other plants depend on their ability to defend themselves against hungry animals. Desert plants must endure extremely dry conditions, while plants in mountain regions cope with extremely cold temperatures.

What about me?
You should never touch or eat any plant that you are unsure about because it may be poisonous.

Plant parasites
More than 4,000 plant species have stems or roots that enter other plants and then, like vampires, suck out sugars, minerals, and water from their hosts.

Plant survival techniques

Defensive hairs
Lamb's ears is a herb covered with tiny hairs that stop small insects from eating it.

Chemical weapons
Dumb cane contains sharp crystal chemicals that can stick in an animal's throat.

Stinger
Nettles are covered with sharp hairs. The hairs jab into the skin of any animal that brushes past.

Fearsome fluid
Fireglow spurges can ooze a milky fluid called latex, which is dangerous for animals to eat.

Plant armour
Sea holly consists of tough, spine-tipped leaves that keep most plant-eaters at bay.

Camouflage
The fleshy, mottled leaves of living stones make them look like pebbles.

How to: survive as a cactus

01. Reduce your leaves to spines to cut down on water loss.

02. The spines will also protect you against hungry plant-eaters.

03. Make food by trapping sunlight in your green stem.

04. When it rains, store water in your stem for later use.

RECORD BREAKER
Rafflesia – a parasitic plant from southeast Asia – has the world's **heaviest flower**. It weighs up to 7 kg (15 lb) and can reach 1 m (3 ft) in diameter.

Surviving the snow

The dogtooth violet is able to grow through a blanket of snow. The snow forms a protective layer that shields the plant from the worst of the cold and wind. As spring arrives and the snow begins to melt, the dogtooth violet's flower begins to bloom.

WHAT'S IN A NAME?

The ants that live in the swellings at the base of the **whistling thorn tree** ward off animals that try to eat its leaves. On windy days, the swellings make a whistling sound, which is how the tree gets its name.

Epiphytes

01: Epiphytes are plants that grow high up on trees and other plants. This gives them a share of the sunlight without having to spend lots of energy growing tall.

02: They are common in rainforests, but they also grow in cool, damp woodlands.

03: Epiphytes include liverworts, mosses, lichens, as well as flowering plants.

04: Epiphytes aren't parasites, they just use their roots to hold on to the tree.

05: They get water from rain and food from airborne particles, or things that drop onto them.

06: Some large epiphytes, called bromeliads, collect water in a tank-like hollow at the centre of the plant.

07: Bromeliad tanks are important habitats. Some frogs lay their eggs in them and tadpoles hatch in them, high up in the tree.

I don't believe it!

In October 2006, visitors to the Botanical Gardens in Lyon, France, reported an unpleasant stink from a group of pitcher plants native to the Philippines. Staff discovered the smell was a part-digested mouse in one of the pitchers.

06. Spread your long roots wide and deep to collect water.

05. Waterproof yourself with your stem's waxy covering.

Poisonous plants

Cherry laurel
A fast-growing garden shrub, the cherry laurel has thick, evergreen leaves that are well protected from insects because they give off cyanide if they are pierced or crushed.

Poison ivy
A thick, sticky poison called urushiol causes severe swelling if it touches bare skin.

Foxgloves
If a mammal eats this plant's leaves, it risks a heart attack. When administered with care, however, digitoxin (the poison found in a foxglove) can be used as a medicinal drug to treat people with heart failure.

Deadly nightshade
A family containing hundreds of plants that produce poisons called alkaloids. Although important in medicines, in large amounts they can kill.

castor-oil plant

Castor-oil plant
The world's deadliest plant releases ricin, a poison that is 10,000 times more deadly than the venom of a rattlesnake.

Four parasitic plants

Instead of growing on their own, parasitic plants live by stealing from other host plants.

Dodder (devil's thread)
Slender brown stems twist around and penetrate their host plant.

Broomrape
Its roots attach to the roots of neighbouring plants to rob them of nutrients.

Mistletoe
Grows latching on to branches of its host tree and steals water and minerals.

Australian Christmas tree
It can flower during the hot, dry southern Christmas because it taps in to nearby plant roots.

Desert survival

The sack-of-potatoes tree grows in the desert on the island of Socotra in the Indian Ocean. Its fat, sack-like trunk stores water and is topped with several short, stubby branches that produce pink flowers.

How to: catch a fly

Carnivorous (meat-eating) plants, such as the brightly coloured pitcher plant, live in boggy soils that are low in nutrients. They get extra nutrients by trapping insects and other small animals. Pitcher plants lure insects to jug-shaped traps on the end of their leaves.

01. Use your colourful appearance to lure all kinds of insects, from large cockroaches to tiny, tasty flies.

02. Produce nectar around the rim. This attracts insects to walk on and over the rim as they search for the source of the nectar.

A sticky end

Sundews have a very sticky weapon – their hairs. Lured in by the plant's attractive colours, an unsuspecting fly soon finds itself stuck to beads of glue at the tips of the sundew's hairs.

Snatch: The fly is attracted by the glistening, sticky droplets, but soon finds itself stuck.

Grab: Now it's in big trouble. As the fly struggles to free itself, the sticky hairs curls round it.

06. Absorb the nutrients that are released by the insects inside the pool then let their hard, indigestible parts sink to the bottom of your pitcher.

05. Release digestive enzymes. Fluids released from your walls, aided by bacteria, turn the fly's soft parts into a mushy goo.

04. Make sure you have a sufficient amount of fluid to drown the fly. A sea of other insect victims will be the last thing it sees.

03. Make the rim slippery so the unwary fly loses its grip and falls into your trap.

Feed: The sundew digests the fly and absorbs nutrients. Any indigestible parts remain stuck to the leaf.

Meal time: Digestive enzymes break down the damselfly's body.

No escape: The pads snap together when the damselfly touches two of the triggers.

Touch down: Once the damselfly lands on the plant, three small bristles in the middle of each pad activate the trap.

Snappy trap

The Venus flytrap's hinged trap imprisons an unwary damselfly. After about a week, the trap re-opens, letting the dead remains fall to the ground. Each trap digests several meals, and then withers away.

Are bacteria important?

Bacteria are the most plentiful living organisms on the planet. They are also the smallest, each consisting of a simple, single cell. A few types of bacteria, often called germs, cause disease in humans. But most bacteria are harmless, and some are very useful, including those used in making foods and drugs.

Tell me more: anatomy of a bacterium

Flagellum: Rotates to propel bacterium through its surroundings

Loop of DNA: Contains instructions for building and running bacterium

Cytoplasm: Contains chemicals that bring the bacterium to life

Cell membrane: Controls substances that enter and leave

Ribosomes: Produce bacteria-building proteins

Capsule: Slimy jacket helps to protect bacterium

Cell wall: Rigid and shapes bacterium

I don't believe it!

When it infects the body, bacterium *Clostridium botulinum* releases a poison that causes a rare paralytic disease called botulism. Just one drop of botulinum toxin, as it is known, could kill 100,000 people.

PRODUCTION LINE

Bacteria reproduce by binary fission (splitting in two). Reproduction by division means that bacteria can multiply fantastically quickly, if the conditions are just right.

Shaping up

Bacteria come in three shapes:

Cocci (one is called a coccus) are spherical

Bacilli (one is called a bacillus) are rod-shaped

Spirilla (one is called a spirillum) are spiral-shaped

Reasons to like bacteria...

✔ They are used to make yoghurt and cheese.

✔ **Chemicals made by bacteria are used in the processes of baking.**

✔ Some bacteria produce antibiotics that are used to kill other harmful bacteria.

✔ **Bacteria at sewage works help to break down smelly human waste.**

✔ Soil bacteria break down dead organisms so their components can be recycled.

✔ **Some bacteria release life-giving oxygen into the air.**

Five diseases that bacteria cause in humans

Acne Pimples can be sore and erupt (pictured)

Dental caries Tooth decay that form cavities

Cholera The major and most deadly symptom is severe diarrhoea

Diphtheria A terrible, but rare, respiratory illness

Tetanus Serious disease causing muscle spasms

What about me?

Always remember to wash your hands after a trip to the toilet. Around half the weight of your faeces (poo) is made up of bacteria, some potentially harmful.

WEIRD OR WHAT?

Light-producing bacteria live inside the Hawaiian squid. At night, the **bacteria mimic moonlight** shining through the water, making the squid invisible to nearby, hungry predators.

Lucky break

In 1928, British scientist Alexander Fleming was studying harmful bacteria by growing them in glass dishes. Returning from a holiday, he noticed that some dishes were infected with a blue penicillin fungus. This fungus released a chemical that killed harmful bacteria. The discovery lead to the development of penicillin – the first bacteria-killing drug, or antibiotic.

Clear zone: Where penicillin has killed harmful bacteria

penicillin fungus

harmful bacteria

Where *don't* bacteria live?

Bacteria appear in many places, but not everywhere. Can you guess where they don't appear?

(*answers below*)

a) Inside your brain and kidneys

b) In the Dead Sea, which is 10 times saltier than the Atlantic Ocean

c) In Antarctica, where the temperature can plummet to −60°C (−76°F)

d) On your teeth

e) In solid rock, 3 km (1.9 miles) below Earth's surface

f) In clouds

g) On a sandwich

h) On the planet Mars

i) In hot springs where the water temperature is near boiling point

Blasts from the past

3.6 billion years ago
First bacteria appear, more than 900 million years after Earth forms

2.7 billion years ago
Cyanobacteria use sunlight energy to make food, releasing oxygen into the atmosphere

1683
Dutch scientist, Antoni van Leeuwenhoek, using his home-made microscope, becomes the first person to see bacteria (in scrapings from his teeth)

1860s
French scientist Louis Pasteur shows that some bacteria cause disease

1990s
Scientists research genetically modified bacteria to produce useful substances, including anti-cancer vaccines

In numbers

0.0001 cm
(0.00004 in) The average length of a bacterium

99%
The percentage of bacterial species that don't cause disease

10,000
The number of bacteria-laden droplets that you will breathe out in the next five minutes

100,000
The number of bacteria living on 1 sq cm (0.16 sq in) of your skin

2.5 billion
The number of bacteria in 1 g (0.04 oz) of soil

1,000 trillion
The number of bacteria on and inside the human body

5 billion trillion
The number of offspring that, in theory, a single bacterium dividing every 20 minutes produces in 24 hours

Answers: a) and (probably) h)

How do mushrooms grow so fast?

Mushrooms belong to a unique group of living things called fungi. They consist of a network of hair-like threads called hyphae, which spread unseen through the soil. When the conditions are right, hyphae push upwards out of the soil with incredible speed to form a mushroom.

- Fungi includes mushrooms, toadstools, moulds, yeasts, and mildews.
- **Unlike plants, fungi cannot make their own food.**
- They feed on either living or dead organisms.
- **Most of the time fungi remain hidden from view as they grow through their food.**
- It is only when fungi produce fruiting bodies, such as mushrooms, that they become visible.
- **Fruiting bodies have only one purpose – reproduction. They make and release tiny spores that enable fungi to reproduce.**

Hidden hyphae

- The fine threads of the hyphae spread through whatever it is feeding on, be it dead leaves, stale bread, rotting fruit, or damp skin.
- Hyphae release enzymes that digest their surroundings into a soupy mix of nutrients.
- The nutrients are absorbed by the hyphae, which provides the fungus with energy and building blocks for growth.

How to: **qualify as a mushroom**

01. You will need a cap that, like an umbrella, protects your gills from the rain.

02. Make sure you have gills to produce and shed millions of tiny spores. This is how you reproduce.

03. You should have a stem ring, which is the remnant of the membrane that covered the young gills as you were growing.

04. Your stem should lift the cap and gills above the ground so that spores can be carried away by the wind.

05. From your stem base, a network of hair-like threads, called hyphae, will penetrate the soil.

There are more than **100,000 species of fungi** in three main groups:
* black bread moulds
* spore shooters
* spore droppers

Five reasons fungi are good

01: Some types of fungi are delicious to eat.

02: Moulds put the blue into blue cheeses, and the rind on brie and camembert.

03: Yeast makes bread rise, and the alcohol in wine and beer.

04: Some moulds produce bacteria-killing antibiotics, such as penicillin.

05: Cyclosporin, isolated originally from a fungus, is a drug used to stop the body rejecting transplanted organs, such as kidneys.

VS

What about me?

Only handle wild fungi if an adult with expert knowledge checks that it is OK first — and always wash your hands after touching fungi.

Gone in a puff

A puffball is a type of fungus that releases billions of spores. A slight tap from, say, a raindrop causes clouds of spores to puff out through a hole in the puffball's cap.

Five reasons fungi can be bad

01: Some fungi are highly poisonous and can even kill.

02: Dry rot fungus destroys wood and timber in houses.

03: Fungi cause diseases such as athlete's foot and ringworm.

04: Fungi can attack paper, clothes, and other household items.

05: Mildews, smuts, and rusts infect and destroy valuable crops.

I don't believe it!

The most valuable fungus is the white truffle. Prized by chefs for its pungent smell, by weight it is five times more expensive than silver.

Menacing mushrooms

The Death cap may look harmless but less than 28 g (1 oz) can kill a person in just a few hours. Likewise, Coffin web cap, Destroying angel, and False morel are all poisonous mushrooms and should never be eaten.

Four curious fungi

Bridal veil fungus
Although they do not smell nice, they are eaten in some parts of southern China.

Scarlet elf cup
Bright in appearance, these fungi are easily visible in damp woodlands in winter.

Devil's fingers
Native to Australia, this strange red fungi has an unpleasant rotting meat smell.

Jelly Antler
Usually found on roots and trunks of conifer trees, Jelly antlers look like sea coral.

How to: fill a balloon with yeast breath

01. Take the top off a bottle of cola and allow it to go flat overnight. Blow up a balloon and let the air out to soften it.

02. Put a teaspoon of dried yeast into the bottle and shake. Stretch the balloon over the mouth of the bottle and place it in a warm spot.

03. The yeast feeds on the sugar in the cola. As it feeds it breathes, releasing carbon dioxide, which inflates the balloon.

A rotten job

One of the most important functions of mould is to break down dead animal and plant remains. Without these fungi we would be knee-deep in dead organisms. As this pepper shows, mould breaks down the remains, leaving it to rot.

day 1   day 5   day 10

RECORD BREAKER

The **world's biggest fungus** – and, possibly, biggest living organism – is a specimen of honey fungus known as the "humongous fungus". It grows beneath a forest in Oregon, USA, covering an area of 9 sq km (3.5 sq miles), and may weigh up to 600 tonnes.

What's the connection between a slug and an octopus?

Both animals are members of a diverse group of animals called molluscs, which also includes mussels, oysters, limpets, whelks, periwinkles, and squid. There are more than 100,000 species of molluscs. Many live in the sea, but some live in fresh water or, like the garden snail, on land.

Tell me more: **molluscs**

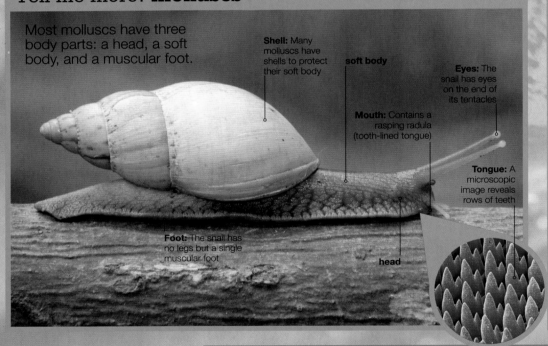

Most molluscs have three body parts: a head, a soft body, and a muscular foot.

Shell: Many molluscs have shells to protect their soft body

soft body

Eyes: The snail has eyes on the end of its tentacles

Mouth: Contains a rasping radula (tooth-lined tongue)

Tongue: A microscopic image reveals rows of teeth

Foot: The snail has no legs but a single muscular foot

head

Record breakers

The **largest of all molluscs** is the aptly named colossal squid, which can reach 14 m (46 ft) in length. That's one scary predator.

The **biggest bivalve** (a mollusc with a shell in two parts) is the giant clam, which can reach 1.5 m (5 ft) in width. In the past, its half shell was used as a baby bath.

The **largest gastropod** is the giant African land snail, which can reach 30 cm (12 in) in length.

The **fastest mollusc** is the squid, which can speed away from danger at 35 kph (22 mph).

One of the **slowest land molluscs** is the garden snail, which travels at 0.05 kph (0.03 mph). That means it covers a distance of 1 km (0.6 miles) every 20 hours.

The world's **oldest living animal** is a mollusc – it's a type of clam called an ocean quahog. In 2006 and 2007 scientists found specimens off Iceland that are estimated to be between 405 and 410 years old.

WEIRD OR WHAT?

Slipper limpets live in stacks of up to 12 animals with the biggest (oldest) shells at the bottom and the smallest (youngest) at the top. Each limpet **starts off male** but then, when another lands on it, **changes sex** to become female.

Five types of molluscs

Molluscs are invertebrates (animals without backbones) and come in a wide range of shapes and sizes.

Chitons
A family of marine grazers with an armadillo-like shell

Tusk shells
These marine burrowers have a long, tapering shell

Bivalves
Molluscs with a shell in two hinged parts, called valves

Gastropods
Most gastropods have a spiral shell, tentacles, and a muscular foot

Cephalopods
Big, intelligent, fast-moving animals with tentacles

Spectacular shells

Nautilus
Inside this shell are pearly chambers of air that help the mollusc float.

Spiny oyster shell
Archaeologists believe these shells were used 5,000 years ago to make ornaments.

Venus comb murex
The spines of this shell may prevent it from sinking into sandy mud.

Cuban land snails
Now protected by law, overcollecting of these shells once threatened their future.

Giant clams
The leaf-like scales of these shells are used for shelter by crabs and others.

What about me?

If you spot a small, cute octopus with blue rings in the rock pools off the Australian coast, don't pick it up. The blue-ringed octopus is one of the world's most venomous animals and one bite could kill you.

Cowries are sea-living gastropods with pretty round shells that were used in many places as a form of **currency**, from the time of the pharaohs in Ancient Egypt, up to the 20th century.

I don't believe it!

Shipworms are not worms at all, but weird-looking bivalves with their shells at the front end of their body. Also called boring clams, shipworms burrow into and weaken any wooden structure in the sea. Their handiwork has even sunk boats!

Feeding methods

Gastropods use a radula (tooth-lined tongue) to eat algae or plants, or to dig into other animals.

Bivalves open and shut their shells and filter tiny food particles from the water.

Cephalopods stalk their prey and then grab it and pull it into their mouth with tentacles and suckers, and crush it with their horny beaks.

Mollusc moves

- Slugs and snails creep and glide on a muscular foot.
- Some sea snails simply float on the ocean's surface.
- Bivalves like cockles burrow into sand or mud using their muscular feet.
- Scallops (above) push themselves through the water by opening and closing their valves.
- Cuttlefish and squid swim by rippling their fins.
- The octopus swims by pulling his arms and suckers through the water.
- Octopus and squid can also make a quick getaway using jet propulsion, squeezing water out of their bodies at speed.

Three cuttlefish facts

01 Cuttlefish can change colour at will in less than a second. They do this to hide from predators and communicate their mood.

02 Their brown ink, which they squirt at enemies when making an escape, has been used by artists for centuries.

03 Pet birds are given cuttlefish skeletons to peck for their calcium content.

For self-defence, the cunning mimic octopus changes its shape, colour, and texture in order to appear like dangerous or unappetizing animals.

01. If a hungry mantis shrimp is on the prowl, change from your natural form (pictured) and turn yourself into one as well, by pulling in your tentacles and changing colour.

02. If predators are lurking nearby, then change quickly to look like an unfriendly sea snake to scare them off.

03. If that doesn't work, try looking like a starfish – they are not very pleasant to eat.

04. Have a go at impersonating a flat fish – you really are a camouflage expert!

Which are the most successful animals on Earth?

There are more insects living and flying inside an area the size of a small town than there are human beings on Earth. They live just about everywhere – only the oceans are insect-free. Insects have six legs, four wings, and a body divided into three parts.

Tell me more: wasp anatomy

Cuticle: A hard, waterproof exoskeleton that supports and protects the body

Thorax: Middle section of the body, with two pairs of wings attached

Compound eye: Made up of lots of tiny lenses to give a wide field of vision

Antenna: One of two, flexible antennae, used to feel, smell, and taste

Head: Houses the brain and sense organs

Leg: One of six jointed legs, attached to the thorax

Abdomen: Contains the intestines and reproductive organs, and is long and slender to help with balance when in flight

Wing: One of two pairs of wings, attached to the thorax

A BIGGER GROUP

Insects, along with crustaceans, arachnids, and centipedes, belong to an even bigger group of invertebrate animals called **arthropods**. All arthropods have a hard outer skeleton (exoskeleton) and flexible legs with joints.

Light show

Fireflies are beetles with an unusual ability: they have a special organ in their abdomens that produces flashes of light. As fireflies fly around at night they flash signals to attract mates.

In numbers

10 quintillion*
Estimate of how many insects there are on Earth

300,000,000
Number of years ago that the first flying insects appeared

30,000,000
Estimate of how many insect species there actually are

1,017,018
Number of named insect species (this is increasing all the time)

*10,000,000,000,000,000,000

10 types of insect

Dragonflies and damselflies
5,500 species
Large eyes and wings, and slender bodies

Grasshoppers and crickets
20,000 species
Powerful hind legs and chewing mouthparts

Mantises
2,000 species
Triangular head, large eyes, extendable front legs for catching prey

Cockroaches
4,000 species
Oval, flattened bodies with a leathery casing

Seven insect movies

Deadly Mantis (1957)
The Fly (1958, remade 1986)
The Swarm (1978)
Antz (1998)
A Bug's Life (1998)
Bugs (2003)
Bee Movie (2007)

Insect snacks

Insects are cheap, plentiful, and rich in protein. Here's a sample of insect snacks.

Fried queen termites
From Africa, they are rich in fat as well as protein.

Mopani worms
These moth larvae are eaten sun-dried or in tomato sauce.

Jumiles
Stink bugs, used as a taco filling in Mexico.

Three insects to avoid

Mosquitoes
Suck blood and may spread diseases such as malaria and dengue fever

Bed bugs
These suckers feed on the blood of people sleeping in bed

Botflies
They lay eggs that hatch into maggots under your skin

How to: change from an egg into a butterfly

01. As a newly laid egg, find yourself stuck on the leaf of a plant that will provide you with constant food when you hatch.

02. Hatch from your egg and enjoy the leafy feast in front of you. You need your strength for all the coming changes to your body. Shed your outer coat several times so that your body can keep expanding.

03. On your last and final moult you'll find it difficult to move, as a hard outer coat forms around you in the pupa stage. Over the next week or so, your body tissues reorganize into those of an adult insect.

04. Split open the pupa casing and emerge as a beautiful butterfly. Wing it over to a flower and use your new sucking mouthparts to drink its nectar.

I don't believe it!

Some doctors use specially bred blowfly larvae (maggots) to treat flesh wounds. The maggots clean a wound by eating dead tissue and harmful bacteria.

Termites
2,750 species
Soft bodies, chewing mouthparts and short antennae. Live in colonies

Bugs
82,000 species
Two pairs of wings, and long "beaks" that pierce and suck

True flies
122,000 species
Single pair of wings, with small balancing organs called halteres

Beetles
370,000 species
Toughened front wings encase and protect hind wings

Butterflies and moths
165,000 species
Special feeding mouthparts, scales on body and wings

Ants, bees, and wasps
198,000 species
Many live in colonies, but some are solitary

What are arachnids?

This is the group of invertebrates (animals without backbones) that includes spiders, scorpions, harvestmen, mites, and ticks. There are about 65,000 species of arachnid, half of which are spiders.

How to: qualify as an arachnid

01. You will need a tough outer skeleton (exoskeleton), like insects and crustaceans.

02. Eat other animals.

03. Have eight legs.

04. Make sure your body is divided into two parts with the legs attached to the front part, and, in spiders, silk-making glands in the back part.

05. See using up to eight eyes.

RECORD BREAKER

A **spider web** in Lake Tawakoni State Park in Texas, USA, covered 180 sq m (1,940 sq ft) of trees and bushes. What was once a white web soon turned dark when hundreds of mosquitoes got caught in it.

Top five biggest spiders

01: **Goliath bird-eating spider** (right)
leg span: 30 cm (12 in)

02: **Honduran curly hair spider**
leg span: 30 cm (12 in)

03: **Bolivian pink bird-eating spider**
leg span: 20 cm (8 in)

04: **Goliath pink toe spider**
leg span: 18 cm (7 in)

05: **King baboon spider**
leg span: 17 cm (6.7 in)

WHAT'S IN A NAME?

Bird-eating spiders do occasionally eat birds, but usually they go for insects, frogs, mice, and lizards. Tasty!

Hair flair

Spiders sense the world around them through their hairs, which can detect tiny vibrations, and some are even able to taste. If threatened, a tarantula brushes its legs against its body to send tiny barbed hairs into the eyes, nose, or mouth of the predator. So never stroke a tarantula! They use their hairs for:

- **sensing the world around them**
- **courtship displays**
- **moving around**
- **self-defence**
- **catching prey**

Good enough to eat

Male spiders, which are usually smaller than females, sometimes get eaten by their partner after mating. It's not a lover's tiff – it's usually because the female mistakes her mate for prey.

Five super scorpion facts

01: Scorpions glow in the dark. They glow bright blue or yellow-green under ultra-violet light.

02: The largest scorpion, the African, can grow to more than 20 cm (8 in).

03: Scorpions grab prey with their claws and crush them into a mush that they then suck up.

04: The sting in a scorpion's tail is used mainly for self-defence.

05: Several thousand people die each year from scorpion stings.

I don't believe it!

Spider's silk is five times stronger than a steel strand of the same width. It's also elastic, stretching to four times its original length before breaking. A pencil-thick strand of spider silk could, in theory, stop a jumbo jet in flight.

Scary spider stats

01: Some large spiders lay more than 2,000 eggs in a single egg sac.

02: The average spider can weave a web in less than one hour.

03: An empress of China once demanded a robe made entirely out of spider web silk. It took 8,000 spiders to make her coat.

04: Out of about 20,000 species of spider in the USA, only 60 are capable of causing harm to humans.

05: The black widow spider's bite is reported to be 15 times stronger than that of a rattlesnake.

Top five most dangerous spiders

01: Funnel web spider Australia

02: Black widow spider North America

03: Red back spider Australia

04: Brown recluse spider USA

05: Brazilian wandering spider Central and South America

Hunting techniques

Trapdoor spiders hide in burrows concealed under a trapdoor, which flies open when the spider leaps out to grab prey.

Orb web spiders make circular webs to catch prey.

Jumping spiders stalk and jump on prey.

Wolf spiders are night-time hunters.

Spitting spiders squirt sticky stuff at prey to trap it.

Hairy tarantulas and **bird-eating spiders** ambush prey as big as lizards and mice.

Funnel web spiders lure their prey into a funnel-shaped web.

What about me?

Arachnophobia is an over-the-top fear of spiders, and it's the world's commonest phobia – even though most spiders are harmless.

Five tasty arachnid dishes from around the world

Central America: Char-grilled bird-eating spider with pepper sauce

China: Fried crispy scorpion

Cambodia: Fried Thai zebra tarantula

China: Scorpion soup

Brazil: Roasted tarantula eggs

How to: spin a spider's web

01. Climb to a suitable spot and use the glands on your abdomen to release a length of thread into the wind.

02. If the thread catches and sticks to another surface, walk across the thread and release a second, looser thread.

03. Lower yourself onto the second thread and then abseil down on a vertical thread to form a Y-shape.

04. Attach threads to the corners of the web to build up the frame.

05. Spin more radius threads out from the centre. Strengthen the web with five circular threads.

06. Add a sticky spiral of threads to complete the web. You are now ready to trap unlucky prey.

Why do crabs walk sideways?

A crab has eight walking legs. The joints on the legs on one side pull the crab, and those on the other side push, producing the sideways-scuttling movement they're famed for. Like their lobster and shrimp relatives, crabs are crustaceans – a group of animals that are extremely numerous in seas, rivers, and ponds.

RECORD BREAKER

With a leg span of up to 4 m (13 ft) and weighing up to 20 kg (44 lb), the giant spider crab is the **biggest crustacean**.

Crustaceans

01: This very diverse group of animals includes crabs, lobsters, shrimps, prawns, barnacles, and woodlice.

02: Like insects and arachnids, crustaceans are arthropods – invertebrates with a hard outer skeleton and jointed limbs.

03: The outer skeleton (cuticle) in many species is reinforced by chalky calcium carbonate.

04: More than 40,000 species live in the sea and fresh water, and a few species are land-dwellers.

05: Crustaceans range in size from microscopic water fleas to giant spider crabs.

Three cunning crustaceans

Valet service
Cleaner shrimps team up with fish like this moray eel to get food. They use their tiny pincers to perform a valet service by picking off parasites, dead skin, and scraps of uneaten food.

Camouflage
Decorator crabs collect tiny shells, bits of seaweed, sponges, sea anemones, and other small animals, which they attach to the hooks that cover their shell for the perfect camouflage.

Lopsided male
Male fiddler crabs have one very big claw, and one tiny one. They signal to females that they will make good mates by waving the big claw up and down, and use it in ritual fights with rival males.

How to: **qualify as a lobster**

01. You will need a jointed abdomen ending in a telson (tail fan) that flicks downwards for rapid swimming.

02. Have four pairs of jointed walking legs, just like those of crabs and prawns.

Odd one out

There are more than 40,000 different species of crustacean. Can you tell at a glance from this line-up of creatures which one is not a crustacean? (answers on opposite page)

goose barnacle

brine shrimp

common shrimp

horseshoe crab

pill woodlouse

Planktonic performers

Plankton is made up of tiny living things that float in the surface waters of oceans, ponds, and rivers. Crustaceans make up an important part of plankton.

 Crab larvae float in the sea before settling on the seabed to mature.

Copepods (tiny crustaceans) are superabundant in the plankton and are an important source of food for fish, seabirds, and whales.

Tiny shrimps provide food for small fish.

Mantis shrimp

■ This marine crustacean is a ferocious predator that lives in tropical oceans.

■ Its second pair of legs is hinged and normally folded up, just like a praying mantis insect.

■ It hides in crevices and ambushes prey by flicking out its folded limbs with lightning speed.

■ In captivity, it has smashed through thick aquarium glass.

How to: **move house** (if you are a hermit crab)

01. Realize that you have outgrown your present home (a mollusc shell) and need to find somewhere bigger.

02. Clamber out of your shell and look for a new home. You're a walking snack for passing predators, so beware.

03. Identify a potential new shell. Tentatively probe the new, bigger shell with a pincer to make sure it isn't occupied.

04. Curl your abdomen into the spiral shell for protection. Fully retreat into your new home if danger threatens.

04. Have two compound (many-faceted) eyes on stalks.

03. Make sure you have a carapace (shield) covering the front part of your body (cephalothorax).

05. Use your two pairs of antennae to feel your way around and detect food.

06. Break up and handle food with your powerful pincers.

Antarctic krill

These 6-cm- (2.4-in-) long, shrimp-like crustaceans live in the nutrient-rich ocean around Antarctica, feeding on tiny plant-like phytoplankton.

They live in massive swarms that provide a major source of food for many animals, including seals, penguins, and massive baleen whales, which filter krill out of the water.

The total weight of all Antarctic krill in the oceans is more than 500 million tonnes. It is the most successful species on Earth.

Krill have tiny light-producing organs that flash pinpoints of yellow-green.

A blue whale, which is 10 billion times bigger than its prey, can eat more than 2.5 tonnes of krill daily.

I don't believe it!

Christmas Island in the Indian Ocean is home to 1.2 million red crabs. In November they walk en-masse through houses, shops, and across roads to breed at the coast.

ANSWERS: The intruder is the horseshoe crab – it is actually a close relative of arachnids, not a crustacean.

Crustaceans 112|113

How do fish breathe?

Fish are vertebrates (animals with backbones) that live in the sea and in fresh water. Like all animals they have to breathe in oxygen. Lungs would simply fill up with water, so instead fish have feathery gills at the back of the head that extract oxygen from water as it flows over them.

I don't believe it !

The eel-like pearlfish has a strange relationship with sea cucumbers, sausage-like relatives of starfish. The fish hunts for food at night, and lives inside the sea cucumber by day, going in and out of the creature's bottom!

FISH

- A goldfish can live up to 40 years.
- A shark's skin is covered in tiny, backward-pointing tooth-like structures which feel like rough sandpaper.
- When flatfish are young they swim upright, but when they settle on the sea bed, one side becomes their ventral (lower) surface, and the other becomes the dorsal (upper) surface. Their left eye moves up to the top of their head to join the right one.
- With fins almost as long as its body, the Atlantic flying fish, can skim above the waves at up to 60 kph (37 mph) to escape predators.

Tell me more: fish features

Streamlined body: The ideal shape to move through water

Overlapping scales: These form a smooth surface for water to flow over

Dorsal fin: This controls how much the fish rolls to one side or the other

Tail fin: The tail gives forward thrust to push fish through the water

Slimy mucus: This makes fish slippery and protects against parasites

Lateral line: Sensors here detect sound vibration and water movement

Fish families

"Fish" is a general name given to a range of vertebrates with streamlined bodies that live in water. There are three types of fish.

Jawless
These long, thin fish have a sucking mouth to grasp food. The group includes lampreys (pictured) and hagfish.

Cartilaginous
Rays (pictured), skates, and sharks all have a skeleton made of flexible cartilage instead of bone.

Bony
This is the largest group of fish. They have a skeleton made of bone and come in all shapes and sizes.

In numbers

13 m
(43 ft) The length of the whale shark, the world's biggest fish

7.9 mm
(0.3 in) The length of *Paedocypris progenetica*, the world's smallest fish. It lives in peat swamps on the Indonesian island of Sumatra

110 kph
(68 mph) The speed of the sailfin

20,000 km
(12,430 miles) The distance the great white shark migrates on its return trip between South Africa and Australia

140
The age in years of the longest-living fish – the rougheye rockfish

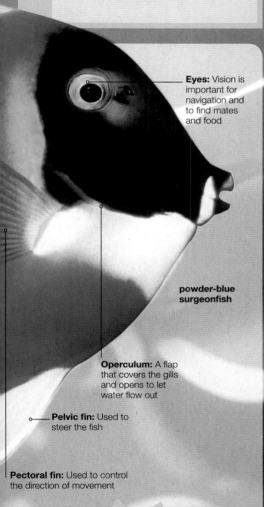

Eyes: Vision is important for navigation and to find mates and food

powder-blue surgeonfish

Operculum: A flap that covers the gills and opens to let water flow out

Pelvic fin: Used to steer the fish

Pectoral fin: Used to control the direction of movement

The **stonefish**, found in the Indian and Pacific Oceans, has **spiny fins filled with venom** that can be fatal to people who step on them.

Seahorses

- Seahorses are slow movers and never exceed 0.0016 kph (0.001 mph).

- To anchor themselves in strong currents, they can wind their tail around a piece of weed.

- The male has a pouch in his body into which the female lays up to 600 eggs. He incubates the eggs in his pouch until they hatch.

- Although seahorses are bony fish, their skin is not covered with scales.

Slithery slime

Hagfishes are jawless fish that are also known as slime eels. Here's why:

- An average sized hagfish can produce enough gooey mucus to fill an 8-litre (14-pint) bucket.

- They use slime as a defence against predators while they feed on dead and dying fish.

- Hagfish get rid of their own mucus by tying a knot in their bodies and then sliding it forwards.

Reef life

Many fish that live on coral reefs have bright colours and patterns to break up their outlines, making it harder for predators to catch them or for prey to see them coming.

Monsters of the deep

Down in the cold, dark gloom of the ocean depths lurk some very strange fish. This deep-sea **anglerfish** can emit light in order to attract prey. It also has flexible bones, allowing the jaws and stomach to expand and create room for prey twice the size of its entire body.

Electric shockers!

- **Electric eels** live in the murky waters of South American rivers and produce 500 volt electric pulses to stun prey and deter predators.

- **Electric catfish** from tropical Africa are nocturnal hunters that use their electric organs to generate 300 volts to stun prey.

- **Electric rays** can release 220 volts to stun other fish.

- **Elephantnose fish** produce weak electrical currents to help with navigation.

- **Sharks and rays** detect the weak electric currents produced by some prey and go in for the kill.

Sharks are more **at risk** from humans than we are from them. Shark **fishing**, especially for shark fins, has seriously **depleted numbers** of some species.

Four sharks to avoid

Great white shark
This scary predator does attack humans, though it doesn't really like the taste.

Hammerhead shark
With widely spaced eyes, this shark is prone to making unpredictable attacks.

Tiger shark
A stripy scavenger found in coastal waters, and known to attack people.

Blue shark
The most widespread of all sharks, the blue commonly circles prey before attacking.

How does a **toad** differ from a frog?

Most frogs are active jumpers that live near water, have long back legs, webbed feet, and smooth, moist skins. Toads are generally less active, have dry, warty skins, and prefer to live on land. Frogs and toads are amphibians – animals that typically prefer moist surroundings, spend part of their life in water and part on land, lay their shell-less eggs in water, and breathe through lungs and their skin.

Tell me more: **amphibians**

Wide mouth: Accommodates large prey

Eardrum: Enables salamander to hear mates and rivals

Skin: Smooth and moist skin to take in oxygen

Bulging eye: Provides a wide range of vision to look for prey

Leg: Each of four legs ends in toes, and are webbed in frogs

fire salamander

In numbers

9.8 mm
(0.4 in) The length of the tiny Brazilian gold frog

33 cm
(13 in) The length of the massive goliath frog, which is found in west Africa

180 cm
(5.9 ft) The length of the biggest amphibian, the Japanese giant salamander – that's as tall as an adult human

Five fantastic frogs **and** tremendous toads

Asian horned toad
It looks like a leaf and is perfectly camouflaged in its forest home.

Madagascan tomato frog
No surprise where it gets its name from.

Darwin's frog
From Chile, the male carries young in its vocal sac.

Budgett's frog
A scary looking frog from Argentina, it screams and grunts to frighten off attackers.

Chilean red-spotted toad
This small toad can be found as high as 4,000 m (13,000 ft) in the Andes mountains.

Types of amphibian

great crested newt

red-eyed tree frog

caecilian

Newts and salamanders
Number of species: 360
Features: slender bodies; long tails; legs the same length

Frogs and toads
Number of species: 3,500
Features: short, compact bodies; long powerful hind legs; no tail

South American horned toad

tiger salamander

Caecilians
Number of species:
more than 200
Features: worm-like; legless; burrowers and swimmers; resemble snakes and live mostly underground

WHAT'S IN A NAME?

If you look underneath a **glass frog**, its skin looks as though it is made of frosted glass. You can even see the frog's heart, liver, and intestines through it.

How to: grow up if you're a frog

01. Start your life as one of a mass of fertilized eggs called frog spawn.

02. After a few days start to wiggle inside your transparent egg.

03. By day six it is time to hatch out from the egg. Stick on to pond weed to feed and breathe through external gills.

04. After a few more days start swimming around – but look out for predators, such as ferocious dragonfly larvae.

05. Your external gills should disappear after seven weeks and your back legs pop out. Eat small animals.

07. Your tail disappears, and you hop out of the pond to join the other froglets. The growing up process, called metamorphosis, is over.

06. Grow front legs during the next nine weeks so you look like a frog with a tail.

HIP HOP
A group of frogs is called a "chorus".

Don't lick them!
Poison dart frogs from Central and South America and mantellas from Madagascar have bright colours to warn predators that their skin is deadly poisonous.

strawberry poison dart frog

green mantella

green and black poison dart frog

Panamanian golden frog

painted mantella

WEIRD OR WHAT?
The male midwife toad winds strings of fertilized eggs around his legs and back and carries them until they are ready to hatch.

I don't believe it!
Snakes are not the most venomous animals in the world. This title belongs to the gold poison dart frog, which carries enough poison to kill 20 people or two bull elephants!

Big mistake
The big South American cane toad was introduced to Australia in 1935 to eat beetles that were destroying sugar cane crops. It didn't eat the beetles but managed to scoff lots of other animals, including native frogs, snakes, and mammals, making some extinct.

Newts

Newts spend most of their lives on land, but return to water to breed.

Newt eggs hatch into larvae with small feathery gills.

The larvae lose their gills and switch to using internal lungs to breathe air. They then take to the land.

Newts can regenerate damaged eye tissue and heart tissue.

Many newts produce toxins as a defence against predators.

FAST FACTS

Do snakes feel slimy?

No, their scaly skin feels cool and dry, a feature snakes share with other reptiles including lizards, turtles, and crocodiles. Reptiles have backbones and are cold-blooded. This means they rely on the Sun's heat to warm them up. Most reptiles lay eggs with waterproof shells, although some snakes give birth to live young.

RECORD BREAKER

The world's **largest (and heaviest) reptile** is the saltwater crocodile, found in Australia. It can reach 7 m (23 ft) in length.

Tell me more: chameleons

Long tail: Can be used to hold onto a branch and aid balance

Scales: Tough, waterproof scales protect the body

Skin: As the reptile grows it sheds its old skin to reveal a new one below

Leg: Limbs bend outwards to the side of the body

Foot: Each foot has five toes with claws

Five reasons not to fall asleep under a tree on Komodo Island

01: The Indonesian island is home to the Komodo dragon, at 3 m (10 ft) long, the world's biggest lizard.

02: Although it prefers rotting flesh, the lizard is not averse to fresh meat, even human flesh!

03: The lizard has a great sense of smell, flicking its tongue to detect scent molecules in the air.

04: If it finds you dozing, the dragon will use its sharp, serrated teeth to bite off chunks of flesh.

05: The incredibly toxic bacteria in its saliva can kill you simply by infecting a wound.

One in the eye

A snake that you should definitely avoid is the spitting cobra, which can open its mouth and squirt venom droplets into the air from tiny openings in its fangs. This venom can cover a distance of 2 m (6.5 ft), and if the venom spray hits a predator's eyes it can cause permanent blindness. They also bite!

Types of **reptiles**   There are four different groups of reptiles:

Lizards and snakes
Lizards, snakes, and amphisbaenians (worm-lizards that live underground) are all closely related.

Crocodilians
This group of semi-aquatic predators includes alligators, crocodiles, caimans, and the gharial.

Tortoises and turtles
These reptiles have a bony shell to protect the soft parts of the body, four limbs, and a toothless beaky mouth.

Tuataras
Only found on islands off New Zealand, tuataras look very like lizards but can put up with colder conditions.

1.6 cm
(0.75 in) The length of the smallest reptile, the dwarf gecko of the Dominican Republic

2
The number of species of tuataras, ancient lizard-like reptiles

10 m
(33 ft) The length of the longest snake, the reticulated python, found in southeast Asia

23
The number of species of crocodiles and alligators

175
The age of the longest lived reptile, the Galápagos tortoise

294
The number of species of turtles and tortoises

2,900
The number of species of snakes

4,500
The number of species of lizards

How to: eat lunch if you're a python

01. Sneak up to your prey and, before it can get away, coil your muscular body around it.

02. Each time your victim breathes out, tighten the coils a bit more.

03. When your prey stops breathing, loosen the coils and find its head.

04. Open your mouth wide by unhinging your jaws, and swallow the prey head first. Lie still and digest.

Big bite

Crocodiles have amazingly powerful jaws, with the strongest bite in the whole animal kingdom. The force of their bite is:

- six times that of a bone-crushing hyena dismembering its prey
- thirteen times that of a great white shark in a feeding frenzy
- fifteen times that of a Rottweiler dog eating meat

Eye: Each eye moves independently, so the animal can look in opposite directions at the same time

Tongue: A long, sticky tongue flicks out to catch prey

Diary of a green turtle

Day 1
I feel the time has come to breed. Had a last snack of sea grasses off the coast of Brazil, then together with many other green turtles, started to swim east across the Atlantic Ocean.

Day 20
Swimming at 5 kph (3 mph), have covered the 2,250 km (1,400 miles) and arrived at Ascension Island.

Day 21
Found a male turtle, mated, then under cover of darkness, crawled up the beach. Dug a hole with my flippers, laid 150 eggs, covered them up, and headed back to sea.

Day 22
Swam home to Brazil using the stars and Sun to navigate.

Day 42
Back to eating sea grasses. Will migrate again in three years' time.

Day 71
My eggs should now be hatching and my offspring will be making their way to the sea. I hope they can dodge the hungry gulls.

Ascension Island

Brazil

Top five most deadly snakes

If you want to avoid the snakes with the deadliest poison, don't go to Australia!

01: Taipan
(Australia)
The most poisonous snake in the world, prey is paralyzed the instant it is bitten.

02: Brown snake
(Australia)
Though less poisonous, the brown snake is more common than the taipan.

03: Tiger snake
(Australia)
Just to confuse you, this snake sometimes has stripes, but often does not.

04: Beaked sea snake
(Arabian Sea to coast of northern Australia)
Will attack and bite divers if disturbed.

05: Malayan krait
(southeast Asia and Indonesia)
This snake is slow to strike, but its poison can be fatal.

Why do birds have feathers?

Feathers help to keep birds warm and enable them to fly. Their wings are equipped with stiff flight feathers to provide both lift and, when the wings are flapped, forward thrust to propel these masters of flight through the air. Something else common to all birds is that they lay eggs with hard shells.

Tell me more: **bird features**

Eyes: Provide bird with a keen sense of vision

Beak: Lightweight, and without any teeth

Feathers: Cover the body

Body: Shaped by a lightweight skeleton

Wings: Powerful chest muscles move the wings

Tail: Short tail has feathers growing from it

Legs: Two scaly legs for walking, and for taking off and landing

Feet: Adapted to bird's lifestyle, and can be used to run, perch, and grasp

Flight checklist

- You will need a strong but light skeleton with hollow bones
- Your wings, carefully curved by their feathers, give you lift when air flows over them
- Strong wing muscles to power your wings, and create the thrust that pushes you forward
- Strong leg muscles to launch you into the air
- Contour feathers make flying more efficient by streamlining your body
- A tail that works as a rudder so you can change direction as you fly through the air

Weird or what?
An ostrich's eyeball is bigger than its brain, and as wide as the bee hummingbird – the world's smallest bird – is long.

In numbers

1.5 billion
The number of red-billed quelea in Africa that form a flock. It takes five hours for this huge flock to fly past

10,000
Species of birds

40,000 km
(24,850 miles) The distance of the Arctic tern's incredible migration. Every year, it flies from its Arctic breeding grounds to the Antarctic and back again

60%
The percentage of all birds that belong to the Passeriformes group (perching birds)

Bird life

Birds come in all shapes and sizes. Their behaviour is also wonderfully diverse. Here is just a sample of the types of birds that are found throughout the world.

Flightless birds
What ostriches lack in flight, they make up for in running speed.

Gamebirds
These birds include wild turkey and pheasants, and are often hunted for food.

Penguins
Flightless birds found in the Southern Hemisphere spend equal time on land as water.

Waterfowl
They are strong swimmers, and include ducks, geese, and swans.

Diary of a duck egg

Day 1
Just laid – I'm an embryo resting on a yolk food store.

Day 12
It's safe and warm in this hard shell, and at last I'm beginning to feel like a bird.

Day 20
I've been growing fast and things are getting a bit cramped in here – I'm planning to break out, but I can't find the door.

Day 21 morning
In desperation, I have begun to bash my way out with a toothy bit on my beak – I can see the light at last.

Day 21 afternoon
I'm free! My feathers have dried out, and I've found my legs and am running around. I am starting to feel a bit peckish, so will start looking for food.

RECORD BREAKER

The ostrich is the **biggest bird**, growing to a height of 2.7 m (9 ft). It also lays the **biggest egg**, up to 18 cm (7 in) long, and is the **fastest runner**, reaching speeds of up to 72 kph (45 mph).

Right beak for the job

Finch
Tough and sharp to crack open seeds

Parrot
Hook pulls flesh off fruit and beak cracks open nuts

Flamingo
Acts as a filter to sieve out tiny animals

Gull
All-purpose beak catches fish and tears food apart

Eagle
Hooked to rip flesh of prey that cannot be eaten whole

I don't believe it!

Australian lyrebirds are fantastic mimics. They copy not only other bird songs to attract mates, but also mobile phone ring tones, camera shutters, chainsaws, crying babies, barking dogs, and even car alarms.

Nesting materials

Some birds just lay their eggs on the ground, but most build a nest to keep them safe. The materials birds use to make their nests include the following:

- **spiders' webs (for glue)** • moss
- **lichen** • grass • **feathers** • mud
- **animal hair** • old snake skin
- **sticks** • stones • **dead beetles**
- anything useful humans leave behind like string and soft materials

Four feathers

Down
Grow close to the skin to keep the bird warm

Contour
Cover the body to give a streamlined shape

Tail
Stiffer feathers that help in flight

Wing
Stiffer feathers that cover the wings

Shorebirds
Thought to have an internal compass to help them migrate over long distances.

Wading birds
Flamingos often stand on one foot, but nobody knows why

Owls
Most owls are night hunters, using their sharp hearing and eyesight to catch food.

Parrots
Their ability to imitate human voices makes them popular pets.

Swifts and swallows
These graceful flyers both catch their insect prey in flight.

Perching birds
They are also known as songbirds because of their whistling tunes.

Why do cats have fur?

Cats, like all other mammals, are warm-blooded, and a furry coat helps to insulate the body and keep them warm. Mammals produce milk to feed their young, and look after them until they are able to fend for themselves. Many mammals have different types of teeth, for cutting, piercing, and grinding food.

Meet the family

The closest relatives of humans, apes are highly intelligent mammals, adept at performing tasks with their flexible limbs.

Gorilla: Lives in mountains and lowland forests of central Africa; eats leaves and fruit

Chimpanzee: Lives in the forests of west and central Africa; eats leaves, fruit, insects, and small mammals

Bonobo: Lives in the rainforest of central Africa in female-dominated societies; eats vegetation

Orang-utan: Lives in the forests of Borneo and Sumatra; eats fruit

FAST FACTS

Mammals

01: There are nearly 4,500 species.

02: Mammals are very diverse and include plant-eaters, insect-eaters, meat-eaters, and omnivores (who eat everything).

03: Mammals are found on the land, in water, and in the air.

04: There are five species of egg-laying monotremes, such as echidnas.

05: There are 292 species of pouched marsupials, such as the koala.

06: The remainder are placental mammals (young develop inside their mother's uterus), such as hyenas and humans.

07: Nearly half of all mammal species are rodents.

08: Around one-fifth of all mammal species are bats.

Tell me more: mammal anatomy

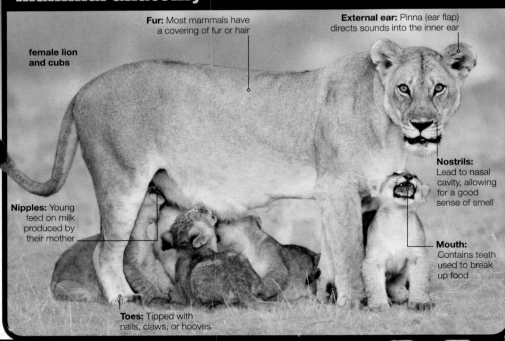

Fur: Most mammals have a covering of fur or hair

External ear: Pinna (ear flap) directs sounds into the inner ear

female lion and cubs

Nostrils: Lead to nasal cavity, allowing for a good sense of smell

Nipples: Young feed on milk produced by their mother

Mouth: Contains teeth used to break up food

Toes: Tipped with nails, claws, or hooves

Types of mammals

There are 21 different groups of mammals. Here are some of the major ones.

Monotremes
Include the platypus and echidna and are the only mammals to lay eggs

Marsupials
Produce undeveloped young that grow in mother's pouch

Rodents
Small mammals with paired chisel-like incisor teeth

Primates
Intelligent, long limbed, with flexible fingers and toes

Bats
The only mammals capable of sustained flight

Insectivores
Small, nocturnal, and feed on invertebrates, especially insects

In numbers

20 million
The number of Brazilian free-tailed bats that group together to form one colony

2,000 m
(6,600 ft) The depth to which a sperm whale can dive, staying there while it hunts for squid and other prey

600 kg
(1320 lb) The weight of the biggest land carnivore (meat-eater), the polar bear

12 tonnes
The weight of an African elephant, the biggest land mammal

180 tonnes
The weight of a blue whale, the biggest animal that has existed on Earth. They can be as long as 33.6 m (110 feet)

100 kph
(62 mph) The top running speed of the cheetah – the fastest land mammal

0.16 kph
(0.1 mph) The speed of the three-toed sloth – the world's slowest mammal

5.5 m
(18 ft) The height of the tallest mammal, the giraffe

RECORD BREAKER

Snow leopards are the world's **greatest leapers**. Found in central Asia, they can hurdle over ravines and pounce on their prey, such as sheep and deer, over a distance of 15 m (49 ft).

I don't believe it!

Arabian or dromedary camels can go for months without drinking and then consume 60 litres (13.2 gallons) of water in just a few minutes.

Five facts about feeding

01: An adult **elephant** munches its way through 250 kg (550 lb) of vegetation daily. Sixty per cent of that comes out of the other end undigested.

02: **Blue whales** can filter up to 3,600 kg (8,000 lb) of shrimp-like krill from the sea every day.

03: **Hyenas** can swallow a third of their body weight in half an hour.

04: **Shrews** have to consume their own weight in food every day.

05: A **star-nosed mole** can snaffle an insect larva in a quarter of a second.

Furry **patterns**

Some mammals have distinctive coat markings that help camouflage them in their native environments.

jaguar   zebra   giraffe   eastern chipmunk   tiger

How to: **find food like a giant anteater**

01. Using your sense of smell (your sight isn't too good) find a nice big termite or ants' nest.

02. Use your strong front legs and big, sharp claws to break open the nest (but don't destroy it – you'll probably pay a return visit).

03. Put your lengthy, toothless snout near the nest and extend your 60-cm (2-ft) long tongue to probe for prey.

04. Flick your sticky, spiky tongue in and out of the nest 150 times a minute to trap insects.

WEIRD OR WHAT?

Male Dayak fruit bats from southeast Asia are the only **male mammals** known to **lactate** (produce milk) and suckle their own young.

Carnivores
Active hunters and meat-eaters with sharp, cutting teeth

Pinnipeds
Aquatic carnivores that breed on land and feed on marine life

Hoofed: even-toed
Have feet with two toes capped with hooves, such as gazelles and camels

Cetaceans
Aquatic mammals that spend their life in water, blubber keeps them warm

Hoofed: odd-toed
One or three toes on each hooved foot, such as zebras and rhinos

Elephants
Large mammals that collect food with a trunk

Do **animals** have a **sixth** sense?

Yes, while humans traditionally have five senses – sight, hearing, taste, touch, and smell – many animals possess one or more extra senses. These might include detecting electrical fields or heat to find prey, or magnetic fields in order to navigate.

Tell me more: finding the way

Migrating animals often travel on long, dangerous journeys from breeding to feeding grounds. They rely on a variety of senses to find their way.

◆ **Sight:** Using visual clues such as coastlines and mountain ranges, bar-headed geese (pictured) fly over the Himalayas twice a year to avoid storms in winter and monsoon rains in summer.

◆ **Smell:** Salmon use their excellent sense of smell to find the stream they were born in, which can be up to 3,200 km (1,988 miles) inland.

◆ **Sound:** Baleen whales listen to the sound of waves crashing on beaches to help them navigate around islands.

◆ **Heat:** When spiny lobsters feel the waters cooling, they know it is time to move to deeper waters to avoid the stormy autumn season.

◆ **Touch:** Boree moth caterpillars leave a trail of silk for their siblings to follow as they swarm off in search of food.

Listen up

Big ears
Mammals collect sound using large external ear flaps. Hares can even turn their ears to scan for sound.

Dish face
The great grey owl's large dish-shaped face channels sound waves into its ears.

Eardrums
Frogs do not have protruding ears, but large eardrums behind each eye.

Insect ears
The cricket has an "ear" just below the knee of both its front legs.

WHAT'S IN A NAME?

Many animals have what is called a **Jacobson's organ** located on the roof of the animal's mouth. This organ **senses chemicals in the air** and is named after Danish scientist Ludwig Jacobson.

A tasty smell?

☀ A sense of smell helps animals to find food or sniff out a mate from a distance, while taste helps them to check things out up close.

☀ **Flies have taste receptors all over their bodies, from their wings to their feet.**

☀ A catfish's whiskers are covered in taste buds and it can identify another catfish by smell alone.

☀ **Whales have no sense of smell, but a very good sense of taste.**

☀ Rats smell in stereo and, in a single sniff, can work out exactly where a smell is coming from because the odour reaches one nostril around 50 milliseconds before the other.

Keep in touch

👆 Animals use touch to find food, communicate, or navigate in the dark.

👆 **The sensitive hairs on a spider's legs help it detect prey.**

👆 The star-nosed mole (pictured) uses the 22 pink, fleshy tentacles on its nose to hunt for worms and leeches.

👆 **Snakes press their lower jaw to the ground to sense vibrations.**

👆 A raft spider sits on dry land and dangles its four front legs in the water to detect prey.

👆 **Mammals like to caress each other for comfort.**

Why senses make sense

An animal's survival depends on it being able to sense what is happening around it.

Finding food
The duck-billed platypus uses receptors in its bill to sense the electric fields of underwater prey.

Hibernating
Feeling chilly is the sign for some animals, like the dormouse, that it is time to hibernate.

Avoiding predators
Sensitive whiskers help nocturnal mammals, like the rat, avoid predators in the dark.

Detecting injury
Senses inform this duck its wing is broken, so its body can begin healing processes.

Finding a mate
Hyenas stick out their tongues to taste information about other individuals.

Migrating
The migration of monarch butterflies is triggered by changes in temperature and the length of the day.

Eye to eye

❶ The large red eyes of the **nocturnal tree frog** help it to see in the dark and may startle predators if the frog is disturbed during the day, giving it a split second to leap away.

❷ The **chameleon**'s protruding eyes can roll from side to side, each independent of the other, so the animal can work out exactly where prey is.

❸ The eyes of the **cuttlefish** are very similar to human eyes, except for the distinctive curved black pupil. They have excellent vision.

❹ Like many insects, the **hoverfly** has a compound eye made up of many thousand lenses, which enable it to spot the slightest movement.

❺ The **southern ground hornbill** has long eyelashes to protect the eye from the Sun and dust as it forages for food on the ground with its beak.

❻ Cats, such as the **tiger**, are able to see well in the dark because they have a mirror-like layer in their eyes.

I don't believe it!

Scientists have discovered that cats can heal themselves by purring, as vibrations between 20–140 Hz can help heal fractures, mend torn muscles, and relieve pain.

Hot stuff
Pit vipers have heat-sensitive organs between the eyes and the nostrils with around 7,000 nerve endings. Using these organs, they create a "heat picture" of warm-blooded prey when hunting at night.

How to: see in the dark (like a bat)

01. Produce a loud, incredibly high-pitched sound by rushing air from your lungs past your vibrating vocal chords.

02. The squeaky sound wave you've created rushes forward at the speed of sound – 1,193 kph (741 mph) – and bounces back off any objects around you.

03. Direct the echo into your inner ear using the strange folds on your nose and ears.

04. Work out how long it takes the noise to return to build up a picture of how far away objects are, and if any of them are prey.

05. Keep calling until you are close enough to grab yourself a tasty snack.

WEIRD OR WHAT?

Bats' calls are **ultrasonic**, which means they're so high-pitched human ears can't hear them. The calls are also so loud the **bats risk deafening themselves**, so their ears have special muscles that close to protect the ear, and then open to listen to the echo.

Can **animals talk?**

Animals can pass on all sorts of messages using touch, smells, and sounds, or visual signals, such as light, colour, and body language. Some signs are clear, like a gorilla smiling at her baby, or subtle, such as a female wolf spider leaving a trail of silk woven with her scent to lure males.

Reasons to communicate

✔ Make an impression
Wolves howl to declare their territory, to call to each other, and to show they are part of a pack.

✔ Find a mate
Polar bears in the vast Arctic wilderness won't bump into each other by accident, they need to leave behind a trail of smells.

✔ Defend your territory
Tigers urinate on trees to mark their territory and avoid competition.

✔ Warn of danger
Prairie dogs have a range of warning calls to tell others what the threat is, and how fast it's approaching.

✔ Care for young
A chick taps its parent's beak to say "Feed me!"

✔ Intimidate opponents
A male gorilla beats its chest to show how big and strong it is.

How to: **read the signs**

01. Feel threatened if a hippopotamus yawns to show off its teeth.

02. Get even more worried if it splashes or scoops the water to add to the effect.

03. If you notice the hippo is shaking its head, lunging forward and then rearing back, prepare to flee.

04. When you hear roaring and grunting it is time to run away!

Cool call
The howl of a coyote reveals its identity, its gender, and how it is feeling.

Male Madagascan ring-tailed lemurs compete for mates by trying to outstink each other.

Causing a stink
🐾 Most animals (except birds) give off chemicals known as "pheromones". These trigger a reaction in other members of the species and can even affect how their bodies grow.

🐾 Once given off, pheromones can travel very long distances when carried by the wind.

🐾 Leaving chemical messages behind is a good way to let other animals know you're in the neighbourhood.

A guide to **making faces**

Much like humans, chimpanzees use facial expressions to communicate with each other.

Fear grin
This is a non-threatening signal used to diffuse an explosive situation.

Pout
By pouting its lips, a chimp expresses anxiety, frustration, or distress.

Play face
An open mouth is a sign that the chimp wants to play.

This **poison dart frog**'s colours say: "Don't eat me – I'll poison you!"

The **firefly**'s bright colours tell predators it tastes bad and should be left alone.

The male leader of a troop of **mandrill** has a vivid red stripe on his nose, reminding the rest of the troop who's boss.

A **skunk**'s black and white colours warn of its foul-smelling spray.

A male **frilled lizard** fans out a huge flap of skin to show females how attractive he is.

Keeping in touch

Touch is used by social animals, such as ants, spiders, and crabs, and especially mammals and birds that care for their young.

Bugs vibrate plants to communicate with other bugs, burrowing animals make the ground vibrate, while alligators produce a deep sound that can travel more than a kilometre in still waters.

Licking and grooming keeps a mammal family clean, but also shows affection.

Scout honey-bees perform a complicated "waggle dance" to direct other members of the hive to a good patch of flowers. Wing vibrations pass on the message even in the dark.

Making a noise

01: Amphibians, reptiles, birds, and mammals combine lung power, and vibrating or echoing body parts, to produce an amazing range of cries and calls.

02: Fish scrape their gills together, birds flutter their wings, while insects buzz, squeak, and click by vibrating wings or rubbing body parts against their hard outer skeleton.

03: Low sounds travel furthest and forest animals often have deeper calls than creatures living out in the open.

04: Birdsong travels up to 20 times further in the early morning when the air is stiller and cooler than it is in the middle of the day.

Showing off

Colouring and pattern are used by most animals to tell male from female. Different markings also help avoid confusion when similar species live in the same habitat.

Body language is great for scaring off predators or attracting a mate, such as the intricate courtship dance of the Japanese crane (pictured). Intelligent species use body language to deal with complicated family relationships.

Flashing signals on and off attract more attention, such as a sudden display of peacock feathers or the flash of the brightly coloured patch of skin under an anole lizard's neck.

Highs and lows

Sounds are pressure waves travelling through the air. When they disturb air particles close to us, the vibrations are picked up by ears and translated back into sound. These vibrations are measured in Hertz (Hz). 1 Hz is one vibration in a second. The more vibrations there are, the higher the sound.

- elephants rumble at 8 Hz
- human ears hear sounds from 20 Hz to 20,000 Hz
- dogs can hear sounds up to 45,000 Hz
- dolphins communicate with sounds well over 100,000 Hz
- moths can hear sounds as high as 240,000 Hz

What is a food chain?

All animals must have food to give them the energy they need to survive, and they get it by eating other living things. This transfer of energy from one living thing to another is called a food chain. Every animal is either a predator or prey for other animals. Those at the top of the food chain are called top predators.

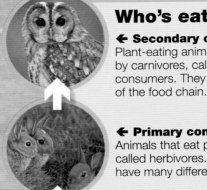

Who's eating who?

← **Secondary consumers:** Plant-eating animals are eaten by carnivores, called secondary consumers. They are at the top of the food chain.

← **Primary consumers:** Animals that eat plants are called herbivores. They may have many different predators.

← **Primary producers:** At the bottom of most food chains are plants, which get their energy from the Sun.

How to: **be a top predator**

A frogfish can open its mouth and snap it shut in just 6 milliseconds. **Gulp!**

01. Locate your prey, then watch, wait, and try to look invisible while you work out what's going on.

02. Identify a likely victim and try to isolate it from the rest of the herd. Slowly approach.

03. Move in, with only your eyes showing above the surface of the water, until close enough to launch your attack.

04. Seize the prey with your massive jaws and drag it into the water. Hold until it has drowned, then tear apart and eat.

69 billion
The estimated number of locusts in a swarm that devastated parts of northwest Africa in 2004

50,000
The number of bees in a typical domestic beehive

30
The number of minutes a marine iguana can hold its breath while grazing on seaweed underwater

99%
The percentage of a giant panda's diet that is bamboo

In numbers

Loaded larders

Acorn woodpecker
These sensible birds drill holes in a tree trunk and fill them with acorns for winter.

Red-backed shrike
Also known as the butcher bird, this shrike keeps its food on thorns or barbed wire.

Honeypot ants
Worker honeypot ants are living larders, storing nectar in their huge bellies to regurgitate later.

Honey bees
Bees turn nectar to honey, which they hoard in the hexagonal cells of their hive.

I don't believe it!

About 140 species are known to eat their own kind. Some insects, fish, and amphibians eat their relatives when food is rare, and the female black widow spider, praying mantis, and scorpion eat the males after mating.

Koalas eat almost nothing but eucalyptus leaves. These aren't very nutritious so they need to **sleep 16 hours a day** to save energy.

Dinner is served

🍽 Spiders inject flies with juices that **turn their insides to mush**, then suck out the resulting soup.

🍽 Snakes can't chop or chew their food so they have highly flexible necks and jaws that dislocate, so they can swallow prey whole.

🍽 **Killer whales, polar bears, and big cats all play with their prey before or after killing it.**

🍽 Leopard seals shake a captured penguin's body and smash it against the surface of the water to break it up into manageable pieces.

🍽 Crocodiles sometimes store drowned prey underwater, waiting for its body to rot before eating it.

Horrible ways to die

01: Dismembered
The tough jaws of a praying mantis (pictured) slice through its victim's body with ease.

02: Strangled
Lions clamp their jaws around a zebra's throat and throttle it to death. Anacondas squeeze prey until it stops breathing.

03: Impaled
The cone snail impales its prey by firing a harpoon with explosive speed.

04: Poisoned
Jellyfish, spiders, and scorpions are all master poisoners.

05: Stunned
An electric eel can stun or kill its prey with a powerful 500V shock.

06: Crushed
Secretary birds stamp on large prey to kill it.

07: Thumped
The tiny peacock mantis shrimp thumps its prey with its club-like limbs, with a force thousands of times its body weight.

08: Wrapped
The uloborid spider wraps its prey in silk so tightly that it breaks their legs and bursts their eyes.

FAST FACTS

Plant-eaters

01: Many animals get energy from plants, not other animals.

02: Animals eat all parts of plants – the leaves, nuts, seeds, fruits, roots, and nectar.

03: Fruits, seeds, and nectar are rich in energy, but leaves and grasses are not very nutritious so animals need to consume large amounts of them.

04: To try to avoid being eaten, some plants have developed toxic leaves or thorns.

05: Some plants benefit from being animal food – animals pollinate flowers, help seeds to germinate by digesting them and softening their tough coatings, and disperse seeds in their droppings.

Choose your weapon

Animals use a wide variety of weapons to grab their prey.

The great white shark has several rows of serrated **teeth**. New ones move to the front to replace teeth that fall out.

The scorpion grabs prey in its claws, then arches forward its tail to stab the victim with its venom-filled **sting**.

A heron uses its **beak** to pluck a fish from the water, knock it out, and then flip it head first down its throat.

The bald eagle has hooked **talons** and often snatches its prey feet first, before ripping it apart with its beak.

Crabs use their powerful **claws** to crack and prise open the tough shells of their seafood.

10 masters of disguise

In the animal kingdom everyone is hungry and only the strongest, or most cunning, survive. To snap up an unsuspecting meal or escape becoming lunch yourself, the best advice is to lay low and blend in, like these cool customers... if you can spot them.

01: The Arctic fox's winter coat is white so it blends in with the snow, but for the summer season, its fur turns brown so it merges with the earth and rocks.

02: Stalking through long grass in search of a tasty meal, tigers go unnoticed as their irregular stripes blend with their surroundings.

03: The great grey owl perches on a tree, safe in the knowledge that its mottled markings merge with the bark.

04: Even at close range the stick insect is easily mistaken for a twig or leaf. In a really sticky situation, they will also pretend to snap off and drop to the ground.

05: The devil scorpion fish hides motionless in reefs looking like a rock or piece of dead coral. Its skin can even change colour to blend in with its surroundings.

06: Tree trunks in bright sunlight spell danger, but the leaf-tailed gecko's skin texture and colour means he disappears into the bark background.

07: Clever camouflage provides extra protection for the leafy seadragon. The fish looks like seaweed and is ignored by predators.

08: If you live on the forest floor there's a high risk of meeting predators, so the European nightjar's streaky-patterned feathers blend with the leaf litter.

09: Also known as bush crickets, katydids are easily mistaken for leaves, and even have specks of mould, chewed corners, pretend blemishes, and fake veins.

10: The beautiful orchid mantis is disguised to resemble a flower. Pastel pink with petal-like legs, it waits to catch insects, untroubled by predators.

How do animals reproduce?

In most animal species, males and females mate to reproduce. This is called sexual reproduction. Some animals can reproduce without mating. They simply "split" themselves into two or more individuals. This is asexual reproduction. There are also a few species where the female can produce young on her own.

Best buddies
A sea anemone can reproduce asexually by a process called budding. This means that the offspring grow as small parts attached to the mother's body, before dropping off.

Ways to make a good impression

✔ **Horns and antlers**
Male stag beetles battle with their horns to win the right to mate. Deers, antelopes, and other hoofed mammals sport a range of spectacular horns.

✔ **Shouting match**
Red deer stags bellow day and night to prove how strong they are.

✔ **Put on a show**
The long-tailed manakin bird judges pairs of hopeful males on a 20-minute display of singing and gymnastics. She may rule out as many as 80 males before making her final choice.

✔ **Presents**
The male wolf spider catches a fly, then wraps it up in silk before offering it to the much larger and fearsome female. This food will help her to lay more eggs.

Tell me more: how a blue-footed booby finds a mate

Sky-pointing: By pointing his bill to the sky and raising his tail, the male blue-footed booby shows the female that he's a bird to be reckoned with

Wings: The male spreads and rotates his wings

Territory: The male chooses a small nesting territory and parades around it to warn rivals and advertise himself to females

Dancing: A stately dance is a good way to show off his feet

Feet: Colour is vital – males with the bluest feet stand the best chance of finding a partner

A dangerous game

⊗ Crushed
One in 1,000 female elephants is crushed to death by heavy partners during mating.

⊗ Munched
The female praying mantis inflicts a fatal "love bite" on her male partners, eating his head while his body continues mating.

⊗ Suicide
During mating, a male red-back spider somersaults so that his abdomen is right between the female's fangs. She can't resist and usually impales him before sucking his body dry.

⊗ Stabbed
A male rattlesnake attaches hooks to a female during mating. These injure the female, preventing her from mating with a rival.

I don't believe it!

Male Kobs (a type of African antelope) gather in groups of 12–40 and wait for females to come to them. The females are attracted less by the male's body and more by the amount of urine sprinkled on his home patch, which reveals how popular he is.

Eggs

01: Birds and most reptiles lay eggs with a protective shell that allows them to survive outside water.

02: Fish and amphibians lay their jelly-like eggs in water as they don't have a shell and would dry out in the air.

03: A female cod fish can produce 4–6 million eggs in one spawning. The eggs are usually left to develop on their own.

04: Some snakes and lizards keep their eggs inside their bodies until they are just about to hatch.

05: Nearly all birds incubate (warm) their eggs with their own bodies. Meanwhile the developing embryo inside feeds on the egg yolk.

06: When hatching, some chicks have an egg tooth to crack the eggshell.

How to: move in... and move out

01. Get your mother cuckoo to lay your egg in the nest of a likely family, like a reed warbler. Don't worry that your new mum will spot that your egg is bigger, as they never suspect a thing.

02. Once you have hatched, you must chuck out any rival eggs. There's only room in this nest for one – and it's got to be you.

03. Eat everything and never stop screeching for more. Strangely, your new mum still won't spot that something's up, even though you're larger than she is and growing all the time.

04. You'll know when it's time to leave home – the nest will collapse under your great weight. Don't bother to say thank you.

Mobile home

Marsupials, such as kangaroos, wallabies, possums, koalas, and wombats keep their young safe in pouches.

A newborn kangaroo is the size of a peanut and squirms through its mother's fur until it reaches her warm pouch.

Safe inside the pouch, the youngster feeds on her milk and grows bigger.

By six months old, the young, or joey, hops in and out of the pouch.

Top breeder
Female aphids (greenfly) can reproduce both sexually (by mating with a male) and asexually (by producing perfect clones).

Reasons to stick together

01: Breeding
From sea birds to fish, gathering together in large numbers in the breeding season makes it easier to find a partner.

02: Feeding
Wolves, hyenas, and lions co-ordinate their hunting in order to make it easier to catch prey to feed their young.

03: Babysitting
Adult meerkats (pictured) take turns looking after all the young pups in their group, feeding them and teaching them new skills.

Home sweet home

Tower block
Worker termites attend the egg-laying queen and transport the eggs through the mound to the nurseries.

Paper house
Common wasps chew dry wood into a pulp to make their waterproof nests. The cells inside each house an egg.

Warm nest
Pairs of white storks build a huge nest from sticks, rags, and paper. Fresh cattle dung helps to keep the nest warm.

Dam builders
Inside the beaver's lodge is a sleeping chamber above water where the mother nurses her young.

Underground
Moles burrow tunnels underground. Females breed and give birth in chambers lined with soft grass.

Why worry about extinction?

Levels of risk

The World Conservation Union ranking, with each listing giving examples of affected species:

Extinct Tasmanian tiger, dodo

Extinct in the wild
South China tiger

Critically endangered
Arakan forest turtle, Javan rhino, Brazilian merganser

Endangered blue whale, snow leopard, tiger, albatross

Vulnerable cheetah, lion

Near threatened
blue-billed duck, solitary eagle

Least concern pigeons, spiny dogfish

Paths to extinction

✗ **Growing population**
The more people there are, the less space there is for animals.

✗ **Habitat destruction**

✗ **Pollution**

✗ **Hunting and fishing**

✗ **Alien invaders**
When humans bring alien animals or plants into a new habitat, the native species often can't compete or will catch diseases they can't fight.

✗ **Climate change**
Global warming is attacking animals and plants in many ways – from melting the sea-ice that polar bears need for hunting to bringing tropical rains early, so plants blossom too soon to feed the animals that depend on them.

There have been five mass extinction events in Earth's history (the last time, 65 million years ago, the dinosaurs vanished). A sixth mass extinction is taking place thanks to humans. As we drive more animals and plants to extinction, we destroy the life support systems that all species depend on – including us.

WHAT'S IN A NAME?

The phrase "**dead as a dodo**" refers to a flightless bird native to the island of Mauritius in the Indian Ocean that was wiped out little more than a century after it was first discovered by humans in 1581.

A quarter of all mammal species may disappear in the next 100 years.

Tell me more: endangered animals

Polar bear
Global warming is a serious threat as their natural habitat melts away.

Iberian lynx
With just 150 left in the wild, this is the most threatened cat species in the world.

Bison
Millions were shot in the 19th century and there are now only 3,000 truly wild bison. They are being saved from extinction by a breeding programme.

Giant armadillo
Hunted for food, up to 50 per cent of the population have been killed in the last 10 years.

Mountain gorilla
Expanding farms have left their forest homes isolated and they are also threatened by poaching. There are less than 700 in the wild.

Aye-aye
This nocturnal Madagascan primate is threatened by the destruction of rainforests.

Amazing animals you'll never see

Irish elk
Extinct for 7,700 years, this was the largest deer that ever lived. It was 2.1 m (6.9 ft) tall at the shoulders and its giant antlers measured 3.65 m (12 ft) across.

Mammoth
Due to climate change and hunting, woolly mammoths vanished from Europe around 10,000 BCE. A small group survived on Wrangel Island (Siberia) until 1,650 BCE.

Great auk
This flightless bird had white and black feathers. It was once numerous along North Atlantic coastlines, but was eventually hunted the great auk to extinction in 1844.

Quagga
A zebra with stripes at the front of the body, it roamed South Africa's Cape Province in large numbers until the 1840s, when it was hunted to extinction by Boer settlers.

Five ways to save a species

01 Setting up nature reserves and parks so that enough numbers of rare animals live in the wild to survive on their own.

02 Building up populations of rare animals in zoos through captive breeding that can be released into the wild.

03 International agreements on hunting can protect endangered animals such as blue whales.

04 Using alternatives in place of products from rare animals, like the rhino horns used in some Chinese medicines.

05 Storing an animal's genetic material in a gene bank so that in future scientists may be able to "grow" a new animal of an extinct species.

I don't believe it !

Could an extinct species, like a mammoth, be brought back to life? Scientists are looking at many different ways this might work, including combining the DNA from a frozen mammoth and an elephant to create an elephant-mammoth creature.

Back for good

From time to time extinct animals are rediscovered:

■ The **La Gomera giant lizard** (pictured) was thought to be long extinct, but it was rediscovered in 1999, living on two cliffs on the island of La Gomera.

■ The **Cyprus spiny mouse** was thought to be extinct, but four were caught in 2007.

■ The **Barkudia limbless skink lizard** has no legs and looks like a giant earthworm. It was seen again in 2003 after a gap of 86 years!

■ A scientific expedition in 2003 rediscovered the **Rancho Grande harlequin frog** breeding along a mountain stream in Venezuela – the first time it had been seen since 1982.

Bengal tiger
A growing human population has hunted out the tiger's natural prey. The tigers are also poached for the illegal fur trade and Asian medicine market. There are now less than 1,500 in the wild.

Orang-utan
Poaching and massive deforestation due to oil palm plantations means just 60,000 survive in the wild.

Blue whale
Almost wiped out by whaling ships in the 1960s, less than 5,000 remain. Populations have recovered since a whaling ban was implemented.

Poaching for the **pet trade** threatens apes such as orang-utans, as well as small creatures like reptiles, fish, and spiders. The poachers usually kill the adult apes and **steal their babies** because they are small and easier to manage.

Human body

Why don't haircuts hurt?

Because hairs are made of dead cells, so you don't feel a thing. The dead hair cells are filled with a tough, waterproof protein called keratin, as are nails, and the skin flakes that you lose daily in their millions from your skin's surface. All these things are part of the fantastic protective overcoat that covers and protects your body.

What about me?

Spots form when oily sebum blocks a hair follicle. Bacteria move in and their activities alert the body's defences, so the spot becomes inflamed. Spots are common during puberty, when the skin is more oily.

Six reasons you need skin

01 It provides a waterproof covering around your body.

02 It forms a barrier between your delicate tissues and the harsh outside world.

03 It stops germs getting into your body.

04 It filters out harmful ultraviolet radiation in sunlight that can damage your cells.

05 It helps your body maintain a steady temperature.

06 It houses receptors that enable you to detect touch, pressure, vibrations, heat, and cold.

In an average lifetime **a man will shave 20,000 times** (unless, of course, he has a beard).

Tell me more: what's in skin?

Skin is really thin but also quite complex. It's made of two layers: The epidermis provides protection, and is constantly worn away and replaced. The dermis glues the epidermis to the rest of the body, and deals with feeling, temperature control, and food and oxygen supplies.

Hair shaft: Grows above the skin's surface

Upper part of the epidermis: Made of dead cells

Nerve ending: Detects touch and other sensations

Epidermis: The thin, upper layer of skin

Lower part of the epidermis: Produces new cells to replace those lost from the surface

Dermis: The thicker, lower part of the skin

Hair follicle: A pit in the skin from which hair grows

Blood vessel: Supplies oxygen and food to skin cells

Sebaceous gland: Releases oily sebum, which keeps hair and skin moist and flexible

Sweat gland: Produces sweat, which is released onto the skin's surface

In numbers

2 sq m
(21 sq ft) The total surface area of an adult's skin

3.2 kg
(7 lbs) How heavy an adult man's skin is

300 million
The number of cells in the skin

4.7 mm
(0.2 in) The thickness of the thickest skin (on the soles of the feet)

0.12 mm
(0.005 in) The thickness of the thinnest skin (on the eyelids)

2.5 million
The number of sweat pores a person has

50,000
The number of skin flakes lost every minute

100,000
The number of hairs on a person's head

80
The average number of head hairs lost and replaced daily

10 mm
(0.4 in) The amount head hair grows in a month

5 mm
(0.2 in) How much fingernails grow in summer (less in winter)

RECORD BREAKERS

The **longest fingernails** ever grown had a combined length of 9.05 m (29.7 ft) – not so good for picking your nose.

The **longest head hair** on record extends for more than 5.5 m (18 ft).

A man in Cuba has a **record 230 piercings** on his body, including 175 rings in the skin of his face.

Armpit **sweat glands** produce a thicker sweat than the body's other sweat glands. When bacteria feed on this sweat they release chemicals that can smell musky and unpleasant – **body odour**.

I don't believe it!

People who suffer from a rare inherited condition called congenital generalized hypertrichosis have hair covering almost their entire body. The only hairless parts are the palms of their hands and soles of their feet.

Your **skin is coloured** by a brown pigment called **melanin**. It protects you by absorbing harmful ultraviolet rays in sunlight. When your skin is exposed to sunlight, it automatically makes more melanin and gives you a suntan. But you should always protect it from excessive sunlight by covering up and applying suncream.

How to: **warm up**

01. Go for a run on a chilly day. Instruct your body to implement temperature-regulating tricks.

02. Pull the hairs in your skin upright to trap heat. The goosebumps will die down once you're warm again.

03. Narrow the blood vessels in your dermis, helping them to lose less heat through your skin's surface.

How to: **cool down**

01. You're all hot and bothered after your run. Cool down by employing more temperature regulation.

02. Pour sweat onto the skin's surface so it can evaporate and draw heat from your body.

03. Widen your blood vessels in the dermis so that they lose heat like radiators through the skin's surface.

Six skin dwellers

Fleas
Feed on blood and then leap on to the next unsuspecting victim.

Head lice
Grip hairs, lay eggs, and then pierce the scalp to feed on blood.

Eyelash mites
Live harmlessly in the eyelash follicles of everyone.

Scabies mites
Burrow under the skin to lay eggs, which causes intense itching.

Ticks
Attach to the skin and blow up like a balloon as they feed on blood, then drop off.

Bacteria
Present in their trillions, but usually harmless unless they get inside you through a cut.

Why do **bones** remain for centuries after a person dies?

Bones are made of two main materials: calcium salts make bones hard, and collagen fibres make them strong but also a bit flexible. After death the collagen rots away, leaving just the durable hard parts behind. In life, the bones of a person's skeleton support the body and protect its internal organs.

Skull and crossbones

Because bones endure after death, skeletons – and the skull and crossbones – have for centuries been symbols of disease, danger, and death.

Tell me more: **inside a bone**

The bones in your skeleton are moist, living organs with their own blood supply. If you look inside a bone you can see that it is not solid. If bones were solid they would be so heavy you would not be able to move.

Compact bone: Made of parallel tubes of bony tissue, it is dense, strong, and forms the outer layer of the bone

Bone marrow: Jelly-like substance that fills the spaces inside bones; yellow bone marrow stores fat, while red bone marrow makes blood cells

Spongy bone: Made of bony struts and spaces filled with bone marrow, it is strong but light

Periosteum: The outer layer of tissue that surrounds the bone

Blood vessels: Supply osteocytes (bone cells) with food and oxygen

TWO SKELETONS

■ **Axial (central) skeleton (the skull, backbone, and ribs):** Consists of 80 bones that run down the centre of the body and protect the heart and lungs

■ **Appendicular skeleton (the arms, legs, shoulder girdle, and hip girdle):** Consists of 126 bones that hang on to the axial skeleton and move the body

I don't believe it !

The Paris Catacombs are underground bone stores that contain many thousands of skulls, femurs, and other bones. In fact, the walls of the catacombs are made from bones! They were brought there for storage in the 18th century, from cemeteries that were overflowing with dead people.

In numbers

206 The number of bones in an adult skeleton

300 The number of bones in a newborn baby's skeleton (as a baby grows, some bones fuse together)

106 The number of bones in hands and feet – more than half the number of bones in the body

99% The percentage of calcium in the body, found in bones and teeth

6 The number of times a living bone is stronger than a piece of steel of the same weight

How to: **fix a fracture**

01. Allow blood to clot, stopping bleeding inside the break and starting the process of self-repair.

02. Link up the broken ends of the bone so that blood vessels can invade the area along with bone-making cells.

03. Cheer on bone-making cells to build new compact and spongy bone. Within months the fracture is repaired.

Blood-making bones

In babies, blood cells are made by red bone marrow inside all bones. In adults, they are made only in certain bones, shown here.

- cranium
- collar bone
- shoulder blades
- top end of each humerus
- breast bone
- ribs
- vertebrae
- top end of each femur

Six flexible joints

Ball and socket joint
Allows movement in any direction and is found in the shoulder and hip

Ellipsoidal joint
Allows movement from side to side, backwards and forwards, and is found in the wrist and knuckles

Hinge joint
Allows movement in just one plane, like a door hinge, and is found in knees and elbows

Pivot joint
Allows the end of one bone to rotate in or on another, found between the top two vertebrae to allow the head to turn

Plane joint
Allows short sliding movements and is found in the wrist and ankle bones

Saddle joint
Provides rotation in all directions, found at the base of the thumb, allowing it to touch the other fingers

Bone

01: The smallest bone in the body is the stapes or stirrup bone. Found inside the ear, it is smaller than a grain of rice.

02: The femur or thighbone is the body's longest bone, at about a quarter the body's total length.

03: The skull is the body's most complex bone.

04: Our most complex joint is the knee.

FAST FACTS

Your "**funny bone**" isn't a bone at all; it's a spot on the outer bit of your elbow that, if you hit or knock it, gives you a weird tingly pain. This is because the ulnar nerve crosses the bone at that point.

NECK BONES
Humans and giraffes have the same number of neck bones, or cervical vertebrae. They both have seven, although each of the giraffe's vertebrae are much longer!

BONE HEAD

There are 22 skull bones, 21 of which have wiggly edges that lock together in sutures (immovable joints) like pieces in a jigsaw. Sutures stop skull bones from moving, making the skull really strong. The only skull bone that does move freely is the mandible or lower jaw. If it didn't, you would not be able to eat, drink, or speak.

Occipital bone: Forms the rear and base of the skull

Frontal bone: Forms the forehead

Parietal bones: Two bones that together form the sides and top of the skull

Suture: Immovable joint that locks the skull bones together

Humerus (upper arm bone): Connects the forearm bones to the shoulder joint, a ball-and-socket joint that allows the arm to move in all directions

Sternum (breast bone): Forms a plate to protect the heart

Backbone: Flexible column of 26 bones called vertebrae that forms the main axis of the body and supports the head

Skull: Protects the brain and gives shape to the head and face

Temporal bone: Encloses the inner part of the ear, which enables us to detect sounds and maintain balance

Mandible: Lower jaw bone is the only movable part of the skull. It enables us to chew our food

Cervical vertebra: One of seven vertebrae that make up the neck, the uppermost of which allow the head to nod and shake

Clavicle (collar bone): Connects the scapula to the sternum

Scapula (shoulder blade): Forms a joint with the humerus that attaches the arm to the body

Ribs: 12 pairs surround and protect the heart and lungs

Tell me more: **skeleton**

Pelvic girdle: Hip girdle consists of two linked bones that anchor the legs and, with the sacrum, form the basin-shaped pelvis, which supports abdominal organs

Femur (thigh bone): The longest bone in the body, which runs from knee to hip

Knee joint: Hinge joint that allows the leg to bend and straighten. It is protected by a small bone called the patella, or kneecap

Metatarsal: One of five that form the sole of the foot

Phalanx (toe bone): One of 14 which have hinge-like joints that help the foot push off the ground during walking

Talus (ankle bone): Forms a hinge joint with the tibia and allows the foot to point up and down

Tibia (shin bone): The larger of two lower leg bones that connects the knee to the ankle

Calcaneus (heel bone): The largest bone in the foot

Navicular: One of seven tarsal bones that form the back part of the foot

Fibula (smaller lower leg bone): Carries little body weight but helps the foot to swivel

Sacroiliac joint: One of two plane joints between the sacrum – part of the backbone – and the pelvic girdle

Elbow joint: Straightens or bends like a hinge to allow movement. This helps us to pick up an apple and bring it to our mouth to eat

Ulna: Long inner bone of the forearm

Radius: A bone of the forearm

Wrist: An ellipsoidal joint that allows movement from side to side and back and forth. This helps us to wave

Phalanx (finger bone): One of three (called phalanges) that make up each finger. The thumb has two

Why does your head flop when you sleep?

When you are awake the muscles in your neck and back hold you and your head upright. When you nod off, those muscles relax and your head falls to one side. Muscles do more than just support you – by pulling your bones they produce every movement from lifting a pen to running a marathon.

Three types of fitness

Stamina
Measures how efficiently your heart pumps blood

Strength
Measures how strong your muscles are

Flexibility
Measures how flexible your joints, tendons, and muscles are

What about me?

Stretch before exercise to prevent cramp, which is when a muscle stays contracted when it should have relaxed and causes pain.

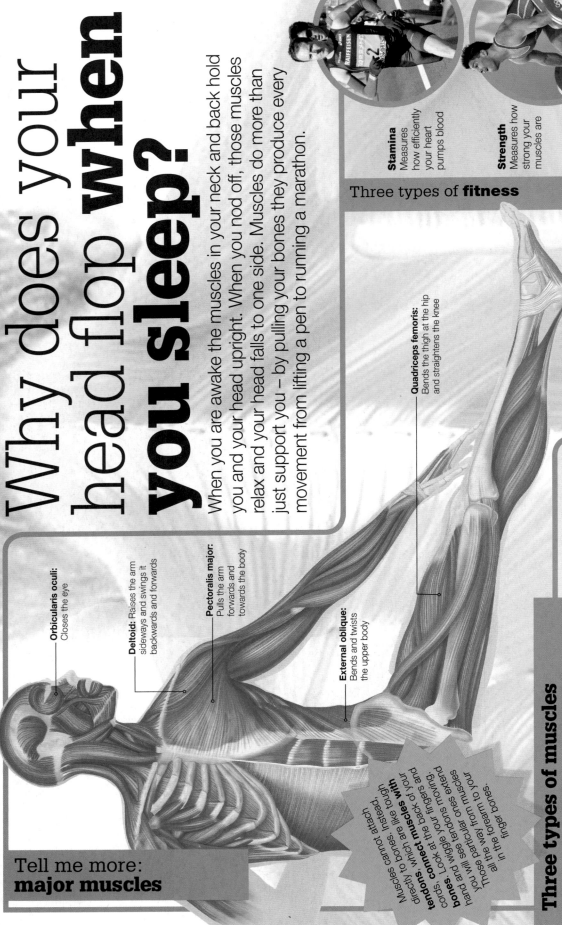

Quadriceps femoris:
Bends the thigh at the hip and straightens the knee

Tell me more: major muscles

Orbicularis oculi:
Closes the eye

Deltoid: Raises the arm sideways and swings it backwards and forwards

Pectoralis major:
Pulls the arm forwards and towards the body

External oblique:
Bends and twists the upper body

Muscles cannot attach directly to bones. Instead, tough muscles like with tendons, which connect the back and bones. Look at your fingers and hand and wiggle your fingers moving. Those particular ones extend cords. tendons extend muscles you will see from your to your all the forearm bones. in finger bones.

Three types of muscles

Skeletal muscle
Pulls on bones so you can move your body

Smooth muscle
Found in the walls of hollow organs, such as the bladder

Cardiac muscle
Found in the wall of the heart, it constantly contracts to pump blood

Latissimus dorsi: Pulls the arm downwards, inwards, and backwards

Triceps brachii: Straightens the arm from the elbow

Gluteus maximus: Straightens the hip by pulling the thigh back

Hamstrings: Straighten the thigh at the hip and bend the knee

Gastrocnemius: Pulls the Achilles tendon to point the foot downwards

Achilles tendon

Tell me more: inside a muscle

Muscles are made up of long cylindrical cells called fibres.

Nerve fibres: Carry signals from the brain that make the muscle fibres contract

Blood vessels: Carry oxygen and food to the muscle fibres

muscle contracts to pull bones

bundle of parallel muscle fibres

How to: straighten and bend your arm

biceps

triceps

01. Straighten your arm with your triceps muscle, which will pull your forearm downwards.

02. To bend your arm, contract (shorten) your biceps so it pulls your forearm upwards.

03. As your biceps keeps contracting (feel the bulge!), relax your triceps muscle to enable your arm to keep bending from the elbow.

04. Your biceps is now fully contracted and your arm bent... time to straighten it again?

In numbers

640
The number of skeletal muscles in the human body

50 cm
(20 in) The length of the longest muscle in your body, the sartorius, which is a thigh muscle

40–50%
The proportion of the male body's weight that is made up by muscles

30–40%
The proportion of the female body's weight that is made up by muscles

0.5 cm
(0.25 in) The length of the shortest muscle in your body, the stapedius, which is located in your ear

Five facial expressions

More than 30 small muscles pull on the skin of the face to produce the expressions that reveal how we feel.

Fear
Muscles pull the lower jaw downwards to open the mouth wide.

Anger
Muscles pull the eyebrows downwards, making them wrinkle.

Joy
Muscles pull and lift the corners of the mouth.

Surprise
Muscles raise the eyebrows and make the forehead wrinkle.

Sadness
Muscles pull the corners of the mouth downwards.

Why is blood red?

Blood is red because most of its cells are packed with a red-coloured substance called haemoglobin. Using this, the red blood cells pick up vital oxygen and deliver it to the body's cells. To achieve this and other roles, such as removing waste, blood is pumped along blood vessels by the heart.

Blood composition

If blood is poured into a glass tube and spun in a centrifuge (a spinning device), its main components separate into three layers.

Plasma (55 per cent):
A watery liquid containing food, wastes, hormones, and many other substances

White blood cells and platelets (1 per cent):
White blood cells fight infection, and platelets prevent bleeding by causing blood clots

Red blood cells (44 per cent):
Transport oxygen from lungs to tissues

Tell me more: circulation

Blood travels through blood vessels, from the heart, to all parts of the body. Oxygen-poor blood (blue) is pumped to the lungs, where it picks up oxygen. This oxygen-rich blood (red) is then pumped to the rest of the body.

WHAT'S IN A NAME?
In the past, people of noble birth were described as being "**blue-blooded**". Back then, only poor people who worked outdoors had suntans. Posh people had pale skins through which you could see their blue-coloured veins, hence "blue-blooded".

upper body

pulmonary artery

aorta

right lung

left lung

right side of heart

left side of heart

liver

stomach

lower body

02: Oxygen-poor blood flows from the heart along a pulmonary artery to one of the lungs

01: Oxygen-poor blood arrives in the heart

03: Newly oxygenated blood zooms along a pulmonary vein to the heart's left side

04: Oxygen-loaded blood gets the big push out of the heart and into the aorta – the body's biggest artery – for carrying around the body

05: Small arteries branch off to the body's organs, where blood travels along tiny capillaries and gives up oxygen to the organs' cells

06: Inferior vena cava – a large vein – carries oxygen-poor blood back to the heart to start its journey again

FAST FACTS

01: On average, women's hearts beat faster than men's.

02: On an average day your two kidneys process the equivalent of 12 bathtubs of blood. Kidneys remove wastes and excess water, which are then released from the body in up to a litre (two pints) of urine.

03: A single drop of blood contains 250 million oxygen-carrying red blood cells, 16 million blood-clotting platelets, and 375,000 infection-fighting white blood cells.

WEIRD OR WHAT?
In 1991, British artist Marc Quinn made a frozen sculpture of his head using 4.25 litres (9 pints) of his own blood collected over a period of five months.

Five creatures that want your blood

Sheep ticks
These balloon after a feed, and can cause Lyme disease in humans.

Leeches
Use their slicing mouthparts to cut through the skin.

Tsetse flies
Biting flies that feed on blood and spread the sleeping sickness disease.

Kissing bugs
These come out at night and suck your blood while you're asleep.

Dracula
A fictional vampire created by Victorian novelist, Bram Stoker.

HAVE A HEART

More than 2,300 years ago, Greek philosopher Aristotle stated that the heart was the part of the body that makes us feel emotions. Today we know the brain is responsible for the way we feel but, although Aristotle's ideas are long gone, people still express their love with hearts on Valentine's day.

Blood vessels

valves prevent backflow

Arteries
Carry oxygen-rich blood from the heart to the tissues and have thick, muscular walls.

Veins
Thin-walled, they carry oxygen-poor blood from the tissues to the heart.

Capillaries
Microscopic and one cell thick, they carry blood through tissues and link arteries and veins.

How to: pump blood through the heart

Your heart is mainly made of a special kind of muscle that never tires. It has two sides – left and right – each divided into an upper chamber called an atrium, and a larger, lower chamber called a ventricle.

01. Receive oxygen-poor blood from the body into your right atrium.

02. Push the blood down into your right ventricle, through the tricuspid valves which prevent any backflow.

03. From your right ventricle, pump the blood to your lungs.

04. Receive the oxygen-enriched blood from the lungs into your left atrium.

05. From your left ventricle, pump the oxygen-rich blood to the body.

Beat it

The noises made by closing valves produce the sound of a heartbeat, which can be heard through a stethoscope.

atrium
tricuspid valve
semilunar valves
ventricle
bicuspid valve

01: Atria and ventricles relax and blood flows into both sides of the heart, with the semilunar valves closed.

02: Atria contract and push blood through the tricuspid and bicuspid valves into the ventricles.

03: Ventricles contract, pushing blood out through the semilunar valves, while the bicuspid and tricuspid valves shut.

In numbers

25 trillion
The number of red blood cells in the blood

2.5 billion
The number of times the heart beats without resting during a 70-year lifetime

1 billion
The number of oxygen molecules carried by one red blood cell

250 million
The number of molecules of haemoglobin inside a red blood cell

150,000 km
(93,000 miles) The total length of all the body's blood vessels stretched out

120 days
The lifespan of a red blood cell

99%
The proportion of all blood cells that are red blood cells

5 litres
(11.5 pints) The amount of blood in an average adult's body

Blasts from the past

1628
English doctor William Harvey proves that blood is pumped around the body by the heart

1663
Italian doctor Marcello Malpighi identifies blood capillaries

1667
Blood transfusion (transfer) performed between a sheep and a human – both survive

1900s
Austrian-American doctor Karl Landsteiner discovers blood groups (A, B, AB, and O)

Why do I need to eat?

Your body's trillions of tiny cells work day and night to keep you alive. To keep going they need energy, which comes from the food you eat. Food also provides the building materials that your cells use to make you grow, but first your body must digest the food, releasing the simple nutrients that your body can use.

What about me?

Digestion begins the moment you put food in your mouth: If you chew on some white bread for a few minutes, an enzyme in your saliva breaks down starch – a bland-tasting carbohydrate in the bread – into sweet-tasting sugars. You've just witnessed digestion in action!

I don't believe it!

The world's human population deposits an incredible two million tonnes of faeces every day, equivalent to the weight of 5,000 completely full jumbo jets.

How to: eat and digest your food

01. Use your teeth to chop and crush food into small pieces.

02. Release watery, slimy saliva into your mouth from the salivary glands. Try not to dribble!

03. Really put your food through the mix, using your tongue to swill it in saliva and push it into the throat for swallowing.

04. Squeeze food along your oesophagus, running from your throat to your stomach.

05. With food in your stomach, churn it into creamy liquid chyme (partially digested food).

06. Release bile from your liver and process any digested food here, storing some of the nutrients and dispatching the rest to the body's cells.

07. Squirt bile, stored in your gall bladder, into the small intestine to help digest any fats.

08. From your pancreas, release more digestive enzymes into the small intestine for breaking down food even further.

Four tooth types

Incisor: Cuts and chops food

Canine: Grips and tears food

Molar: Crushes and grinds food into small pieces

Premolar: Crushes food

WE:IRD OR WHAT?

Michel Lotito (1959-2007), better known as **Monsieur Mangetout** ("Mister Eat Everything"), was a man who consumed indigestible items such as metal and glass. His crowning achievement was to eat a Cessna 150 aircraft – a feat that took him just over two years. Oddly, bananas and hard-boiled eggs made him sick.

09.
With semi-digested chyme working its way through your sausage-shaped small intestine, absorb any remaining nutrients into your blood, which speeds them along to the liver for processing.

10.
With food-remnants now entering the final part of your digestive system – the large intestine – absorb any water from them into the blood, leaving behind solid faeces.

11.
Store the faeces in your rectum until such time as you can get to a toilet...

12.
...and now open your anus, pushing the faeces out of your body. Job done!

Fart facts

- Farts are made up of air that you swallow, and gases released by bacteria in the intestines.
- Farts smell because of certain stinky gases released by bacteria.
- Eating cauliflower, eggs, or meat produces the smelliest farts.
- Eating beans produces the largest volume of farts. Bacteria love beans!
- An average person farts 14 times a day.

Vomiting step-by-step

01: An unsuspecting person eats food that contains nasty bacteria or toxins (poisons).

02: The stomach lining becomes irritated by the intruders.

03: The irritated lining sends signals to the "vomiting centre" of the brain.

04: The person feels sick and makes for the nearest toilet. Quickly.

05: The abdominal muscles contract and squeeze the stomach.

06: Soupy food is forced up the oesophagus and out of the mouth. Yuck!

Your **small intestine** is the most important part of the digestive system. Its ridged lining is covered with tiny, finger-like villi that increase the surface area for absorbing nutrients from the semi-digested food passing through.

Nutrients you need from food

what?	why?	which foods?
carbohydrates	to provide energy	pasta, bread, rice, potatoes
proteins	growth and repair	meat, fish, beans
fats	energy, insulation	dairy foods, plant oils, meat, fish
vitamins	to help cells work	fruit, vegetables, eggs, meat, fish
minerals	to help cells work	dairy foods, meat, fish, nuts, beans
fibre	to help intestines work	fruit, vegetables
water	essential for life	all foods and drinks

WHAT'S IN A NAME?

Borborygmi is the name used by doctors to describe stomach rumblings and other digestive noises because, if you say it, it sounds like the odd noises coming from your tummy region.

In numbers

100 trillion
The number of bacteria living in your colon

100 ml
(3.4 fl oz) The volume of water a person loses in their faeces each day

20
The number of teeth in a set of milk (baby) teeth, which are replaced from age six onwards

32
The number of teeth in a full set of adult teeth

30 tonnes
The weight of food eaten in an average lifetime

11.5 litres
(24 pints) How much food, liquid, and digestive fluid flows through your digestive system every day

---

10 things your liver is doing right now

01: Processing digested food

02: Controlling levels of glucose (sugar) in your blood

03: Storing and transporting fats

04: Processing amino acids (protein building blocks) and making proteins

05: Making green bile, which flows into the small intestine to help digest fats

06: Storing vitamins A, B₁₂, D, E, and K

07: Removing hormones (chemical messengers) from the blood once they've done their job

08: Removing and breaking down drugs and poisons

09: Removing bacteria (germs)

10: Removing worn-out red blood cells

Why can't you ever **take a break from breathing?**

Breathing takes air in and out of your lungs, and that air contains the gas oxygen. Every one of your trillions of body cells needs a constant supply of oxygen, 24 hours a day, and oxygen is something your body cannot store – so, no break! Breathing also removes carbon dioxide from the body – a waste gas that your cells are releasing all the time.

Tell me more: the respiratory system

Nasal cavity: Split in two by cartilage running down its middle, it warms and cleans the air flowing through it

Nostril: One of two hairy entrances to the nasal cavity

Larynx (voice box): Produces sounds

Trachea: Carries air to and from the lungs and is held open by cartilage rings

Intercostal muscles: Connect and move neighbouring ribs

Five ways the nose freshens air

01: Nostril hairs work like a net to catch pollen, insect bits, and skin flakes.

02: Sticky mucus lining the nasal cavity traps bacteria, viruses, and dust particles.

03: Hair-like cilia in the nasal lining move from side to side to waft germ-laden mucus to the throat, where it is swallowed and treated to an acid bath in the stomach.

04: Blood vessels lining the nasal cavity act like radiators to warm the air – especially useful on cold days.

05: The nasal lining loses water vapour to make even the driest air moist.

RECORD BREAKER

Freedivers dive underwater to considerable depths without an air supply. American **freediver** Tanya Streeter has descended to a lung-crushing 160 m (524 ft), and has held her breath for more than six minutes.

In numbers

600 million
The number of alveoli in our two lungs

25,000
The average number of breaths we take each day

9,000 litres
(1,980 gallons) The volume of blood that flows through the lungs to pick up oxygen every day

8,500 litres
(1,869 gallons) The average volume of air breathed in and out daily

100 sq m
(1,076 sq ft) The area of the lungs' alveoli, which is equivalent to the area of a tennis court

12–15
The number of breaths a person makes each minute when at rest. This can double during exercise

0.5 litres
(1 pint) The amount of water we lose from the body each day in breathed-out air

Cell respiration

FAST FACTS

01: Inside every body cell are small, sausage-shaped structures called mitochondria.

02: These mitochondria use oxygen to release energy from fuels, such as glucose, that you get from food.

03: The released energy is used to power the cell activities that keep you alive and healthy.

04: This energy release process, called cell respiration, produces waste carbon dioxide.

Throat: Carries air to and from the larynx

Epiglottis: Closes the entrance to the larynx during swallowing

How to: **make sounds and speak**

04. Using your tongue, teeth, and lips, shape the sounds that the vibrations produce into understandable speech.

01. Breathe normally so that the vocal cords that stretch across your larynx are wide open to let air pass through.

03. Breathe controlled bursts of air from your lungs through the closed vocal cords so that they vibrate.

02. Now pull your vocal cords taut so that they close like curtains.

Bronchus: Branch of the trachea that branches repeatedly into smaller bronchi

Bronchiole: Very fine branch of the smallest bronchi

Alveoli: Microscopic air sacs clustered at the end of each bronchiole, through which oxygen enters the bloodstream

Diaphragm: Dome-shaped muscle sheet under the lungs

Alternative breathing movements

Coughing
To clear mucus and other matter from the upper airways, air from the lungs builds up behind the closed vocal cords and is forced out through the mouth.

Sneezing
This movement is the same as for a cough, but air is forced out through the nasal cavity (instead of the mouth) to clear mucus or relieve an irritation.

Hiccupping
An irritation to the diaphragm (perhaps due to eating too quickly) makes it contract suddenly, causing air to rush into the lungs and the vocal cords to slap shut noisily.

Yawning
A deep breath taken into the lungs when you are tired, probably to "flush out" excess carbon dioxide from the blood.

I don't believe it!

Setting the record for non-stop sneezing, a British girl sneezed more than one million times in 978 days between January 1981 and September 1983.

No choke
Why can't you swallow food and breathe at the same time? A built-in safety device – a flap called the epiglottis – automatically covers the entrance to your trachea. If it didn't, food would get into your trachea, preventing air from reaching your lungs and causing you to choke.

Tell me more: cerebral cortex

The cerebral cortex is the thin outer layer of each of the brain's hemispheres. It is within the cortex that incoming information is processed and stored and instructions sent out. Each part of the cortex has a particular job to do.

1. Auditory association cortex identifies sounds

2. Primary auditory cortex receives signals from the ears

3. Broca's area controls speech production

4. Prefrontal cortex is involved in planning, problem solving, and thinking

5. Premotor cortex controls complex movements such as riding a bike

6. Motor cortex tells muscles to contract to move the body

7. Primary sensory cortex receives signals from receptors in the skin

In numbers

2%
The weight of the brain compared to the weight of the body

20%
The proportion of the body's oxygen supply that is used by the brain

100 billion
The number of neurons (nerve cells) in the brain

83%
The proportion of the brain that the cerebrum makes up

100 trillion
The number of connections between the brain's neurons

350 kph
(218 mph) The speed impulses travel along the fastest neurons

2,500
The number of times the fastest neurons "fire" each second

80%
How much of the brain is made up of water

WEIRD OR WHAT?

An explosion shot a rod that went through mild-mannered Phineas Gage's left cheek and out through the front of his brain. He survived but became bad-tempered, proving that the front of the brain controls personality.

Why do I feel pain if I step on a pin?

Because as the pin sticks into your skin, receptors send signals along nerves to your spinal cord and brain where those signals are analyzed, causing you to feel pain. Your nervous system enables you to move, think, feel, and controls all the activities going on inside your body.

Tell me more: nervous system

Brain stem: Controls automatic activities such as heart and breathing rates

Cerebrum: The main part of the brain. It is divided into linked left and right halves (hemispheres)

Cerebellum: Co-ordinates muscle movement and balance

Spinal cord: A downward extension of the brain that relays signals to and from the brain

Brain: The control centre of your nervous system

Nerves: Bundles of long neurons (nerve cells) that relay signals between all parts of the body, and the brain and spinal cord

8. Sensory association cortex interprets skin sensations

9. Wernicke's area makes sense of written and spoken language

10. Visual association cortex forms images

11. Primary visual cortex receives signals from the eyes

Top five types of intelligence

01: Spatial intelligence
The ability to use the mind to turn around shapes. It is useful in map-reading and understanding how machines are put together.

02: Verbal intelligence
This measures how good someone's writing and reading skills are, and how rapidly they can take in information.

03: Numerical intelligence
Someone who is good at mathematics, with a logical sort of mind that's good at analyzing things, has a high level of numerical intelligence.

04: Lateral intelligence
With this aplenty, a person can easily solve problems using their imagination, and are probably also creative.

05: Emotional intelligence
Scoring well in this department means that you are good at understanding how other people think or feel.

Left is right and right is left

The left cerebral hemisphere controls the right side of the body, and the right cerebral hemisphere controls the left. Each hemisphere also has its own specialities. The left side is usually dominant, which is why most people are right-handed.

Right hemisphere
✓ thinking spatially (visually)
✓ appreciation of art and music
✓ recognizing faces and objects

Left hemisphere
✓ written and spoken language
✓ numbers and maths
✓ problem solving and logical thinking

What about me?

Although it's at the centre of your nervous system, your brain cannot feel pain. A headache is not your brain aching; headaches are commonly caused by muscle tension in the neck and under the skin of the scalp.

I don't believe it!

A nerve impulse takes just one-hundredth of a second to travel from the spinal cord to the big toe.

Four types of memory

You forget many of the things you experience, but important things are stored in long-term memory. Without memory you would not be able to learn, think, or create.

1: Working (short-term) memory provides you with an awareness of your surroundings to help you function.

2: Procedural memory stores skills such as riding a bike.

3: Semantic memory deals with facts, learned words, and languages.

4: Episodic memory remembers life events such as holidays and birthdays.

How to: test your reflexes

01. Locate a cactus with sharp spikes.

02. Touch a spike! This alerts receptors in your skin to send nerve impulses along sensory neurons to your spinal cord.

03. When the nerve signal hits your spinal cord, relay it to a motor neuron, plus send on to the brain.

04. Send the nerve message to your upper arm muscle through the motor neuron.

05. Before you realize what's happening your upper arm muscle will automatically pull your hand away. Good reflexes!

06. Message reaches your brain and you feel pain. Ouch!

KEY
→ sensory neurons
→ relay neurons
→ motor neurons

Why is ice cream sweet, smooth, and cold?

Receptors in your tongue's surface detect tastes and they pick up the sweetness of the ice cream. Touch receptors detect the ice cream's smooth texture, and other receptors sense how cold it is. They all send signals to your brain, which allows you to feel the sweet, smooth, and cold sensations.

Tell me more: anatomy of an eye

Ciliary muscle: Adjusts the thickness of the lens so it can focus light from any distance

Fovea: The point on the retina that produces the most detailed images

Iris: Automatically controls the size of the pupil

Cornea: Lets light into the eye and helps to focus it

Pupil: Lets light into the back part of the eye

Lens: Fine focuses light onto the retina

FAST FACTS

Seeing clearly

- You may think that you see with your eyes, but it's actually the brain that does the seeing, just as it does the hearing, smelling, tasting, and touching.

- Your eyes detect the light that comes into them from outside, and turns it into tiny electrical signals.

- Your brain then turns the signals back into images so you can "see" moving, 3-D pictures of what's going on around you.

The five senses

Vision
Eyes detect light and send signals to the brain, which produces moving images of your surroundings.

Hearing
Ears detect sounds and send signals to the brain, which identifies them as sounds you can hear.

Smell
The nose detects odour molecules in the air and sends signals to the brain so that you can smell them.

Taste
The tongue's taste buds detect taste molecules in food and send signals to the brain so that you taste what you're eating.

Touch
Receptors in your skin sense different types of touch and send signals to your brain so that you feel your surroundings.

WEIRD OR WHAT?

Years ago, sailors believed that wearing a gold earring would improve their eyesight (and pay for their funeral if they drowned and got washed up on a beach).

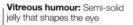

What colour is that word?

Approximately 1 in 23 people experience **synaesthesia**, which means their **senses intermingle**. They might see words or music as colours, taste sounds, or hear a picture.

I don't believe it!

Sometimes people who have had an arm or leg amputated (cut off) can still feel pain in the body part that's missing. This weird and ghostly phenomenon is called phantom pain. And phantom itches are even more frustrating – there's nothing to scratch!

Tell me more: skin sensors

Free nerve ending: Detects pain, heat, or cold

Meissner's corpuscle: Detects light touch

Merkel's disc: Detects light touch and pressure

Ruffini's corpuscle: Detects deep and continuous pressure

Pacinian corpuscle: Detects vibrations and deep pressure

Vitreous humour: Semi-solid jelly that shapes the eye

Optic nerve: Carries nerve signals to the visual cortex in the brain, which produces the images you "see"

Retina: Thin layer that contains rods and cones (light detectors)

Sclera: Tough, white outer layer of eye

Five tastes your tongue's taste buds pick up

Sweet
Cakes, biscuits peaches, mangoes

Sour
Lemons, vinegar, fresh orange juice

Salty
Crisps, bacon, pizza, ready-made meals

Bitter
Coffee, dark chocolate

Umami
The savoury taste of meat, meaty stocks, and cheese

What about me?

Have you eaten anything spicy lately? Chilli peppers contain a substance called capsaicin, which triggers pain receptors in your tongue when you eat them. That's why they feel painfully hot.

The muscles that move your eyes are the body's most active muscles. **They contract (pull) 100,000 times a day.**

In numbers

10,000 The number of taste buds on the tongue

5 The number of tastes detected by the tongue

10,000 The number of odours detected by the nose

25 million The number of smell receptors in the nose

10,000 The number of times more sensitive that the sense of smell is than taste

70% The proportion of the body's sensory receptors that are in the eyes

10,000 The number of different colours that the eyes can distinguish

120 million The number of rods (light-sensitive receptors that work in dim light and cannot detect colour) in each eye

7 million The number of cones (light-sensitive receptors that work in bright light and detect colours) in each eye

1.6 km (1 mile) The distance over which an eye can detect a burning candle in the dark

Why do identical twins look exactly the same?

Identical twins happen when a single sperm (male cell), fertilizes a single egg (female cell) that then splits in two. Each one goes on to grow into a baby, but both cells share exactly the same genetic instructions (DNA).

FAST FACTS

Double (or triple) trouble!

The numbers of births in which twins or triplets are likely to occur naturally:

01: Identical twins
4 in 1,000 births

02: Non-identical (fraternal) twins
15 in 1,000 births

03: Identical triplets
1 in 100,000 births

04: Non-identical triplets
1 in 8,000 births

Born 25 July 1978 in Oldham, England, Louise Brown was the **world's first baby to be conceived by IVF** (in vitro fertilization). One of Louise's mother's eggs was fertilized by Louise's father's sperm in a laboratory, and the resulting embryo transferred back to the uterus (womb) of Mrs Brown.

Reproduction

All humans follow the same path through life. We are born, go through childhood, get older, and eventually die. Reproduction makes sure that we produce children to succeed us when we are no longer here. This sequence reveals how the resulting baby grows inside its mother's uterus, from fertilized egg through the embryo and fetus stages, until it is ready to be born.

Fertilized egg
Travels towards the uterus, ready to start dividing

16-cell stage
Three days after fertilization, the egg has become a ball of 16 cells

Embryo at 4 weeks
Pea-sized embryo is embedded in the lining of the uterus

Fetus at 8 weeks
All its organs in place and it has a beating heart, and arms and legs

Fetus at 12 weeks
The lemon-sized fetus has recognizable facial features, and separate fingers and toes

Cell
One of
a hundred trillion
microscopic living
units inside
your body

Nucleus
The cell's control
centre, which
contains the
instructions to
build and run it

Chromosome
One of 46
instruction
packages (23
came from your
mother and 23
from your father)
inside the cell

DNA
A very long
molecule that
is coiled up to form
a chromosome

Gene
A short section of
DNA that controls
one of your
features, such as
eye or hair colour

Where are the instructions for making a human?

Bony bits

A baby's bones have lots of bendy cartilage in them. As he or she grows, the cartilage is replaced by hard bone tissue – which looks dark on an X-ray.

1 year old
There are wide spaces
of cartilage between each
finger bone.

3 years old
Wrist bones are starting
to form and palm bones
are thickening.

13 years old
Bones are nearly fully formed,
although some bone ends
are still separated by cartilage.

20 years old
The bones are fully grown;
the only cartilage is covering
the ends of the bones.

In numbers

6.72 billion
The number of humans in the world in November 2008

16 million
The number of living direct male descendants of Mongol emperor Genghis Khan (1162–1227)

300 million
The daily number of sperm produced by a man's testes

800,000
The number of eggs in a girl's ovaries when she is born

69
The number of children born to one Russian woman between 1725 and 1765

122 years, 164 days
The longest (confirmed) human lifespan, lived by Louise Calment (1875–1997)

Brain growth

At birth: All of its 100 billion neurons (nerve cells) are in place, but communication between them is poor. Gaps between the skull bones allow it to expand.
At six years: After a rapid growth due to lots of connections being made between neurons, the brain is now nearly full size. Gaps between the skull bones are closed.
At 18 years: The full-sized brain has a complete network of neuron connections.

Peak ages

Childhood and teens: Peak age for learning

Mid-20s to 30s: Peak age for fitness

Mid-20s to early 30s: Peak age for fertility

That's life!

6 months: Baby sits up unsupported, eats semi-solid food, and can pick up small objects

12 months: Infant can walk with help, understand simple commands, drink from a cup, and will speak his/her first words

2 years: Child can walk, speak about 300 words, and recognize itself in a mirror

3 years: Child can run, kick a ball, open doors, and speak simple sentences

5 years: Child can catch a ball, dance in time to music, start to read and write, and form more complex sentences

10 years: Child develops a sense of identity, starts to reason, and can perform skills such as cycling

11–17 years (girls): Puberty and adolescence sets in (when her body becomes adult)

13–17 years (boys): Puberty and adolescence sets in (when his body becomes adult)

20s–30s: Young adult at his/her fittest and healthiest

40s–50s: Older adult begins to show the first signs of ageing

60s–80s: Visible signs of ageing include wrinkles, thinning and greying hair, weaker muscles, poorer sight and hearing

I don't believe it!

The average weight of a newborn baby is 3.5 kg (7.5 lbs), but one baby, born in Italy in 1955, weighed a massive 10 kg (22 lbs)! There doesn't seem to be anything to prevent unborn babies growing bigger and bigger; instead, the onset of labour is linked to the unborn baby's maturity.

Fetus at 20 weeks
Starts to kick, can be felt by its mother, and can hear sounds

Fetus at 30 weeks
The eyes are open and it can hear the sound of its mother's voice

Newborn after about 40 weeks
The baby is born and can breathe, suck, and swallow immediately

What stops the body working normally?

Your body is made from trillions of cells that work together within tissues, organs, and systems to keep you alive. Keeping healthy helps ensure that cells work normally. But sometimes things go wrong and you get ill. Usually, modern medicine can treat and cure these malfunctions.

Bleeding used to be employed as a (useless) way of treating illness, by **cutting a vein** or by applying a **bloodsucking leech**. Today, leeches have made a comeback, used by doctors to stimulate blood flow where, for example, severed body parts have been sewn back on.

I don't believe it!

Testing urine using chemical tests to look for signs of disease is routine these days. Centuries ago doctors examined a patient's urine by smelling it, looking at its colour, and seeing if it was cloudy or not – and they also tasted it. Yuck!

Tell me more: a balanced diet

Follow the guidelines of the food pyramid! The proportion of space in the pyramid given to each category shows how much of each food type the body needs to provide it with energy and to keep it working and healthy.

Sugary foods: Fats, sugars, and junk foods

Dairy: Milk, yoghurt, cheese, and butter

Proteins: Meat, fish, eggs, and nuts

Fruit and vegetables: Include apples, bananas, carrots and cabbage

Starchy foods: Potatoes, bread, pasta, rice, and grains

Six key branches of medicine

 Anatomy: The structure of the body

 Epidemiology: How diseases are caused and spread

 Immunology: The immune system and its disorders

 Neurology: The nervous system and its diseases

 Physiology: How cells, tissues, organs, and systems work

Psychiatry: Mental illness and its treatment

WEIRD OR WHAT?

Thousands of years ago, people with mental problems were sometimes subjected to a particularly brutal "treatment" called **trepanning**. A stone knife was used to cut a hole in the person's skull to let "evil spirits" escape from the brain.

Blasts from the past

1796 First vaccination (against deadly smallpox) is carried out by English doctor Edward Jenner

1846 First anaesthetic (to make a patient unconscious) is used during an operation in Boston, USA

1860 French scientist Louis Pasteur shows how bacteria cause infectious diseases

1865 English doctor Joseph Lister uses antiseptics to prevent wound infection during operations

1895 German physicist Wilhelm Roentgen discovers X-rays

1928 Scottish bacteriologist Alexander Fleming discovers penicillin – the first antibiotic (drug that kills bacteria)

1967 South African surgeon Christiaan Barnard performs the first heart transplant

1980 Introduction of "keyhole" surgery to perform operations through tiny openings in the body

Four types of pathogens

Pathogens are micro-organisms that cause disease.

Viruses
Colds, influenza (flu), measles, chickenpox

Bacteria
Dental caries (tooth decay), whooping cough, tuberculosis (TB)

Protists
Malaria, sleeping sickness, giardiasis (severe diarrhoea)

Fungi
Athlete's foot, ringworm, candidiasis (thrush)

How to: vaccinate against a nasty disease

01. Make a vaccine – a liquid that contains a pathogen that has been made harmless so that it doesn't make you ill.

02. Inject the vaccine into your body.

03. Muster up your body's immune system, which will react to the harmless pathogen and make billions of antibodies, ready to disable it.

04. Cheer on the antibodies surging around your body, mopping up the harmless pathogens.

05. Be amazed when your body becomes infected by the "real" nasty, disease-carrying pathogen and…

06. …your fully prepared immune system pours out antibodies to combat the pathogen and prevents you from becoming ill.

RECORD BREAKER

Before pain relief and anaesthetics, the best surgeons were regarded as the ones that worked **fastest**. On 21 December 1846, Scottish surgeon Robert Liston performed a thigh **amputation** in just 25 seconds.

Alternative therapies

Acupuncture: Sticks fine needles into the skin at specific points to treat disorders

Aromatherapy: Uses scented plant oils to treat disorders or help relaxation

Chiropractice: Manipulates the joints of the backbone to give pain relief

Herbalism: Uses certain plants and their extracts to treat illnesses

Homeopathy: Patients given incredibly dilute doses of a remedy that undiluted produces symptoms similar to the illness being treated

Naturopathy: Holistic (whole body) treatment by changing the patient's lifestyle or diet

Reflexology: Massaging specific parts of the feet that are supposed to be linked to the afflicted body parts

Five ways to improve your health

01 Eat a balanced diet with the right mix of foods in the right quantities.

02 Only eat small amounts of fatty, sugary, or salty foods.

03 Take regular exercise.

04 Avoid spending hours in front of a television or computer.

05 Avoid alcohol, cigarettes, and all other types of drugs.

Looking inside the body

These imaging techniques allow doctors to see inside the body without having to cut it open.

X-ray
Passes X-rays through the body to show its bones

Angiogram
A special kind of X-ray, used to show arteries

CT scan
Uses X-rays and a computer to show body tissues

MRI scan
Uses magnets and radio waves to show body tissues

PET scan
Uses radioactive substances to show the brain at work

Ultrasound scan
Sound waves produce images of organs and developing babies

Endoscopy
Puts a tiny camera inside a body opening

Science and technology

What's the matter?

Everything! Well not quite. Matter is everything in the Universe that takes up space and has mass. An atom is the simplest part of matter. It can't be split apart by normal chemical or physical processes – only by a nuclear reaction.

Nucleus: The central core of an atom

Protons: Inside the nucleus there are particles called protons that carry a positive electric charge

Quarks: Protons and neutrons are made of smaller particles called quarks. Quarks always exist in triplets

Neutrons: The nucleus also contains neutrons, which have no charge

A proton is about 0.000000000001 mm (1/25,000,000,000,000 in) in diameter

Electrons: Whizzing around the nucleus is a cloud of negatively charged electrons. Electrons are about 1,800 times lighter than protons and neutrons

Types of quarks:

up
down
top
bottom
charm
strange

Up and down quarks make up protons and neutrons. Top, bottom, charm, and strange quarks are believed to have decayed within a fraction of a second after the Big Bang, although they can be artificially created by scientists.

In a single drop of water there are **2 sextillion** – that's **2,000,000,000,000,000,000,000** – oxygen atoms and twice the number of hydrogen atoms.

How to: **split an atom**

Equipment needed:
nuclear reactor

01. Fire neutrons at high speed at the nucleus of a large atom.

02. The atom is smashed into two smaller atoms, giving off energy and more neutrons.

03. These neutrons hit other atoms of the original material, starting a chain reaction.

Warning!
Nuclear reactions involve unstable atoms that give off streams of radiation that can damage and kill body cells and alter genes.

Nuclear reactions produce massive amounts of energy. A lump of uranium about the size of a tennis ball will produce as much energy as about 4 million litres (1 million gallons) of petrol – that's about enough to fill two Olympic-sized swimming pools.

What about me?

A human hair is about 1 million atoms wide. You have around 100,000 hairs on your head, so that makes… You do the maths!

Most of an atom is made of empty space. If the atom were the size of a sports stadium, the nucleus would be a pea at the centre, with the electrons orbiting at the outer stands.

You can't see atoms because they are **invisible**. They are thousands of times smaller than the wavelengths of light, so they don't reflect light. If you really want to observe individual atoms, try a **scanning tunnelling microscope**.

Blasts from the past

5th century BCE
Greek thinker Democritus guesses that everything must be made from very tiny particles too small to be seen and which could not be destroyed or split into anything smaller. The word "atom" comes from the Greek for "uncuttable"

1661
Irish philosopher Robert Boyle argues that matter is made up of different "corpuscles" (atoms) rather than the classical elements of air, earth, fire, and water

1803
English scientist John Dalton comes up with an atomic theory: that all elements are made up of tiny particles called atoms and that the atoms of each element are different from the atoms of every other element

1897
British scientist Joseph John Thomson discovers the electron

1911
New Zealander Ernest Rutherford shows that atoms have a dense, positively charged nucleus, with negatively charged electrons surrounding it

1913
Danish scientist Niels Bohr explains how atoms share or exchange electrons to make chemical bonds

1932
English physicist James Chadwick discovers the neutron

1963
American physicist Murray Gell-Mann suggests the existence of quarks

---

An atom usually has exactly the same number of positively charged protons as it does negatively charged electrons.

Sand grains are made of two kinds of atom – oxygen and silicon. Humans are made of about 28 different kinds of atom.

Most of the atoms that exist on Earth today were present when the Solar System formed 4.6 billion years ago.

I don't believe it!

Scientists can study subatomic particles using a **particle accelerator**.

01: Beams of subatomic particles are sent around in circles by powerful electromagnets and speeded up by pulses of electricity.

02: When the particles are travelling fast enough (at almost the speed of light), they are extracted and made to smash into each other to create smaller particles.

03: The world's largest particle accelerator is run by CERN (the European Organization for Nuclear Research) and is a 27-km- (16.7-mile-) long underground loop on the border of Switzerland and France.

Thinking big

Atoms make up about 4 per cent of the total matter of the Universe.

The remaining 96 per cent is made up of dark matter, which scientists can so far only observe by seeing how known matter reacts to it.

For every type of particle of matter a corresponding type of particle of anti-matter exists, which is like a mirror image of it.

Light, heat, and sound do not take up space or have mass so are not made of matter but are forms of energy. Even though it isn't matter, don't waste energy as that does matter.

What is an element?

An element is a pure substance made up of only one type of atom. The atoms of every element are different from the atoms of every other element. 117 elements have so far been discovered or created. Of these, 91 occur naturally on Earth. The others can be created in laboratories. The atoms of one element can combine with atoms of other elements to form compounds. For example, hydrogen and oxygen can combine to form water.

Tell me more: element symbols

Each element has a one- or two-letter symbol as well as its name. Some of the elements have symbols that come from Latin words. For example, the symbol for iron is "Fe" as the Latin word for iron is *ferrum*. Elementary!

Tell me more: the periodic table

The periodic table arranges elements according to their atomic number (the number of protons each element has in its nucleus). This arrangement results in elements with similar properties (characteristics) being grouped together.

Atomic number: How many protons are in the atom's nucleus

Symbol: Used as shorthand when writing chemical equations

Mass number: The total number of protons and neutrons in the nucleus of each atom

The symbol for **tungsten**, "W", comes not from Latin, but from its alternative name: **wolfram**.

Key

The elements in the Periodic Table can be colour coded to show the nine different groupings. Hydrogen does not belong to any one group.

- alkali metals
- alkali-earth metals
- transition metals
- rare earths
- radioactive rare earths
- other metals
- semimetals
- non-metals
- noble gases
- hydrogen

Elements named after scientists

Curium
Marie Curie
Discovered radium and polonium

Mendelevium
Dmitri Mendeleyev
Invented the Periodic Table of elements

Bohrium
Niels Bohr
Worked out how atoms bond

Seaborgium
Glen Seaborg
Created 10 new elements

ELEMENTARY FACTS

Mercury and bromine are the only elements that are liquid at room temperature.

Silver has antibacterial properties – you can buy silver-treated socks to control foot odour.

Lasers using the gas **xenon** can cut through materials so tough that diamond-tipped blades can not cut them.

Gold is so soft that people used to bite coins to check they were real gold – if they were, they left teeth marks.

Burning **potassium** gives off a violet flame.

Helium is lighter than air, which is why it's used to fill balloons.

Osmium is used to make hard-wearing points on fountain pens.

Most common elements in the Universe
(estimated percentage of atoms)

hydrogen 92.4%
helium 7.4%
oxygen 0.06%
carbon 1.03%
nitrogen 0.01%
neon 0.01%

Most common elements in Earth's atmosphere
(estimated percentage of atoms)

nitrogen 78%
oxygen 21%
argon 0.93%
carbon 0.03%
neon 0.0018%
helium 0.00052%

Record Breakers

H Hydrogen is the simplest and lightest of all the elements. If it is not attached to other elements, hydrogen on Earth floats away into space.

Os A 30-cm (1-ft) cube of osmium weighs 640 kg (1,410 lb). That's the same as ten 64-kg (140-lb) adults!

Li Lithium is so soft it can be cut with a knife, and is light enough to float on water.

I don't believe it!

Want to buy some of the element californium? You will need a lottery win as it costs US$27 million for just one gram! Elements at the end of the Periodic Table have to be artificially created in a nuclear reactor and some only last for a fraction of a second, hence the high price tag.

Elements in a human

hydrogen 61%
oxygen 26%
carbon 10.5%
nitrogen 2.4%
calcium 0.23%
sulphur 0.13%
phosphorous 0.13%

In numbers

5,596°C
(10,104.8°F) The boiling point of rhenium
3,550°C
(6,422°F) The melting point of carbon
-268.93°C
(-452.074°F) The boiling point of helium

Why are most gases invisible?

In the air around us, the molecules of gases are usually so far apart that our eyes can't detect them – although with a few, it's possible to detect them by smell. Gases have no firm shape or form. Their molecules move rapidly in every direction to fill whatever container they are in, or escape if the container has no lid.

How to: fly a hot-air balloon

01. Inflate the envelope of the balloon using a large fan.

02. Blast the burner to heat the air in the envelope. The heat causes the air molecules to move faster and further apart, causing the envelope to swell.

Tell me more: states of matter

Solid
The molecules in a solid object are tightly packed together. Solids have a fixed volume and a definite shape that is not easy to change.

Liquid
Molecules in a liquid can move past each other, allowing the substance to flow. Liquids have a fixed volume but no definite shape.

Gas
Molecules in a gas are free to move around, filling all the space around them. Gases have no fixed shape or volume.

How does popcorn pop?
Inside each kernel of corn there is a small amount of moisture. When the corn is heated, the moisture changes to steam and expands. The pressure from the expanded gas creates an explosion and the kernel is blown inside out.

What about me?
Sound travels three times faster in helium gas than in air. So if you take a gulp from a helium balloon, the resonant frequency (speed of vibrations) of your voice increases, making it sound squeaky.

When a **gas condenses** into a **liquid**, on average, the liquid takes up **1,300 times less space** than the gas.

03. While ground crew hold the balloon's basket down, climb aboard.

04. Hot air rises because it is less dense than the colder air around it and this causes the balloon to lift off. Enjoy your flight!

05. Fire the burner to heat the air more so the balloon lifts higher.

06. When ready to land, open a valve in the balloon's envelope to release the air. The balloon will descend to the ground.

The one who smelt it dealt it!

Gases travel very fast and mix rapidly and completely with one another in a process called diffusion. So when you open a bottle of something strong-smelling – or let rip with a fart – the scent molecules diffuse into the air and soon reach your nose.

Parp power!

The flatulence of a single sheep could power a small truck for 40 km (25 miles) a day. It contains methane gas, which can be burned as fuel.

I don't believe it!

Gas particles move at more than 1,600 kph (1,000 mph) at room temperature – that's faster than the speed of sound.

The gases in a fart

nitrogen
20–90%
hydrogen
0–50%
carbon dioxide
10–30%

oxygen
0–10%
methane
0–10%

sulphur compounds
(they cause the pong!)

Ever wondered how your soda drink gets its fizz?

Carbon dioxide gas is dissolved in the drink at low temperatures under pressure. When the bottle or can is opened, the pressure is released and the gas escapes in bubbles of fizz.

DON'T TRY THIS AT HOME!

If you shake a fizzy drink bottle, the dissolved gas is released and rises to the top of the bottle creating enormous pressure. When the lid is released, gas – together with quite a lot of the drink – shoots out!

Greenhouse gases

✸ Gases in the atmosphere, such as water vapour, carbon dioxide, and methane, let radiation from the Sun through to warm the Earth and trap some of the heat, which would otherwise be reflected back into space.

✸ This "greenhouse effect" has always happened and is vital to keep the planet warm enough for life to exist.

✸ As the amount of greenhouse gases in the atmosphere increases due to pollution, burning fossil fuels, and cutting down forests, more heat is trapped and global temperatures rise.

What is a force?

A force is a push or a pull that gets something moving or changes the way it moves. Flicking a marble creates a force that sends the marble rolling across the table. Putting out your hand to stop it falling off the table's edge creates a force that sends it spinning in another direction. If the marble rolls off the table, gravity pulls it to the ground – another force, of course!

WHAT'S IN A NAME?

Sir Isaac Newton's three laws of motion, often called **Newton's Laws**, explain how forces make objects move. Legend has it that an apple fell on Newton's head while he was sitting under a tree, which led to his discoveries about motion and gravity.

Newton's first law

An object will stay still or move along at the same speed and in the same direction unless a force acts upon it. This law is sometimes referred to as the law of inertia.

In action: If you brake too hard on your bike, you may go flying over the handlebars. The force exerted by the brakes has stopped the bike, but you keep moving forwards at the same speed.

Newton's second law

The amount an object's speed or direction changes depends on its mass and the size of the force acting upon it.

In action: If you exert a force on a marble by pushing it, it begins to move. But it takes more force to move a heavier object or to move something faster. So if you push a giant boulder it won't move so far.

Newton's third law

Whenever a force acts, an equal force acts in the opposite direction.

In action: When you jump, you push the ground with your feet, and the ground pushes back, propelling you into the air.

Tell me more: **friction**

According to Newton's first law, a rolling ball ought to go on rolling for ever, but it actually slows down and stops. That's because there's another force stopping it – **friction**. Friction is the rubbing force created between a moving object and whatever it touches.

Drag snag

Vehicles moving through air or water are affected by friction caused by the air or water around them – this is called **drag**. Giving the vehicle a smooth surface and **streamlined shape**, designed to make air or water flow over the vehicle smoothly, can reduce drag.

Four reasons why **friction** is useful

Friction produces heat. For thousands of years, humans have rubbed dry sticks together to **make fire**.

The patterned tread on tyres creates a rough surface to increase friction, so they **don't slip** on smooth surfaces.

The ridges of your fingerprints create friction between your fingers and whatever you are holding, **helping you grip**.

Brakes rubbing against moving wheels create friction, which causes the wheels to **slow down**.

When you go up in a lift you feel your body's **inertia** acting downwards as it resists the change in its direction. This makes you feel heavier. When you go down, inertia acts upwards, making you feel lighter. You are actually feeling the **acceleration** (the change in speed or direction) your body is experiencing, but because it feels like the force of gravity, it is called a **g-force**.

Every time a roller coaster changes speed or direction, *g*-force affects every part of your body. As you plummet down, your stomach is pushed up against the base of your lungs – let's hope you haven't eaten too many hot dogs!

I don't believe it !

Snow is made up of such tiny particles sliding past each other that they act as a lubricant – that's why you can ski down it.

You can beat **friction** by coating the moving parts of machines with slippery substances called **lubricants**. Lubricants such as oil prevent moving parts sticking and wearing out due to friction. Because friction also creates heat, lubricants also stop machines from **overheating**.

While you are reading this book, you might think you're not moving at all... but think again!

🌐 You are sitting on the Earth, which is spinning at 1,600 kph (1,000 mph).

🌐 The Earth is going around the Sun at more than 110,000 kph (70,000 mph).

🌐 The Solar System is travelling through space at 2,000,000 kph (1,300,000 mph).

How to: **move the tablecloth and not break anything**

01. Find a table, a large cloth, and some cheap objects. Lay the cloth on a table and place the objects on it.

02. Hold the end of the cloth with both hands and give it a quick, firm tug.

03. You should be able to pull out the cloth leaving the objects where they are. Their inertia stops them from moving with the cloth.

need **gravity?**

Yes! Without it there'd be no Universe as we know it. Gravity is what keeps you, and everything else, on Earth. It is the tendency of objects with mass to be attracted to each other. An object's mass is the amount of material it contains. The bigger the mass of an object, the stronger its force of gravity.

Five reasons why gravity is good

01 Gravity makes things fall when they are dropped. At least you know where to start looking for your socks!

02 It's the force that keeps the water on Earth and makes the rain and snow fall to the planet's surface.

03 The Earth's gravity holds the atmosphere in place.

04 The Sun's gravity keeps the Earth and other planets in orbit around it.

05 Gravity keeps everything else in the Universe in orbit around some other object. Without it there'd just be a chaos of floating matter.

Great escape
The speed needed to break free of an object's gravitational pull is called "escape velocity". Escape velocity from the Earth is 11.2 km/sec (6.96 miles/sec).

Watch your weight

The pull of gravity varies across the Universe, so your weight (your mass in the presence of gravity) will vary depending on where you are. Multiply your weight by the figure below to find out how heavy you'd be in other parts of the Solar System.

Sun	multiply by 28	**Jupiter**	multiply by 2.54
Mercury	multiply by 0.38	**Saturn**	multiply by 1.08
Venus	multiply by 0.91	**Uranus**	multiply by 0.91
Mars	multiply by 0.38	**Neptune**	multiply by 1.19
Moon	multiply by 0.17	**Pluto**	multiply by 0.06

Zero gravity

↓ Zero gravity does not really mean no gravity at all – that's impossible as there are always objects with mass exerting gravity, even in space.

↓ It is the feeling of weightlessness when a person is falling freely without ever reaching the ground.

Four ways to achieve zero gravity

01 Orbit around Earth in a spacecraft.

02 Travel to the centre of the Earth.

03 Ride in a "vomit comet" – a specially modified aircraft that zooms downwards towards the Earth.

04 Jump on a trampoline. For a fraction of a second, while you're at the top of your jump, just before you start to come back down, you experience weightlessness.

Brain boxes

Some of the biggest brains in history have struggled to understand the invisible force of gravity.

Galileo Galilei
Italian scientist Galileo Galilei, who lived from 1564–1642, knew that there was a mysterious force making things move, but he just couldn't work out what it was.

Isaac Newton
In 1687, English brainbox Sir Isaac Newton did the maths and told the world it was a force called gravity that made things fall to Earth, and planets move through the night sky.

Albert Einstein
In the early 20th century, German-born genius Albert Einstein was developing revolutionary theories to explain gravity and the Universe. Mind-boggling stuff!

01. Jump out of a plane (make sure you have a parachute strapped to your back first!) You will at first accelerate then, as drag (resistance) balances the pull of gravity, you will reach a steady speed called terminal velocity.

02. Keep your limbs spread wide to maintain terminal velocity of about 200 kph (124 mph). To change speed, reduce drag by altering body posture.

03. By standing straight up or diving headfirst with your arms and legs behind you, you can reach speeds of 290 kph (180 mph).

04. To slow down for landing, you will need to increase the drag and reduce your speed to around 20 kph (12 mph). To do this, pull the parachute cord to open the canopy.

05. As soon as your toes make contact with the ground, slightly bend your knees, tuck your elbows in close to your body, and allow yourself to safely fall.

X300

What about me?

You may not know it, but you regularly experience big *g*-forces. A sneeze exerts a force of 3 *g* on your body, and a cough can punch a mighty 3.5 *g*.

Mars's moon, Deimos, has such a small force of gravity that if you were standing on it and you jumped hard, you could achieve escape velocity.

In numbers

The *g*-force is the force you feel under acceleration. It is measured in "*g*", but you experience it as the heavy feeling when you swoop up the curve of a roller coaster. Hold on tight!

0 *g*
Weightlessness

1 *g*
Force of gravity at Earth's surface

2–3 *g*
Space shuttle astronauts experience between 2–3 *g* on launch

3 *g*
Roller coasters are designed to not to exceed 3 *g*, though there are a few hair-raising exceptions

4–6 *g*
Fighter pilots, who often have to make sharp turns, may wear anti-*g* suits to protect them from the effects of high *g*-forces. If forces between 4–6 *g* are experienced for more than a few seconds a person might lose consciousness

5 *g*
Experienced by Formula One racing drivers when braking

9 *g*
Pilots pulling out of a dive may experience as much as 9 *g*

Problems with living in zero gravity...
as experienced by astronauts

◂ Drinks must be kept in sealed containers and drunk through a straw or they'll float off.

◂ **Avoid crumbly food as crumbs float away around the spacecraft and can get into everything.**

◂ When you sleep you have to be strapped tightly into a sleeping bag attached to the wall.

◂ **It's confusing – there's no up or down in zero gravity, so ceilings, walls, and floors are all the same.**

◂ You have to be firmly attached to a space toilet with Velcro and a good air seal so nothing floats away! The toilet is flushed with a jet of air.

◂ **Long-term weightlessness causes weakening of a person's muscles and bones. You need to exercise, or you'll be too weak to walk out of the spacecraft when you get back to Earth.**

I don't believe it!

On a diet? Well then plan the weigh-in for a night with a full Moon overhead. The weak pull of the Moon's gravity works against the pull of the Earth's gravity, reducing your weight very slightly. Every little helps!

Why do objects look different colours?

The white light around us is made up of a mixture of different colours of light. The surfaces of objects absorb some colours and reflect others back. Our eyes see only the colours that are reflected. An object that reflects all the colours of light appears white. An object that absorbs all the colours, looks black. A tomato absorbs all the colours except red, which it reflects back to us. You get the picture!

Tell me more:
electromagnetic spectrum

Light is part of a continuous band of energy called the electromagnetic spectrum, which is made up of waves of radiation with different wavelengths (distance between two peaks or troughs of the waves). Apart from light, all electromagnetic waves are invisible to the human eye.

Television: Uses radio waves

Radio waves: Used to carry radio signals around Earth

Microwaves: Cooking is a common use for microwaves

Radar transmitter: Sends microwaves through the air

Visible light: What humans can see – red, orange, yellow, green, blue, indigo, violet

Infrared rays: We cannot see, but can feel the heat emitted by these rays

What about me?

Even if you could travel at the speed of light (which scientists are pretty sure is impossible), light would always be travelling away from you at the same speed.

WHAT'S IN A NAME?

"Laser" is short for Light Amplification by Stimulated Emission of Radiation. A laser passes light or electricity through a gas or a crystal to produce a concentrated jet of light powerful enough to cut through metal and precise enough to perform surgery.

Primary colours of light

red green blue

- When beams of all three of the primary colours are mixed together in equal quantities they form white light.

- By combining the primary colours in different proportions any colour can be made. This is how the colour is produced on a TV screen.

Secondary colours of light

When mixed together in equal quantities, the primary colours of light form the secondary colours.

red + green = yellow

blue + red = magenta

green + blue = cyan

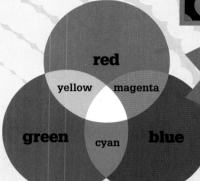

red
yellow magenta
green cyan blue

Printing colour
We can see the different colours in this book because the ink pigments absorb certain colours of light and reflect others. Printers mix yellow, magenta, and cyan ink to create colours. Mixing all three together creates a muddy brown, so printers must also use a black ink.

Ultraviolet rays:
Invisible rays that can cause damage to our eyes and skin

Gamma rays:
Harmful, cancer-causing rays produced by radioactivity

X-rays:
High-energy rays used in medicine to check people's bones

Rainbows

01: A rainbow appears when light passes through raindrops.

02: Inside each raindrop, the sunlight is bent and split into the colours of the spectrum:

- **red**
- **orange**
- **yellow**
- **green**
- **blue**
- **indigo**
- **violet**

03: You can only see a rainbow when the Sun is behind you and the rain is falling in front of you.

04: From an aeroplane, a rainbow forms a complete circle.

05: There are "mnemonic" word tricks to help you remember the colours of a rainbow:

- *Richard Of York Gave Battle In Vain*

- *Roy G Biv (the rainbow guy)*

Colourful triangle
Just like a raindrop, a prism (triangle of glass) changes the direction of light passing through it. This is called **refraction**. The prism bends the wavelengths, splitting the white light into a spectrum of colours.

I don't believe it!

Light travels through space at 300,000 km/sec (186 miles/sec). A beam of light can travel around the world seven times in one second.

In numbers

8
The number of minutes it takes for the Sun's light to travel the 149,000,000 km (93,000,000 miles) to reach Earth. We see the Sun the way it looked eight minutes ago

2000
The number of light waves that would fit in a millimetre (0.04 in)

20
The number of times more men than women that are affected by red/green colour blindness. The ability to detect colour depends on cells in the retina at the back of the eye that detect particular parts of the spectrum. Some of these are missing or inactive in a colour-blind person

What is electricity?

Inside all atoms, there are particles called protons, which have a positive electric charge, and particles called electrons with a negative charge. Usually there are equal numbers of protons and electrons, so the charges cancel each other out. But sometimes, an atom gains or loses electrons, giving it a positive or negative charge. Electricity is the presence or flow of this electric charge.

What about me?

Combing hair can strip it of negatively charged electrons, giving it a positive charge of static electricity. Like charges repel, causing your hair to stand on end.

The word "electricity" comes from Greek elektron, meaning amber. The Greeks noticed that when a piece of amber is rubbed with wool it attracts light objects. This is static electricity.

Static electricity makes clingfilm clingy.

Conductors

are materials where the electrons are free to move, creating an electric current. Some good conductors:

magnesium

copper

silver

steel

gold

aluminium

lead

mercury

Insulators

are materials where electrons cannot move as freely as they can in a metal, so they cannot conduct electricity. Some good insulators:

plastic

rubber

ceramic

fibreglass

wool

Lighten up!

As night falls the lights go on. Energy-saving light bulbs use less energy and last longer than regular light bulbs. Here's how they work.

Visible light: Produced when UV light passes through tube's phosphor coating

Electrons: Interact with mercury gas in tube, producing ultraviolet (UV) light

Tungsten electrodes: Generate electrons from electric current

Wires: Carry electricity to electrodes

Fitting: Connects to mains electricity supply

Bright sparks

These scientists have all had electrical measurements named after them.

André Marie Ampère
(1775–1836)
amp
electric current

Charles Coulomb
(1736–1806)
coulomb
charge

James Joule
(1818–1889)
joule
energy

Georg Ohm
(1789–1854)
ohm
resistance

Alessandro Volta
(1745–1827)
volt
electric pressure

James Watt
(1736–1819)
watt
power

I don't believe it!

When different types of metals come into contact, they can generate an electric current. Biting aluminium foil when you have metal fillings can give you an electric shock!

In numbers

25%
The amount of power a disposable battery may lose in a year even if it is not taken out of its packaging

600 volts
The amount of electricity an electric eel can produce by mixing different chemicals in its body

432 kph
(268 mph) The speed of the electric currents that send messages via the nerves to and from the human brain

10%
The amount of electricity wasted by items left in standby mode in households in the USA

What's the point?

Earth is a giant magnet with a magnetic field driven by molten material circulating beneath its surface. Any magnet hanging so that it can move freely – including the needle of a compass – will point in a north-south direction, attracted by Earth's magnetic field.

RECORD BREAKER

At 4.11 m (13.5 ft) tall, the world's **biggest light bulb** sits on top of the Edison Memorial Tower in New Jersey, USA. It marks Thomas Edison's role in inventing the light bulb.

Weird or what?

Earth's magnetic north pole is not the same as the geographical North Pole. At the moment it's in northern Canada, but it is gradually moving northwest at a rate of 40 km (24 miles) per year.

Tell me more: magnets

■ A magnet is a material that will attract objects made of iron and certain other materials.

■ **Magnets attract and repel other magnets.**

■ Every magnet has two ends called the north and south poles where its magnetic forces are strongest.

■ **Like poles (north and north or south and south) repel each other.**

■ Unlike poles (north and south) attract.

■ **When an electric current moves through a wire it creates a magnetic field around it. A magnet created in this way is called an electromagnet.**

How to: get a shock

01. Walk across a nylon carpet with shoes on. As you do so, your shoes rub electrons off the carpet.

02. These electrons collect on your body, giving it a negative electric charge.

03. When you touch something that is an electrical conductor, such as a metal door handle, the electrons flow away into the handle very quickly, giving you a tingling shock. Ouch!

Why has my bicycle gone rusty?

You probably left it out in the rain again didn't you? A chemical reaction took place as the iron in the bike reacted with oxygen in rainwater and in the air to create a new substance called iron oxide – also known as rust.

Tell me more: chemical reactions

01: The atoms that make up matter are joined together in clumps called molecules.

02: In a chemical reaction, the bonds that join the atoms in molecules are broken apart and new molecules are formed.

03: The starting materials in a chemical reaction are called reactants and the materials that are formed are called the products.

04: Chemical reactions never create or destroy atoms, they only rearrange them.

05: There are chemical reactions going on around you all day, every day, in the kitchen, in car engines, and inside you.

Chemical equation

hydrogen molecules usually contain two hydrogen atoms

oxygen molecule contains two oxygen atoms

water molecules contain two hydrogen atoms

$$2H_2 + O_2 \rightarrow 2H_2O$$

two hydrogen molecules

plus sign shows that the molecules are reacting together

arrow shows reaction has taken place

the product of the reaction is two molecules of water

water molecules contain one oxygen atom

What about me?

When things burn they react with oxygen and give out energy in the form of heat. What's this got to do with you? The food you eat combines with oxygen in your body, and the heat released provides you with the energy you need to live.

I don't believe it!

Mints combine with saliva in your mouth in an endothermic reaction – that's a reaction that draws in heat in order to work. The heat is drawn from your mouth and tongue, which is why mints taste cool.

pH scale   A substance's pH is a measure of how acid or alkaline it is.

pH 1	pH 1.5	pH 2	pH 2.8	pH 3	pH 3.7	pH 4.3	pH 5.6	pH 6.5	pH 7
car battery acid	the worst acid rain	digestive juices	vinegar	lemon juice	orange juice	tomato juice	normal rainfall	milk	pure water

Chemicals that make you look good

chemical	found in	what it does
mica	eye shadow	gives sparkle
ammonium lauryl sulphate	shampoo	removes dirt and grease
calcium carbonate	toothpaste	abrasive that grinds away plaque
sodium fluoride	toothpaste	strengthens teeth enamel
hydrated magnesium silicate	face powder	known as talc, gives a smooth sheen
aluminium chlorohydrates	deodorant	controls perspiration

What a blast!

A firework display is really a series of dramatic chemical reactions. The rainbow of sparks is produced by using compounds that burn with different colours.

strontium or lithium compounds

calcium compounds

sodium compounds

barium compounds

copper compounds

potassium or strontium with copper compounds

aluminium, titanium, or magnesium compounds

Explosive reactions

Alkali metals such as potassium, sodium, rubidium, caesium, and francium are so reactive that just putting them in water makes them explode.

Salt (sodium chloride) and vinegar (acetic acid) is an explosive combination when mixed in large quantities.

If you set light to thermite (a mixture of aluminium and iron oxide), the reaction produces extremely bright light containing dangerous levels of UV and can reach temperatures of 2,400°C (4,350°F). As the reaction produces its own oxygen, it will even burn underwater!

When nitrogen compounds revert to nitrogen gas in chemical reactions, masses of energy is released. The nitrogen compound nitroglycerine is often used in explosives.

Six ways to make a reaction go faster

Reactions happen when molecules bump into each other. Increasing the rate at which molecules collide speeds up the reaction. You can do this by:

01: Using more concentrated solutions, which means there are more molecules in a smaller space.

02: Increasing the pressure of gases, which forces more molecules into a smaller space.

03: Heating, which makes molecules move faster.

04: Light, which makes some molecules move faster.

05: Breaking a solid up to increase the surface area exposed to other reactants.

06: Adding a substance called a catalyst, which speeds up a chemical reaction by reducing the energy needed for the reaction to take place but does not itself change during the reaction.

How to: write a secret message

01. Dab a cotton bud or small paint brush into a bowl of lemon juice. Use the bud or brush to write a message on a piece of white paper and let it dry.

02. Pass your secret message to a friend and instruct them to hold the paper up to a heat source, such as a light bulb.

03. The lemon juice is slightly acidic and when the paper is held near heat, the acidic parts of the paper turn brown before the rest of the paper does, revealing the hidden message.

pH 7.3
human blood

pH 8
sea water

pH 9
toothpaste

pH 9.5
bleach

pH 10.5
milk of magnesia

pH 11
household ammonia

pH 12
soap

pH 12.8
hair remover

pH 13.8
oven cleaner

How do we measure time?

By observing the Earth's movements relative to the Sun. One complete spin of the Earth on its axis takes a day. Approximately 365.26 spins (days) make one complete revolution of the Sun, or one solar year. Units of time smaller than a day, such as hours, minutes, and seconds, are measured using clocks. Weeks, months, and years, are measured using calendars. Time to find out more...

Tell me more:
time zones

If everyone in the world set their clocks to the same time, when it was midnight it would be daylight in one part of the world and the middle of the night in another. To avoid this, Earth is divided into time zones.

- Time zones generally follow lines of longitude (imaginary lines running from pole to pole), but usually bend to include entire countries or states in one time zone.

- There are 24 time zones, each 15° of longitude and one hour apart.

- India straddles more than one time zone but has chosen a time halfway between those on either side so that the whole country can use one time.

- Russia has 11 time zones – more than any other country.

- China stretches across four time zones but uses only one time.

- The International Date Line dividing one day from the next follows the 180° meridian (longitude line) on the globe.

- Countries east of the date line are a day ahead of those to the west.

- The International Date Line runs mostly through the ocean, but where it would pass through or near land it bends to avoid dividing a region into two days.

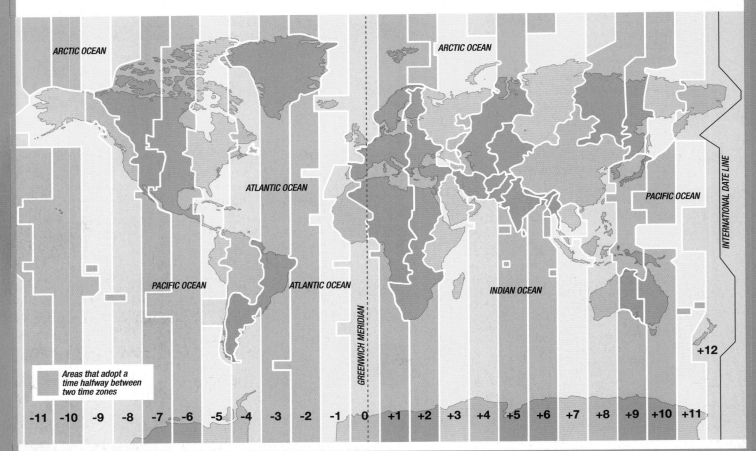

ARCTIC OCEAN · ARCTIC OCEAN · ATLANTIC OCEAN · PACIFIC OCEAN · PACIFIC OCEAN · ATLANTIC OCEAN · INDIAN OCEAN · GREENWICH MERIDIAN · INTERNATIONAL DATE LINE · +12

Areas that adopt a time halfway between two time zones

-11 -10 -9 -8 -7 -6 -5 -4 -3 -2 -1 0 +1 +2 +3 +4 +5 +6 +7 +8 +9 +10 +11

Blasts from the past

1500 BCE
Sundials are used in Egypt to define time periods such as morning and afternoon, and to measure the longest and shortest days of the year

1400 BCE
Water clocks are used in Egypt. Water drains from a vessel, reaching different levels that represent periods of time

1000s CE
Arab engineers invent the first mechanical clocks driven by weights and gears

1100s
Monks use the hourglass to show the times of prayer

1325
The first clock with a dial is installed in Norwich Cathedral, England

1335
The first clock to strike the hours is made in Milan, Italy

1350
The oldest known alarm clock is made in Würzburg, Germany

1650
Dutch scientist Christiaan Huygens invents a pendulum clock with an error of less than one minute per day

1759
British clockmaker John Harrison makes an accurate marine chronometer. Timekeeping is vital at sea for calculating position

1949
The first atomic clock is built. This precise timekeeper measures the vibrations of an atom

TICK TOCK

Clocks keep time by measuring a **constantly repeating motion**. This may be the swing of a pendulum or the vibrations of atoms.

A.M. is short for the Latin phrase *ante meridiem* meaning "before midday".

P.M. is short for the Latin phrase *post meridiem* meaning "after midday".

COUNTING TIME

picosecond = 0.000,000,000,001 seconds
nanosecond = 0.000,000,001 seconds
microsecond = 0.000,001 seconds
millisecond = 0.001 seconds
minute = 60 seconds
hour = 60 minutes = 3,600 seconds
day = 24 hours = 86,400 seconds
week = 7 days = 604,8000 seconds
fortnight = 14 days = 2 weeks
month = 28 to 31 days
quarter = 3 months
year = 12 months = 365 days = 52 weeks + 1 day
leap year = 366 days = 52 weeks + 2 days
decade = 10 years
century = 100 years
millennium = 1,000 years

I don't believe it!

Air passengers crossing from Tonga to Samoa – a two-hour flight across the International Date Line – often arrive the day before they left!

Time leaps

Most calendar years are 365 days long. In leap years, a day is added to the end of February to account for the extra quarter day in each solar year.

Leap years happen in years divisible by four, except years ending in 00, which must be divisible by 400 to be a leap year.

Earth's rotation is slowing down at a rate of about 0.6 seconds per year, so the solar day (the time it takes Earth to spin once) and the time on the most accurate atomic clocks gradually diverges.

Since 1972, about every 18 months a leap second is added at the end of June or December to compensate for the slowdown.

Just a phase

01: Months are based on the phases of the Moon.

02: A phase is the time it takes for the Moon to orbit the Earth – about 29.5 days.

03: Calendar months are not very accurate and can vary between 28 and 31 days. So, in a year of 12 calendar months there are 12 and a bit lunar months.

RECORD BREAKERS

01: First demonstrated in February 2008, the world's **most accurate clock** uses strontium atoms and is accurate to one second in 200 million years.

02: The Colgate Clock in Jersey City, USA, has a diameter of 15.24 m (50 ft) and is the **world's largest clock**.

03: The **tallest clock tower** is 239.9 m (787 ft) high and tops the NTT DoCoMo Yoyogi Building in Tokyo, Japan.

In numbers

0.01 second
a flash of lightning

0.1 second
blink of human eye

1 second
human heartbeat

15 seconds
space shuttle to travel 120 km (75 miles)

497 seconds
light reaching the Earth from the Sun

1,000 seconds
a snail to move 10 m (32.8 ft)

800 million seconds
a lifetime's sleep

2.5 billion seconds
human lifetime (80 years)

How do computers store data?

All the data stored in your computer – every word, picture, number, and sound – is captured as a series of electrical pulses that are either on or off. A number system called binary is used to represent these pulses with "1" meaning "on" and "0" meaning "off". A single binary digit, known as a "bit", switches a single switch on or off. By linking together these switches, the computer can carry out the complex operations we demand.

Bits and bytes

1 bit = a binary digit, either 1 (on) or 0 (off)

1 byte = 8 bits

1 kilobyte = 1,000 bytes

1 megabyte = 1,000,000 bytes

1 gigabyte = 1,000,000,000 bytes

1 terabyte = 1,000,000,000,000 bytes

How much data?

10 bytes = one word
2 kilobytes = one typewritten page
100 kilobytes = a low-resolution photograph
1 megabyte = a short novel
2 megabytes = a high-resolution photograph
100 megabytes = a shelf of novels 1 m (3 ft) long
1 gigabyte = 17 hours of digital music
10 terabytes = all the printed works in the US Library of Congress (the world's largest library)

Tell me more: computer anatomy

Monitor: LCD screen displays text and images made up of individual dots of colour called pixels

Ports: External devices such as flash sticks, printers, scanners, and digital music players can be plugged in

Keyboard: Contains microprocessor that detects which key has been pressed and sends a signal to the control processing unit (CPU)

Mouse: As the mouse is moved it sends co-ordinates to the computer, which moves the cursor on the screen

Moore's Law
"Computers double in capacity and complexity about every 18 months." (An observation made by Gordon E Moore, co-founder of Intel, in 1965.)

I don't believe it!

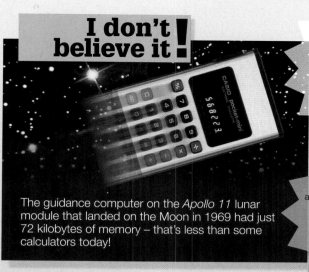

The guidance computer on the *Apollo 11* lunar module that landed on the Moon in 1969 had just 72 kilobytes of memory – that's less than some calculators today!

Q:
What is an astronaut's favourite key on a computer keyboard?

A:
The space bar

WEIRD OR WHAT?

The first computer **"bug"** was actually a moth that got trapped inside a computer at Harvard University, USA, in 1945. Perhaps it was looking for a "byte" to eat!

1945

ENIAC
The first electronic computer used so much power that all the lights in a nearby town dimmed every time it was switched on. It weighed in at about 30 tonnes.

2008

MacBook Air
This ultra-thin laptop computer fits in a bag and weighs just 1.4 kg (3 lb).

ROM vs RAM

Read Only Memory
This holds permanent data that remains even when the computer is switched off.

Random Access Memory
This holds data temporarily. The data is lost when the computer is switched off, unless the user has saved it.

Top 10 computer-owning countries

- Russia 2.52%
- Canada 2.63%
- Italy 2.87%
- South Korea 3.14%
- France 3.58%
- UK 4.27%
- Germany 5.58%
- China 7.03%
- Japan 8.5%
- USA 25.49% of world total

Motherboard: This is the main circuit board. It connects the computer's key components and passes on instructions

Hard disk: This magnetic disk is located within the main body of the computer and stores the computer's programs and data

CPU: The central processing unit is the brains of the computer and carries out calculations and instructions

Data storage

1940s
punched cards

1950s
magnetic tape

1950s
hard disk drive

1970s
floppy disks

1990s
rewritable CDs

2000s
DVDs

2000s
USB flash sticks

Geek speak

Programs are sets of instructions that tell a computer what to do, written in a code called a programming language. There are lots of languages, all designed to suit different types of programs.

Ada: Named after Ada, Countess of Lovelace, a pioneer of programming

BASIC: Beginners All-purpose Symbolic Instruction Code

C#: pronounced C-sharp, it gets its name from music

COBOL: Common Business Oriented Language

FORTRAN: FORmula TRANslation

JAVA: Named after Java coffee, because inventors thought their language just as strong and rich!

PASCAL: Named after French mathematician and writer Blaise Pascal

Blasts from the past

1972
Atari releases *Pong*, the first commercial video game, which sells 100,000 copies

1973
Robert M Metcalfe at Xerox creates the Ethernet, a way of connecting computers in a local-area network (LAN)
■ The minicomputer Xerox Alto is the first with GUI (Graphics User Interface), the desktop system that allows users to navigate using a mouse instead of typing in words

1975
Ed Roberts designs the first popular microcomputer, the Altair, named after a planet in *Star Trek*

1978
Micropro International launches WordStar, the first commercially successful word processing software

1980
Paul Allen and Bill Gates buy the rights to a simple operating system, QDOS. They use it to develop MS-DOS, which becomes the standard operating system in PCs

1947
Physicist William Shockley and his team invent the transistor at Bell Laboratories in the USA. Transistors miniaturize electronic circuits and help to make PCs in the future small, reliable, and affordable

1948
British engineer Andrew Donald Booth invents magnetic drum memory for computers

1949
Maurice Wilkes builds the EDSAC, the first practical stored-program computer, at Cambridge University. It contains 3,000 vacuum tubes and uses mercury delay lines for memory

1951
T Raymond Thompson and John Simmons develop the first business computer, the Lyons Electronic Office (LEO)
■ The UNIVAC is the first business computer made in the USA

1959
John Kilby and Robert Noyce work out how to manufacture complete networks of components on to a single crystal of semiconductor material. Their invention, the integrated circuit, kick-starts the computer revolution

1961
Richard Mattessich develops computerized spreadsheets for use in accounting

1962
Steve Russell invents *SpaceWar!* – the first game intended for computer use

1848
George Boole works out how to write logical problems using algebra

1868
The modern QWERTY keyboard layout is designed by Christopher Latham Sholes, to avoid jamming when typing fast

1869
Using Boolean algebra, William Stanley Jevons designs the first practical machine that can solve a logical problem faster than someone without the machine!

1873
The first successful direct current electric motor is designed by Zenobe Theophille Gramme. Without it, there would be no hard disk drives or fans to keep PCs cool

1884–1892
Americans Dorr E Felt and William S Burroughs pioneer new adding machines called Comptometers. They are operated by pressing keys and have a printing device

1906
Lee De Forest develops a new electronic tube, the triode, which could be used as a switch – a key development in computing

1918
The German Enigma encryption machine can "scramble" a message by a complex system of substituting letters

50,000–20,000 BCE
Pebbles and human fingers are the first tools for calculation. The Latin word *digit* means finger (or toe) as well as a number, and the Latin word for pebble is *calculus*, giving us the word "calculate"

20,000 BCE
The oldest-known objects used to represent numbers are bones with carved notches

c 2400 BCE
The abacus – the first known calculator – is invented in Babylonia

c 500–300 BCE
Ancient Indian writer Pingala describes the first binary (two digit code) numbering system

87 BCE
A mechanical computer used to predict the movement of stars is built. It is discovered in a shipwreck off the coast of the Greek island of Antikythera in 1901

724 CE
Chinese engineer Liang Ling-Can builds the first mechanical clock (driven by water) with parts that make a ticking sound. More than 1,300 years later, early computers and robots inherit the technology from the clock's gear and spring mechanism

820
In Baghdad, Muhammed idn Musa Al-Khwarizmi introduces the decimal numbering system and use of zero into Arabic mathematics

1492
Italian Leonardo da Vinci designs the first mechanical calculator and a humanoid robot (dressed in a suit of armour and programmed to sit up, wave its arms, and move its head)

1984
Jon Postel, Paul Mockapetris, and Craig Partridge pioneer the Domain Name System (DNS) used to access websites over the Internet. Seven "top-level" domain names are introduced: edu, com, gov, mil, net, org, and int

▪ Apple introduces the Apple Macintosh, the first affordable computer that uses a mouse to navigate through drop-down menus, tabs, and icons

▪ Microsoft Windows and Excel (the first graphical spreadsheet software) are released

1986
The first PC virus, known as the Brain virus, is written in Pakistan

1989
Tim Berners-Lee develops a "hypertext" system, creating the modern Internet

1992
Wolfenstein 3D video game begins a revolution in PC gaming

2000
There are unfounded fears of a "Millennium Bug" causing computers to crash as they switch from 31/12/99 to 01/01/00

2003
Skype software allows people to make free international phone calls via their computers

2007
Increasing convergence of different technologies into single small gadgets as Apple's iPhone is released

2008
The world's first biodegradable computer, the Iameco, is produced in Ireland, built from waste products from the lumber and pulp industry

1963
Douglas Engelbart invents and patents the first computer mouse

▪ The American Standard Code for Information Interchange (ASCII) is developed to standardize data exchange

1965
Ted Nelson develops an idea for an interconnected network of documents with embedded links to each other, which he calls "hypertext"

1967
David Noble at IBM creates the first floppy disk

1969
Seymour Cray develops the CDC 7600, the first supercomputer (a computer designed to receive and process vast amounts of data)

▪ The forerunner of the Internet, the Advanced Research Projects Agency Network (ARPANET), is the first to connect researchers in universities in the United States

1970
Music-lover and inventor James T Russell patents the first CD-ROM

1971
▪ Computer engineer Ray Tomlinson sends the first e-mail message between two machines

▪ James Fergason invents the first practical Liquid Crystal Display (LCD)

▪ Intel introduces the first microprocessor, the Intel 4004. The 4-bit silicon chip packs as much processing power as the first electronic computer – the ENIAC – into a space smaller than a thumbnail

▪ The first truly pocket-sized electronic calculator, the LE-120A "HANDY", is launched by Busicom

1937
Alan Turing develops the first software using binary

1938
German Konrad Zuse creates the first working binary digital computer, the Z1. On his Z2 and Z3 machines, he punches holes in old movie film to store his data

1939
John Vincent Atanasoff and Clifford Berry develop the ABC (Atanasoff-Berry Computer), the first computing machine to use electricity, vacuum tubes, binary numbers, and capacitors. It's the size of a desk, weighs 315 kg (694 lb), and contains a kilometre of wire

1943
To counter the German Enigma machine, Alan Turing and engineer Tom Flowers develop the code-breaking machine Colossus, so-called because it filled an entire room

1945
John Presper Eckert and John W Mauchly develop the ENIAC (Electronic Numerical Integrator and Computer), a monster machine with 18,000 vacuum tubes. It's the first to contain gates, buffers, and a high-speed storage-and-control device

1946
F C Williams develops the cathode-ray tube (CRT) storing device, forerunner to the Random-Access Memory (RAM) device

1614
Scotsman John Napier invents a system of movable rods based on logarithms, which could do sums

1642
Frenchman Blaise Pascal invents the "Pascaline", the first serious calculating machine, to help his father, a judge in the tax court

1679
German Gottfried Leibniz perfects the binary system

1801
Joseph-Marie Jacquard invents an automatic sewing loom controlled by punched cards. During its first demonstration in Lyon, France, the machine is destroyed by an angry mob

1834
Charles Babbage designs the Analytical Engine – the world's first computer, with punch card input devices, an arithmetic processor, and a memory to store numbers. He runs out of money before it is ever built

1843
Augusta Ada Lovelace (daughter of the poet Lord Byron) creates the first ever computer program for Babbage's Analytical Engine

Where is the Internet?

The Internet is everywhere. It's a network linking millions of computers all over the world. With a computer, the right software, and a phone connection, anyone anywhere in the world can set up a website for anyone else to look at. There's no one in charge of the Internet and since there's no limit to the number of computers that can be linked, there's no limit to the amount of information that can be held on it.

untitled folder

What's in a name?

HTML *(Hyper Text Mark-up Language)*
The computer language websites are written in

WWW *(World Wide Web)*
All the interlinked pages that exist on the Internet

URL *(Uniform Resource Locator)*
A web address

TCP/IP *(Transmission Control Protocol/ Internet Protocol)* The standard method of communication that all Internet sites use

HTTP *(HyperText Transfer Protocol)*
A request to retrieve a linked document on the Web

ISP *(Internet Service Provider)*
The hub that connects a user to the Internet

Top ten Internet nations

USA
211,108,086 users

China
137,000,000 users

Japan
86,300,000 users

Germany
50,471,212 users

India
40,000,000 users

UK
37,600,000 users

South Korea
34,120,000 users

Brazil
32,130,000 users

France
30,837,592 users

Italy
30,763,848 users

Rapid growth

In numbers

year	number of Internet users
1982	**200**
1991	**600,000**
1995	**45,000,000**
1999	**150,000,000**
2008	**1,500,000,000**

untitled folder

How to: **set up a search engine**

hard drive

untitled folder

CD

untitled folder

01. Develop a "web spider" – a software program to browse the Internet.

02. Instruct the spider to begin its "web crawl" at popular websites, building an index of the words on the pages.

03. By following the links on the sites, the spider will quickly spread out across much of the web.

04. Build up an index of search words found by the spider and encode and store the data for users to access.

05. Develop search engine software – a program to sift through the millions of entries in your index and rank them in order of relevance.

Name game

Top domain names (the letters after the dot at the end of a website address) work like international phone numbers, grouping websites.

.aero	aviation industry
.biz	business
.com	commercial
.edu	educational (US)
.gov	government
.info	general information
.int	international organization
.mil	US military
.net	major service provider
.org	non-profit organization

untitled folder

RECORD BREAKER

The world's **biggest and most-used search engine**, Google has an index of millions of web pages and handles 250 million searches every day. The company was set up in 1998 and today has around 20,000 employees.

I don't believe it!

It took 46 years after the invention of household electric power to wire 30 per cent of American homes. Just seven years after the World Wide Web was created, 30 per cent of American homes were connected to the Internet.

Going the long way round

Before data is sent through the Internet, the computer breaks it up into small pieces called packets.

The packets are labelled with the address they are going to, then each packet travels separately to the destination by the best and quickest route available.

That means part of your message may go via a computer in the next town, while another part goes via a location on the other side of the world!

When the packets reach their destination, they are sorted and joined up again.

Internet pioneer
British scientist Tim Berners-Lee invented a simple computer language (HTML) that allowed pages to be linked together and designed an addressing scheme (URL) to locate each page. He then created the first web browser to allow people to access his creation, the World Wide Web, making all the resources of the Internet available to everyone in the world.

Blasts from the past

1969 Distant computers first communicate with each other when Arpanet is set up, linking computers at four US universities

1971 The first email message is sent between computers

1983 A new computer language called TCP/IP allows all computers on the network to communicate with each other. The network is called the Internet and governments and universities begin to use it

1991 The World Wide Web is created, giving people a simple way to navigate through the information on the Internet

2008 There are more than 100 million websites

Why did Archimedes shout "Eureka"?

The Ancient Greek scientist was trying to find a way of determining whether a crown was made of pure gold. While pondering the problem Archimedes climbed into his bath and saw the water level rise. He realized that he could compare the volume of gold in the crown with a lump of pure gold of the same weight by submerging them and comparing the rise in water level. He leapt out of his bath and cried "Eureka!" ("I have found it!")

Tell me more: **Nobel Prizes**

The Nobel Prizes are named after Alfred Nobel, who left almost all of the enormous fortune he had made from inventing and manufacturing dynamite to establish the awards. Each year, prizes are given for:

- ⚛ **physics**
- 🧪 chemistry
- 💉 **medicine or physiology**
- 💵 economics
- 📚 **literature**
- ✈ peace

How to: **be a scientist**

01. Find something you are interested in investigating. Ask yourself questions about your subject: "Why does this happen?", "What is this made of?"

02. Think up a possible answer to your question based on what you already know about the subject. This idea is called a "hypothesis" – it's really just a kind of guess.

03. Scientists only consider things to be facts if they can be proved to be true, so you need to think up an experiment to test whether your hypothesis is true.

04. As you carry out the experiment, you need to observe everything that happens carefully and keep records. If your hypothesis is true, this data will be the proof.

10 sciences you've never heard of

01 **Biometrology**
Effects of weather on people

02 **Cryology**
Snow, ice, and freezing ground

03 **Eremology**
Deserts

04 **Ethology**
Animal behaviour

05 **Ethnobotany**
How people use plants

06 **Googology**
Large numbers

07 **Malacology**
Shells

08 **Nephology**
Clouds

09 **Osmology**
Smells

10 **Xylology**
wood

Before the word **scientist** was invented in 1833, scientists were known as **natural philosophers**.

Timely designs

Renaissance artist Leonardo da Vinci kept notebooks crammed full of notes for new inventions. Many of these were way ahead of his time:

 helicopter

 tank

 solar-power generator

 scuba diving suit

 robot

hang gliding

Ingenious but useless

The word *chindogu* (the Japanese for "weird tool") describes an invention that does actually work, but which no one would ever really use.

Duster slippers for cats – for helping with housework

Hayfever hat – a toilet roll headpiece

Butter in a tube – like a stick of glue

Solar-powered torch (think about it...)

Noodle eater's hair guard – stops hair trailing in the noodles

Five ways to win a Nobel Prize

01: **By mistake!** Enrico Fermi received the 1938 Nobel Prize in Physics for discovering new radioactive elements, but it turned out he had just found fragments of existing elements produced by nuclear fission.

02: **Not for the theory of relativity.** Albert Einstein's theory of relativity is a major scientific discovery, but he won his Nobel Prize in 1921 for proving that light exists in particles called photons.

03: **Find the structure of DNA.** James Watson, Francis Crick, and Maurice Wilkins won the 1962 Nobel Prize for Physiology when they discovered the double-helix shape of DNA.

04: **Campaign for peace.** Linus Pauling won the 1954 Nobel Prize for Chemistry then followed this with the 1962 Nobel Peace Prize for working to end nuclear weapons testing.

05: **Keep it in the family.** Nobel Prize winners in the Curie family include Marie, her husband Pierre, daughter Irène Joliot-Curie, and Irène's husband Frédéric Joliot-Curie.

10 everyday inventions

date	invention	inventor	where
100	central heating	unknown	Rome
500s	toilet paper	unknown	China
1597	flushing toilet	John Harrington	England
1863	breakfast cereal	James Caleb Jackson	USA
1787	fridge	William Cullen	Scotland
1890	hairdryer	Alexandre F Godefroy	France
1913	zip	Gideon Sundback	USA
1928	sliced bread	Otto Rohwedder	USA
1943	ballpoint pen	Lázló Biró	Argentina
1956	velcro	Georges de Mestral	Switzerland

Five **accidental** inventions

Ice-cream cones: An ice-cream stall at the 1904 World Fair in St Louis, USA, ran out of dishes. The neighbouring stall sold wafer-thin waffles and the stall holder came up with the idea of rolling them into a cone and topping with ice cream.

X-ray: While setting up a cathode ray generator in 1895, Wilhelm Roentgen noticed a faint fluorescent effect on a chemical coated screen in the room. He had discovered invisible X-rays, which pass through cardboard, wood, and paper, but not through bones.

Synthetic dye: In 1856, William Perkin was attempting to produce synthetic quinine to treat malaria but the experiment produced nothing but a purple mess. Perkin spotted an opportunity at once, and set up a factory to produce the first synthetic dye.

Microwave: A chocolate bar in Percy Spencer's pocket melted as he stood in the path of radiation from a radar-generating machine in 1945. He put corn kernels in the path of the beams, and they popped. He had discovered the principle behind the microwave oven.

Post-it® notes: In 1968, Spencer Silver was trying to find a new strong adhesive and came up with a glue that didn't even hold pieces of paper together firmly. In 1974, co-worker Arthur Fry thought of a use for the non-sticky adhesive and the Post-it® note was born.

What is a skyscraper?

The term "skyscraper" was first used in the 1880s to describe a building with more than ten storeys. Today a building isn't considered to be a skyscraper unless it has at least 40 storeys. Humans have constructed buildings for shelter for thousands of years and they come in all shapes and sizes.

Dome sweet **dome**

Pantheon
Rome, Italy
125 CE

Hagia Sofia
Istanbul, Turkey
537

Dome of the Rock
Jerusalem, Israel
691

The Duomo
Florence, Italy
1502

Pantheon
Rome, Italy
125 CE

St Peter's Basilica
Vatican City
1593

Building high

It wasn't until the first lift was developed in 1857 that the first skyscrapers began to be built.

Modern skyscrapers have a central core made of reinforced steel containing lifts, staircases, and air ducts.

Steel and concrete floors extend from the core to a steel perimeter structure.

The outside is covered with a lightweight curtain wall of glass and metal.

Building types

- agricultural
- commercial
- residential
- educational
- leisure
- industrial
- government and social
- military
- religious
- transit ports

WHAT'S IN A NAME

"**Architect**" comes from the Greek term *arkhitekton*, meaning "master builder".

Top 10 tallest buildings

01: Burj Dubai Dubai, United Arab Emirates, 780 m (2,559 ft)

02: Taipei 101 Taipei, Taiwan, 509 m (1,670 ft)

03: Petronas Towers Kuala Lumpur, Malaysia, 452 m (1,483 ft)

04: Sears Tower Chicago, United States, 442 m (1,450 ft)

05: Jin Mao Building Shanghai, China, 421 m (1,380 ft)

06: Two International Finance Center Hong Kong, China, 416 m (1,362 ft)

07: CITIC Plaza Guangzhou, China, 391 m (1,283 ft)

08: Shun Hing Square Shenzhen, China, 384 m (1,260 ft)

09: Empire State Building New York City, United States, 381 m (1,250 ft)

10: Central Plaza Hong Kong, China, 374 m (1,227 ft)

Taj Mahal
Agra, India
1653

St Paul's Cathedral
London, UK
1708

United States Capitol
Washington DC, USA
1866

Louisiana Superdome
New Orleans, USA
1975

Stockholm Globe
Stockholm, Sweden
1989

The O2
London, UK
2000

Eden Project
Cornwall, UK
2001

Styles of architecture

- ⊙ Classical
- ⊙ Byzantine
- ⊙ Moorish
- ⊙ Gothic (pictured)
- ⊙ Georgian
- ⊙ Expressionist
- ⊙ Art Nouveau
- ⊙ Bauhaus
- ⊙ Modern
- ⊙ Art Deco
- ⊙ Deconstructivist
- ⊙ Post-modern

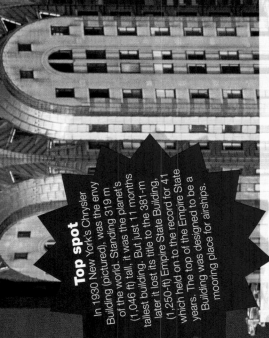

Top spot

In 1930 New York's Chrysler Building (pictured), was the envy of the planet's. Standing 319 m (1,046 ft) tall, it was the planet's tallest building. But just 11 months later it lost its title to the 381-m (1,250-ft) Empire State Building, which held on to the record for 41 years. The top of the Empire State Building was designed to be a mooring place for airships.

State homes

official residence	country	rooms
Palacio Real de Madrid	Spain (monarch)	2,800
Buckingham Palace	UK (monarch)	775
Abdeen Palace	Egypt (president)	500
Rashtrapati Bhavan	India (president)	340
White House (pictured)	USA (president)	132
The Lodge	Australia (prime minister)	40
24 Sussex Drive	Canada (prime minister)	34

How to: build an igloo

01. Use a long-bladed snow-knife to cut blocks of compacted snow.

02. Lay a circle of blocks on a flat bed of snow.

03. Shave off the top of the blocks at a sloping angle to form the first part of a spiral.

04. Add blocks to the spiral, gradually placing them further inwards to form a dome shape.

05. Fill in the joints between the snow blocks with loose snow and leave a hole at the top for ventilation.

06. Build a narrow tunnel to lead into the igloo and your shelter is finished!

Types of **building materials**

stone

adobe

wood

concrete

glass and steel

brick

Where can you drive above the clouds?

Reaching 270 m (890 ft) above the Tarn River at its highest point, the deck of the Millau Viaduct in southern France is higher than any other road bridge in the world. It is counted among the planet's super structures – the most amazing feats of human design and engineering.

Types of bridge

Beam
The flat roadway rests on solid piers. Beam bridges are usually only used for short distances.

Cantilever
This type of beam bridge balances on a supporting pier embedded in the river.

Suspension
The deck or roadway hangs from long steel cables attached to towers.

Cable-stayed
The deck is supported by steel cables connected to towers, but it also rests on piers.

Arch
A strong arch usually supports a flat roadway.

Bascule
Two sections are raised to allow traffic to pass underneath.

Pontoon
The bridge rests on floating hollow concrete blocks, anchored to the river bed.

SKY HIGH
The Millau Viaduct's massive, curved roadway is 2,460 m (8,100 ft) long and 32 m (100 ft wide). It is supported by seven concrete pylons, but appears to float delicately across the valley.

What's in a name?

The Latin word *aqueduct* means "a channel for carrying water". An aqueduct can be as simple as a canal or a tunnel, but the most spectacular aqueducts are huge arched bridges carrying the water over uneven terrain. The 49-m- (161-ft-) high, three-level Pont du Gard at Nîmes, France, was built by the Romans in the 1st century CE.

Bridges

FAST FACTS

01: There are 23,000 km (14,290 miles) of wires in the cables of New York's Brooklyn Bridge.

02: Akashi-Kaikyō Bridge in Japan spans 1.9 km (1.2 miles), making it the world's longest suspension bridge.

03: The Ponte Vecchio bridge in Florence, Italy, is more than 600 years old, but there are still houses and shops on it.

04: The first iron bridge (pictured) was built in 1779 in England. It is a UNESCO World Heritage Site.

How to: go uphill in a boat

01. Open the lock gates. Move the boat into the lock and close the watertight gates behind it.

02. Open valves in the gate ahead, which allows water from the upper level into the lock.

03. When the water level inside the lock is the same as the higher level of the canal, open the gates in front.

04. Drive the boat through and make sure that you close the gate behind you.

05. To go downhill, pump water out of the lock once the gates are closed.

Or take the elevator!
The Falkirk Wheel in Scotland is a rotating boat lift. It raises barges 24 m (79 ft) from one canal to another – the equivalent of an eight-storey building.

Three canals that link seas

Suez Canal built 1869
Links Red Sea with Mediterranean Sea
174 km (108 miles) long

Kiel Canal built 1895
Links North Sea with Baltic Sea, Germany
99 km (61 m) long

Panama Canal built 1914
Links Atlantic Ocean and Caribbean Sea with Pacific Ocean
81 km (50 miles) long

Swamp city

The city of Venice in Italy is built on 118 separate islands in a seawater lagoon. The swampy land was made habitable by digging drainage channels, which became the city's 150 canals. The islands are linked with 400 bridges. The foundations of Venice's massive brick and stone buildings rest on wooden piles buried in the damp ground.

WEIRD OR WHAT?
To protect Venice from rising sea levels, 79 **inflatable gates** are being installed in the seabed around the city. When **high tides** are predicted, the gates will inflate, blocking off the incoming water.

Super-structure landmarks

Stonehenge
Wiltshire, UK

Great Wall of China
Beijing, China

Eiffel Tower
Paris, France

Statue of Liberty
New York, USA

CN Tower
Toronto, Canada

London Eye
London, UK

Five artificial islands

Kansai International Airport Japan
Three mountains were excavated to provide landfill for this airport island, which has a terminal building and two runways.

Flevoland Netherlands
This island was built on an inland sea between 1957 and 1968. It is the largest artificial island in the world and home to 370,000 people.

Uros Islets Peru
There are 42 small islands on Lake Titicaca constructed from bundled dried reed by the Uros people hundreds of years ago.

Kamfers Dam South Africa
This S-shaped island was built as a breeding ground for flamingos. An estimated 9,000 chicks were born on it in 2008.

Palm Islands United Arab Emirates
These islands off the coast of Dubai are the largest artificial islands in the world and function as luxury holiday resorts.

Why go by bike?

The bicycle is the perfect form of transport. It's a relatively simple machine that can be made and bought cheaply. Not much can go wrong with a bike, and if it does it's usually easy and inexpensive to repair. Driven by human leg-power, a bike gives off no pollution and keeps you fit as you ride. What more do you want?

Most people travel between **16 and 24 kph** (10-15 mph) on a bike – that's about **four to five times faster than they can walk**.

I don't believe it!

Cyclists in a long road race ride in a line one behind the other. This is called drafting and it reduces the effect of air resistance on the group, cutting energy use by up to 40 per cent. Each rider takes a turn at the front, where the drag is greatest.

Putting bikes to work

On the beat
Police bikes patrol the streets and can get almost anywhere quickly and quietly.

Special delivery
In busy cities, a bike courier can dodge the traffic to get an urgent package delivered.

Commuting
Office workers keep fit by cycling to work. If they need to take the train, they can just fold up the bike and take it with them.

Loaded
No job is too big or too small for a determined delivery bike.

Taxi!
A bicycle rickshaw, a human-powered taxi, is a cheap and pollution-free way to travel.

Record breakers

In 2008, German Günter Mai created the world's **lightest bike**, weighing just 3.1 kg (7.04 lb).

The world's **longest bike** is 28.1 m (92 ft) – almost the length of a basketball court. It was built in 2002 at Delft University of Technology in the Netherlands.

The **first circumnavigation of the globe by bike** took place between 1884 and 1887, when American Thomas Stevens rode a penny-farthing around the world.

In 1995, Dutch cyclist Fred Rompelberg reached a **record speed** of 268.831 kph (167 mph), riding behind a dragster to reduce air resistance.

How to: ride a bike

01. Push your feet down on the pedals. This moves a set of levers called cranks.

sprocket
pedal

02. The cranks turn a chainwheel, the teeth of which fit into the links of a chain. The chain is also linked to the teeth of a sprocket on the back wheel.

chainwheel
chain
crank

WEIRD OR WHAT?

To steer a bike you turn the handlebars to turn the front wheel, yes? Think again! The handlebars are more to help you balance. To turn left, you turn the handlebars very slightly right and then tip your body to the left. This is called countersteering, and you do it automatically.

In the mid-1890s, so many people were coming up with improvements for the **design of the bicycle** that the USA had **two patent offices** – one for bicycles and one for everything else!

Tour de France

The world's greatest cycle race covers more than 3,500 km (2,200 miles) split into 21 daily stages. To help people identify them, the race leaders are awarded **coloured jerseys** each day.

The 1989 Tour de France was the **closest in Tour history**. After three long weeks of cycling, American cyclist Greg LeMond stole victory over Frenchman Laurent Fignon by **just eight seconds**, with a time of 87 hours, 38 minutes, and 15 seconds.

Yellow jersey
Worn by the race leader – the rider with the quickest time overall

Green jersey
Worn by the rider who has gained most points from sprints

Polka-dot jersey
Worn by the rider with the most points from the climbing stages

handlebars

brake cable

stem

Yellow jersey legends

Number of days the cyclist has worn the yellow jersey in their career:
Eddy Merckx (Belgium) 96
Lance Armstrong, (pictured) (USA) 83
Bernard Hinault (France) 78

Lance Armstrong (USA) 7 consecutive wins
Miguel Indurain (Spain) 5 consecutive wins
Eddy Merckx (Belgium) 5 wins
Bernard Hinault (France) 5 wins
Jacques Anquetil (France) 5 wins

Top Tour winners

04. The back wheel pushes down on the ground as it turns, propelling you forwards. Keep turning those pedals!

03. As the chain moves, it drives the sprocket, which in turn drives the wheel.

Tell me more: **the right gear**

Most bikes have a set of different toothed wheels, called gears, that makes it possible to turn the wheels faster, or with more force.

When you change gear, the chain shifts onto different sizes of chainwheels and sprockets.

high gear (12 teeth) — **pedal**
rear sprocket — **chainwheel with 48 teeth**

■ **Problem: Want to speed along a flat road**
■ **Solution: Switch to a high gear**

If you select a rear sprocket, or gear, with 12 teeth, it only takes a quarter-turn of the chainwheel to turn the rear sprocket, so one turn of the pedals results in four turns of the rear wheel.

low gear (24 teeth) — **pedal**
chainwheel with 48 teeth

■ **Problem: Want to cycle uphill**
■ **Solution: Switch to a lower gear**

If you select a rear sprocket, or gear, with 24 teeth, it takes half a turn of the chainwheel to turn the rear sprocket, so one turn of the pedals results in two turns of the rear wheel.

Blasts from the past

1813
The Draisienne is invented by German Carl Von Drais. It has a steerable front wheel but no pedals

1839
The pedal bicycle is invented by Scottish blacksmith Kirkpatrick Macmillan. It can reach speeds of 22.5 kph (14 mph)

1863
French blacksmith Pierre Michaux develops the velocipede bike. It sparks a craze in Paris and is nicknamed the "boneshaker"

1871
English inventor James Starley creates the first penny-farthing bicycle. Named after British coins, it has a huge front wheel

1885
John Kemp Starley builds the Rover Safety Bicycle, with pedals linked to the rear wheel by a chain and gears

1920s
In the age of the car, bikes are out of fashion and are primarily built for children

1960s
Racing bikes with dropped handlebars, narrow tyres, and multiple gears become popular

1970s
BMX bikes are launched

1970s
Mountain bikes are invented in California. They are first known as "clunkers"

Can a car run on chocolate?

It may sound ridiculous, but it's true. In 2007, two British environmentalists drove a car 7,200 km (4,500 miles) from Britain to Timbuktu in Mali, Africa, powered by 4,000 kg (8,800 lbs) of chocolate converted into a biofuel.

Top 5 car manufacturers
1 Toyota
2 General Motors
3 Volkswagen
4 Ford
5 Honda

Safe driving

01: Seat belts (restrain passengers on impact)

02: Safety glass in windscreens (cracks rather than shatters)

03: Windscreen wipers (improve visibility)

04: Traffic lights (control traffic flow)

05: Airbags (inflate on impact)

Top 10 countries with the longest road networks

  USA 6,430,366 km (3,995,643 miles)

  India 3,383,344 km (2,102,312 miles)

  China 1,930,544 km (1,199,584 miles)

  Brazil 1,751,868 km (1,088,560 miles)

  Japan 1,193,000 km (741,296 miles)

  Canada 1,042,300 km (647,655 miles)

 France 950,985 km (590,915 miles)

  Russia 854,000 km (530,650 miles)

Australia 812,972 km (505,157 miles)

Spain 681,224 km (423,293 miles)

In numbers

¼
The proportion of the world's cars that are in the United States

5
How many cents it cost to park for one hour at the world's first parking meter. It was installed in 1935 in Oklahoma City, USA

50 million
The number of new cars built worldwide each year

WEIRD OR WHAT?

An English law of 1878 said that powered vehicles could only travel at walking pace, and had to have a man walking in front of them carrying a red flag to warn pedestrians and horse traffic ahead. Fortunately the law was repealed in 1896, or the traffic jams would be horrendous!

Popularity contest

 In 1921, 50.4 per cent of all the cars made in the world were **Model-T Fords**, making the car, nicknamed the "Tin Lizzie", the most popular ever built.

 More **Toyota Corollas** have been sold than any other type of car. The Corolla began production in 1966 and is still being built today, with more than 31 million cars sold so far.

The Corolla has substantially changed over the years, whereas the 21,529,464 **Volkswagen Beetles** sold between 1983 and 2003 all had the same basic design, making it the true winner.

In a jam

The average commuter spends 46 hours a year in jams.

The longest traffic jam ever was 176 km (109 miles), stretching from Lyon to Paris, France, on 16 February 1980.

In Athens, Greece, only cars with odd-numbered licence plates can drive in the city on odd-numbered days, and vice versa on even-numbered days.

Blasts from the past

1400s	**1885**	**1886**	**1895**	**1896**	**1899**	**1901**	**1979**	**1997**
Italian inventor and artist Leonardo da Vinci considers the idea of a self-propelled vehicle	German Karl Benz builds the first car with an internal combustion engine	German engineer Gottlieb Daimler builds the first four-wheeled car	The French Michelin brothers produce the first pneumatic (air-filled) tyres	The British Arnold is the first car fitted with an electric starter motor	Steering wheels are fitted. Before this cars were steered with a "tiller" handle	The first mass-produced car, the Oldsmobile, begins production in the USA	The catalytic converter is introduced to reduce pollution from car exhausts	Toyota releases the first hybrid car, the Prius. It is powered by both petrol and electricity

The most popular car colour in the world is silver.

The **most expensive car in the world** is a Bugatti Veyron 16.4. Produced by Volkswagen, it costs about US$1.4 million.

The **cheapest car in the world** is the Nano, made by Indian car manufacturer Tata. It costs just US$2,500.

Mad motors

The **Jeep Hurricane** has a steering system that allows all four wheels to move in different directions.

The **Commuter Cars Tango** is so narrow it can fit sideways into a parking space. It can carry two people.

The **Gibbs Aquada** is a car that can float. It travels at 160 kph (100 mph) on land and 50 kph (30 mph) on water.

The **Rinspeed SQuba** is a convertible car that can move underwater like a submarine.

The triple crown of motorsports

Indianapolis 500 Nicknamed "The 500", this 805-km (500-mile) annual race is held in Speedway, Indiana, USA. It is the largest single-day sporting event in the world.

24 Hours of Le Mans A 24-hour endurance race held annually near the town of Le Mans, Sarthe, France.

Formula One World Championships The cars are known for the deafening roars of mighty engines, screeching tyres, and breathtaking speeds reaching 360 kph (225 mph). The driver with the most points at the end of a 17-race season is the winner.

Types of car

saloon

estate

hatchback

convertible

coupé

limousine

4x4

people carrier

How do boats float?

Boats come in all shapes and sizes, from small canoes to giant supertankers. A boat pushes away a certain amount of the water beneath it. The water pushes back against the boat with an upwards force, called buoyancy, which is equal to the weight of the displaced water. This upwards force keeps the boat floating.

Mainsail: The boat's most important sail

Rigging: A system of ropes used to control the sails

Mast: Vertical pole support for sails

Size matters

▲ Some tankers and container ships are so big that the **crew ride** around them on **bicycles**.

▲ The world's biggest container ships can carry more than 14,500 truck-sized containers. Stacked end to end, one ship's containers would **tower over Mount Everest**.

▲ The world's largest container ship, the *Emma Maersk*, is 397 m (1,302 ft) long. Its **anchor is as heavy as five African elephants**.

▲ The largest oil tankers carry about **500,000,000 litres (133,000,000 gallons)** of crude oil.

▲ The largest cruise ship, *Genesis of the Seas*, can carry **5,400 passengers**, has 16 decks, a tropical park in the centre, and is about the same height as a 25-storey building.

▲ An aircraft carrier can carry **85 small fighter aircraft**.

Stern: Rear part of the vessel

Around the world
In 1522, Portuguese explorer Ferdinand Magellan's crew completed the **first** **circumnavigation** of the globe. The journey took just over **three years and 27 days**. In 2005, French yachtsman Bruno Peyron sailed around the globe in just **50 days, 16 hours, and 20 minutes**.

WEIRD OR WHAT?
In 1992, several containers on a ship bound for the USA fell overboard, spilling their contents. As a result, nearly **30,000 plastic bath toys** were left floating in the sea!

Types of boat

canoe

rowing boat

yacht

barge

speed boat

tug

junk

dhow

trawler

cruise liner

Deck: The surface of the boat that people can stand on

Hull: The body of the boat

Sailing boats cannot sail straight into an oncoming wind. To get around this you must use a zig-zag manoeuvre called tacking.

01. Make sure the sails are properly trimmed (set) for maximum speed.

02. Push the tiller (lever that turns the rudder) until the boat sails to the port side at an angle of between 35 and 45 degrees to the oncoming wind.

03. When your sail is flapping in the wind you are halfway through the manoeuvre.

04. The boom will move as you sail the boat to the starboard side, so remember to duck as it swings around.

05. The zig-zag from port to starboard makes the sailing boat curve gently into the wind.

How to: **sail into the wind**

Boom: Pole jutting out from the bottom of the mast to support the sail

Bow: Front part of the vessel

I don't believe it!

By hollowing out giant pumpkins and attaching motor engines, intrepid mariners can compete in pumpkin boat races. They are a bit of a squash though!

Finding your way around on a boat

forward	at or near the bow
aft	at or near the stern
port	left-hand side
starboard	right-hand side

Sea time

At sea, the 24-hour day is divided into seven watches. Each crew member is on duty for one or more of these periods.

first watch	middle watch	morning watch	forenoon watch	afternoon watch	first dog watch	last dog watch
8pm – midnight	midnight – 4am	4am – 8am	8am – noon	noon – 4pm	4pm – 6pm	6pm – 8pm

ferry

paddle steamer

oil tanker

container ship

Types of train

Electric
Get their power from an overhead pick-up or an electrically live third rail

Steam
Powered by steam generated by burning coal

Diesel
Powered by diesel-fuelled internal combustion engine

Maglev (magnetic levitation)
Electromagnets create magnetic fields providing an air cushion for the train to ride friction free

Subway
Train running through underground tunnels

Funicular
Tram-like vehicle that ascends or descends a steep slope

Which is the fastest train?

A train is a series of carriages pulled along a track by a locomotive engine. The top speed record-holder is a Japanese maglev (magnetic levitation) train, which reached 581 kph (361 mph) in 2003. When not setting records, trains provide an efficient means of transporting people and goods across land.

Tell me more: train anatomy

Passenger carriage: Seating for commuters and baggage racks

Pantograph: Picks up an electric current from overhead cables

Carriage connector: Flexible connections between carriages allow train to make turns

WHAT'S IN A NAME?
British rail pioneer George Stephenson's engine *Rocket* was worthy of its name – it won an 1829 competition to find the world's fastest locomotive, reaching 56 kph (35 mph).

Wheels: Metal wheels ride on the rails

Blasts from the past

1803
British inventor Richard Trevithick builds the world's first steam railway locomotive

1825
The first passenger train service is set up, running 40 km (26 miles) between Stockton and Darlington in the north of England pulled by a locomotive built by George Stephenson

1830
The first cities to be linked by railway are Liverpool and Manchester in England. They are 64 km (40 miles) apart

1863
The first underground railway opens in London. It runs 6 km (3.75 miles) between Paddington and Farringdon Street

Longest rail networks

🇺🇸	**USA**	226,612 km (140,810 miles)
🇷🇺	**Russia**	87,157 km (54,157 miles)
🇨🇳	**China**	75,438 km (46,875 miles)
🇮🇳	**India**	63,221 km (39,284 miles)
🇩🇪	**Germany**	48,215 km (29,959 miles)
🇨🇦	**Canada**	48,068 km (29,868 miles)
🇦🇺	**Australia**	38,550 km (23,954 miles)
🇦🇷	**Argentina**	31,902 km (19,823 miles)
🇫🇷	**France**	29,370 km (18,250 miles)
🇧🇷	**Brazil**	29,295 km (18,203 miles)

In numbers

500
The number of cars on the world's longest freight train. It stretched for 6.4 km (4 miles) and ran on a track in Ohio, USA, in 1967

295
The number of stations on the Trans-Siberian railway, which stretches 9,300 km (5,778 miles) from Moscow to Vladivostock

1,370,782 km
(851,764 miles) The combined length of railway track in the world

Driver's cab: Contains controls to power and steer train

365521

Subway systems

city	stations	passengers (per day)
New York	468	6.5 million
London	268	4.25 million
Seoul	266	5.9 million
Mexico	185	3.8 million
Moscow	177	6.8 million
Beijing	123	3.4 million

RECORD BREAKER

The world's **deepest railway** is in the Seikan tunnel between the Japanese islands of Honshu and Hokkaido. It reaches 240 m (787 ft) below sea-level in the middle.

Five amazing trains

01: Possibly the most famous train ever, the **Orient Express** was introduced in 1883, running between London, Paris, Vienna, Budapest, and Istanbul. Today the train only runs from Strasbourg to Vienna.

02: Introduced in 1939, the **Blue Train** runs along 1,600 km (1,000 miles) of rail track between Pretoria and Cape Town in South Africa. It is one of the most luxurious trains in the world. Its carriages have gold-tinted windows and many of its compartments have full-sized baths!

03: From 1902 to 1967, the **20th Century Limited** was an American express train running between New York City and Chicago. The train covered the 1,550-km (960-mile) journey in about 16 hours.

04: Since 1970, the **Indian Pacific** has covered the 4,352 km (2,704 miles) between Perth and Sydney, Australia, twice each week.

05: The **Flying Scotsman** has been running between London, England, and Edinburgh, Scotland, since 1862. The original journey took 10.5 hours, but today it takes about 4.5 hours.

1869
A railway crossing the United States is completed, cutting a six-month wagon journey to just seven days on a train

1879
The first electric railway to supply power through the rails is a miniature locomotive demonstrated by German Ernst Werner von Siemens at an exhibition in Berlin

1912
Diesel locomotives are developed in Germany. Over the next two decades they replace steam trains

1964
The Japanese Shinkansen (bullet train) is introduced. These electric trains can reach speeds of 300 kph (187 mph)

1991
The first maglev train is installed in Birmingham, England. This short-distance, low-speed train shuttles people between the airport and the city railway station

2003
The first high-speed maglev railway opens in Shanghai, China, with speeds up to 501 kph (311 mph)

Who invented the helicopter?

Renaissance artist Leonardo da Vinci sketched an idea for a "helical air screw" – a craft that would spin in the air – in 1480. However, Frenchman Paul Cornu achieved the first successful helicopter flight in 1906. The craft lifted off the ground for 20 seconds.

Air rescue More than **3 million lives** have been saved by **rescue helicopters**. They can reach remote, inaccessible areas other vehicles can't.

Tell me more: helicopter anatomy

Rotor blades: Provide lift and thrust. Tilting the blades allows the helicopter to change direction

Vertical fin: Protects the tail rotor

Horizontal fin: Helps stabilize the tail during flight

Tail boom: Hollow carbon fibre or aluminium tube that contains tail rotor mechanism

Cabin: Enclosed compartment where passengers are carried

Tail rotor: Spins in an opposite direction to the main rotor to prevent a twisting force called torque, which makes the helicopter spin around

RECORD BREAKER

The Westland Lynx holds the record as the **world's fastest helicopter** – a slightly modified version reached 400.87 kph (249.09 mph). At 40.025 m (131.3 ft) in length, the Mil Mi-26 is the **world's largest helicopter**. It is designed to carry up to 150 people or 20,000 kg (44,000 lbs) of cargo.

What a helicopter can do that most planes can't

- take off and land vertically
- hover
- fly backwards
- fly sideways

VIPs on board

The US president travels in a Sikorsky VH-3D Sea King helicopter. When the president is on board, the helicopter's call sign is "Marine One".

Pope Benedict XVI has a pilot's licence and flies the papal helicopter from the Vatican to his summer residence, Castel Gandolfo.

WEIRD OR WHAT?

Viewed from above, helicopters from the United States, Britain, and Germany **spin anticlockwise**, while helicopters from all other countries **spin clockwise**.

How to: **fly a helicopter**

01. Start the engine and ensure rotor blades are whirring at a flat pitch (with no angle).

02. Raise the collective control stick (a lever at your side) to increase the pitch (angle) of both blades. The blades force air downwards and create an upwards force, lifting the helicopter vertically.

03. To fly forwards, backwards, and to either side adjust the cyclic pitch (a control stick just in front of you) to vary the angles of the rotor blades. Move the stick to the left and the rotor tilts in that direction.

04. To control the pitch of the tail rotor (essential for straight flight), use the pedals on the cockpit floor.

Cockpit: Contains flight controls and pilot's seat

Landing wheels: Support the weight of the craft when it lands on the ground

In a spin

Tandem rotor helicopters have two main sets of rotors and no tail rotor.

Coaxial rotor helicopters have two rotors mounted on the same mast.

FAST FACTS

Helicopter uses

- transport
- search and rescue
- air ambulance
- aerial crane (to carry heavy loads to high or inaccessible places)
- aerial firefighting (carrying loads of water to dump on wilderness fires)
- law enforcement
- armed forces (used to attack ground-based targets with missiles)
- surveillance
- aerial photography
- traffic control

Mass production

Russian-American Igor Sikorsky produced the first fully operational rotary-bladed helicopter in 1939. He founded a successful manufacturing company that still carries his name.

There are **more than 45,000** military and civilian helicopters operating worldwide.

Robo-copter

The Yamaha RMAX helicopter is a UAV ("Unmanned Aerial Vehicle"). It can perform tasks that are too dangerous for a human pilot to undertake, such as filming a volcano erupting from close range.

Safe landing

If the engine turning a helicopter's blades **stop working**, the pilot can pivot the blades so that they **rotate automatically** as the air flows upwards through them. This is called autorotation and enables the pilot to land safely.

Why do **planes fly above clouds?**

Aeroplanes are powered, heavier-than-air aircraft with fixed wings. Most planes are flown above cloud level because there is not as much air resistance higher up in the atmosphere, so they use less fuel. There is also less turbulence above the clouds, meaning passengers don't get thrown about so much and there is less demand for sick bags!

Types of **aeroplane**

Propelled plane
Small planes powered by propellers that can take off from short runways

Light aircraft
Small planes used for leisure and short trips and powered by piston engines similar to small cars

Biplane
Small propeller-driven planes with double wings that are often used for aerobatic displays

Seaplane
Propeller-driven planes that can take off and land on water

VTOL
Vertical take-off and landing jet used by the military

Jet aircraft
Powered by jet engines and used to transport passengers and cargo and as military craft

Supersonic plane
Military jets that can fly faster than the speed of sound

What about me?

As an aircraft ascends, the change in pressure can cause your ears to hurt. Your body equalizes the pressure, causing your ears to "pop" as they return to normal.

WEIRD OR WHAT?

At altitudes over 3,000 m (10,000 ft), **air pressure** is too low for people to absorb oxygen so air is pumped into the cabin. If the plane's door opened, the air would be sucked out along with anything loose in the cabin, the temperature would plummet, and people would quickly begin to suffer from **lack of oxygen**. Gulp!

I don't believe it!

Some Boeing 747s can carry 243,120 litres (64,225 gallons) of fuel – enough to fill the petrol tanks of more than 5,000 small cars.

Wing: Generates the lift (upward force) to hold the plane in the air

Jet engine: Generates thrust to push the aeroplane forwards

Rudder: Steers the plane

Elevator: Controls the plane's ascent and descent

How to: **fly an aeroplane**

RECORD BREAKER

The **largest passenger aircraft** is the Airbus A380. It has a wingspan of 79.8 m (261.8 ft) and can carry 853 passengers.

Runways must be at least 2,430 m (8,000 ft) long to accommodate large jets. The world's **longest runway** is at Qamdo Bangda Airport, China. It stretches 5,500 m (18,045 ft).

01. Taxi on to the runway and line up the plane. Apply full power. As you speed forward, the nose will begin to rise and the plane will take-off.

02. To pitch the plane up or down, raise or lower the elevator flaps on the tail wing.

03. To roll the plane, raise the ailerons on one wing and lower them on the other.

04. To make the plane yaw (swerve) to the left or right, turn the rudder.

05. To land, align the plane with the runway and lower the flaps. Just before touchdown, raise the nose so that the main wheels make contact with the ground first. Reduce power to idle and apply the brakes.

Tell me more: **anatomy of an aeroplane**

Cockpit: Where the pilot sits to control the plane

Spoiler: Used during landing to slow the plane down

Fuselage: Body of the plane

Flaps: Used at take-off and landing to increase the amount of lift

Aileron: Hinged part of wing used to bank (roll) the plane

PILOT CHECK LIST

✈ To qualify as a pilot you must have good hearing and vision, pass a strict medical, and can't be colour blind. Some airlines also have strict height and weight restrictions.

✈ Pilots (and air traffic controllers) must be able to speak English – it is the international language for aviation.

✈ Pilots have to be clean-shaven as a beard could stop the oxygen mask from fitting tightly enough if the cabin pressure dropped suddenly.

✈ Passenger jet pilots and co-pilots are never given the same in-flight meal in case of food poisoning.

CABIN CREW

✈ The first female flight attendants had to be registered nurses.

✈ The senior flight attendant on a jumbo jet is responsible for carrying top secret diplomatic mail from country to country. There is a special lock-up to keep the documents safe.

✈ The number of attendants on a flight is determined by the number of emergency exits on the plane.

RECORD BREAKER

The world's **fastest ground-launched aircraft** is the Lockheed SR-71A *Blackbird*, which achieved the record speed of 3,529 kph (2,193 mph) in July 1976.

Places

SVALBARD
(to Norway)

Franz Josef Land

Severnaya Zemlya

New Siberian Islands

Novaya Zemlya

JAN MAYEN
(to Norway)

ICELAND

FAEROE ISLANDS
(to Denmark)

SWEDEN

FINLAND

RUSSIAN FEDERATION

European
Russia

Asiatic Russia

NORWAY

ESTONIA

ISLE OF MAN
(to UK)

DENMARK

RUSS.
FED.

LATVIA

LITHUANIA

UNITED
KINGDOM

IRELAND

NETH.

GERMANY

POLAND

BELARUS

BELG.

SLOVAKIA

UKRAINE

KAZAKHSTAN

MONGOLIA

CHANNEL ISLANDS
(to UK)

LUX.

CZ. REP.

LIECH.

FRANCE

SWITZ.

AUSTRIA

SLOVENIA

HUNGARY

MOLDOVA

ROMANIA

MONACO

CROATIA

S.M.

SERBIA

UZBEKISTAN

KYRGYZSTAN

ANDORRA

VATICAN
CITY

ITALY

B.&H.

MON.

ALB.

KOSOVO (disputed)

BULGARIA

GEORGIA

ARMENIA

AZERBAIJAN

TURKMENISTAN

TAJIKISTAN

Azores
(to Portugal)

PORTUGAL

SPAIN

MACEDONIA

GREECE

TURKEY

AZERBAIJAN

CHINA

NORTH KOREA

JAPAN

GIBRALTAR (to UK)

TUNISIA

MALTA

CYPRUS

SYRIA

LEBANON

IRAQ

IRAN

AFGHANISTAN

SOUTH
KOREA

Madeira
(to Portugal)

ISRAEL

NEPAL

BHUTAN

Canary Islands
(to Spain)

MOROCCO

ALGERIA

LIBYA

EGYPT

JORDAN

KUWAIT

PAKISTAN

Ryukyu Islands
(to Japan)

WESTERN SAHARA
(disputed)

BAHRAIN

QATAR

U.A.E.

SAUDI
ARABIA

OMAN

BANGLADESH

MYANMAR
(BURMA)

LAOS

NORTHERN
MARIANA
ISLANDS
(to US)

CAPE
VERDE

MAURITANIA

MALI

NIGER

CHAD

ERITREA

YEMEN

INDIA

THAILAND

VIETNAM

GUAM
(to US)

Socotra
(to Yemen)

Laccadive
Islands
(to India)

Andaman
Islands
(to India)

Paracel
Islands
(disputed)

SENEGAL

BURKINA
FASO

SUDAN

DJIBOUTI

CAMBODIA

PHILIPPINES

GAMBIA

GUINEA-
BISSAU

GUINEA

NIGERIA

BENIN

CENTRAL
AFRICAN
REPUBLIC

ETHIOPIA

SRI LANKA

Nicobar
Islands
(to India)

Spratly
Islands
(disputed)

MICRO

SIERRA LEONE

LIBERIA

CAMEROON

MALDIVES

BRUNEI

PALAU

CÔTE D'IVOIRE
(IVORY COAST)

GHANA

EQ. GUINEA

UGANDA

KENYA

SOMALIA

MALAYSIA

TOGO

GABON

CONGO

SINGAPORE

SAO TOME & PRINCIPE

DEMOCRATIC
REPUBLIC
OF CONGO

RWANDA

BURUNDI

I N D O N E S I A

PAPUA
NEW
GUINEA

Cabinda
(to Angola)

TANZANIA

SEYCHELLES

Agalega Islands
(to Mauritius)

BRITISH INDIAN
OCEAN TERRITORY
(to UK)

CHRISTMAS ISLAND
(to Australia)

EAST TIMOR

ASCENSION ISLAND
(to St Helena)

ANGOLA

MALAWI

COMOROS

ASHMORE &
CARTIER ISLANDS
(to Australia)

MAYOTTE (to France)

COCOS (KEELING) ISLANDS
(to Australia)

ST HELENA
(to UK)

ZAMBIA

MOZAMBIQUE

MADAGASCAR

MAURITIUS

A T L A N T I C

NAMIBIA

ZIMBABWE

REUNION (to France)

I N D I A N

AUSTRALIA

O C E A N

BOTSWANA

SWAZILAND

O C E A N

SOUTH
AFRICA

LESOTHO

Prince Edward Islands
(to South Africa)

FRENCH SOUTHERN
& ANTARCTIC TERRITORIES
(to France)

Tasmania

HEARD & MCDONALD ISLANDS
(to Australia)

S O U T H E R N   O C E A N

A N T A R C T I C A

ARCTIC
OCEAN

Queen Elizabeth Islands

GREENLAND
(to Denmark)

Baffin Island

Arctic Circle

Alaska
(to US)

C A N A D A

ST PIERRE
& MIQUELON
(to France)

ATLANTIC
OCEAN

Kurile Islands
(to Russ. Fed.)

Aleutian Islands (to US)

PACIFIC
OCEAN

UNITED STATES
OF AMERICA

BERMUDA
(to UK)

PUERTO RICO (to US)

MIDWAY ISLANDS
(to US)

Guadelupe
(to Mexico)

DOMINICAN REPUBLIC

BRITISH VIRGIN ISLANDS (to UK)

VIRGIN ISLANDS (to US)

ANGUILLA (to UK)

Tropic of Cancer

Hawaii
(to US)

TURKS & CAICOS ISLANDS
(to UK)

CAYMAN ISLANDS
(to UK)

BAHAMAS

ST KITTS & NEVIS

ANTIGUA & BARBUDA

WAKE ISLAND
(to US)

*Revillagigedo
Islands*
(to Mexico)

HONDURAS
BELIZE

CUBA

MONTSERRAT (to UK)

GUADELOUPE (to France)

MEXICO

JOHNSTON ATOLL (to US)

JAMAICA

NAVASSA I.
(to US)

HAITI

DOMINICA

MARTINIQUE (to France)

MARSHALL
ISLANDS

WALLIS & FUTUNA
(to France)

KINGMAN REEF (to US)

GUATEMALA

NETH. ANT.
(to Neth.)

ST LUCIA

BARBADOS

BAKER &
HOWLAND
ISLANDS
(to US)

PALMYRA ATOLL (to US)

EL SALVADOR
NICARAGUA
COSTA RICA

ARUBA
(to Neth.)

ST VINCENT & THE GRENADINES

GRENADA

TRINIDAD & TOBAGO

NAURU

JARVIS ISLAND
(to US)

CLIPPERTON ISLAND
(to French Polynesia)

PANAMA

VENEZUELA

FRENCH GUIANA
(to France)

Equator

TUVALU

K I R I B A T I

COLOMBIA

Galapagos Islands
(to Ecuador)

ECUADOR

GUYANA
SURINAME

SOLOMON
ISLANDS

TOKELAU
(to NZ)

P
E
R
U

B R A Z I L

VANUATU

COOK
ISLANDS
(to NZ)

PACIFIC

BOLIVIA

NEW
CALEDONIA
(to France)

FIJI

FRENCH POLYNESIA
(to France)

OCEAN

San Felix Island
(to Chile)

PARAGUAY

Tropic of Capricorn

CORAL SEA ISLANDS
(to Australia)

TONGA
SAMOA

NIUE (to NZ)

AMERICAN
SAMOA
(to US)

Easter Island
(to Chile)

Sala y Gomez
(to Chile)

*San Ambrosia
Island*
(to Chile)

CHILE

A
R
G
E
N
T
I
N
A

URUGUAY

NORFOLK ISLAND
(to Australia)

PITCAIRN
ISLANDS
(to UK)

Lord Howe Island
(to Australia)

Kermadec Island
(to NZ)

Juan Fernandez Island
(to Chile)

NEW
ZEALAND

Chatham Island
(to NZ)

Bounty Island
(to NZ)

FALKLAND ISLANDS
(to UK)

Campbell Island
(to NZ)

Macquarie Island (to Australia)

SOUTH GEORGIA &
SOUTH SANDWICH ISLANDS
(to UK)

Key

North America

South America

Africa

Europe

Asia

Oceania

ANTARCTICA

Countries of the world

What makes up North America?

This continent is home to three very large countries – Canada, the USA, and Mexico – and 20 smaller countries. It stretches all the way from the Arctic Circle to Central America (the narrow strip of land that joins South America) and includes Greenland and the long chain of Caribbean islands.

Canada's national emblem is the **maple leaf** – fair enough, as more than 85 per cent of the world's supply of maple sugar comes from Canadian maple trees. Yummy on pancakes!

Tell me more: ancient origins

Humans first arrived in North America about 20,000 years ago. They entered Alaska from Asia and spread throughout North America to become the ancestors of today's Native Americans.

There are about 3 million Native Americans living in the USA and Canada.

The Native Americans of Mexico and Guatemala are descended from the ancient Aztec and Maya people, conquered by the Spanish 500 years ago.

Many Caribbean people are descendants of African slaves forced to work on sugar plantations.

"Straight on" and "tout droit"

Canada has two official languages so road signs must be written in **English and French**. The first European settlers in Canada were French, followed by the British. In Québec, Canada's largest province, French is the only official language.

Five most populated countries in North America

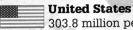
United States
303.8 million people

Mexico
109.9 million people

Canada
33.2 million people

Guatemala
13 million people

Cuba
11.4 million people

WEIRD OR WHAT?

Greenland belongs to Denmark. It is the second largest island in the world (after Australia), but only 56,000 people live there!

Most popular spectator sports

American football (nearly half of American households watch the Super Bowl championship on TV)

Baseball

Basketball

 NASCAR (stock car auto racing)

 Ice hockey (it's a national obsession in Canada, where the modern game was invented)

Name that hurricane

🌀 The US National Hurricane Center has six lists of names to identify the hurricanes that batter the Caribbean islands and the Gulf of Mexico from July to November each year.

🌀 **The lists are alphabetical and alternate male and female names.**

🌀 If a hurricane causes heavy destruction, its name is retired.

🌀 **In 2005, Hurricane Katrina flattened New Orleans. When the list of names from that year comes up again in 2011, Katia will replace Katrina. Other changes will be Don for Dennis, Rina for Rita, Sean for Stan, and Whitney for Wilma.**

How to: elect a US president

01. Every four years, choose two candidates – one from the Republican Party, one from the Democrat Party. Begin in January with the first state primaries – elections in which each of the 50 states vote to choose delegates to go to the party conventions.

02. There can be a lot of presidential hopefuls, so keep a running total of the primary results to see which candidate is winning the most pledges of support. Some states wait until June to hold their primaries and it may take some time to find a clear frontrunner.

03. Have lots of balloons and banners ready for the national conventions when the lucky candidates accept their nominations and announce vice president running mates.

04. Raise lots of money from backers for the final run to the White House. This is when the two presidential candidates confront each other in TV debates and rush backwards and forwards across the country shaking as many voters' hands as possible.

05. The presidential election always takes place on the first Tuesday in November. Stay glued to the TV as the results come in.

Melting pot

Most Americans can trace their family roots back to other countries. The United States has opened its doors to immigrants from all over the world, making it an exciting mix of cultures and traditions. More than 28 million Americans speak Spanish as their first language.

Mexico City stands on the site of the **Aztec city** of **Tenochtitlan**, built in 1325 on an island in Lake Texcoco – that makes it 300 years older than New York City.

FAST FACTS

North America

Total land area
24,454,000 sq km
(9,442,000 sq miles)

Biggest country
Canada
9,970,610 sq km
(3,848,655 sq miles)

Smallest country
St Kitts and Nevis
269 sq km
(104 sq miles)

Highest mountain
Mount McKinley,
Alaska
6,194 m (20,322 ft)

Longest river
Mississippi/Missouri
6,019 km (3,740 miles)

Biggest lake
Lake Superior USA/
Canada 82,414 sq km
(31,820 sq miles)

Most populated city
Mexico City
20,450,000 people

Tallest building
CN Tower, Toronto
553 m (1,815 ft)

Blasts from the past

1000 Leif Erikson, a Viking explorer, visits the coast of Canada

1492 Christopher Columbus lands on Hispaniola and Cuba

1519 The Spanish conquer Mexico and Central America

1620 Pilgrim Fathers found Plymouth colony, New England

1776 US declares independence from Britain

1821 Mexico gains independence from Spain

1865 USA abolishes slavery

1867 Dominion of Canada created

1914 Panama Canal opens. It cuts across the country of Panama, linking the Pacific and Atlantic Oceans

1960s Caribbean islands win independence from Britain

I don't believe it!

Guatemala's unit of currency, the quetzal, is named for a bird. With its brilliant golden-green feathers and long tail, the forest-dwelling quetzal was sacred to the Aztecs and Mayas.

Treasure ahoy!

Disney's three *Pirates of the Caribbean* movies grossed a record-breaking US$2.79 billion – riches beyond the wildest dreams of Blackbeard, Sir Henry Morgan, Calico Jack Rackham, and the rest of the villainous pirates who once sailed the waters of the Caribbean in search of real treasure!

Why do people in Brazil speak Portuguese?

The tango is more than a dance for Argentines, it's a way of life. As the saying goes, **"El tango no está en los pies. Está en el corazón."** ("Tango isn't in the feet. It's in the heart.")

Olá! In the 16th century, European nations conquered overseas lands to create empires. Portugal ruled Brazil, which is why Portuguese is spoken there today. Spain ruled the western half of South America from Venezuela to Argentina, bringing the Spanish language. More than 100 Native American languages are still spoken in the continent.

Tell me more: continent of extremes

- South America stretches from just north of the Equator almost to Antarctica. At one end are tropical rainforests, at the other glaciers.

- **There are 12 countries, of which Brazil is by far the largest.**

- Chile and Ecuador are the only countries that do not border Brazil.

- **Bolivia and Paraguay are the only countries without access to the sea.**

- Suriname and Guyana are former Dutch and British colonies. French Guiana is an "overseas department" of France – that means it's part of France and the people are French citizens.

- **The island of Tierra del Fuego ("Land of Fire") at the southern tip of the continent is divided between Argentina and Chile. Ushaia, on the Argentine side, is the most southerly city in the world.**

FAST FACTS

South America

Total land area
17,838,000 sq km
(6,887,000 sq miles)

Biggest country
Brazil 8,511,965 sq km
(3,285,618 sq miles)

Smallest country
Suriname 163,265 sq km
(63,020 sq miles)

Highest mountain
Aconcagua, Argentina
6,960 m (22,835 ft)

Longest river
Amazon
6,570 km (4,080 miles)

Biggest lake
Lake Maracaibo, Venezuela
13,312 sq km
(5,140 sq miles)

Most populated city
São Paolo, Brazil
18,333,000 people

Tallest building
Costanero Centre,
Santiago, Chile
257 m (843 ft)

Brazilian **Pelé** is the only footballer to have played in **three World Cup winning teams**, the first in 1958. His career total of **1,281 goals** – 77 for Brazil and 12 in World Cups – is still the highest ever achieved in the sport.

Under threat

- There are probably fewer than 100,000 native people living in the vast Amazon rainforest today.

- Experts believe as many as 50 or 60 tribes have never had contact with the outside world.

- Illegal forest clearance for logging and farming, and pollution from oil drilling is threatening their existence.

Football crazy

South American countries have won the FIFA World Cup – soccer's premier event – nine of the 18 times it has been contested since 1930:

Argentina (1978, 1986)

Brazil (1958, 1962, 1970, 1994, 2002)

Uruguay (1930, 1960)

WHAT'S IN A NAME?

Not many people can claim to have had an entire country named for them, but **Simón Bolivar**, the liberator of South America, can do just that. Bolivia was named in his honour in 1825.

Top attractions

The Incan city of Machu Picchu, high in the Andes, is the most visited site in South America, with more than 400,000 tourists a year.

An international poll in 2007 named the famous statue of **Christ the Redeemer (shown here)**, which stands on a peak overlooking the Brazilian city of Rio de Janeiro, as one of the Seven New Wonders of the World.

Chips with everything!

Potatoes were first cultivated on the high plains of the Andes more than 2,000 years ago. From there they have conquered the globe.

Other South American foodstuffs: **chocolate, pineapples, peanuts, lima (butter) beans**

Five most populated countries in South America

Brazil
196.4 million people

Colombia
45 million people

Argentina
40.4 million people

Peru
29.1 million people

Venezuela
26.4 million people

The spaceport of the European Space Agency is at Kouru in French Guiana. Its proximity to the Equator makes it an ideal place for launching the *Ariane 5* launch vehicle, which places satellites in orbit above the Earth.

The Andes is the world's **longest mountain range**, stretching 4,500 km (7,200 miles).

The world's **highest free-falling waterfall**, with a clear drop of 807 m (2,647 ft), is the Angel Falls in Canaimo National Park, Venezuela.

The world's **driest desert** is the Atacama (Peru/Chile). Some parts haven't seen a drop of rain since records began.

Bolivia's capital La Paz is 3,682 m (11,916 ft) above sea level, making it the world's **highest capital city**.

The **highest lake** is in the crater of the Licancábur volcano (Chile/Bolivia), 5,930 m (19,455 ft).

Weighing up to 91 kg (200 lb), the capybara, a native of the Amazon, is the world's **largest rodent**.

The Andean condor has the **largest wingspan of any living bird** – up to 3 m (10 ft).

Blasts from the past

1200s–1500s
Inca civilization flourishes in Peru region

1499
Italian explorer Amerigo di Vespucci explores northeast coast of Brazil

1531–1535
Spanish soldier Francisco Pizarro conquers the Inca Empire

1534
The first African slaves are landed in Brazil

1545
Spain grows rich after world's biggest silver mine is discovered at Potosi in the Andes

1565
The Portuguese found Rio de Janeiro

1816–1822
South America wins its independence from Spain and Portugal

1888
Brazil abolishes slavery

Where does Europe end?

That's a bit of a tricky one. Europe isn't a continent on its own but is attached to the western end of Asia. It is usually said to end at the Ural and Caucasus Mountains in Russia. Europe is the second smallest continent (only Australia is smaller). It occupies just 7 per cent of the Earth's surface, but contains 25 per cent of the world's population. There are 47 countries.

Big Ben, London, UK

Your royal highness…

These European countries still have monarchies. In most, the monarch has no political powers but is the official head of state.

- ♛ Belgium
- ♛ Denmark
- ♛ Liechtenstein
- ♛ Luxembourg
- ♛ Monaco
- ♛ Netherlands
- ♛ Norway
- ♛ Spain
- ♛ Sweden
- ♛ UK

Cross countries

The River Danube flows through four capital cities – Vienna, Bratislava, Budapest, and Belgrade – on its journey from central Germany to the Black Sea.

Despite its name, you'll never run out of hot water in **Iceland**! This volcanically active island has many geysers and hot springs, including the Strokkur geyser, which spouts boiling water high into the sky.

Eiffel Tower, Paris, France

Record breakers

▲ Mont Blanc, 4,807 m (15,771 ft), is the **highest peak in the Alps**, Europe's greatest mountain range and home to some of the world's top ski resorts.

● The **longest tunnel in Europe** is the Channel Tunnel linking England and France, which stretches 50 km (31 miles). The Gotthard Base Tunnel under the Alps (due for completion in 2012) will be 57 km (35 miles).

WHAT'S IN A NAME?

The **Iron Curtain** was a widely used term for the political division of Europe during the Cold War (1948–1989). It was coined by British wartime prime minister Winston Churchill.

Membership of the European Union (EU)

The EU works for greater economic, political, and social cooperation between its member-states.

6 in 1958 Belgium, France, West Germany, Italy, Luxembourg, Netherlands

9 in 1973 Denmark, Ireland, and UK join

10 in 1981 Greece joins

12 in 1986 Portugal and Spain join

15 in 1995 Austria, Finland, and Sweden join

25 in 2005 Cyprus, Czech Republic, Estonia, Hungary, Latvia, Lithuania, Malta, Poland, Slovakia, and Slovenia join

27 in 2007 Bulgaria and Romania join

Going up…

Blasts from the past

How to: eat spaghetti like an Italian

01. Tie a large napkin around your neck and carefully lower your fork into the dish of steaming hot spaghetti in front of you. Pick up several strands between the tines (spikes) of the fork.

02. Raise the spaghetti-loaded fork several centimetres above the dish to make sure the ends of the strands are clear of the mass of spaghetti. Give your fork a quick twist to secure the strands.

03. Place the pointed end of your fork against the bottom of the dish and deftly turn the fork around and around until the spaghetti strands twist themselves into a roll.

04. Place the fork in your mouth and slide the spaghetti off. You'll probably find there are a few dangling ends of spaghetti left in mid-air. You can guide them into your mouth with your fork or simply suck them up – much greedier and more satisfying!

Leaning Tower of Pisa, Italy

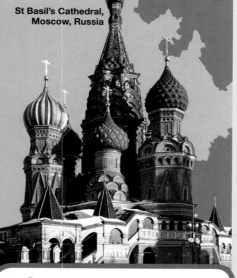

St Basil's Cathedral, Moscow, Russia

Five most populated countries in Europe

 Russia 140.7 million people

 Germany 82.3 million people

 France 62.1 million people

 UK 60.9 million people

 Italy 58.1 million people

Europe's newest countries

After the Cold War ended, many regions declared independence and formed their own nations.

Belarus: Established 1991, was part of Soviet Russia

Estonia: Established 1991, was part of Soviet Russia

Latvia: Established 1991, was part of Soviet Russia

Lithuania: Established 1991, was part of Soviet Russia

Moldova: Established 1991, was part of Soviet Russia

Ukraine: Established 1991, was part of Soviet Russia

Croatia: Established 1991, was part of Yugoslavia

Serbia: Established 1991, was part of Yugoslavia

Slovenia: Established 1992, was part of Yugoslavia

Bosnia and Herzegovina: Established 1992, was part of Yugoslavia

Czech Republic: Established 1993, was part of Czechoslovakia

Slovakia: Established 1993, was part of Czechoslovakia

Macedonia: Established 1993, was part of Yugoslavia

Montenegro: Established 2006, was part of Yugoslavia

I don't believe it!

The town of Oulu in Finland hosts the annual Air Guitar World Championships. Competitors from all over the world pretend to play rock guitars, and marks are given for technical merit, stage presence, and "airness" (artistic interpretation).

Delhi, **India**

Hong Kong, **China**

Bali, **Indonesia**

Which is the largest continent?

Asia – it covers one-third of the total land area of the Earth. North to south it extends from the Arctic Circle to just south of the Equator and at its widest point it measures 8,500 km (5,300 miles). Four billion people – three out of every five of the world's population – live in Asia.

Five most populated countries in Asia

China
1.3 billion people

India
1.1 billion people

Indonesia
237 million people

Pakistan
173 million people

Bangladesh
154 million people

Tell me more: sumo wrestling

- It is Japan's national sport.
- **Professional sumo wrestlers live in "training stables" known as *heya* and eat a special high-protein diet to put on weight.**
- The heaviest weight ever recorded for a sumo wrestler was 212 kg (469 lb) – no wonder they spend most of their time asleep when they're not fighting or eating!

Indonesia has about 13,000 islands, which makes it the **largest archipelago** (chain of islands) in the world. Fewer than 1,000 are inhabited, and 60 per cent of the country's population live on one island – Java.

FAST FACTS

Asia

Total land area
44,493,000 sq km
(17,179,000 sq miles)

Biggest country
(Asiatic) Russia
12,780,000 sq km
(4,934,385 sq miles)

Smallest country
Maldives
300 sq km (120 sq miles)

Highest mountain
Mount Everest, Nepal/China 8,850 m (29,050 ft)

Longest river
Yangtze, China
5,980 km (3,720 miles)

Biggest lake
Caspian Sea, Iran/Russia/Turkmenistan/Kazakhstan/Azerbaijan 371,000 sq km
(143,240 sq miles)

Most populated city
Tokyo, Japan
34,327,000 people

Tallest building
Burj Dubai, Dubai, United Arab Emirates
780 m (2,559 ft)

Nara, **Japan**

Gojal, **Pakistan**

Aitaura, **Nepal**

Great Wall, **China**

WHAT'S IN A NAME?

In the past, the Maluku (Moluccas) islands in Indonesia were the world's only source of cloves and nutmegs. Europeans called the region the "Spice Islands".

Holy land

Asia is the birthplace of six of the world's major religions:

Buddhism, Christianity, Islam, Judaism, Hinduism, Sikhism

Slick states

Five Middle Eastern countries possess some 70 per cent of the world's oil reserves between them:

✳ **Saudi Arabia**
✳ **Iran**
✳ **Iraq**
✳ **United Arab Emirates**
✳ **Kuwait**

Sky high

Nine of the 10 highest mountains in the world are in the **Himalayas**, the gigantic mountain range that divides the Indian subcontinent from the rest of Asia.

The Great Wall of China

01: It is a myth that astronauts can see the wall from space.

02: It is a chain of fortified walls and towers about 6,400 km (4,000 miles) long.

03: Most of the wall standing today was built 500 years ago by the Ming emperors.

04: Parts of the wall were torn down and used as a quarry on the orders of communist leader Mao Zedong in the 1960s.

In numbers

Lake Baikal, Siberia, is the world's deepest lake.

20% Percentage of the world's entire supply of unfrozen freshwater stored in the lake

336 The number of rivers that drain into the lake (only one drains out)

500 The number of species of fish that live in the lake

2,100 km (1,304 miles) The total length of coastline

23,600 km³ (5,662 cubic miles) The amount of water in the lake – enough to fill all the Great Lakes of North America

25 million years The age of the lake – the oldest in the world

More than 50 per cent of the world's silk comes from China and Japan.

The Chinese learned how to make silk 3,000 years ago but kept it a closely guarded secret for centuries. The Romans, who imported Chinese silk, thought it grew on trees!

How to: **make silk**

01. You'll need a clean, warm environment, plenty of mulberry leaves, and lots of silkworm eggs. Silkworms are the caterpillars (larvae) of the white silkmoth, *Bombyx mori*.

02. The eggs will hatch in about a week. You will need to feed the larvae three times a day on chopped mulberry leaves – they're fussy eaters and won't touch anything else. They grow very fast.

03. After 25 days they are ready to spin cocoons. Each silkworm spins around 1.6 km (1 mile) of silk filaments from tiny openings in its head. The silk comes out as a liquid and hardens on contact with the air.

04. When the silkworm is completely enclosed in a cocoon, free the outside end of the filaments and start winding them onto a reel, twisting several filaments together to form yarn.

05. Each cocoon will produce approximately 3,650 m (12,000 ft) of yarn. After it has been carefully dried and graded, the raw silk yarn can be dyed various colours, ready for weaving into silk cloth.

Where can you find pyramids, palm trees, and penguins?

Africa. The Nile valley and delta in the north was home to the Ancient Egyptians, who constructed huge pyramids. At the southern end of Africa, the Cape of Good Hope is famous for its colonies of penguins. In the vast Sahara Desert, palm tree oases provide occasional shelter for travellers. Equatorial rainforests cover the centre of Africa.

Africa

Total land area
30,293,000 sq km
(11,696,000 sq miles)

Biggest country
Sudan 2,504,530 sq km
(966,749 sq miles)

Smallest country
Seychelles 453 sq km
(175 sq miles)

Highest mountain
Kilimanjaro, Tanzania
5,895 m (19,340 ft)

Longest river
Nile 6,695 km (4,160 miles)

Biggest lake
Lake Victoria, Tanzania
69,500 sq km (26,827 sq miles)

Most populated city
Lagos, Nigeria 8,715,000 people

Tallest building
Carlton Tower, Johannesburg
(South Africa) 223 m (732 ft)

Five most populated countries in Africa

 Nigeria
146.2 million people

 Ethiopia
82.5 million people

 Egypt
81.7 million people

 Democratic Republic of Congo
66.5 million people

 South Africa
48.7 million people

The **Sahel** is a belt of dry grassland that runs for 3,862 km (2,400 miles) along the southern edge of the Sahara from Senegal to Sudan and Eritrea. Droughts are frequent in this region, bringing devastating famine to millions of people.

Six of the ten **poorest countries in the world** are in Africa:

Malawi

Somalia

Comoros

Congo

Burundi

Tanzania

African hero

Nelson Mandela spent 27 years in jail for his part in leading the struggle against apartheid (segregation of blacks and whites) in South Africa. He was released in 1990 and four years later became South Africa's first black president.

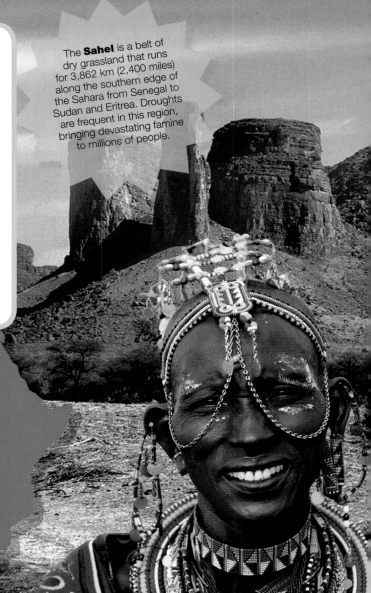

Blasts from the past

3000–300 BCE Egyptian civilization flourishes in Nile Valley

814 BCE Phoenicians found a trading city at Carthage (modern Tunis)

202 BCE Romans destroy Carthage and colonize North Africa

350 CE Ethiopia is converted to Christianity

700 Arab rule established in North Africa

1350 Kingdom of Great Zimbabwe at its height

1500 Portuguese found trading posts on the African coast

1871 Diamonds discovered at Kimberley, South Africa

1884 European race to colonize Africa begins

1960 First African states gain independence

Hot facts about the Sahara

01: The Sahara is HUGE – the whole of Australia could fit into it.

02: *Sahara* is the Arabic word for "desert".

03: Most of the Sahara is bare rock or gravel.

04: Camels are not native to the Sahara. They were brought from Asia 2,000 years ago.

05: About 15 billion litres (4 billion gallons) of water lies deep beneath the desert in underground pools called aquifers.

06: Desert-living plants can sink their roots up to 24 m (80 ft) to find water.

07: The highest recorded temperature was 57°C (136°F) in September 1922.

08: Wind-blown dust from the Sahara ends up in the Caribbean.

RECORD BREAKER

The Great Mosque at D'jenne, Mali, is the **largest mud structure in the world**. Arab traders who crossed the Sahara from North Africa brought Islam to the region about 1,000 years ago.

Fossils show that **early humans** (*Homo sapiens*) were living in Africa about 150,000 years ago. They began to migrate out of Africa about 100,000 years ago and spread around the world by about 10,000 years ago.

I don't believe it!

The welwitschia plant grows only in the Namib Desert of southwest Africa. It lives for 2,000 years or more, and produces a single pair of leaves – they just keep growing… and growing.

What about me?

In 1960, Ethiopian Abebe Bikila ran the Olympic marathon barefoot and won gold. East African athletes have dominated long-distance running events ever since.

Five top animal reserves

Name: Serengeti
Country: Tanzania
Key attraction: wildebeest migrations

Name: Masai Mara
Country: Kenya
Key attraction: big cats; lion, leopard, cheetah

Name: Kruger
Country: South Africa
Key attraction: buffalo, elephant, leopard, lion, rhino

Name: Luangwa
Country: Zambia
Key attraction: antelope, zebra, crocodile

Name: Selinda
Country: Botswana
Key attraction: elephant, lion

How big is Australia?

Australia covers 7,692,300 sq km (2,969,228 sq miles), making it the 6th largest country in the world and just slightly smaller than the United States. Depending on how you look at it, Australia is the smallest continent or the largest island in the world – and the least populated. It is located in the geographical region of Oceania, along with more than 25,000 islands. The islands are scattered across the enormous expanse of the South Pacific.

WHAT'S IN A NAME?

Aotearoa, the Māori name for New Zealand, means **"the long white cloud"**. Legend has it that after many days' sailing, Polynesian explorers saw a cloud low on the horizon and decided to settle there.

Tell me more: Easter Island

🧍 Polynesian voyagers sailed 4,000 km (2,500 miles) across unknown seas from Tahiti to settle on Easter Island (Rapa Nui) 1,000 years ago.

🧍 **They carved giant stone heads, called *moai*, which they erected around the island.**

🧍 They felled the island's trees to use as rollers to transport the stone heads. This eroded the soil, causing food to become scarce. When Europeans arrived in 1722 (on Easter Day), there were few islanders left.

🧍 **Today the island belongs to Chile.**

Five famous New Zealanders

Russell Crowe
(b.1964)
Movie actor

Sir Edmund Hillary
(1919–2008)
Climber, conqueror of Everest, explorer

Peter Jackson
(b.1961)
Oscar-winning film director

Bruce McLaren
(1937–1970)
Grand Prix racer, founder of McLaren cars

Ernest Rutherford
(1871–1937)
Atomic physicist, Nobel Prize winner

Blasts from the past

c.40,000 years ago The ancestors of today's Aborigines spread throughout Australia

6,000 years ago Farming begins in New Guinea

500 BCE Polynesian sailors begin to colonize the Pacific Islands

1000 CE Polynesians (Māori) settle New Zealand (Aotearoa)

1520–1521 Portuguese explorer Ferdinand Magellan is the first European to sail across the Pacific

1768–1771 English navigator Captain Cook proves that Australia is a separate continent

1788 British found the colony of New South Wales in Australia

1840 British lay claim to New Zealand

1908 Canberra becomes the capital of Australia

2000 Olympic Games held in Sydney

Five most populated countries in Oceania

 Australia
21 million people

 Papua New Guinea
5.9 million people

 New Zealand
4.1 million people

 Fiji
932,750 people

 Solomon islands
581,300 people

Five things you may not know about Australia

01: It is compulsory to vote in Australian **political elections**.

02: The **Sydney Harbour Bridge** is known locally as "the coathanger".

03: 29 per cent of **red back spider** bites come when people are putting on their shoes – the spiders hide in them.

04: The **largest cattle station** (farm) in Australia is the same size as the country of Belgium.

05: There are **58 million kangaroos** – more than twice the number of humans.

Oceania

Total land area
8,945,000 sq km
(3,454,000 sq miles)

Biggest country
Australia 7,692,300 sq km
(2,969,228 sq miles)

Smallest country
Nauru 21 sq km (8 sq miles)

Highest mountain
Mount Wilhelm, Papua New Guinea 4,509 m (14,793 ft)

Longest river
Murray/Darling, Australia 3,718 km (2,310 miles)

Biggest lake
Lake Eyre, Australia 9,000 sq km (3,475 sq miles)

Most populated city
Sydney, Australia 4,297,100 people

Tallest building
Q1 Tower, Gold Coast, Australia 323 m (1,059 ft)

Uluru

Called Ayers Rock by European settlers, Uluru is a huge sandstone monolith in the centre of Australia. It covers 3.3 sq km (1.3 sq miles) and is 348 m (1,141 feet) high. It is sacred to the Aboriginal people.

Q: WHAT DO YOU CALL A BOOMERANG THAT WON'T COME BACK?
A: A stick

How to: **throw a boomerang**

Australian Aborigines used boomerangs for hunting and sport. With a little practice you'll be able to get a boomerang to come back to you.

boomerang

01. Grip one end of the boomerang as if you were holding a tennis racket. Make sure the curved side is towards you (it doesn't matter which end you grip).

02. Face directly into the wind, and then turn about 45 degrees to the right. Fix your eye on a tree or building a little above the horizon. Aiming at that point, raise your arm back over your shoulder with your wrist bent backwards.

wind   45°

03. Release the boomerang with a strong snap of the wrist. It should cartwheel forward, end over end. To catch it, hold one hand in the air, palm down, and the other below it, palm up. As the boomerang floats back towards you, slam your hands together.

Who owns Antarctica?

No one – it doesn't have a government. The Antarctic Treaty, signed by 46 countries, requires that the continent is used only for peaceful scientific research. Antarctica is very dry, cold, and windy, and about 98 per cent of its land surface is covered by ice. Very few plants grow there except mosses, lichens, and seaweed.

Tell me more: South Pole

❄ **The South Pole is the southernmost point on Earth.**

❄ It is located in the middle of a windswept icy plateau.

❄ **The ice at the South Pole is 2,700 m (9,000 ft) thick.**

❄ A plaque records the dates when Roald Amundsen and Robert Falcon Scott first reached it.

❄ **The Ceremonial South Pole, surrounded by the flags of Antarctic Treaty countries, is a short distance away.**

How to: survive the cold (if you are a penguin)

01. Grow densely packed, overlapping feathers. They will keep out the wind and make you waterproof. Downy feathers below the outer layer trap air and provide insulation during dives.

02. Your thick layer of fat (blubber) will provide extra insulation, but even so you need to stay active in water to generate body heat.

03. On land, the dark feathers on your back will absorb heat and help you warm up.

04. Tuck your flippers in close to your body – this will reduce heat loss. Shivering will also help.

05. If you are an Emperor penguin, rock back on your feet and rest your entire weight on your heels and tail so that only a tiny part of your body is touching the ice.

06. Huddle up to your neighbours. Male Emperor penguins crowd together in groups of up to 6,000 when the females go off feeding, leaving them to incubate the eggs.

FAST FACTS

Antarctica

Total land area
14,400,000 sq km
(5,400,000 sq miles)

Highest point
Vinson Massif
4,897 m (16,055 ft)

Average depth of ice sheet
1.6 km (1 mile)

Lowest temperature
-89.2°C (-128.6°F)

Closest city
Ushaia, Argentina
1,238 km (769 miles) away

Permanent population
about 1,000 research scientists (5,000 in summer)

Winter blues
In winter, the area of frozen sea water, or **pack ice**, around Antarctica roughly **doubles in size** to 20 million sq km (7.2 million sq miles) – one and a half times the size of the USA.

Creature comforts

During the summer, a blue whale eats 4 million krill (small shrimp-like creatures) a day.

Penguins are such good swimmers that early explorers mistook them for fish.

Four species of penguin breed in the Antarctic – Adélie, Chinstrap, Emperor, and Gentoo.

Many Antarctic fish have antifreeze in their blood to survive the cold waters.

Fears that dogs were passing on diseases to seals led to their being banned in 1994.

Seven cool facts about the Antarctic ice sheet

01: It is the single largest mass of ice on Earth.

02: It contains about 60–70 per cent of the fresh water on Earth.

03: Most of the ice sheet rests on land.

04: More than 70 lakes lie deep below the surface of the ice sheet.

05: Snow falling at the South Pole takes about 100,000 years to "flow" to the coast, where it drops off as part of an iceberg.

06: The Ross Ice Shelf is a large mass of floating ice, about the size of France, attached to Antarctica.

07: There are about 3 million icebergs in the Southern Ocean around Antarctica.

Ice tours

✦ Around 37,000 tourists visit the waters of Antarctica every year, and numbers are growing.

✦ **There are fears that tourism may be putting the fragile Antarctic environment at risk.**

✦ Strict rules for disposing of wastes, including human waste, are enforced – organic matter can take decades to disappear. All recyclable and non-recyclable waste must be separated and removed.

I don't believe it !

More than 500 million years ago, when Antarctica was part of the supercontinent of Gondwana, it lay almost on the Equator.

RECORD BREAKER

The **first baby to be born on Antarctica** was Emilio Marcos Palma in 1978. His parents were working on the Argentine Base Esperanza at the time.

Scientific research

❆ There are nearly 40 research stations in Antarctica.

❆ **The biggest research station is the US McMurdo Base on Ross Island (home to about 1,000 scientists in summer and 250 in winter).**

❆ Ice cores – long cylinders of ice drilled from the ice sheet – give information about the global climate going back tens of thousands of years.

❆ **Meteorites (lumps of rock or metal that crash to Earth from space) found buried in the ice sheet contain valuable clues about the Solar System.**

Blasts from the past

1911 Norwegian party led by Roald Amundsen wins the race to be the first humans at the South Pole

1912 British explorer Robert Falcon Scott and four others reach the South Pole a month after Amundsen. All die of extreme cold and starvation on the return journey

1929 US Admiral Richard Byrd is first to fly over the South Pole

1956 The US Navy lands a party by air to set up the Amundsen-Scott South Pole Station

1958 Edmund Hillary and Vivien Fuchs meet at the South Pole during the Commonwealth Trans-Antarctic expedition

1989 Arved Fuchs and Reinhold Messner are the first to reach the South Pole travelling on skis

2007 Hannah McKeand sets the record for the fastest unsupported walk to the South Pole – 1,111 km (690 miles) in 39 days

How many **countries** are there in the **world?**

The United Nations (UN) recognizes 193 countries. They all have international land borders (though these are sometimes disputed) and an independent government. Countries usually have their own flag, official emblem, and national anthem. Size doesn't matter: the Vatican City, in Italy, the world's smallest country, is no bigger than a city block, and has a tiny population, too – about 1,000.

There are **58 dependencies or territories** in the world – countries or areas (most often islands) that are (usually) self-governing but come under the economic and military protection of another country. The largest is **Greenland**, which is **part of Denmark**.

Top ten countries by population

China 1.3 billion people

India 1.1 billion people

USA 303 million people

Brazil 187 million people

Indonesia 237 million people

Largest countries

01: Russia
17,175,400 sq km
(6,591,000 sq miles)

02: Canada
9,970,610 sq km
(3,848,655 sq miles)

03: USA
9,161,923 sq km
(3,537,438 sq miles)

04: China
9,596,960 sq km
(3,705,406 sq miles)

05: Brazil
8,511,965 sq km
(3,285,618 sq miles)

How experts predict the top ten countries will look in 2050:

India 1.62 billion people
China 1.47 billion people
USA 404 million people
Indonesia 338 million people
Nigeria 304 million people
Pakistan 268 million people
Brazil 207 million people
Bangladesh 205 million people
Russia 118 million people
Japan 101 million people

Countries with the largest reserves of oil
(billions of barrels)

- **Saudi Arabia** 265.3
- **Iraq** 115
- **Kuwait** 98.8
- **Iran** 96.4
- **United Arab Emirates** 62.8
- **Russia** 54.3
- **Venezuela** 47.6
- **China** 30.6
- **Libya** 30
- **Mexico** 26.9

Smallest countries

01: Vatican
0.4 sq km (0.2 sq miles)

02: Monaco
1.95 sq km (0.75 sq miles)

03: Nauru
21 sq km (8 sq miles)

04: Tuvalu
26 sq km (10 sq miles)

05: San Marino
61 sq km (24 sq miles)

Land of two names

The people of Bhutan call their country Druk Yul, which means "Land of the Thunder Dragon". Bhutan is the name given it by outsiders and is thought to come from a Sanskrit word meaning "high land".

Right or left?

🚗 62 per cent of countries drive on the right side of the road, 38 per cent on the left.

🚗 At one time the USA and Canada drove on the left.

🚗 Most of the countries that drive on the left are in Africa, Asia, Australia, and Oceania.

🚗 The majority are former British colonies, but Indonesia, Thailand, and Japan are not.

🚗 The UK, Ireland, Cyprus, and Malta are the only European countries to drive on the left. They are all islands.

🚗 Sweden was the last country in mainland Europe to drive on the left. It changed to the right on 3 September 1967. All cars were kept off the roads for five hours while the traffic signals were rearranged.

Of thee I sing: national anthems

♪ Greece has the longest national anthem – 158 verses. Luckily they don't sing them all!

♪ Japan can claim the world's oldest national anthem – the words are a poem written in the 9th century.

♪ South Africa's anthem, *Nkosi sikelel' iAfrika*, has words in five languages – Xhosa, Zulu, Sesotho, English, and Afrikaans.

♪ Spain's national anthem, *La Marcha*, doesn't have any words at all.

♪ Uruguay's anthem takes five minutes to play.

♪ The tune of the US anthem *The Star Spangled Banner* was originally a popular drinking song. The words refer to an incident in the War of 1812.

WHAT'S IN A NAME?

Libya's full name in Arabic is **Al Jamahiriya al-Arabiya al-Libya al-Shabiya al-Ishtirakiya**, the longest official name of any country in the world. Roughly translated it means "Great Socialist People's Libyan Arab Republic of the Masses".

Seven countries that end in "stan"
("stan" means nation or land)

Afghanistan
Kazakhstan
Kyrgyzstan
Pakistan
Tajikistan
Turkmenistan
Uzbekistan

Pakistan
173 million people

Nigeria
146 million people

Bangladesh
154 million people

Russia
140 million people

Japan
129 million people

Where in the world?

More than 20,000 people in **Japan** are over 100 years old.

India has the most universities in the world with 8,507.

The **USA** has the biggest pet cat population in the world – 76 million.

People in **Thailand** watch more TV than anyone else – an average of 22.4 hours a week.

Switzerland recycles 52 per cent of its waste – more than any other country.

The Netherlands has the best road safety record in the world.

In numbers

12 countries in South America

14 countries in Australia and Oceania

23 countries in North America

44 countries in Asia

47 countries in Europe

53 countries in Africa

Ten countries that have changed their names:

new name	old name
Benin	Dahomey
Burkina Faso	Upper Volta
Democratic Republic of the Congo	Zaire
Ethiopia	Abyssinia
Ghana	Gold Coast
Moldova	Moldavia
Myanmar	Burma
Sri Lanka	Ceylon
Taiwan	Formosa
Thailand	Siam

How many people live in cities?

For the first time in history, more people live in cities than in rural areas, with 3 billion city dwellers. There are 22 megacities (with more than 10 million inhabitants) and upwards of 300 cities with a population greater than 1 million.

Top 10 megacities

01: Tokyo, Japan
34 million people

02: Seoul, South Korea
23 million people

03: Mexico City, Mexico
22.4 million people

04: New York City, USA
21.9 million people

05: Mumbai, India
21.6 million people

06: Delhi, India
21.5 million people

07: Sao Paolo, Brazil
18.3 million people

08: Los Angeles, USA
18 million people

09: Shanghai, China
17.5 million people

10: Osaka, Japan
16.7 million people

World's most polluted cities

Sumgayit Azerbaijan
Linfen China
Tianjing China
Sukinda India
Vapi India
La Oroya Peru
Dzershinsk Russia
Norilsk Russia
Chernobyl Ukraine
Kabwe Zambia

Do you know these capital cities?

1. Antananarivo
2. Bishkek
3. Bandar Seri Begawan
4. Dili
5. Nouakchott
6. Nuku'alofa
7. Ouagadougou
8. Port Moresby
9. Tbilisi
10. Tegucigalpa
11. Ulaanbaatar
12. Vaduz

(answers bottom right-hand page)

How the world's urban population has grown

1800
3 per cent of people live in cities; 1 city has a population of more than 1 million

1900
9 per cent of people live in cities; 13 cities have populations of more than 1 million

2000
50 per cent of people live in cities; 330 cities have populations of more than 1 million

In 1900 only **four Asian cities** had populations of more than **1 million**; today the number is 194, with the majority of them in China.

By 2015 there are predicted to be **253 cities in Asia** with more than **1 million** people, plus 65 in South and Central America, and 59 in Africa.

Cities with the most **skyscrapers**

Hong Kong
China

New York City
USA

Tokyo
Japan

Shanghai
China

Chicago
USA

Bangkok
Thailand

Guangzhou
China

Chongqing
China

Shenzhen
China

High altitude cities

🏔 Wenzhuan in Tibet, China, is the **highest city in the world**, with an altitude of 5,100 m (16,730 ft).

🏔 La Paz, Bolivia, is the **highest capital city in the world** at 3,600 m (11,811 ft).

🏔 **Highest city in Africa** is Dinsho, Ethiopia, at 3,207 m (10,522 ft).

🏔 **Highest city in the USA** is Alma, Colorado, at 3,156 m (10,355 ft).

🏔 Andorra la Vella, Andorra, is **Europe's highest capital city** at 1,023 m (3,356 ft).

I don't believe it !

Nauru is the only country without a capital city, which is down to the centre of this tiny Pacific island being a phosphate mine. Its population of 13,000 lives on the narrow coastal strip fringing the shore.

Cities destroyed by major earthquakes

c.1400 BCE
Ancient Troy and Armageddon (Megiddo)

1138
Aleppo, Syria

1755
Lisbon, Portugal

1906
San Francisco, California

1923
Tokyo, Japan

1960
Agadir, Morocco

1963
Skopje, Macedonia

1976
Guatemala City, Guatemala

1995
Kobe, Japan

2003
Bam, Iran

WHAT'S IN A NAME?

According to an old Malay legend, a prince was shipwrecked and washed ashore on an island. He saw an animal he mistook for a lion and called the place **Singa pura** ("Lion city"). It's doubtful if the story is true, but today the national emblem of **Singapore** is a **lion**.

Blasts from the past

3,500 BCE
First cities appear in Mesopotamia (Iraq)

1,600 BCE
First cities in China

1 CE
Rome's population reaches 450,000 people

500
Teotihuacan (Mexico) is the largest city in ancient America

800
Population of the city of Baghdad reaches 700,000

1800
London is world's first city to top a population of 1 million people

1950
New York is world's largest city with a population of 12.4 million

1965
Tokyo is first city to top 20 million

1985
The average living space in the crowded city of Shanghai, China, is the size of a small car

Think twice before moving to...

Istanbul, Turkey
Since it was founded (as Constantinople) in 330 CE, this city has been hit by 15 major earthquakes – the last was in 1999.

Naples, Italy
Some experts believe that Vesuvius, the volcano that buried Pompeii in 79 CE, will erupt again. Naples would be right in its path.

Mumbai, India
When it rains heavily in India's largest city, whole sections of the city flood as the drains cannot cope with the volume of water.

Shanghai, China
China's showplace city is sinking by 1.5 cm (0.5 in) a year due to the weight of skyscrapers built in the past decade.

Phoenix, USA
This city of 1 million people, built in the middle of the desert in Arizona, is in danger of running out of water.

ANSWERS: 1. Madagascar / **2.** Kyrgyzstan / **3.** Brunei / **4.** East Timor / **5.** Mauritania **6.** Tonga / **7.** Burkina Faso / **8.** Papua New Guinea / **9.** Georgia / **10.** Honduras **11.** Mongolia / **12.** Liechtenstein

Cities | 226|227

Which flag has flown the highest?

The **stars and stripes** of the US flag have special meaning. There are **13 stripes** for the original 13 states of the Union and **50 stars** for the number of states today. Alaska and Hawaii were the last to make their mark on the flag. Two stars were added in 1959 when they became states.

A national flag is the symbol of a country and an emblem of its people and history. The Stars and Stripes – the flag of the United States – star-trekked 383,400 km (238,855 miles) in July 1969 to the surface of the Moon, where it was planted by the *Apollo 11* astronauts.

Under ice
In 2007 Russia planted its flag 4,200 m (14,000 ft) **below the North Pole**. Why? Because the Arctic seabed is thought to be rich in oil and gas and the country was making a somewhat controversial claim to the ownership of these reserves.

Ten things you can find on flags

01: Carpets
Turkmenistan

02: Temple (Angkor Wat)
Cambodia

03: Yin-yang symbol
South Korea

04: Shield
Kenya, Lesotho, and Swaziland

05: Cedar tree
Lebanon

06: Wheel
India

07: Star of David
Israel

08: Dragon
Bhutan

09: Maple leaf
Canada

10: Trident
Barbados

How to: fold the US flag

The US flag is lowered at the end of each day. Then it is folded into the shape of a tricorner to symbolize the hats worn by soldiers in the American Revolution. As day becomes night, so the red and white stripes are folded into the dark blue section of stars.

06. ...until only a triangular blue section of stars is visible.

01. Hold the flag waist-high between two people, so that its surface is parallel to the ground.

02. Fold the lower half of the stripe section lengthwise over the stars section. Fold again, with the stars section on the outside.

03. Make a triangular fold by bringing the striped corner of the folded edge to meet the open edge of the flag.

04. Turn the triangular end inward, parallel to the open edge, to form a second triangular fold.

Birds that appear on flags

eagle
Albania, Egypt, Mexico, Moldova, Montenegro, Kazakhstan, Serbia, Zambia

quetzal
Guatemala

frigate bird
Kiribati

crane
Uganda

parrot
Dominica

Sun and stars

☀ The flags of **Antigua and Barbuda**, **Kiribati**, and **Malawi** all feature a **rising sun**.

★ The stars of the **Southern Cross** – the brightest constellation in the southern skies – appear on the flags of **Australia, Federated States of Micronesia, New Zealand, Papua New Guinea, Samoa,** and **Solomon Islands**.

★ There are **nine stars** on the **Tuvalu** flag, one for each of the country's islands.

RECORD BREAKER

The **largest flag ever flown** was a US flag measuring 78 m by 154 m (255 ft by 505 ft)—more than big enough to cover an entire football field.

Flag rules

⚑ If you wash a Finnish flag, you must be sure to dry it indoors.

⚑ **The flag of Chile can only be flown from a white pole.**

⚑ The flag of Iceland should never be raised before seven o'clock in the morning.

⚑ **The South African flag must never be used as a tablecloth.**

Colourwise

There are **six colours** on the flag of **South Africa**—more than on any other national flag.

Green, the symbolic colour of Islam, features prominently on the flags of **Bangladesh, Libya, Mauritania, Pakistan, Saudi Arabia,** and **Turkmenistan**.

Many African nations have flags of **green, yellow,** and **red**, symbolizing independence and unity.

Eight European nations have flags of **blue, white,** and **red** stripes. France is the only one on which the stripes are vertical.

Red appears on about **75 per cent** of national flags.

Libya is the only country to have a flag of a **single colour**. It is a solid green rectangle.

The study of flags is called **vexillology**, so a flag buff is known as a vexillologist. It can be a vexing hobby!

Flag nicknames

Auriverde
("**gold and green**") Brazil

Ay Yildiz
("**moon star**") Turkey

Dannebrog
("**Danish cloth**") Denmark

Estrella Solitaria
("**lone star**') Chile, Cuba

Hinomaru
("**circle of the sun**") Japan

Jalur Gemilang
("**stripes of glory**") Malaysia

Old Glory; Stars and Stripes
United States of America

Tricolore
("**tricolour**") France

Union Jack
United Kingdom

05. Continue the triangular folding along the length of the flag…

What about me?

Since ancient times, people have painted their faces to show tribal allegiance. At international sporting events today, many people paint their faces with their national flag.

bird of paradise
Papua New Guinea

The flag of **Zimbabwe** has a statue of a **stone bird**.

Tell me more: flags of the world

Canada | United States of America | Mexico | Belize | Costa Rica | El Salvador | Guatemala | Honduras

Nicaragua | Panama | Antigua and Barbuda | Bahamas | Barbados | Cuba | Dominica | Dominican Republic

Grenada | Haiti | Jamaica | St Kitts & Nevis | St Lucia | St Vincent and the Grenadines | Trinidad and Tobago | Colombia

Guyana | Surinam | Venezuela | Bolivia | Ecuador | Peru | Brazil | Argentina

Uruguay | Chile | Paraguay | Algeria | Egypt | Libya | Morocco | Tunisia

Benin | Burkina | Cape Verde | Gambia | Ghana | Guinea | Guinea-Bissau | Ivory Coast

Liberia | Mali | Mauritania | Niger | Nigeria | Senegal | Sierra Leone | Togo

Cameroon | Central African Republic | Chad | Congo | Democratic Republic of Congo | Equatorial Guinea | Gabon | Sao Tome and Principe

Burundi | Djibouti | Eritrea | Ethiopia | Kenya | Rwanda | Somalia | Sudan

Tanzania | Uganda | Angola | Botswana | Lesotho | Malawi | Mozambique | Namibia

South Africa | Swaziland | Zambia | Zimbabwe | Denmark | Finland | Iceland | Norway

Sweden | Ireland | United Kingdom | Belgium | Luxembourg | Netherlands | Germany | France

Monaco
Andorra
Portugal
Spain
Italy
San Marino
Vatican City
Austria

Liechtenstein
Slovenia
Switzerland
Czech Republic
Hungary
Poland
Slovakia
Albania

Bosnia and Herzegovina
Croatia
Kosovo (disputed)
Macedonia
Montenegro
Serbia
Bulgaria
Greece

Moldova
Romania
Ukraine
Belarus
Estonia
Latvia
Lithuania
Cyprus

Malta
Russian Federation
Armenia
Azerbaijan
Georgia
Turkey
Iraq
Israel

Jordan
Lebanon
Syria
Bahrain
Kuwait
Oman
Qatar
Saudi Arabia

United Arab Emirates
Yemen
Iran
Kazakhstan
Kyrgyzstan
Tajikistan
Turkmenistan
Uzbekistan

Afghanistan
Pakistan
Bangladesh
Bhutan
India
Nepal
Sri Lanka
China

Mongolia
North Korea
South Korea
Japan
Myanmar (Burma)
Cambodia
Laos
Philippines

Thailand
Vietnam
Brunei
Indonesia
East Timor
Malaysia
Singapore
Comoros

Madagascar
Maldives
Mauritius
Seychelles
Australia
New Zealand
Papua New Guinea
Fiji

Solomon Islands
Vanuatu
Marshall Islands
Micronesia
Nauru
Palau
Kiribati
Tuvalu

Tonga
Samoa

Key
North America
South America
Africa
Europe
Asia
Oceania

What do **900 million people** do a year?

Take a vacation. Tourism is one of the biggest businesses in the world, generating at least 200 million jobs. It is vital for the economies of many countries. The downside is that tourism is a major contributor to climate change through the carbon emissions it creates. Sheer weight of tourist numbers threatens the survival of many of the Earth's most fragile ecosystems and ancient historical sites.

Take a break (at a price!)

For **US$1 million** you can enjoy a **seven-day** "once-in-a-lifetime" **stay** at the Emirates Palace Hotel, Abu Dhabi. For your money you get:

- accommodation in a 680 sq m (7,310 sq ft) suite
- a deep-sea fishing trip
- a sunset and desert island tour
- gifts including fine champagne, rare pearls, and a choice of the world's best sporting guns
- first-class travel from and to any international airport of your choice
- chauffeur-driven car at your disposal

Top 10 most visited countries (2007)

01: France
81,900,000 visitors

02: Spain
59,200,000 visitors

03: USA
56,000,000 visitors

04: China
54,700,000 visitors

05: Italy
43,700,000 visitors

06: United Kingdom
30,700,000 visitors

07: Germany
24,400,000 visitors

08: Ukraine
23,100,000 visitors

09: Turkey
22,200,000 visitors

10: Mexico
21,400,000 visitors

Have a blast!
What do Dennis Tito, Mark Shuttleworth, Gregory Olsen, Anousheh Ansari, and Charles Simonyi have in common? They are the first **space tourists**. They flew to and from the International Space Station on Soyuz spacecraft. Cost of a trip? Around US$25 million.

Six of the world's top dive sites

- **Yongala** Shipwreck dive off coast of Queensland, Australia
- **Blue Corner, Palau** Sharks and barracudas
- **Sharm el Sheikh, Egypt** Best reef diving in the Red Sea
- **Sipadan, Borneo** Matchless marine life, including turtles, barracudas, and sharks
- **Protea Banks, South Africa** Dramatic reef walls and coral gardens
- **Great Blue Hole, Belize** Exhilarating dive in the crystal clear waters of an underwater sinkhole

I don't believe it !

On Mount Huashan in China, trekkers cling to a rusty iron chain while clambering along a 30-cm (1-ft) wide wooden plank above a 2,090 m (6,857 ft) cliff face without a safety barrier. The 24-hour hike attracts thousands of visitors, though it is said to claim 100 victims a year. That's extreme!

Extreme vacations

trekking

mountaineering

abseiling

Eiffel Tower, Paris, France

Blasts from the past

100s Romans tour monuments of Greece and Egypt

1200s Medieval pilgrims are the first mass tourists

1700s Rich young noblemen make the Grand Tour of Europe

1811 The word "tourist" is used for the first time

1830s Karl Baedeker publishes the first tourist guides for travellers in Germany

1841 Thomas Cook becomes the first travel agent when he organizes rail excursions for workers in Britain

1860s Railways bring growing numbers of tourists to the French Riviera

1900 First Michelin Guide published for drivers

1902 First packaged winter sports holiday

1950s Mass tourism takes off with cheaper air flights

In numbers

25 million
The number of international tourists in 1950

903 million
The number of international tourists in 2007

1.6 billion
The forecasted number of international tourists by 2020

1 trillion
The global income in US dollars generated by tourism in 2007

54%
The percentage of international tourists that visited Europe in 2007, making it the most popular continent for vacations

82.9 billion
The amount in US dollars spent by German tourists in 2007 – the global top-spenders

Going green

Ecotourism is one of the fastest growing areas of tourism. It offers wilderness adventures in some of the most **remote parts of the world**, with top priority given to the protection of traditional **cultures** and the careful management of **wildlife**. Top destinations are:

- ✪ **Alaska**
- ✪ **Galapagos Islands**
- ✪ **Serengeti, Tanzania**
- ✪ **Komodo Island, Indonesia**
- ✪ **rainforests of Madagascar**
- ✪ **Tasmanian wilderness**

The top 10 commandments of ecotourism

01 Respect the frailty of the Earth so that unique and beautiful places are left for future generations to enjoy.

02 Leave only your footprints behind. No graffiti, no litter!

03 Learn about the customs and cultures of the region you plan to visit.

04 Don't photograph people without asking them first.

05 Don't buy products made from endangered plants or animals.

06 Always follow marked trails. Never disturb animals, plants, and their habitats.

07 Support conservation programmes and organizations.

08 Where possible, cycle or walk.

09 Use hotels and tour operators that conserve water and energy, recycle, and manage waste safely.

10 Encourage others to think environmentally.

Some holidaymakers seek adventure. Here are some of the most popular thrill-seeking vacations:

mountain biking

white-water rafting

bungee jumping

zip lining

rock climbing

surfing

snow boarding

Society and culture

Tell me more:
major world religions

✹ Buddhism
360 million followers
Place of origin: India,
2,500 years ago
Inspired by the teachings of
the Buddha

✝ Christianity
2,000 million followers
Place of origin: Palestine,
2,000 years ago
Christians believe Jesus Christ
to be the son of God

ॐ Hinduism
830 million followers
Place of origin: India, more than
3,000 years ago
Embraces many gods and beliefs

☾★ Islam
1,250 million followers
Place of origin: Arabia,
1,400 years ago
Followers, called Muslims,
obey the teachings of one God,
Allah, as revealed to the
Prophet Muhammad

✡ Judaism
14.5 million followers
Place of origin: Israel,
3,000 years ago
Believe in one God, who appeared
to Abraham and Moses and set
out his laws

☬ Sikhism
24.3 million followers
Place of origin: India,
500 years ago
Sikhs believe in one God, Sat Guru
("true teacher"), and the teachings
of the 10 Gurus

Pilgrims in the Islamic holy city of Mecca

What is a religion?

A set of beliefs, shared by a group of
people, that gives meaning to life and
death is called a religion. Some
religions are monotheistic – their
followers believe there is only one
god. Polytheistic religions
have many gods.

Traditionally, **Muslims are called to their daily prayers** by a cry that goes out from the tower of a mosque. Today, however, many imams (prayer leaders) use **text messages** to summon the faithful instead.

World percentages

This bar chart shows the percentages of
followers of the major world faiths. A further
12 per cent of people follow other religions,
while 12 per cent of people
are non-religious.

Judaism	Sikhism	Buddhism	Hinduism	Islam	Christianity
0.23%	0.4%	5.8%	13.2%	21%	33.3%

The five Ks

As a sign they have dedicated themselves
to their faith, Sikh men wear five "Ks".

01. Kirpan
A short ceremonial sword,
kept in a sheath

02. Kara
A circular steel
bracelet

03. Kachha
White undergarment

04. Kangha
A small wooden comb

05. Kesh
Punjabi for "uncut hair".
Sikhs often wear turbans to
keep their long hair tidy

Hindu gods and their animals

Hindus believe that their gods and goddesses ride on a particular animal, known as a *vahana*. Here are just a few gods and their animals:

Brahma
The Hindu god of creation, rides on a white swan

Vishnu
The protector, flies with Garuda and is half-man, half-eagle

Lakshmi
Goddess of wealth and beauty, flies on an owl

Shiva
The creator and destroyer, sits on Nandi the bull

Ganesh
The god of prosperity, Ganesh travels with a rat

Indra
The god of storms and war, rides on Airaveta – a white elephant

Varuna
The god of the sky and ocean, travels on Mukura – a sea monster

---

Places people go to worship

Buddhist temple
Relics (remains) of the Buddha, such as his robes, are often found in Buddhist temples.

Church
Christians meet together to worship in churches. Some churches have domes, others are topped with tall spires.

Hindu temple
Hindus worship images of their gods both in temples and in their homes.

Synagogue
The Jewish place of worship is called a synagogue. It is a place of prayer and study.

Mosque
Muslims pray in a mosque facing towards Mecca, the birthplace of Muhammad, in Saudi Arabia.

Gurdwara
A Sikh temple is called a Gurdwara, which means "gate to the guru". (A guru is a religious guide.)

Shinto is the ancient religion of Japan. Followers worship many gods (*kami*) found in nature, such as waterfalls, rocks, and islands.

Followers of the Indian Jain religion believe that every living thing has a soul. Some Jains sweep the ground as they walk, to avoid harming insects.

In numbers

3
A pilgrimage – a journey to worship at a holy place or shrine – is believed to bring special benefits to the traveller.
The number of steps some Buddhist pilgrims take before kowtowing (kneeling and bowing so low their heads touch the ground)

44,000
The number of tents erected by the Saudi Arabian government to accommodate Muslims making the Haj – a pilgrimage to the holy city of Mecca. All Muslims are expected to make the pilgrimage once in their life

500,000
The number of sheep and cattle sacrificed by pilgrims in the world's largest abattoir in Mecca during the week-long Haj festival

60 million
The number of Hindus who make the journey to the largest religious gathering in the world at Allahabad in India. During the 12-day Kumbh Mela festival, worshippers bathe in the sacred waters of the River Ganges

---

Sacred books

- Christianity: **Bible**
- Hinduism: **Vedas**
- Judaism: **Torah, Talmud**
- Islam: **Qur'an, Hadith**
- Buddhism: **Dharma**
- Sikhism: **Adi Granth**

Patron saints

Saints are people who led holy lives and are revered by Christians.

saint	patron of
Andrew the Apostle	fishermen
Christopher	travellers
Apollonia	dentists
Hubert of Liege	mad dogs
Martin de Porres	hairdressers
Clare of Assisi	television
Drogo	the really ugly

A very holy city

Jerusalem, in Israel, is a holy city for three major religions.

✝ For **Christians**, it is where Jesus, the son of God, died and came back to life.

✡ **Jews** pray at the Western Wall, also called the Wailing Wall, which is all that remains of the Jewish people's ancient Second Temple in Jerusalem.

☪ **Muslims** believe that the mosque of the Dome of the Rock marks the place where their prophet Muhammad was taken up into heaven.

One of the fastest-growing religions is **Baha'i**, founded in Iran in the 19th century. It seeks to unite all religions and has 7.5 million followers worldwide.

What is a festival?

People get together at festivals to enjoy themselves. Many festivals have their origins in the agricultural past and mark the changing seasons, while others celebrate key events in the religious year. Festivals may be solemn or fun – or both – and often they are occasions for eating special foods or giving presents.

Tell me more: carnivals

■ **A carnival is a street party held in many Catholic countries in the days leading up to Lent (a traditional time of fasting), when people dance, wear masks, and parade in costumes.**

■ The Galo de Madrugada (Cockcrow Parade) in Recife, Brazil, is the biggest carnival parade in the world.

■ **Steel bands are an essential part of Trinidad's carnival celebrations.**

■ The word "carnival" may come from an Italian phrase *carne levare*, meaning "take away the meat".

■ **Revellers in the Italian city of Venice traditionally wear elaborate masks at the annual carnival.**

RECORD BREAKER

The **biggest festival in the world** is the Chinese New Year, celebrated in China and parts of Asia where there are large Chinese communities. People travel to be at home with their families, and the festivities last for several days, with dragon and lion dances, food, and fireworks.

I don't believe it!

In Sweden, people hold parties in August in honour of the crayfish, a lobster-like crustacean that is fished at that time of year. They wear silly hats and sing songs about the crayfish!

Eid

01: Eid al-Fitr marks the end of Ramadan, the Muslim month of fasting.

02: **This festival is a three-day celebration with prayers and gifts.**

03: Eid al-Adha (the big Eid, or festival of sacrifice) marks the end of the Haj (pilgrimage to Mecca).

04: **A sheep, goat, or camel is slaughtered and the meat is shared with family and given to the poor.**

FAST FACTS

Every year the Japanese weather bureau announces when the **cherry blossoms** are in bloom. Special parties (*hanami*) are held beneath the trees to view the flowers at their most beautiful.

Food with meaning

For Passover, Jewish people eat a symbolic ritual meal, the seder. The food they eat recalls the sufferings of the Jews during their exile and slavery in Egypt and their exodus (journey) to Israel.

Lamb shank bone:
A reminder of the lamb sacrificed on the first Passover

Horseradish:
Represents the bitterness of slavery

Parsley dipped in salt water:
To remember the tears of the slaves

Green vegetable:
Represents new life

Roasted egg:
To remind Jews of temple sacrifices in Biblical times

Apple and nut mix:
Represents the mortar that held buildings together

Some things people do **at festivals**

Holi (Hindu)
Spray each other with brightly coloured powders and water

Setsubun (Japan)
Throw handfuls of beans into dark corners shouting "Fortune in, devils out!"

Purim (Jewish)
Wear different types of fancy dress and eat cakes filled with poppyseeds

Easter (Christian)
Hunt around for hidden chocolate eggs and bunnies

Moon Festival (East Asia)
Carry lanterns and eat moon cakes under the Full Moon

Diwali (Hindu, Sikh, Jain)
Clean homes and light small oil lamps

In numbers

Thanksgiving in the USA is held on the fourth Thursday in November. A turkey feast is central to the celebrations.

45 million
The number of turkeys consumed across the USA at Thanksgiving

295 million kg
(650 million lbs) The amount of cranberries used to make sauce

700 million kg
(1.6 billion lbs) The number of sweet potatoes eaten

453 million kg
(998 million lbs) The amount of pumpkins consumed

RECORD BREAKER
The **biggest food festival in the world** is Oktoberfest, held in Munich, Germany. More than 6 million people taste the famous beers and foods.

Santa legends

Santa Claus (also known as Saint Nicholas, Father Christmas, or Kris Kringle) delivers gifts at Christmas.

Most people think of him as a fat, white-haired gentleman wearing a red suit with white cuffs and collar. He was first portrayed in this way in a 19th-century US cartoon.

Traditions in some countries have Santa living at the North Pole. Other people believe he lives in Lapland.

Dutch children believe that Sinterklaas comes just before the feast day of Saint Nicholas on 6 December and put their shoes out for him to fill with candy treats and little gifts if they have been good – if not, they get a small bag of salt!

Colours that light up New York City's Empire State Building on holidays:

Chinese New Year
St Valentine's Day
St Patrick's Day
Easter
Hanukkah
Thanksgiving
Eid al-Fitr
Christmas

What is money?

We exchange money for goods and services. In the past, people bartered (exchanged) goods of equal worth, but it's not very convenient to swap a chicken and two bags of corn for that DVD you want. That's why we use money – either cash (notes and coins), or a virtual payment using a debit or credit card.

In numbers

5
The number of sacks of grain it took to barter for a pig in Ancient Egypt

12
The number of sides on an Australian 50-cent piece (more than any other coin)

1 billion
The value in US dollars of the amount of Iraqi dinar currency that was stolen from the Central Bank of Iraq in Baghdad the day before the US bombings in 2001. US$650 million was later found hidden in the walls of Saddam Hussein's palace

12 billion
The number of coins made by the US mint every year

56 billion
The net worth in US dollars of Microsoft founder Bill Gates – the richest man in the world

The Euro is used by 320 million Europeans in 20 countries.

Money around the world

A currency is the form of money used in a particular country. Here are some examples:

£	**UK**	Pound	100 pence
$	**USA**	Dollar	100 cents
L	**Albania**	Lek	100 qindarka
Tk	**Bangladesh**	Taka	100 paisa
元	**China**	Yuan	100 jiao
D	**Gambia**	Dalasi	100 butut
Rs	**India**	Rupee	100 paise
₪	**Israel**	Shekel	100 agorot
RM	**Malaysia**	Ringgit	100 sen
₮	**Mongolia**	Tugrik	100 mongos
zł	**Poland**	Zloty	100 groszy
руб	**Russia**	Ruble	100 kopecks
﷼	**Saudia Arabia**	Riyal	100 halalat
฿	**Thailand**	Baht	100 stang
ЛВ	**Bulgaria**	Leva	100 stotinki

What's in a name?

The word "salary" comes from the Latin word *sal*, meaning salt. Roman soldiers used to be paid a *salarium* – an allowance to buy salt.

WEIRD OR WHAT?

There was a time when British householders had to pay a window tax if they had more than a certain number of windows in their house. To avoid paying, people simply bricked some of their windows up – no wonder they called it daylight robbery!

Plastic fantastic

Debit cards can be used to purchase goods instead of money. A simple swipe or input of numbers, and money is debited direct from a bank account.

The first credit card (plastic card used to purchase goods and services on credit, to be paid off at a later date) was introduced in 1949 in New York City. Called the "Diners Club", it was accepted in restaurants.

There are more than 670 million credit cards in circulation in the USA.

RECORD BREAKERS

The **largest denomination banknote** ever issued was a note for 100,000,000,000,000,000,000 pengo. It was issued by the Hungarian National Bank in 1946, when inflation was so high that prices were doubling every 15 hours.

RECORD BREAKER

The **world's first ATM**
(Automated Teller Machine,
or cashpoint) was installed in
London in June 1967.

Funny money

Before money, a variety
of things were used as
payment instead:

cattle · cowrie shells · iron nails · metal armlets

tobacco leaves · wampum · whales' teeth · tea

How to: play the stock market

01. Select stock
to buy. Companies
issue stock (shares in
the company) to raise
money to enable them
to grow.

02. Owning stock in a
company means you own part of
that company. Congratulations!
Don't worry, you won't be expected
to work at the company, but you
will get a vote on important issues.

03. If the company makes a
profit, you get a share of the money
and the value of the stock goes up.

04. Decide whether
to hold on to your stock
or sell it. If the value of the
stock rises, you can sell
it to another investor for a
profit. But if the value of
the stock falls, you could
end up losing money.

A **bear market** is when
stock prices are falling.

V

A **bull market** is
when stock prices
are rising.

Key stock exchanges

country	city	index (shows the price of selected shares being traded)
Japan	Tokyo	Nikkei Average
USA	New York	Dow-Jones
UK	London	FTSE-100
Germany	Frankfurt	DAX

Note worthy

Over the ages and around the world, famous faces have adorned
banknotes and coins. Many in this list are now out of circulation.

name of person	country issued	coin or note
George Washington, US president	USA	1 dollar
William Shakespeare, playwright	United Kingdom	20 pounds
Nelson Mandela, statesman	South Africa	5 rand
Napoleon Bonaparte, emperor	France	5 francs
Albert Einstein, scientist	Israel	5 lirot
Marie Curie, scientist	Poland	20,000 zloty
Galileo Galilei, scientist	Italy	2,000 lire
Karen Blixen, writer	Denmark	50 kroner
Mahatma Gandhi, political leader	India	5,10, 20, 50, 100 rupees

Tell me more: how the economy works

BUSINESS

If a company sells its goods and services for more than they cost to produce, it makes a **profit**. If it sells for less or fails to sell, it makes a **loss**.

Companies can borrow money from banks to **invest** in developing the business. They are charged **interest** (a fixed fee) on the **loan**.

Where there are a number of different businesses producing the same product, there is **competition**. If just one company is producing a product, it has a **monopoly**.

WAGES

LABOUR

GOODS AND SERVICES

Command vs market

In a command economy, the government decides what goods and services should be produced, how many should be produced, and how they should be distributed. In a market economy, each producer makes their own decisions, but these are driven by market forces – consumer demand.

GOVERNMENT

TAXES

The government collects **business taxes** from companies and **income tax** from individuals to fund services such as education, health, law and order, social welfare, transport networks, and national defence.

EDUCATION, HEALTH CARE, LAW AND ORDER, SOCIAL WELFARE, TRANSPORT NETWORKS

Every country has a **currency**. The **exchange rate** is the amount of one country's currency needed to buy a fixed amount of another country's currency.

TAXES

PEOPLE

If the economy is doing well it is called a **boom** and there is **high employment**. When the economy goes into decline, it is in **recession** and **unemployment rises**.

EDUCATION, HEALTH CARE, LAW AND ORDER, SOCIAL WELFARE, TRANSPORT NETWORKS

What is a law?

Laws are rules that spell out how people should behave in society. Throughout history, people have devised ways of settling disputes between neighbours and punishing wrongdoers. The earliest surviving set of laws was issued by Ur-Nammu, king of Sumer (modern Iraq), about 4,000 years ago.

I don't believe it!

In the UK, many lawyers and judges wear wigs made from white horsehair. This tradition dates back to the 17th century. The wigs are very expensive to make, so judges are paid a special wig allowance!

10 fictional sleuths (who have also appeared on postage stamps)

Sherlock Holmes (Arthur Conan Doyle) Wears a deerstalker hat and lives in Baker Street

Hercule Poirot (Agatha Christie) Belgian detective with a distinctive moustache

Inspector Maigret (Simenon) French pipe-smoker

Charlie Chan (Earl Derr Biggars) – Chinese-American sleuth

Father Brown (G K Chesterton) Roman Catholic priest

Sam Spade (Dashiell Hammett) San Francisco's finest

Philip Marlowe (Raymond Chandler) Tough private eye with a penchant for poetry

Dick Tracy (Chester Gould) Fast-shooting comic book hero

Miss Marple (Agatha Christie) Prim English spinster

Inspector Clouseau (Blake Edwards) Bumbling French policeman

Blind justice

The Roman goddess Justitia (Justice) is still used as a symbol of law and order. Her statue can be seen on court buildings around the world. She wears a blindfold, and carries a sword in her right hand and a pair of weighing scales in her left.

Sword: Represents punishment

Blindfold: Symbolizes how justice is impartial

Crime categories

Against people: assault, battery, robbery, rape, kidnapping, manslaughter, murder

Against property: arson, theft, burglary, deception, vandalism

Against the state: tax evasion, espionage, treason

Against justice: obstruction of justice, bribery, perjury, malfeasance (wrongdoing by a public official)

Against international law: apartheid (racism), piracy, genocide, war crimes, slavery

WEIRD OR WHAT?

In **medieval times**, French villagers found a **pig guilty** of murdering a baby and hanged her. They **charged her six piglets** with being accessories, but let them off on grounds of youth and having a bad role model!

Most wanted

? The FBI (Federal Bureau of Investigation) posts photographs of the 10 most wanted fugitives in the USA in public buildings and on the FBI website.

? Since 1950 more than 489 fugitives have been listed, eight of whom were women.

? Occasionally, the FBI adds a "Number Eleven" if a criminal is regarded as extremely dangerous, but none of the other 10 can be removed until caught.

Puzzling case

In 2008, a drugs trial in Australia was halted after members of the jury were found playing Sudoku to pass the time – the judge thought they were taking notes!

Famous outlaws

$ Billy the Kid was a 19th-century frontier gunman

$ Bonnie and Clyde robbed their way across the USA in the early 1930s

$ Jesse James was a legendary 19th-century Wild West bandit

$ Ned Kelly was a 19th-century Australian bushranger and gang leader

$ Robin Hood was the English folklore hero who robbed the rich to feed the poor

Scales: Show how justice weighs up opposing evidence

HOLY LAW
In the Muslim world, the law is called Sharia (meaning "way" or "path"), and it derives from the holy book of the Qur'an. Religious scholars can issue formal legal rulings called fatwas.

Global forces

The United Nations (UN) Police work in some of the most dangerous and unstable places around the world.

The UN's aim is to **restore peace and order** by rebuilding local police forces and promoting fair and humane laws for all citizens.

UN police officers are drawn from more than **90 countries** around the world.

Short for the International Criminal Police Organization, **INTERPOL** is an international crime-busting organization established in 1923 and based in Lyon, France.

INTERPOL has **186 member countries**, whose police forces share information to help bring fugitives to justice across national borders.

Four famous forces

01: **The Mounties (Royal Canadian Mounted Police)** Canada's federal police force is famous for dashing red breeches and wide-brimmed hats. Their real motto is *"Maintiens le droit"* ("Uphold the law"), but the unofficial one is, "We always get our man".

02: **New York City Police Department (NYPD)** The NYPD is the largest police force in the USA, with more than 37,000 officers. It is nicknamed "New York's finest" and is portrayed in many television shows and movies.

03: **New Delhi Police** India's New Delhi Police force has nearly 58,000 officers. Its history stretches back to 1237 when a force was founded for the sultan of Delhi.

04: **Metropolitan Police** New Scotland Yard is the home of London's Metropolitan Police, founded by Sir Robert Peel in 1829.

Who's who in the law

Law makers
Countries have their own laws, which often date back a long time. New laws and changes to existing ones are usually decided and voted on by a nation's government.

Cops
The police enforce the laws by patrolling the streets and investigating crime.

Legal eagles
Lawyers present the evidence in court cases and question witnesses. Some are hired to bring charges against the accused, while others argue the case for the defence.

Hammer time
Judges preside over court proceedings and rule on the law. They sit behind a high desk and sometimes bang it with a hammer. The judge interprets the law and decides the punishment.

Final verdict
In many countries, a jury (a group of ordinary citizens) listens to evidence and decides if the accused is guilty or not.

Most popular **police dog breeds**

The usual police dog retirement age is seven years old.

German shepherd   Dutch shepherd   Belgian malinois   Labrador retriever   Springer spaniel   Bloodhound   Beagle

How many languages are there?

Give or take a few – 6,912. Some languages are used by only a few people. Others, such as Mandarin Chinese and English, are spoken by millions. Many people speak two or more languages. They may use one language at home with family and friends, and another at work or school. Regional variations of a language are known as dialects.

Linguists (people who study languages) believe the **"click" languages** of southern Africa may descend from the earliest speech used by humans. Speakers **click their tongue** fast against the roof of the mouth to make different sounds.

Under threat

One language is said to die every two weeks. Danger hotspots are:

Some endangered languages have only a single speaker left – when that person dies, the spoken language will vanish.

- **Aboriginal** languages of northern and western Australia
- **Amerindian** languages of South American Andes
- **Siberian** languages of northern Russia and China
- **Native American** languages of northwest Pacific (USA and Canada)
- **Amerindian** languages of Brazil, Paraguay, and Argentina
- **Native American** languages of southwest USA
- Languages of **New Guinea and Melanesia**

Tell me more: a fine Romance

- The term "Romance language" sounds like the language of love, but is actually derived from Latin – spoken in much of western Europe during the Roman Empire. The main Romance languages are French, Portuguese, Italian, Romanian, and Spanish.
- English is not a Romance language. The Anglo-Saxons, who conquered Britain at the end of the Roman Empire, spoke a Germanic language, which later became English. Other Germanic languages include Danish, Dutch, German, and Swedish.
- English also contains French-derived words after it was ruled by French-speaking kings following the Norman conquest.

English words with

Germanic roots		French roots	
(modern German equivalent)		(modern French equivalent)	
apple	apfel	beef	boeuf
book	buch	castle	chateau
brother	bruder	law	loi
cow	kuh	parliament	parlement
daughter	tochter	soup	soupe
house	haus	tailor	tailleur

20 ways of saying "I love you"

Ami tomay bhalo bashi (Bengali)
Bon sro lanh oon (Cambodian)
Jeg elsker dig (Danish)
Ik hou van jou (Dutch)
Je t'aime (French)
Hoon tane pyar karoo choon (Gujarati)
Ich liebe dich (German)
Kimi o ai shiteru (Japanese)
Mahal kita (Tagalog)
Mina rakastan sinua (Finnish)
Muhje tumse mohabbat hai (Urdu)
Rwy'n dy garu di (Welsh)
S'agapo (Greek)
Szeretlek (Hungarian)
Taim I'ngra leat (Irish)
Te quiero (Spanish)
Ti amo (Italian)
Tora dust midaram (Farsi)
Wo le ni (Chinese)
Ya vas liubliu (Russian)

Invented languages

Esperanto

Polish linguist **Ludwig Lazarus Zamenhof** came up with Esperanto in 1887. Supposed to be a universal language, it never really took off.

Elvish

Lord of the Rings author **JRR Tolkien** invented Elvish languages for his mythological creation of Middle Earth.

Klingon

Linguist **Marc Okrand** devised Klingon for the *Star Trek* television series. Klingon even has its own dictionary!

Record breakers

☺ The Pacific island of Papua New Guinea has **more languages** than any other country – 832 languages for a population of only 3.9 million.

☺ South Africa has the **most official languages** – 11. An official language has legal status within a country, which means it is used for government business and in the law courts. Many countries have several official languages.

☺ Khmer, the official language of Cambodia, has the **largest alphabet** with 74 letters.

English language

English is an official language in 48 countries, although funnily enough not in the UK and USA, where it is the first language but does not have legal status!

SUPERCALIFRAGILISTEXPIALIDOCIOUS

(invented for the movie *Mary Poppins*) is one of the longest words in the English dictionary, checking in at a whopping 34 letters!

Donaudampfschiffahrtselektrizitätenhauptbetriebswerkbauunterbeamtengesellschaft is a record-breaker from Germany at 79 letters! Don't ask for details, but it has something to do with the management of a steamship company on the River Danube.

Top 10 languages in the world

01: Chinese Mandarin
1,120 million speakers, mostly in China, Malaysia, Taiwan, and Singapore

02: English
510 million speakers, mostly in USA, UK, Australia, Canada, and New Zealand

03: Hindi
490 million speakers, mostly in India

04: Spanish
425 million speakers, mostly in South and Central America, USA, and Spain

05: Arabic
255 million speakers, mostly in the Middle East, Arabia, and northern Africa

06: Russian
254 million speakers, mostly in Russia and Central Asia

07: Portuguese
218 million speakers, mostly in Brazil, Portugal, and southern Africa

08: Bengali
215 million speakers, mostly in Bangladesh and northern India

09: Malay/Indonesian
175 million speakers, mostly in Indonesia, Malaysia, and Singapore

10: French
130 million speakers, mostly in France, Canada, western and central Africa

Why are books important?

They feed our imagination, amuse and inform us, and introduce us to new ways of understanding the world. Most of human knowledge is recorded in books.

Tell me more: printing in the past

The Chinese invented printing. The world's oldest printed book is a copy of the *Diamond Sutra* – one of Buddhism's most sacred texts – which was printed in China in 868 BCE.

Printing didn't take off in China, though, because the Chinese script has thousands of different characters.

Johann Gutenberg of Germany came up with the idea of the "printing press" in about 1450.

The printing press could produce books quickly and in multiple copies – a technological breakthrough that has been compared to the invention of the Internet.

The first book printed was the Bible.

Record breaker

The oldest book in the world dates from 2,500 years ago. It is six pages of gold, hinged together at the top and written in ancient Etruscan – a language no one can read today.

The most expensive book ever sold at auction is the *Codex Leicester* – the manuscript (handwritten) notebooks of Renaissance genius Leonardo da Vinci. It was bought by Microsoft founder Bill Gates for US$30.8 million in 1994.

A copy of James Audubon's *Birds of America* sold for $8.8 million in 2000, making it the world's most expensive printed book.

Do books have a future?

Some people have suggested that the **Internet** threatens the long-term survival of books, as more and more works can be **downloaded**. But books still have many **advantages**: they are more **easily read** than a screen, are good to handle, and can be taken almost* **anywhere** – don't write them off yet.

* until someone invents waterproof books!

What is an ISBN?

An **International Standard Book Number** – a 13-digit number that is printed at the front of **every book** to show where it was published. In this book you'll find the **ISBN on page two**.

ISBN 978-1-40533-732-8

9 781405 337328

10 great children's authors

These authors sold more than 100 million copies of their books.

Enid Blyton
Wrote many popular series such as *Noddy* and the *Famous Five*

Dr Seuss
Author of imaginative rhyming tales, such as *The Cat in the Hat*

JK Rowling
Wrote the immensely popular *Harry Potter* magical adventures

RL Stine
Thrilled many with his horror stories, such as the *Goosebumps* series

CS Lewis
Authored the fantasy novels that made up *The Chronicles of Narnia*

JRR Tolkein
Wrote *The Hobbit*, followed by the *Lord of the Rings* sequel

Beatrix Potter
Wrote 23 small books about animal characters, such as Peter Rabbit

Best sellers

The best-selling book of all time is the Bible, followed by the collected works of Chinese communist leader Mao Zedong.

The world's best-selling novel is thought to be Charles Dickens's *Tale of Two Cities*.

The best-selling book in French is *Le Petit Prince* (The Little Prince) by Antoine de Saint-Exupéry.

The best-selling practical book is *Scouting for Boys* by Robert Baden-Powell, founder of the international scout movement.

In numbers

The Library of Congress in Washington, DC, is the largest library in the world.

853 km (530 miles) The total length of all the bookshelves in the library

32 million The number of books in the library

470 How many different languages the books are written in

2.7 million The total number of recordings stored in the library

13 million The number of photographs

4.5 million How many maps there are

61 million The number of manuscripts in the library

Comic capers

Manga are highly popular **Japanese comic books**, or graphic novels.

Manga is a huge business in Japan – worth about **US$4.4 billion** a year.

Manga is not just for sci-fi and fantasy geeks – you'll see businessmen, schoolchildren, and housewives reading manga books on all kinds of subjects from **sports** and **historical fiction** to **romance** and **cookery**.

Animated game and **movie versions** of manga stories have boosted their popularity around the world.

Comic books in France and Belgium are known as **Bandes Dessinées** (BDs).

The Nobel Prize for Literature, founded in 1901, is given for outstanding work in the field of literature in any language. Moody French philosopher Jean-Paul Sartre is the only person known to have declined it.

WEIRD OR WHAT?

With nanotechnology (engineering on a molecular scale) you can create **books smaller than a grain of salt**. A book called *Teeny Ted from Turnip Town*, made in 2007 at Simon Fraser University, Canada, measures 0.07 x 0.1 mm (0.0027 x 0.0004 in). The only way to read it is with an electron microscope at 8,000 times magnification.

Potty about Potter

The *Harry Potter* series has sold 400 million copies and been translated into 65 languages.

Harry Potter and the Deathly Hallows, the seventh and last book of the series, sold 11 million copies in 24 hours – an all-time record.

JK Rowling penned the final words of the series in Room 652 of the Balmoral Hotel, Edinburgh.

An original copy (where only 500 were printed) of *Harry Potter and the Philosopher's Stone* sold for US$40,355.

16,700 tonnes of paper were used for the first printing of *Harry Potter and the Deathly Hallows*.

JK Rowling dreamed up the names of the Hogwarts houses while flying, and scribbled them on the back of an aeroplane sickbag.

The initials "JK" stand for Joanne Kathleen.

Fact or fiction

Books come in two types:

fact books that tell you about real things, like this one

fiction books, which are made-up stories, or novels

Richard Scarry
Wrote and illustrated many books, such as *Best Word Book Ever*

Roald Dahl
Became a bestseller with novels like *Charlie and the Chocolate Factory*

Roger Hargreaves
Created the *Mr Men* and *Little Miss* books, carried on by his son (pictured)

Who wrote the first play?

Five famous theatres

01: **Amazon Theatre, Manaus, Brazil** This grand Italian opera house has an unusual location – in the middle of the Brazilian rainforest.

02: **Epidauros Theatre, Epidauros, Greece** A stunning ancient theatre where you can see classical Greek tragedies performed today.

03: **Sydney Opera House, Sydney, Australia** An iconic Australian landmark on Sydney Harbour that opened in 1973.

04: **Ford's Theatre, Washington DC, USA** President Abraham Lincoln was fatally shot here during a performance of *Our American Cousin* in 1865.

05: **Globe Theatre, London, UK** This replica open-air Elizabethan theatre is built on the site of the original Globe theatre where Shakespeare's plays were first performed.

People have been going to the theatre to watch plays (stories performed by actors) for thousands of years. The Ancient Greeks were the first to write these plays down. They performed "tragedies" in which characters come to a sticky end, and "comedies" in which characters make audiences laugh.

How to: **stage a play**

01. Select a play to perform and hold auditions to cast the right person for each role.

02. Ensure the cast learns the lines of the script and hold plenty of rehearsals.

03. Appoint people to create the costumes and build the stage scenery.

04. Publicize the play to make sure you get a big audience coming along to watch.

Speak up!

The Ancient Greeks built open-air theatres consisting of rows of stone seats rising one above the other. They were designed so that sound would travel, allowing people sitting at the top to hear every word spoken by the actors on the circular stage. There were no microphones in those days!

I don't believe it!

In silent plays, called mimes, actors tell the stories using only facial expressions and movements of the hands and body. The French mime artist Marcel Marceau made audiences believe he was trapped in a room or taming a lion without saying a word.

Theatre don'ts

✗ **Never say the word "Macbeth".** Actors believe saying it will bring bad luck. Instead, they always call William Shakespeare's play "the Scottish play".

✗ **Never accept flowers before a performance.** Receiving flowers before a play begins is regarded as a bad omen. Don't worry afterwards though – it is a lucky sign to be given flowers after the performance.

✗ **Never wish a fellow actor good luck.** Instead, tell them to "break a leg", although nobody is quite sure why.

06. It is opening night, so take a bow and enjoy the standing ovation. This show could run and run!

05. Hold a final dress rehearsal to run through the script and perfect the performance.

10 longest-running Broadway shows

01: *The Phantom of the Opera* January 1988–present

02: *Cats* October 1982–September 2000

03: *Les Misérables* March 1987–May 2003

04: *A Chorus Line* July 1975–April 1990

05: *Oh Calcutta!* September 1976–August 1989

06: *Beauty and the Beast* September 1976–August 1989

07: *Chicago* September 1976–August 1989

08: *Rent* April 1996–September 2008

09: *The Lion King* November 1997–present

10: *Miss Saigon* April 1991–January 2001

Theatre forms

Plays are stage performances in which actors act out stories

Operas are plays in which the actors sing all the words

Ballets are plays where the story is told through music and graceful dance techniques

Musicals are popular shows packed with singing and dancing

Noh is an old form of Japanese theatre, in which actors retell traditional stories

Kabuki is another form of Japanese theatre, performed only by men

Worldwide Will

William Shakespeare (1564–1616) was an English poet and playwright. Considered by many to be the greatest playwright of all time, his poems and plays have been translated into many languages and are popular all over the world. He was a master of both tragedies and comedies.

Famous Shakespearean tragedies
Romeo and Juliet
Hamlet
Othello
King Lear
Macbeth

Famous Shakespearean comedies
A Midsummer Night's Dream
The Merchant of Venice
The Merry Wives of Windsor
As You Like It
Twelfth Night

RECORD BREAKER

The Mousetrap, a play by murder–mystery writer Agatha Christie has been showing in London since 1952 – more than 55 years!

How do we spend free time?

People have found ways of relaxing and enjoying leisure time since history began. Some of the games we still play today have ancient origins, but the media and technology boom of the 20th century brought a rush of new entertainments and pastimes, with the spread of popular newspapers, cinema, recorded music, radio, television, and computer games.

INTERNET BOOM

The Internet is huge and still growing. It would take about 300 years to index all the current Web pages.

SQUARE EYES

People in the USA watch 250 billion hours of television a year, and two out of three households own three or more television sets.

Ancient games

Mancala
The oldest game in the world, played with stones or shells placed in a series of holes.

Go
A 5,000-year-old Chinese strategy game with black and white playing pieces called "stones".

Senet
A board game enjoyed by the Egyptian pharaohs (kings). Tutankhamun was buried with senet boards.

Knucklebones
Popular in Greece and Rome; players toss bones in the air and catch them on the back of their hands.

Chess
A popular board game that originated in India about 2,000 years ago.

FAST FACTS

- Early computer games ran on university computers. The first was *SpaceWar!* (1962).
- Atari developed home video games in the 1970s. The first, *Pong*, sold 150,000 copies.
- *Pokémon Red, Blue,* and *Green* is the highest selling computer game (20 million copies), followed by *Super Mario Bros 3* (18 million).
- Nintendo's console Wii is the fastest selling console of all time.

Blasts from the past

713 BCE First newspaper printed in China
1605 First newspaper printed in Europe
1880 First photograph in a newspaper
1895 Lumière brothers stage the first commercial screening of a film
1920 The first commercial radio station goes on air in Pittsburgh, USA
1936 BBC launches television service
1951 Colour television in the USA
1954 First transistor radio
1958 Hollywood Walk of Fame opens, studded with stars bearing the names of celebrities
1990 World Wide Web is launched
1994 First online newspapers
1994 First Internet café opens
2001 First podcast

NEWSPAPER INVENTOR

Julius Caesar was first with the news with his *Acta Diurna* ("Daily Acts") – large boards on which information about military victories, coming events, or major trials were displayed in Rome.

Best-selling newspapers, by country

Yomuiri Shimbun
Japan: 14 million

Das Bild
Germany: 3.8 million

Canako Xiaoxi
China: 2.6 million

The Sun
UK: 2.4 million

Chosun Ilbo
South Korea: 2.3 million

USA Today
USA: 2.3 million

Dainik Jagran
India: 1.9 million

Liberty Times
Taiwan: 1.3 million

Thai Rath
Thailand: 1.2 million

Al-Ahram
Egypt: 900,000

Top 10 countries
with the most cinema-goers

01: India 3,591,000,000
02: USA 1,402,700,000
03: France 175,700,000
04: Mexico 165,000,000
05: UK 164,700,000
06: Japan 160,500,000
07: South Korea 143,000,000
08: China 138,000,000
09: Germany 127,300,000
10: Spain 126,000,000

Gem of a gadget

Russian-Canadian millionaire Alex Schnaider owns the world's most expensive MP3 player. Made of 18 carat gold adorned with diamonds, it was a snip at US$20,000!

Heavyweight read
The Sunday edition of the *New York Times* for 14 September 1987 contained 1,612 pages and weighed 5.4 kg (12 lb)!

Radio first

The human voice was first heard on the radio on 24 December 1906. Canadian radio pioneer Reginald Fessenden sang *Oh Holy Night* during a Christmas broadcast to radio operators at sea in the Atlantic.

WHAT'S IN A NAME?

The Academy of Motion Picture Arts and Sciences held its first award ceremony, the **Oscars**, in 1928. Librarian Margaret Herrick gave the Academy – she said the winners' statue for her famous nickname for the reminded her of her Uncle Oscar! her Uncle Oscar!

TELEVISION RECORD BREAKERS

- ☐ *Meet the Press*, a news show, has appeared weekly on US television since 1947.
- ☐ The longest-running soap opera is *Guiding Light*, shown on US television since 1952. It began originally as a radio serial in 1937, making it more than 70 years old.
- ☐ The oldest sports show is *Hockey Night in Canada*, running since 1952.
- ☐ The UK's *Blue Peter* is the longest running children's show, begining in 1958.

What is art?

Art is paintings, sculptures, and a whole lot more. Artists today work with all kinds of media and materials – video clips, computer graphics, piles of bricks, driftwood, old car parts. Art is what the artist says it is. The aim is to make the viewer think and reflect on life and… well… art.

I don't believe it!

It weighs 200 tonnes, is the height of four double-decker buses, and is almost as wide as a Jumbo jet. The *Angel of the North*, a giant steel sculpture by Anthony Gormley stands beside a busy road in northeast England. It is 20 m (65 ft) high and has a wingspan of 54 m (175 ft).

Wall art

You think graffiti art was invented by Banksy? Think again. It's one of the oldest art forms. The Italian word *graffiti* means "scratched", and the first graffiti artists were busy chipping patterns on rocks and pebbles 30,000 years ago. In the 1970s, graffiti got its modern meaning of spray-painted tags on urban buildings.

Some weird and wacky ideas

- Smear your body with honey and fish oil and wait for the swarms of flies (Zhang Huan)
- Put tins of your poo on show (Piero Manzoni)
- Cut a cow and calf in half (Damien Hurst)
- Exhibit your unmade bed and filthy knickers (Tracy Emin)
- Use dried elephant poo in your paintings (Chris Ofili)
- Freeze nine pints of your blood and use it to make a life-size cast of your head (Mark Quinn)

WEIRD OR WHAT?

Vincent van Gogh felt so bad about threatening fellow artist Paul Gauguin with a razor that he cut off part of his own ear. Then he painted a portrait of himself with a bandage around his head.

10 women artists

Until very recently art has been a man's world. These women artists did make it to the top.

Artemisia Gentileschi Italian painter of the 1600s. Specialized in large pictures of heroic women

Elisabeth Louise Vigée-Lebrun French portrait painter; she painted Queen Marie Antoinette who later lost her head (no connection, apparently)

Rosa Bonheur French 19th-century artist known for her animal sculptures and paintings; she liked to dress as a man

Berthe Morisot French Impressionist. The artist Eduard Manet, her brother-in-law, painted a famous portrait of her looking very gloomy

Mary Cassatt American 19th-century artist admired for her sensitive studies of women and children

Grandma Moses Won fame for her folksy paintings of life down on the American farm when she was 80. It's never too late!

Käthe Kollwitz German artist and sculptor haunted by the death and suffering of World War I

Georgia O'Keeffe Pioneering figure in American 20th-century art noted for her paintings of flowers and buildings

Barbara Hepworth English sculptor of abstract works in wood, stone, and metal. She died in a fire in her studio

Frida Kahlo Mexican artist known for her stormy life and for brilliantly coloured paintings

So you want to be an art buff

Impressionism
Began in Paris during the 1860s, with artists painting glimpses of outdoor scenes

Post-impressionism
20th-century developments in French art

Cubism
Abstract paintings with squares and cubes

Fauvism
Artistic preference for strong, bright colours

Expressionism
Exploring feelings and emotions in paintings

Dadaism
Anti-war artists expressing their outrage

Constructivism
Using everyday items in abstract art

Surrealism
Exploring the mind by creating fantasy art

Postmodernism
Giving up on all previous "isms" and experimenting with new types of art

What was Pop Art?

A 1960s movement that turned everyday objects like soup cans and comic strips into cultural icons. Many of its images came from the world of entertainment – like the famous print of Marilyn Monroe by Andy Warhol.

Great art robberies

Most casual art theft
$ In 1911, a thief took Leonardo da Vinci's *Mona Lisa* off the wall of the Louvre in Paris, France, tucked it under his coat and strolled out. It was missing for two years.

Biggest art haul
$ Thirteen artworks worth a total of US$500 million were snatched from the Isabella Stewart Gardner Museum, Boston, USA, in 1990. They are still missing.

Most prolific art thief
$ In 2005, French waiter Stéphane Breitwieser admitted to stealing 239 artworks, said to be worth a total of US$1.4 billion, over a 10-year period.

Most stolen painting
$ Dutch painter Rembrandt's *Portrait of Jacob de Gheyn*, a picture of a man wearing a ruff, has been snatched four times. It has turned up in a taxi, in the luggage rack of a train, under a bench in a graveyard, and on the back of a bicycle.

Most exciting recovery
$ Edvard Munch's masterpiece *The Scream*, seized from the National Gallery in Oslo during Norway's Winter Olympics in 1994, was recovered in a potato cellar three months later after a dramatic sting operation.

Flat out

Contrary to popular belief **Michelangelo** did not paint the magnificent ceiling of the **Sistine Chapel** lying flat on his back – he crouched on a platform jutting out from the walls. The work took him four painful years.

It's a wrap

Avant-garde artists Christo and his wife Jeanne-Claude like to think big. Among their favourite large-scale projects is wrapping huge structures in fabric. In the past they have covered the Reichstag parliament building in Berlin, Germany (pictured), and Pont Neuf bridge in Paris, France.

How do musicians know what notes to play?

When composing a piece of music, the composer writes down all the notes that each of the instruments will play – this is known as the score. The way the notes are written down indicates how high or low, fast or slow they should be played. Special instructions in Italian give the players more information.

Musical instructions

adagio
slow, restful

allegro
lively, fast

andante
at a moderate pace

appassionato
with passion

crescendo
getting louder

forte
loud

legato
smoothly

maestoso
majestic

piano
soft

presto
very fast

prestissimo
very, very fast

rallentando
slowing down

scherzando
humorously

strepitoso
noisy, boisterous

How to: **sing like a superstar**

01. Before you even start singing it is important to relax and stand with your feet shoulder width apart.

02. Breathing properly is crucial. Learn to inhale from the belly up. When you exhale, let the air come out rather than forcing it – imagine there is a candle in front of you and you are trying not to blow it out.

In the past, people made drums, rattles, and whistles out of **wood, seeds, and animal hide**. Simple flutes have been found that are between 22,000 and 35,000 years old. They were made by boring a series of holes into a **hollow animal bone** and blowing down it.

Beyond the grave

These dead musicians are still raking it in...

Elvis Presley
Died 1977
US$49 million
(earnings in 2007)

John Lennon
Died 1980
US$44 million
(earnings in 2007)

George Harrison
Died 2001
US$22 million
(earnings in 2007)

Tupac Shakur
Died 1996
US$9 million
(earnings in 2007)

James Brown
Died 2006
US$5 million
(earnings in 2007)

Types of music

classical · country · jazz · hip hop · latin · rap · reggae · R&B · rock · blues · pop · soul · world · folk · opera · disco · metal · punk · reggae · ska · dance and techno

03. Once you have chosen a song you love (or something you have written), try to sing by making the sound resonate from your cheeks and the roof of your mouth.

WHAT'S IN A NAME?

As Slow as Possible is the appropriate name of a piece of music written by American composer John Cage. The performance, which is being played on a church organ in Germany, started in 2001 and is due to finish in 2639!

04. Practice makes perfect. Do this by standing in front of a mirror and try not to laugh at the faces you find yourself pulling as you sing. Soon you will be performing in front of thousands of adoring fans.

Weird or what?

The **thermin** is an electronic musical instrument that is **played without even touching it**. To play, you must move your hands around various antennas to control the pitch and volume. The instrument generates an eerie sound, which makes it perfect for use in thriller movie soundtracks.

Bob Marley
Died 1981
US$4 million
(earnings in 2007)

88
The number of keys on a piano (36 black and 52 white)

1982
The year compact discs were introduced

US$164,930
The amount a Led Zeppelin fan paid for two tickets for the group's 2007 reunion concert in London

US$3.5 million
The sum paid at a Christie's auction in 2006 for a rare 300-year-old violin made by Stradivarius

1.7 billion
Digital music downloads in 2007

Bum notes

The worst singer ever must be Florence Jenkins Foster who gave recitals to fashionable audiences in New York in the 1930s despite her inability to hold a note. She claimed she could reach top F (that's really high) after being involved in an accident in a taxicab. You can hear her murdering Mozart on YouTube.

William Hung was a contestant on the US television programme *American Idol*. His audition was noteworthy for all the wrong reasons, but it did land him an album deal.

Top ten best-selling albums ever

01: *Thriller*
Michael Jackson 1982
65 million Pop/R&B

02: *Back in Black*
AC/DC 1980
42 million Rock

03: *The Bodyguard*
Whitney Houston 1992
42 million Pop/R&B

04: *Greatest Hits*
Eagles 1976
41 million Rock

05: *Saturday Night Fever*
Bee Gees/various 1977
40 million Disco

06: *Dark Side of the Moon*
Pink Floyd 1973
40 million Rock

07: *Bat Out of Hell*
Meat Loaf 1977
37 million Rock

08: *Come on Over*
Shania Twain 1997
36 million Country

09: *Sgt. Pepper's Lonely Hearts Club Band* Beatles 1967
32 million Rock/Pop

10: *Falling into You*
Celine Dion 1996
32 million Pop

World music

bagpipes *Scottish*

mbira *Southern African*

sitar *Indian*

didgeridoo *Aboriginal Australian*

shaman's rattle *Native American*

tubular bells

02

xylophone

flute

timpani

piccolo

01

violin

06

Tell me more: **anatomy of an orchestra**

01 At the heart of the orchestra, the **string family** makes up the largest part. Played with a bow or by "plucking", they usually lead the way through a musical piece.

02 Comprising anything that makes a noise when struck, the **percussion family** is known as the "kitchen department" and includes both tuned instruments, like the xylophone, and untuned instruments, such as cymbals.

03 With many of its instruments originally made from wood, the **woodwind family** today is a clan of plastic, silver, and gold versions. They mostly make their sound when the player blows against a reed (thin piece of wood) in the mouthpiece.

04 The instruments of the **brass family**, such as the trumpet and trombone, produce a distinctive sound made by the vibration of the players' lips as they blow into their instruments.

05 **Keyboards** include the piano and its relatives, as well as the electronic synthesizer, which can make a variety of weird and wonderful sounds. It stands apart from the rest of the orchestra in producing sounds digitally rather than acoustically.

06 Standing on a raised platform waving a baton to keep time, the **conductor** directs the orchestra through the musical piece. All members of the orchestra must be able to see the conductor for guidance and prompts.

piano

05

drums

french horn

03

oboe

synthesizer

clarinet

viola

bassoon

trombone

04

trumpet

tuba

cello

double bass

Ways to be a good sport

Grrr... it's easy to fly off the handle playing a game. A tricky opponent, a disappointing performance, or a suspicion of cheating can all add fuel to the fire. Show what a good sport you are with these top tips.

01 Learn the rules of the game, so you know what's right and wrong.

02 Listen to your coach so you can improve your game.

03 Shake hands with your opponents and the referee before and after the game.

04 Be prepared to sit out a game so a teammate can have a go, even if you're the star player.

05 Don't show off. Just play your best and people will notice you.

06 Don't cheat or blame your teammates when decisions are not going your way.

07 Keep a clear head. Congratulate your teammates and opponents on their performance, regardless of the outcome.

Tribal traditions

Many rugby teams from the southern hemisphere don war paint and perform traditional dances to prepare themselves and intimidate their opponents before big international matches.

Pelé
Scoring 77 goals for his country (a national record), the legendary Brazilian is regarded as football's perfect player.

Michael Jordan
The US basketball star had an incredible scoring rate and defensive record during the 1980s and 1990s.

Babe Ruth
Playing for 20 years from 1914, Babe Ruth is the most celebrated baseball player in US history.

Jonah Lomu
In 1994, New Zealand rugby player Jonah Lomu became the youngest player for the All Blacks aged 19.

Sporting **superstars**

What game do 250 million people play?

Football. From streets to stadiums, the beautiful game is played all over the world. It's a sport that everyone understands – kick a ball, score a goal. Whether it's hit, struck, passed, or caught, a ball is at the heart of many of the most popular sports. Even those that don't involve a ball still revolve around fixed rules and physical effort. Ready to play?

How to: **serve an ace**

04. Push up with your legs and roll your right shoulder forward to hit the ball.

01. Stand sideways behind the baseline and throw the tennis ball up above you.

The most popular sports could mean most watched, most played, or most revenue-generating. This list considers all three factors, with football topping the charts for all of them.

01: football
02: cricket
03: tennis
04: hockey
05: baseball
06: basketball
07: volleyball
08: table tennis
09: rugby
10: golf

Top ten most popular **sports worldwide**

Cathy Freeman
Australian sprinter Cathy Freeman won gold in the 400m race at the Olympic and Commonwealth Games, and World Championships.

Martina Navratilova
Czech-born Martina Navratilova won 59 tennis titles (18 singles, 31 doubles, and 10 mixed doubles).

Ellen MacArthur
This British yachtswoman broke the world record for fastest solo circumnavigation of the globe in 2005.

Jack Nicklaus
Known as "Golden bear", this US golfer won a record-breaking 18 titles in a career spanning 25 years.

Odd origins

Tennis
French monks first played tennis in about the 11th century. The name "tennis" means "take this" in French, which the monks would shout as they served the ball.

Table tennis
This sport began in Victorian England, when dinner guests turned their tables into mini tennis courts and used their champagne corks as balls.

Croquet
During the 14th century, French peasants used wooden mallets to whack a wooden ball through hoops of bent branches.

Basketball
This game was first played using peach baskets on poles for hoops. If a team scored, the referee climbed a ladder to get the ball.

Bizarre sporting terms

SILLY
A fielder who stands very close to the batter in cricket.

DR IBBLING
Running with a football under close control, mainly using the outside and top of the foot.

SPIKE
When a beach volleyball player jumps above the net to smash the ball hard at the ground.

LOVE
A zero-point score in a tennis game.

BIRDIE, EAGLE, ALBATROSS
These golfing terms refer to the par (standard number of golf strokes) for each hole. "Birdie" means a score of one stroke under par, "eagle" means a score of two strokes under par, and "albatross" is a very rare three strokes under par.

Sound idea
In 2008, the first blind tennis tournament was held in the UK. A bell inside the tennis ball helps the players keep track of it during rallies, while tactile lines around the court assist them in finding their way.

I don't believe it!
The only sport to be played on the Moon is golf. In 1971, Apollo 14's US astronaut Alan Shepard landed on the lunar surface and struck two golf balls. He described the balls as going for "miles and miles and miles!"

02. Raise your racket and start to swing.

03. While bending the knees, drop the racket behind your back.

05. Snap your wrist down and smash your racket against the ball, generating as much speed as possible.

06. Watch the ball fly past your helpless opponent and enjoy your first ace (unreturnable serve)!

In numbers

0.3
The time, in seconds, that it takes a volleyball to travel from one baseline of the court to the other when served by a top player at a speed of 194 kph (121 mph)

1
The total number of paying spectators at the Olympic croquet final in 1900, the first and last time the sport was played at the Games

8
The number of left-handed tennis players to have won a Wimbledon singles title

152
The highest margin in an international rugby match, when Argentina beat Paraguay 152–0 in 2002

173
The number of hits during one 60-second table tennis rally between two female players in 1973

259 kph
(155 mph) The fastest recorded tennis serve, delivered by Andy Roddick at the UK's Stella Artois Championships in 2004

501
The highest ever individual score in a cricket match, made by Brian Lara for Warwickshire in 1994

2,666
The number of strokes in a single squash rally, recorded in the UK in 2004

199,854
How many spectators watched the 1950 World Cup game between Brazil and Uruguay, the highest official attendance at a football match

5 million
Football officials worldwide

20 million
Netball players worldwide

1 billion
The average global audience for football's World Cup final

How to: **win the decathlon**

The decathlon consists of 10 track and field events. It is held over two days and the winner is the athlete with the highest total points across all 10 events. Decathlon contests are open to male athletes. Female athletes compete in the heptathlon, which has seven different sports: 100 metres hurdles, high jump, shot put, javelin, 200 metres, long jump, and 800 metres. Ready, set, go!

Decathlon events

- ☺ 100 metres
- ☺ long jump
- ☺ shot put
- ☺ high jump
- ☺ 400 metres
- ☺ 110 metres hurdles
- ☺ discus
- ☺ pole vault
- ☺ javelin
- ☺ 1,500 metres

Event 1: 100 metres sprint

01. Wear an aerodynamic body suit and very light shoes.

02. Position yourself on the starting blocks. Crouch on one knee with your feet on the pedals of the blocks.

03. With your hands slightly more than shoulder width apart, place your fingers on the track.

04. At the command of "set", push your feet back firmly against the pedals of the blocks.

05. Raise your hips higher than your shoulders.

06. On the starter's gun, explode out of the blocks. Pump your arms, keep your eyes on the track, and run as fast as you can until you cross the finish line.

Event 2: long jump

01. Run as fast as you can down the approach runway.

02. When you reach the take-off board (a white strip in the runway), jump!

03. Move your legs and arms in a rapid cycling motion to maintain an upright body position.

04. Land feet first in the sand pit, leaning forwards to prevent losing distance by falling backwards into the pit.

Event 6: 110 metre hurdles

01. Sprint towards the first hurdle. As you approach, raise the knee on your leading leg.

02. As you jump, the knee on the leading leg should be in line with the centre of your body and the trailing leg kept low to minimize the height of the leap so your speed is not affected.

03. Pull your trailing leg down as quickly as possible when your heel crosses the hurdle.

04. On landing, the trailing leg should go straight into the running stride.

Event 7: discus

01. Grip the discus with the tips of your fingers and your palm resting on top, and extend your throwing arm behind you. Rotate your torso to set a throwing rhythm.

02. Spin around one and a half times from the back of the circle to the front, shifting your body weight from foot to foot.

03. Release the discus at shoulder level. As it spins into the distance, continue to turn your body to avoid overstepping the boundary.

Event 8: pole vault

01. Grasp the pole at one end and hold it aloft. Run up to the crossbar and lower the pole as you approach.

02. Plant the pole in the box in front of the crossbar. The pole will bend as you lever yourself over the crossbar.

03. As you descend, push the pole away so it does not knock down the crossbar.

Event 3: shot put

01. Stand in the throwing circle. Face away from the direction of the throw (the white board marks at the front of the throwing circle), tuck the shot (a heavy metal ball) between your neck and shoulders, and crouch.

02. Shift your weight from right to left side and then spin on the ball of the left foot. Your left arm should come forward and point in the direction you want to throw.

03. Keeping your left side braced, release the shot. Aim to throw it further than any of your competitors.

Event 4: high jump

01. Make a curved run up to the high jump and launch yourself upwards. Twist your legs, hips, and shoulders as you ascend.

02. As you reach the horizontal bar, arch your body backwards and propel yourself over the bar head-first.

03. As your body crosses the bar, flex your hips to bring your legs up and over.

04. Land shoulder first on the cushioned landing area.

Event 5: 400 metres

01. Take up your position on the starting block, following the top tips recommended in the 100 metres sprint.

02. At the sound of the starter's gun, start running, and be sure to stay in your lane for the entire race.

03. This distance is exactly one lap on a standard running track, so pace yourself and build up to your fantastically fast finish!

04. The crossbar height is raised after every round and the winner is the competitor who clears the highest crossbar.

Event 9: javelin

01. Hold the javelin over your shoulder and, as you near the throwing line as you run down the track, cross your legs in preparation for the ultimate throw.

02. Untwist your legs as you reach the throwing line and pull your throwing arm backwards.

03. Thrust the throwing arm forward and release the javelin. The person who throws the javelin the furthest is the winner.

Event 10: 1,500 metres

01. Start running. After the first curve, leave your lane and move towards the inside lane so you can compete for pole position with the other competitors.

02. Stay behind the front runner for as long as possible – they take the full brunt of wind resistance.

03. When you are ready, make a break for the finish line and start accelerating.

Who was the first Olympic champion?

The first Olympic Games were held in Greece in 776 BCE. There was only one event – a sprint of 200 m (600 ft) in which the competitors ran naked! The winning runner was a male cook called Koroibos. The prize for athletes back then, along with great fame, was a wreath of olive leaves and a statue of them placed at Olympia. The modern Olympic Games take place every four years with (fully dressed) competitors from all around the world.

Olympic greats

Lucius An ancient stone records the achievements of this Roman athlete who competed "in all the athletic festivals in a manner worthy of victory".

Jesse Owens At the 1936 Olympics, this US athlete won gold in four events and his long jump world record was held for more than 25 years.

Tanni Grey-Thompson One of the greatest Olympic paralympians, this UK athlete competed in a wheelchair, winning 16 medals, including 11 golds.

Nadia Comaneci In 1976, this 14-year-old Romanian became the first Olympic gymnast to score a perfect 10.0.

Steve Redgrave This British rower picked up five golds in the 1980s, 1990s, and 2000, with all his medals won as part of a team.

Raisa Smetanina In the 1980s, this Russian skier became the first woman in history to win ten winter Olympic medals.

Michael Phelps This US swimmer has won 14 golds, more than any Olympian in history. He holds the record for most golds from a single Olympics, winning eight at the Beijing Games in 2008.

SINCE 1928, OLYMPIC MEDALS HAVE FEATURED THE SAME DESIGN ON THE FRONT.

ribbon

Olympic rings

colosseum of ancient Athens

Greek goddess

The Olympic gold medals are actually sterling silver, covered with a very thin coat of gold.

WHAT'S IN A NAME?

Gymnasium comes from the Greek word gymnos, which means "**school for naked exercise**". The original Olympians did just this, whipping their clothes off to strut their stuff in a range of challenges and competitions.

FAST FACTS

On your marks

01: An **electronic gun** sound generator is used to start races. When the trigger is pulled, a signal is passed to the **sound generator**, which produces a sound and transmits it by cable to a loudspeaker in the back of each competitor's starting block.

02: Electronic starting blocks can distinguish between an athlete's unintentional movement and a **false start**.

03: At the finish line, athletes can be timed to within a thousandth of a second using a **split-video photo-finish system**. An image of the athletes is shown on monitors for judges to study. They can move a cursor over each athlete and read the time from a scale.

In numbers

0 The number of female competitors at the first modern Olympic Games

4 How many years between each Olympics

5 The number of rings on the Olympic logo. They represent the five competing continents – counting North and South America as one continent, and not counting Antarctica as there are no events for penguins – yet

10 The age of the youngest Olympic competitor – Greek gymnast Dimitrios Loundras who competed in Athens in 1896

72 The age of the oldest Olympic medal winner – Swedish shooter Oscar Swahn won silver in 1920

205 How many nations are eligible to qualify

3.5 billion The global television audience of the Olympics, the world's largest broadcast event, made up of people from 220 countries

Summer sports include:
- archery ▪ athletics
- badminton ▪ baseball
- basketball ▪ boxing ▪ canoeing
- cycling ▪ decathlon ▪ diving
- fencing ▪ field hockey ▪ football
- gymnastics ▪ handball
- horseriding ▪ judo ▪ modern
pentathlon ▪ rowing ▪ sailing
- shooting ▪ softball ▪ swimming
- tennis ▪ table tennis
- triathlon ▪ volleyball
- water polo

Winter sports include:
- alpine skiing ▪ bobsleighing
- cross-country skiing ▪ curling
- figure skating ▪ freestyle skiing
- ice skating ▪ luge ▪ short-track
speed skating ▪ ski jumping
- snowboarding
- tobogganing

No horseplay
There was no entry for the neighing nags hoping to compete in Australia's Olympics in 1956. Due to quarantine laws, all events involving horses had to be held 15,500 km (9,600 miles) away in Sweden.

Good sports?
Olympic sports come and go. These weird and wonderful events were once part of the games, but have since bitten the dust.

▪ tug-of-war ▪ croquet ▪ chariot racing ▪ running, wearing armour ▪ jumping, holding weights

Cold conditions, poor publicity, and a lack of international backing resulted in a disastrous Olympics in Athens in **1896**. Not only did some athletes pay their travel expenses themselves, but some **contestants were tourists** who just happened to be on holiday in Greece!

How to: manage the Olympic flame

01. Angle a special mirror towards the Sun to light the wick of the torch.

02. Stay in shape because running is the most common way to transport the famous flame between Olympia, Greece, and the Olympic site of the host city.

03. If you're not up for the run, take your pick from these other popular methods of torch transportation: boats, aircraft, horses, canoes, or camels.

04. Keep the flame burning overnight in special cauldrons along the route.

05. It's the home straight now. On arrival at the host stadium, enjoy a lap of honour before lighting the cauldron of cauldrons with the Olympic flame.

Climate and conditions

Snow shortage
There was **not enough snow** at Innsbruck for the winter Olympic Games in 1964. Instead, the Austrian army **moved 20,000 ice bricks** for the bobsleigh and luge runs, and 40,000 m³ (130,000 ft³) of snow to the ski slopes.

High altitude
When the summer Olympic Games were held in Mexico City in 1968, it proved a challenge for the competitors. At **2,200 m (7,200 ft) above sea level**, the location gave many athletes **breathing difficulties**, as they struggled to adapt to air with **30 per cent less oxygen** than normal.

Extreme weather
Warm sunshine at the winter Olympics in the Swiss town of St Moritz resulted in the **cancellation** of a skating contest in 1928. This was followed by **18 hours of torrential rain**, with all events postponed.

Record breakers

The US has won in excess of 2,400 **summer Olympic medals**, more than any other country.

The country to win the **most winter Olympic medals** is Norway, with almost 300.

Australia, France, Greece, Switzerland, and the UK are the only five **countries to compete in all the modern Olympic Games**, since they began in 1896.

Athletics, cycling, fencing, gymnastics, and swimming are the only five **sports to feature at every modern summer Olympic Games**.

History

Khufu
Ordered the construction of the Great Pyramid

Hatshepsut
Powerful queen who ruled Egypt for 20 years and even wore the pharaoh's ritual false beard

Akhenaten
Banished the traditional gods and set up his own religion

Tutankhamun
In 1922, the tomb of this boy-pharaoh was found with all its magnificent burial goods intact

Rameses II
Reigned over Egypt for 67 years and built more monuments and statues than any other pharaoh

Cleopatra VII
One of the most famous women in history, she killed herself when Egypt fell to the Romans

When did the **pharaohs** rule?

The great Ancient Egyptian civilization arose more than 5,000 years ago among farmers living on the banks of the River Nile. It lasted for 3,000 years – longer than any other civilization on Earth. What is really remarkable is that throughout this long history, the way of life and the art and sculpture of Ancient Egypt remained largely unchanged.

In numbers

The Great Pyramid is the largest stone structure on Earth.

2.5 tonnes
The average weight of each block used in the construction of the Great Pyramid

20
How many years it took to build

146 m
(480 ft) The height from ground to capstone

230 m
(755 ft) The length of each of the four sides

800 km
(500 miles) The distance blocks were transported from the quarry to the pyramid site

4,000
The number of workers involved in building it

2,300,000
The total number of blocks used in its construction

6,500,000 tonnes
The total weight of the pyramid

RECORD BREAKER

The pharaoh Pepy II reigned for 94 years – the **longest reign** in all of recorded history. He was only six when he came to the throne in 2278 BCE and died in 2184 BCE, at the ripe old age of 100.

THE WRITE STUFF
The Egyptians used a form of writing called hieroglyphs, made up of about 700 different picture signs.

River Nile
~ Flood water used to irrigate farmland
~ Was a highway for transporting goods
~ Provided fish for food

Egyptian gods

Ra
The Sun god, who also represented kingship

Amun
Creator god, associated with fertility

Mut
Wife of Amun and goddess of war

Pharaohs

01: The king of Egypt was called the "pharaoh", a word that originally meant "great house" or "palace", but came to describe the man who lived there.

02: He was thought to be a living god and wore a ritual false beard as a symbol of royalty.

03: He also wore a red crown and a white crown symbolizing the union of Upper Egypt (the river valley) with Lower Egypt (the Nile delta).

How to: make a mummy

01. Wash the body as soon as possible after death.

02. Take out the brain. It is useless, so you can yank it out through the nostrils using a hook and throw it away.

03. Remove the internal organs and place them inside special containers called canopic jars. Leave the heart as it contains the soul.

04. Fill the body cavity with a salty mineral called natron to absorb moisture. Cover the body with more natron and leave it to dry for 40 days.

05. Rub the skin with oils, stuff sawdust inside the body to give it shape, and put balls of linen into the eye sockets.

06. Wrap the body in linen bandages, placing amulets (magic charms) between layers to protect the mummy on its journey to the afterlife.

WHAT'S IN A NAME?

The Egyptians knew their country as *Kemet*, which means "the Black Land", from the rich dark soil of the Nile valley. They called the surrounding desert "the Red Land" – *Deshret*.

Royal burials
The pyramids were built as tombs for the pharaohs during the period known as the Old Kingdom, more than 4,500 years ago.

I don't believe it!

Egyptian noblewomen at court tied scented cones of animal fat to the tops of their wigs to make themselves smell nice as the perfumed fat melted. Both men and women wore coloured eye make-up.

The Egyptians worshipped around 2,000 different gods and goddesses.

Tell me more: kingdoms and dynasties

Early Dynastic Period
c 3100–2686 BCE
1st and 2nd dynasties

Old Kingdom
c 2686–2181 BCE
3rd–6th dynasties

First Intermediate Period
c 2181–2055 BCE
7th–11th dynasties

Middle Kingdom
c 2055–1650 BCE
11th–14th dynasties

Second Intermediate Period
c 1650–1550 BCE
15th–17th dynasties

New Kingdom
c 1550–1069 BCE
18th–20th dynasties

Third Intermediate Period
c 1069–715 BCE
21st–25th dynasties

Late Period
c 715–332 BCE
26th–30th dynasties; Persian kings

Ptolemaic Period
333–30 BCE
Macedonian and Ptolemaic dynasties

Anubis
Jackal-headed god of the dead and mummification

Sobek
Crocodile god and ruler of the Nile

Osiris
God of the dead and the afterlife

Isis
Wife of Osiris and goddess of nature and fertility

Horus
Falcon-headed god of the sky, light, and life

Seth
God of deserts, storms, chaos, and evil

Thoth
God of wisdom and writing

Who were the Ancient Greeks?

Ancient Greece was not a single country – the Greeks lived in separate city-states all around the Aegean Sea and often quarrelled violently with each other. They were united by the Greek language and writing, by shared myths and legends about the gods, and by a common enemy, the Persians.

Blasts from the past

2000–1450 BCE
Minoan civilization flourishes on Crete

1450–1100 BCE
Mycenaean civilization rises and falls on mainland Greece

800–600 BCE
Greeks found colonies in Ionia and Sicily and around the Black Sea

776 BCE
First games held at Olympia

c.750 BCE
Homer composes the *Iliad* and the *Odyssey*

508 BCE
Start of Athenian democracy

490 BCE
Battle of Marathon – Athenians defeat a Persian invasion

480–479 BCE
Sparta and Athens combine forces to prevent a second Persian invasion

450 BCE
Parthenon temple is built in Athens

441–404 BCE
War between the city-states ends in Spartan victory

371 BCE
Defeat of Sparta by Thebes

338 BCE
Philip of Macedon makes himself effective ruler of the Greek city-states

334–300 BCE
Philip's son Alexander the Great conquers Persia

Athenian politics
- The Athenians introduced a new form of government called democracy ("rule of the people").
- All male citizens over 18 could speak and vote in the assembly, where laws were made.
- They also made up the juries that heard legal cases.
- Once a year Athenians voted to banish an unpopular citizen from the city.

Places in the Greek world

Mount Olympus: Legendary home of the Greek gods

Delphi: Site of a famous oracle (wise counsel) that the Greeks consulted about the future

Athens: Most powerful of the city-states; birthplace of Greek democracy

Olympia: Where the Olympic Games were held

Sparta: Warrior city-state in southern Greece

Greek gods and goddesses

Aphrodite
Goddess of love

Apollo
God of the Sun, healing, and medicine

Artemis
Goddess of the Moon and hunting

Asclepius
God of medicine and healing

Athena
Goddess of wisdom and war

Demeter
Goddess of corn and the harvest

Good sports

- The Olympic Games was the greatest of four athletic festivals that attracted competitors from all over the Greek world.
- **Events included running, chariot racing, horse races, boxing, wrestling, discus, and javelin.**
- Athletes were naked.
- **They competed for a prize of an olive crown.**
- Wars stopped to allow people to travel to and from the games.

I don't believe it!

According to a famous legend, the playwright Aeschylus was killed when an eagle dropped a tortoise on his head. Seems that the bird mistook the old fellow's shining bald pate for a handy rock to crack open the shell!

Five famous Greeks

Archimedes
Mathematician and inventor. He developed a device for pumping water, which is known as the Archimedes screw

Aristotle
Philosopher who studied the natural world, one of the most influential figures in the history of learning and science

Hippocrates
Physician who believed there was a rational explanation for illnesses and made careful notes of symptoms

Homer
Every Greek knew this poet's most famous works, the *Iliad* and the *Odyssey*, which told the story of the Trojan War

Socrates
Philosopher who was interested in how people should behave. He was condemned to death by drinking a deadly poison

FAST FACTS

Alexander the Great

01: Alexander became king of Macedon when he was only 19.

02: He led a great invasion force of Greeks and Macedonians against the Persians.

03: He made himself master of an empire that stretched from Egypt as far as Afghanistan and northwest India.

04: He founded more than 70 towns, naming 13 of them after himself.

05: He died suddenly at the age of 32.

Spartan living

Sparta, Athens' main rival for power in Greece, was a military state. From age seven, boys lived in army barracks. Spartan girls were also trained in gymnastics and athletics. The aim was to make them healthy mothers of future soldiers.

Greek architecture

Doric columns
Thick and the capitals (top stones) were undecorated

Ionic columns
More elegant – the capitals were decorated with two scrolls (volutes)

Corinthian capitals
Elaborately carved with acanthus leaves

The Greek god Pan was half-man and half-goat.

He played a set of reed pipes – the "panpipes". When humans saw him they were overcome by a terrible fear – from which we get our word "panic".

Dionysius
God of wine, drama, and fertility

Hades (Pluto)
God of the underworld

Hera
Wife of Zeus, protector of women

Hermes
Messenger of the gods

Poseidon
God of the sea and earthquakes

Zeus
King of the gods, master of the sky

How large was the Roman Empire?

At its fullest extent, in the 2nd century CE, it stretched 4,000 km (2,500 miles) from Spain in the west to the Caspian Sea in the east, and from Britain in the north to Egypt in the south. Of course, this didn't happen overnight – in fact, it took more than 700 years for Rome to grow from a small village to a superpower.

Types of gladiators

Gladiators were trained in the art of killing for the entertainment of the Roman crowds in the Colosseum. They mostly fought armed combats with swords (gladii), but some specialized in other weapons and tactics.

Eques
Mounted gladiator who fought with a spear and sword

Retiarius
Carried a trident, dagger, and net to catch his opponent

Bestiarius
Fought wild beasts armed only with a spear

Hoplomachus
Heavily armed with a huge helmet and leg and arm coverings

Secutor
Carried an oblong shield and sword, often pitted against a murmillo

Dimachaerus
Fought with two swords, one in each hand

Murmillo
Wore a helmet decorated with a fish

Thrax
His weapon was the deadly Thracian curved sword

Laquerius
His weapon was a rope and noose

Gore fest
Contests between **gladiators**, mock sea battles, and **fights to the death** with exotic wild animals drew crowds of up to 80,000 to Rome's Colosseum.

Blasts from the past

753 BCE
Traditional date of the foundation of Rome

509 BCE
Romans drive out their kings and found a republic

272 BCE
Rome has conquered all of Italy

145 BCE
Rome's power covers much of the Mediterranean

88–31 BCE
Roman Republic weakened by a series of civil wars

44 BCE
Assassination of Julius Caesar, dictator of Rome

27 BCE
Augustus becomes the first emperor of Rome

117 CE
Roman Empire is at its greatest extent

286
Diocletian divides the Roman Empire into eastern and western halves

324
Constantinople founded as the new capital in the east

410
Visigoths (barbarians) sack Rome

475
The end of the Western Empire

EATING ROMAN STYLE

- At formal dinners, Romans ate reclining on couches.

- The meal usually started with eggs or seafood and ended with fruit. In between came elaborate dishes such as birds garnished with eggs and asparagus or dormice sprinkled with honey and poppyseed.

- Romans loved to pour *garam*, a fish sauce, over their food, much as we use ketchup.

- It was good manners to belch at the end of a meal.

I don't believe it!

Romans went to the toilet in public, sitting on a long stone bench in the street with a row of holes pierced through it. They would chat together while they relieved themselves through the holes.

How to: put on a toga

01. Drape one end of the toga over your left shoulder so that it falls all the way down at the front to your left foot.

02. Holding the rest of the toga about midway along its length, take it under your right arm at waist level.

03. Lift it loosely across the front of your body and throw the remaining length of cloth over your left shoulder.

04. Arrange the folds of cloth neatly and pull the left end up to hang elegantly over your left forearm.

Warning! Better not to attempt toga dressing unless you have a house slave to help you!

Five terrible emperors

14–37 CE — Tiberius
Gloomy and paranoid, he spied on his enemies. Eventually retired to the island of Capri, where he is said to have thrown his victims off a cliff

37–41 CE — Caligula
Tiberius's grandson, famous for his cruelty and probably insane. He tried to have his horse elected to the senate

54–68 CE — Nero
A hated monster who murdered his own mother and fancied himself as a musician even though he was awful

180–192 CE — Commodus
Addicted to gladiatorial combat and even performed in the arena himself (the other gladiators had blunted swords)

218–222 CE — Elagabalus
Loved dressing up and behaving outrageously. At one party he showered so many roses on his guests that many of them suffocated

The Romans invented **concrete** by mixing rubble with lime (burnt chalk) and volcanic ash.

Five strong emperors

27 BCE –14 CE — Augustus
Ended the chaos of civil war (and the Republic) by making himself emperor. Created a lasting system of strong, efficient government

117–138 CE — Hadrian
Travelled throughout the Empire and strengthened its frontiers. He built Hadrian's Wall in Britain as a barrier against the Picts

161–180 CE — Marcus Aurelius
Philosophically minded emperor who wrote a famous book of meditations. Biggest mistake was to make Commodus his heir (see above)

284–305 CE — Diocletian
General who reorganized the army and split the Empire in two to make it easier to govern, then astonished everyone by retiring to the seaside

307–337 CE — Constantine I
The first Christian emperor who founded the city of Constantinople (modern-day Istanbul) as a second capital

Roman army

Legionary
Ordinary foot-soldier. Legionaries were Roman citizens and joined up for 20 to 25 years. They were armed with a shield, sword, and dagger

Contubernium
Unit of eight legionaries led by a decanus

Century
Unit of 10 contubernia (80 men)

Centurion
Commanded a century

Cohort
Usually made up of six centuries (480 men)

Legion
Made up of 10 cohorts (about 5,000 men)

Legate
Commanding officer of a legion

Signifer
Carried the legion's silver eagle standard into battle

Cornicen
Trumpeter who blew a horn to signal each command during a battle

Cavalry soldier
Fought on horseback with spears and javelins. The cavalry were usually non-citizen soldiers, often foreign recruits

The Romans built **aqueducts** to carry water into their cities. One of Rome's aqueducts brought water from 70 km (43 miles) away.

How old is **China?**

Tell me more: **Chinese dynasties**

商 **Shang Dynasty**
c.1766–1122 BCE

西周 **Zhou Dynasty**
1122–221 BCE

春秋 **Springs and Autumns period**
770–480 BCE

戰國 **Warring States period**
480–221 BCE

秦 **Qin Dynasty**
221–206 BCE

西漢 **Han Dynasty**
206 BCE–220 CE

三國 **Three Kingdoms**
220–581

隋 **Sui Dynasty**
581–618

唐 **Tang Dynasty**
618–907

五代十國 **Five Dynasties and Ten Kingdoms**
907–960

南宋 **Song Dynasty**
960–1279

元 **Yuan (Mongol) Dynasty**
1279–1368

明 **Ming Dynasty**
1368–1644

清 **Qing Dynasty**
1644–1911

Chinese history traditionally begins with the Shang Dynasty, nearly 4,000 years ago, but Chinese civilization goes back much further, to around 9,000 years ago when farming started on the Yellow River in northern China. The Shang Dynasty was the first in a line of imperial dynasties that lasted until 1911.

Testing times
The Chinese invented the world's **first written exams** to select candidates to become state officials. The tests lasted up to 72 hours and when a candidate had finished, an official recopied their answers so that their handwriting would not be recognized.

How to: **make paper**

Legend has it that a Han court official, Ts'ai Lun, invented paper in 104 CE. This is how he did it.

01. Take lots of old rags, the inner bark of a mulberry tree, and bits of bamboo.

02. Leave to soak in water and pound thoroughly with a wooden mallet to break up all the fibres.

03. Pour the mixture through a coarsely woven cloth and let the water drain through it, leaving the fibres behind on the cloth.

Boning up
The Shang kings used oracle bones to ask the gods questions, such as "Will this war turn out well?" The question was written on an ox bone or a tortoise shell, which was heated until cracks appeared. The shape of the cracks would reveal the answer.

Chinese inventions

1100 BCE silk

500 BCE cross bow

100 BCE iron plough

c.1600 BCE
First use of pictographic writing in China

c 600 BCE
Iron is first used in China

551–479 BCE
Life of Confucius, philosopher and teacher

221 BCE
China is united under Qin Shi Huang, the First Emperor

100 BCE
Han emperors expand China's frontiers westwards and open up the Silk Road, the overland trade route to the Mediterranean

610 CE
The Grand Canal, built to carry trade between north and south China, is completed; it runs for 1,770 km (1,100 miles)

1000 CE
Science and technology flourish under the Song Dynasty

1275
Venetian explorer Marco Polo arrives at the court of Kublai Khan, Mongol emperor of China

1368
A peasant leader, Zhu Yuangzhang, overthrows the Mongols and becomes the first Ming emperor

1644
Manchu (Mongolian) warriors seize Beijing and establish the Qing Dynasty (until 1911)

Blasts from the past

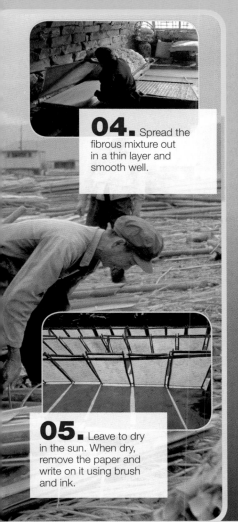

04. Spread the fibrous mixture out in a thin layer and smooth well.

05. Leave to dry in the sun. When dry, remove the paper and write on it using brush and ink.

FAST FACTS

The Forbidden City

01: Built as the imperial palace for the Ming emperors in Beijing

02: Construction took 15 years and employed more than 1 million workmen

03: The world's largest palace complex, it covers an area of 75 hectares (183 acres) and is surrounded by a wall 10 m (33 ft) high and a moat 6 m (20 ft) deep

04: Contains 980 buildings and 9,000 rooms

05: Was the residence of 24 emperors – 14 from the Ming Dynasty and 10 from the Qing

Five facts about the First Emperor

✦ When Ying Zheng became king of Qin, China was divided into seven warring states. He conquered them all and declared himself Qin Shi Huang (the First Emperor) of China, in 221 BCE.

✦ **He determined to make China a single state.** Everyone had to obey the same laws, adopt the same writing style, and use the same coins, weights, and measures.

✦ He ordered the construction of an earth barrier stretching more than 1,600 km (1,000 miles) to keep out invasions – the beginning of the Great Wall of China.

✦ **Qin Shi Huang feared one thing only – death – and** is supposed to have travelled to the islands of Japan in search of a magic elixir to give him eternal life.

✦ It took 700,000 men 36 years to build his massive tomb. It is 60 m (164 ft) high and is said to contain a replica of his capital city.

Buried army

Buried near the tomb of Qin Shi Huang is the Terracotta Army – 7,000 clay soldiers, 600 horses, and more than 100 wooden war chariots to protect the Emperor in the afterlife.

Dates are approximate. Many Chinese inventions predated similar European inventions by several hundred years.

All at sea
In 1405, Chinese admiral **Zheng He** led an expedition to spread Chinese trade and military power around the Indian Ocean. His fleet consisted of more than 200 ships, with a crew of up to 28,000.

200 CE woodblock printing

500 paddlewheel ship

600 porcelain

600 fireworks and gunpowder

950 navigational compass

Who were the ancient Americans?

The Maya and Aztecs of Central America and the Incas of Peru developed remarkable cultures that were swept away by Spanish invaders in the 1500s. They were the final witnesses to the long history of human civilization in ancient America.

How to: play the Maya ball game

01. You need a long, narrow stone court with sloping sides. Fixed to the walls above the ground should be two vertical stone rings.

02. Pick two teams of young adult men.

03. Players must keep the ball in the air at all times by flicking it with their elbows, knees, or hips – never their hands.

04. The aim is to pass a small, hard rubber ball through one of the rings. It is very difficult, so be prepared for a game to last for hours.

05. Once a team scores, the game ends. The winners are rewarded with a lavish feast. The losers are sacrificed to the gods!

I don't believe it!

The Maya thought the height of masculine good looks was to have a flat long head. When a baby was a few days old his head would be squeezed between wooden boards to give it the desired shape. Adults' teeth were filed and inlaid with jade, as were their ears. It all added to their manly allure.

Five facts about the Maya (250–900 CE)

Maya people lived in small city-states in modern-day Guatemala and Yucatán (Mexico). Their kings were called *k'ul ahau* ("supreme and sacred ruler").

They waged war against their neighbours and recorded their conquests on elaborately carved tablets known as "stone trees" using a form of picture-writing (glyphs).

They built tall pyramids of stone where they performed the rituals and human sacrifices that the gods demanded. The victims were prisoners of war, slaves, and children.

Some rituals took the form of painful self-mutilation ceremonies when they would pierce their tongues with sting-ray spines to enter a trance-like state.

They developed a complex calendar based on accurate observation of the Sun, stars, and planets.

Lines in the desert

01: Two thousand years ago, the Nazca civilization in Peru created mysterious designs in the desert.

02: They consist of a series of lines, some up to 300 m (1,000 ft) long.

03: The designs can only be seen from the air.

04: Some depict animals – for example, a hummingbird, monkey, condor, or spider. Others are abstract geometrical shapes.

05: No one knows what the lines mean. Some historians believe they formed part of an astronomical calendar and were connected in some way with irrigation.

FAST FACTS

Aztec gods

There were more than 100 gods in the Aztec religion.

Chalchiuhtlicue
Goddess of lakes and streams

Cihuacoatl
Goddess of fertility and childbirth

Coatlicue
Goddess of life and death

Quetzalcoatl
Feathered serpent, god of the wind

Tlaloc
God of rain who makes things grow

Xipe Totec
God of springtime and agriculture

Xochiquetzal
Goddess of sensual love, pleasure, and art

Choc-tastic!

❖ The Aztecs drank a bitter spicy drink called *chocolatl* made from the beans of the cocoa tree.

❖ Cocoa was first cultivated by the Maya in the rainforests of Central America.

❖ The beans were used as a form of currency – 10 could buy a rabbit, 100 a slave.

❖ The Aztecs believed chocolate had been brought to Earth by the god Quetzalcoatl.

❖ Aztec king Montezuma II is said to have served Spanish invader Cortés with chocolate in a golden goblet.

❖ Cortés took cocoa beans back with him to Spain. The Spanish kept the source of chocolate a closely guarded secret.

Five facts about the **Aztecs** (1300–1519 CE)

The Aztecs were the last people to dominate Mexico before the arrival of the Spanish.

They waged continual war to capture prisoners to sacrifice to the gods and to demand tribute from neighbouring states.

Soldiers were rewarded with elaborate costumes to show how many prisoners they had captured.

The last Aztec ruler was Montezuma II. He believed a rumour that the Spanish commander Hernán Cortés was the god Quetzalcoatl in human form and invited him to his palace.

Bad mistake – the Spaniards took Montezuma prisoner and conquered his empire.

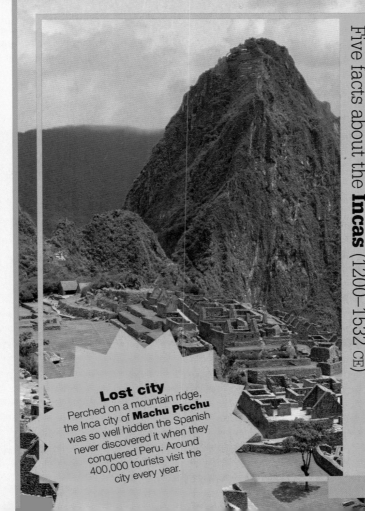

Lost city
Perched on a mountain ridge, the Inca city of **Machu Picchu** was so well hidden the Spanish never discovered it when they conquered Peru. Around 400,000 tourists visit the city every year.

Five facts about the **Incas** (1200–1532 CE)

The Inca Empire extended for 4,800 km (3,000 miles) along the Andes from Ecuador to central Chile.

The Incas loved gold, which they called "the sweat of the Sun". They called silver "the tears of the Moon".

The Incas built more than 40,000 km (24,855 miles) of roads to carry goods, armies, and messages quickly around the Empire.

Although they made wheeled toys for children to play with, they did not have wheeled carts – instead they carried goods on sure-footed llamas and alpacas over the steep mountain roads.

Records were kept on *quipu* – knotted strings of different colours attached to a main cord. The colour of the string and the number of knots along it indicated the nature and quantity of goods and supplies.

Who were the Vikings?

The Vikings were sailors who came from Norway, Sweden, and Denmark. They began raiding places on the coasts of England, Ireland, and France just before 800 CE and later settled there as farmers and traders. Some Vikings voyaged across the Atlantic to Iceland, Greenland, and North America. Others travelled down the great rivers of Russia to the Black Sea.

Story time

On long winter nights poets called skalds entertained the feasters in the king's hall with tales about the gods or the adventures of famous warriors.

These poems were passed down from generation to generation.

By the 1200s most Scandinavians were Christian. Icelandic poet and historian Snorri Sturluson was so worried people might forget the myths he wrote them down in collections known as the *Eddas*.

Around the same time some 40 stories about the histories of Icelandic families were written down. They are called the *Sagas*, and contain stories from the earliest days of the Viking settlement in Iceland.

wool sail

Tell me more: **Viking dress**

- fur hat
- warm wool cloak fastened with brooch
- overshirt of undyed linen
- knife and purse on belt
- baggy woollen trousers

- linen head cloth
- oval brooch
- wool stretched and spun for weaving
- pinafore tunic
- spindle
- raw wool
- long under-dress
- leather shoes

How to: **build a Viking ship**

01. Cut and plane a keel (a long beam that will run along the bottom of the boat) out of oak.

steering oar

Viking sailors didn't have maps or a magnetic compass. They **found their way across the ocean** by observing the positions of the **Sun and stars** and the direction of the **wind**.

05. Erect a mast in the centre of the ship to support a single square sail made of wool. This should be lowered at night and can be used as a tent in bad weather.

02. Construct the sides of the ship using overlapping strakes (side timbers) for strength.

03. Make sure you caulk (waterproof) the gaps between the strakes with a mixture of tar and animal hair.

oarport

04. Add holes for the oars (oarports) along both sides so that the ship can be steered when there is no wind.

Norse gods

Odin
The god of war was said to gather up the warriors who had fallen in battle and carry them back to his hall, Valhalla.

Thor
Armed with his hammer Miollir, the god of thunder defended Asgard (where the gods lived) against giants and dragons.

Loki
Thor's companion, Loki was a mischievous and sometimes nasty creature who made lots of trouble for the other gods.

Freyr
The god of fertility and controller of sunshine and rain, Freyr was responsible for making Viking crops grow.

Freyia
The twin of Freyr, Freyia was the goddess of love. She could turn herself into a bird by putting on a magic falcon skin.

Raiding season

"Dire portents… immense whirlwinds and flashes of lightning, and fiery dragons flying in the air." That's how one monk described the first Viking attack on the monastery of Lindisfarne, northeast England, which came out of the blue on 8 June 793.

The Viking war fleets came every summer, raiding right around the coasts of England, Scotland, and Ireland before returning home with their booty.

They were soon raiding along the coast of France and far inland along its rivers. Paris was attacked and burned several times.

The Viking raiders attacked mercilessly with their long, double-edged swords and battle axes. They wore conical iron helmets, but no horns – that's a 19th-century myth.

They picked on monasteries because they were undefended and contained precious objects.

Blasts from the past

790s Viking raids start in western Europe

841 Viking settlement founded at Dublin, Ireland

856–857 Vikings sail up the Seine to sack Paris for the first time

860s Swedish Vikings found Novgorod and Kiev in Rus (Russia and Ukraine)

870 Farmers from Norway found a settlement on Iceland

886 Eastern England comes under Danish rule (Danelaw)

900 Vikings raid along the Mediterranean coast

911 Viking chief Rollo is granted land in France (Normandy)

941 Rus Vikings attack Constantinople (Istanbul)

986 Erik the Red founds a settlement on Greenland

1000 Leif Erikson explores the coast of Newfoundland

Writing in runes

fehu (f)

unuz (u)

thurisaz (th)

ansuz (a)

raido (r)

kanaz (k)

Vikings wrote in runes – letters that were specially designed for incising into wood and stone.

They carved runic inscriptions on memorial stones and decorated them with fantastic designs of writhing dragons and serpents.

Halfdan, a Viking warrior who travelled to Constantinople (Istanbul), scratched his name on a marble slab in the church of Hagia Sofia – you can still see it there today.

The runic alphabet, or futhark, takes its name from the first six characters – fehu (f), unuz (u), thurisaz (th), ansuz (a), raido (r), kanaz (k).

Go west!

Erik the Red was exiled from Iceland in 982 for murder. Three years later he was back with tales of a land he called Greenland. He set off with about 1,000 volunteers to start a new colony, which flourished for 300 years.

In 1000, Leif Erikson sailed from Greenland and landed at a place he called Vinland. Archaeologists believe it was Newfoundland, making him the first European to reach America.

WHAT'S IN A NAME?

Most chroniclers called the Vikings *Norsemen* or *Northmen* because they came from the north. The name "Viking" may originate from the Scandinavian word *vik*, meaning a creek or inlet.

06. Attach a steering oar to the right or "steering board" side of the ship – the origin of the term "starboard".

07. Decorate the post at each end of the ship. On fighting ships, a carved dragonhead is often fitted to the front post.

mast

When were medieval times?

The period after the Dark Ages (the time that followed the collapse of the Roman Empire in Europe) is called the medieval era (also known as the Middle Ages). Trade and learning revived. The population rose and people became richer. Kings held power by granting their nobles landed estates to live on.

Blasts from the past

800
The Pope crowns Charlemagne, King of the Franks (France), Holy Roman Emperor

1066
William the Conqueror, Duke of Normandy, conquers England

1088
The first European university is founded at Bologna, Italy

1095
Pope Urban II calls for a crusade to the Holy Land

1140
The abbey of St Denis, near Paris, is built in the new Gothic style

1298
Marco Polo publishes his account of his travels in Asia

1326
Cannons are used for the first time in European warfare

1337
The start of the Hundred Years' War between France and England (ends 1453)

1347–1351
Black Death (plague) devastates Europe

1431
Joan of Arc is burned at the stake

Power pyramid
A medieval king agreed to protect his nobles, while the nobles swore to come to his aid when asked. The nobles in turn rewarded their followers with smaller grants of land. This system, which began in France, is known as **feudalism**.

The Crusades

⚐ The Crusades were a series of wars fought between Christians and Muslims for control of the Holy Land (Palestine).

⚐ The word "crusade" comes from the French *croix* ("cross"). European crusader knights wore a red cross on their tunics.

⚐ Crusaders believed they would go straight to heaven if they died fighting on crusade.

⚐ The knights of the First Crusade (1095–1099) captured the city of Jerusalem.

⚐ In 1187 Saladin, a Muslim leader, recaptured Jerusalem. Little by little the crusaders were driven out of the Holy Land.

How to: become a knight

01. Be born the son of a nobleman. At age eight you'll be sent to be a page in another nobleman's castle. You'll be taught how to handle a sword and spear.

02. At age 15 or 16 you'll be made the squire to a knight. Look after him at all times – dress him, prepare his meals, and take care of his horse and armour.

03. So long as you've performed your duties well, when you're 20 or so you'll be made ("dubbed") a knight in a special ceremony.

04. The night before, put on a white tunic and red robe and spend all night praying solemnly in the castle chapel. The chaplain will bless your sword and place it on the altar. Next morning confess your faults to him.

05. You'll be led outside to kneel in front of your lord, who will tap you lightly on each shoulder with his sword. You've been made a knight! Let the feasting begin!

06. A short-cut way to becoming a knight is to perform some brave deed in combat – best of all, save your lord's life. Then he'll take his sword and dub you Sir Lancelot (or whatever) on the field of battle.

A knight was expected to obey the code of chivalry. He promised to:

✶ **protect the poor and weak, especially women**

✶ **obey his lord and show courage, honesty, loyalty, and strength**

✶ **defend the Church and go on crusade**

Monks and monasteries

✝ Only Church people could read and write, so abbots (heads of monasteries) were powerful men who advised the king and sat on his council.

✝ **Landowners gave monasteries grants of land so that the monks would pray for their souls. Some monasteries grew very rich as the monks were highly efficient farmers.**

✝ Monks spent hours copying religious books by hand and decorating them with gold and coloured pictures – these are known as illuminated manuscripts.

✝ **Women who followed a religious life were called nuns. They lived in convents.**

✝ The monks had to pray seven times a day (they also attended mass, the main service of the Church, every day).

Daily prayers:

sunrise	matins ("morning prayer")
6 am	prime ("first hour")
9 am	terce ("third hour")
midday	sext ("sixth hour")
3 pm	none ("ninth hour")
sunset	vespers ("evening prayer")
9 pm	compline ("night prayer")

WHAT'S IN A NAME?

Medieval comes from two Latin words *medium* ("middle") and *aevum* ("age"). It's the filling in the sandwich between the age of the Romans and the modern world.

WEIRD OR WHAT?

One "cure" for the Black Death was to drink a glass of urine twice a day. Placing a live hen next to the black swellings on the patient's body was also believed to help draw the pestilence out.

The Black Death was a deadly outbreak of bubonic plague that raged through Asia and Europe, spread by fleas and rats.

4 years
The time it took to spread through Europe (1348–1351)

5–8 days
Average length of illness

50%
Chance of dying

25–50 million
The number of victims in Europe (30–60 per cent of population)

75 million
The number of victims in Asia

Boom towns

🏰 Towns were on the up as trade and commerce boomed.

🏰 Towns grew rich through the right to hold weekly or seasonal fairs.

🏰 Thanks to the cloth trade, northern Italy and Flanders (Belgium) had the richest towns in Europe.

🏰 Skilled craftsmen and merchants formed guilds – associations to look after their interests.

🏰 Insurance and banking were invented at this time.

Gothic architecture

Cathedrals and churches soared upwards as medieval masons (builders) discovered the pointed Gothic arch.

Spire: Tall and thin, it pointed upwards to heaven

Rounded arch: Romanesque style (Norman in England), used throughout Europe until 1100s

Flying buttress: Stone arch on the outside of the building that supported the high walls

Stained glass window: Windows became larger and were filled with coloured stained glass

Gargoyles: Stone water-spouts in the shape of strange creatures were built along the gutters

Pointed arch: Springing from the top of narrow columns, pointed Gothic arches allowed masons to build much taller structures. The style spread rapidly in Europe after 1150

How to: **joust**

Jousting started as a way for knights to test their horsemanship and weapons skills in preparation for war. Over the centuries it developed into a popular tournament event, attracting hundreds of spectators and offering big money prizes. It was the ultimate extreme sport!

03. Take hold of your lance in your right hand. Keep it upright.

01. Have your squire dress you in your armour and prepare your horse.

02. Mount your horse, sitting hard in the saddle with your feet in the stirrups.

You will need:

Suit of armour
For the very best protection, you should wear a full suit of plate armour. Special jousting armour is available, which has heavier protection on the side facing the opponent.

Helmet
Make sure the eyes are well protected. In 1559, a splinter of lance entered through the visor of King Henry II of France and pierced his brain. He died nine days later.

Horse
The most popular horses are chargers (bred for agility) or destriers (heavy war horses). You will need to dress it in an ornamental covering and protect its head with armour.

04. When the herald signals, ride straight ahead with the tilt barrier to your left. Make sure your lance is still upright.

05. As you near your opponent, lower your lance at an angle across the tilt barrier (fence).

06. Aim for your opponent's torso, clinging tightly to your horse as you strike.

07. Repeat until either you or your opponent falls out of the saddle.

Lance
This should be made of solid oak and decorated with your coat of arms (family symbol).

Tilt barrier
Before tilt barriers were introduced in the 15th century, jousts were a lot more dangerous. The barrier protects the horses and ensures lances are pointed at a safer angle.

Herald
Heralds keep score and act as masters of ceremony by announcing the contests and reading out the rules of the tournament.

Opponent
The knight challenging you in the joust should also be wearing armour, mounted on a horse, and carrying a lance.

A **cannon** used by the Ottomans at the siege of Constantinople was the **largest the world had seen** – its bronze barrel was 8.5 m (28 ft) long and 20 cm (8 in) thick. It could fire a ball weighing 544 kg (1,200 lb) more than 1.6 km (1 mile). A special carriage drawn by 30 oxen and 700 men was needed to drag it into place.

Who were the Ottomans?

A Turkish dynasty of sultans who ruled one of the most powerful Muslim states in modern history. At its height, the Ottoman Empire stretched from Hungary to Egypt and from Algeria to Iraq, putting fear into the hearts of the European powers. Over time it became weaker, but managed to survive from 1301 until 1922.

WHAT'S IN A NAME?

When the Ottomans took over the city of **Constantinople** they would hear the Greek inhabitants say they were going "*eis tin polis*" ("to the city"). This became shortened in Turkish to **Istanbul** – and the name stuck ever since.

Five Ottoman sultans

Murad I
(ruled 1359–1389)
Made inroads into Europe across the Dardanelles and established a capital at Edirne (the former Byzantine city of Adrianople). He was killed after the battle of Kosovo.

Bayezid I "the thunderbolt"
(ruled 1389–1403)
Conquered Bulgaria, Serbia, and Macedonia but was defeated and imprisoned by Tamurlane, a fearsome Mongol warlord.

Mehmed II "the conqueror"
(ruled 1451–1481)
Ended the Byzantine Empire by capturing Constantinople in 1453, which he made his capital.

Selim I "the grim"
(ruled 1512–1520)
After getting rid of his father and killing off all his brothers and nephews, he extended Ottoman rule to Syria, Palestine, Saudi Arabia, and Egypt.

Suleyman I "the magnificent"
(ruled 1521–1566)
The Ottoman Empire reached its largest extent during his 46-year reign.

Top title
Suleyman I called himself: "Slave of God, powerful with the power of God, deputy of God on Earth, obeying the commands of the Qur'an and enforcing them throughout the world, master of all lands, the shadow of God over all nations, Sultan of Sultans in all the lands of Persians and Arabs, the propagator of Sultanic laws, the tenth Sultan of the Ottoman Khans, Sultan, son of Sultan, Suleyman Khan."
A pretty magnificent name!

Safavids of Persia (Iran) 1501–1722

◆ 14-year-old Ismail I declared himself shah (king) of Persia. He had the skull of a defeated Uzbek leader made into a drinking cup.

◆ **The Safavids were followers of the Shia branch of Islam, which became the state religion.**

◆ The greatest Safavid ruler was Abbas I (ruled 1587–1629). He built up an army and seized Baghdad from the Ottomans in 1623.

◆ **Abbas's capital at Isfahan was one of the glories of the Muslim world. It had 162 mosques, 272 public baths, and 48 madrasas (schools).**

◆ In 1722 Afghan invaders captured Isfahan and killed the last shah.

Mughals of India 1501–1857

🔱 Babar (ruled 1501–1531) was the founder of the Mughal dynasty. He invaded northern India in 1526.

🔱 **His grandson Akbar (ruled 1556–1605) expanded the Empire. A wise Muslim ruler, he showed tolerance to his Hindu subjects.**

🔱 Jahangir (ruled 1605–1627) invited Persian artists, writers, and architects to his court.

🔱 **Jahan (ruled 1627–1666) built the Taj Mahal (pictured) as a memorial to his wife.**

🔱 Aurangzeb (ruled 1658–1707), the last of the great Mughal conquerors, was a mean-minded emperor who lost the trust of his people.

FAST FACTS

A soldier's life

01: Janissaries were the Ottoman sultan's crack infantry corps.

02: Their name is made up of two Turkish words – *yeni* (new) *çeri* (soldier).

03: Recruits were drawn from the *devshirme* – the annual tribute of Christian boys sent as slaves to Constantinople and made to convert to Islam.

04: The janissaries were loyal only to the sultan. They lived in barracks and were forbidden to marry.

Ottoman terms

divan council (literally, a low couch)

firman imperial decree

gazi warrior dedicated to fighting for Islam

harem private family quarters of palace

janissary the sultan's infantry guard

kiosk pavilion

pasha high official

Sublime Porte ("High Gate") the sultan's government

sultan Muslim ruler

sultana wife or daughter of a sultan

vizier royal minister

Modern states (or parts of them) that belonged to the Ottoman Empire

❈ Albania
❈ Algeria
❈ Armenia
❈ Azerbaijan
❈ Bosnia-Herzegovina
❈ Bulgaria
❈ Croatia
❈ Cyprus
❈ Egypt
❈ Georgia
❈ Greece
❈ Hungary
❈ Iraq

❈ Israel
❈ Jordan
❈ Libya
❈ Macedonia
❈ Montenegro
❈ Romania
❈ Russia
❈ Saudi Arabia
❈ Serbia
❈ Syria
❈ Tunisia
❈ Turkey
❈ Ukraine
❈ West Bank

Battlefront reports

🗒 The Battle of Kosovo (1389) ended Serbian independence for 500 years and is still bitterly remembered.

🗒 **When a Venetian army laid siege to Athens, Greece, in 1687, the Ottomans used the ancient Parthenon as an ammunitions store. It blew up, destroying much of the temple.**

🗒 Mustafa Kemal (pictured) served as an Ottoman division commander at the World War I Battle of Gallipoli (1915). He became the first president of the Turkish Republic (1923), taking the name of Atatürk ("Father of the Turks").

Under siege!

🔺 Constantinople stood on a triangle of land with water on two sides. The city wall on the land side, built in the 5th century CE, was 20 km (12 miles) long.

🔺 The siege lasted 57 days, from 6 April to 29 May 1453.

🔺 **The defenders had 7,000 men and 26 ships, and the Ottomans an estimated 100,000 men and 126 ships.**

🔺 The fall of the city brought to an end the 1,000-year-old history of the Greek Byzantine Empire, the successor to the Eastern Roman Empire.

🔺 **Constantine XI, the last Byzantine emperor, died defending Constantinople in the final Turkish assault on the city walls. His body was never found.**

🔺 Hagia Sophia ("Holy Wisdom"), the great domed church built by the Emperor Justinian 900 years earlier, was turned into a mosque. Today it is a museum.

What was the Renaissance?

The word Renaissance means "rebirth". It's the name historians give to a cultural movement that started in northern Italy in the 1400s and spread throughout Europe in the course of the next 150 years.

01: At age 14 he entered the workshop of Andrea Verrocchio, a leading sculptor, painter, and goldsmith in Florence.

02: He once wrote to the Duke of Milan offering to work for him as an engineer designing forts, bridges, weapons, and canals – but almost forgot to say he could paint as well. He got the job.

03: It took him four years to paint the *Mona Lisa*. No one knows who she is or why she is smiling. She hasn't any eyebrows – women shaved them off at that time.

04: He was passionately interested in how everything works, from the human body to the movement of water, and filled notebook after notebook with his ideas.

05: His designs for ingenious machines included an armoured car, machine gun, helicopter, and underwater diving suit.

Techniques of Renaissance painting

Perspective: Giving an illusion of distance

lifelike figures

bright colours

Sfumato: Blurring or softening of sharp outlines to give a 3-D effect

Chiaroscuro: Strong contrast of light and dark

Leonardo da Vinci: Renaissance man of genius (1452–1519)

FAST FACTS

Renaissance

01: Wealthy trading and banking cities like Florence, Milan, Urbino, and Venice became hotspots of artistic activity.

02: Artists developed new styles of painting, sculpture, and architecture based on the ideals of the Ancient Greeks and Romans.

03: Scholars began to study Greek and Latin manuscripts. This sparked new interest in philosophy and science.

04: Growing criticism of the corruption of the Church led to a lasting split in Christianity (the Reformation).

Five Renaissance artists

Sandro Botticelli
Painted women with long flowing tresses like his *Birth of Venus*, which shows the goddess appearing from the sea on a large shell.

Albrecht Dürer
Greatest German artist of the Renaissance era. Some of his woodcuts, like *Knight, Death, and the Devil*, are quite spooky.

Michelangelo Buonarroti
Sculptor, painter, and architect who is always called by his first name. His masterpiece is the ceiling of the Sistine Chapel in the Vatican.

Raphael (Raffaello Sanzio)
His greatest works are in Rome, including the frescoes he painted for the Pope's apartments in the Vatican.

Titian (Tiziano Vecellio)
Venetian painter who painted kings and popes and lived to a ripe old age before falling victim to the plague.

Advice for kids

One of Erasmus's bestselling books was *A Handbook on Good Manners for Children*. Among the gems of advice he doled out are these:

✓ **Always put your hand in front of your mouth when you yawn.**

✗ Don't lick your greasy fingers at table or wipe them on your coat – use the table cloth.

✗ **Don't rock your chair backwards and forwards – people will think you are farting.**

✗ Don't look for bogeys in your hanky after blowing your nose.

✗ **Don't lend your filthy hanky to a friend.**

1434 The Medici family of bankers become unofficial rulers of Florence

1455 First printed book in Europe

1492 Fall of Granada, last Muslim kingdom in Spain

1498 Leonardo da Vinci paints *The Last Supper* in Milan

1504 Michelangelo's giant nude statue of *David* goes on show in Florence

1509 Humanist scholar Erasmus publishes *The Praise of Folly*, his most famous essay

1513 Niccoló Machiavelli writes *The Prince*, a handbook for Renaissance rulers

1534 King Henry VIII declares himself Supreme Head of the Church in England

1543 Nicolaus Copernicus publishes a book proving the Earth revolves around the Sun

Blasts from the past

The Reformation in five easy steps

01: German priest Martin Luther composes a list of 95 complaints against the Church (1517).

02: The Pope throws Luther out of the Church and he is hauled before an imperial court at Worms (1521). He refuses to back down and is outlawed by Emperor Charles V.

03: He goes into hiding. Germany is torn apart by conflict and revolt. Support for his reforms (demands that the Church mend its ways) spreads through northern Europe.

04: A number of German princes refuse to give in to pressure from the Emperor to reject the reformers. They are called Protestants.

05: The Peace of Augsburg (1555) gives individual German princes the right to decide what faith (Protestant or Roman Catholic) their subjects should follow.

WHAT'S IN A NAME?

The **Sistine Chapel** in the Vatican is named for Pope Sixtus IV, the pope responsible for building it. There have been five popes called Sixtus. If there had been one more he would have been called Pope Sixtus the Sixth!

Movers and shakers

Nicolaus Copernicus
This Polish astronomer argued that the Earth moves around the Sun, rather than the other way round, contrary to the Church's teachings.

Niccoló Machiavelli
Italian statesman and writer whose name has become a byword for political cunning and intrigue.

Desiderius Erasmus
Foremost Humanist scholar (the Humanists found their inspiration in the works of Plato and other Greek and Roman writers). Erasmus's writings were bestsellers, thanks to the new technology of printing.

How to: **print a book on Gutenberg's press**

About 1450, a German craftsman, Johann Gutenberg, invented a printing press using movable type. Gutenberg's first printed book was the Bible. It took him about a year to print all 180 copies – about the same time it would have taken a copyist to produce a single handwritten copy.

01. Create your movable type (raised metal shapes for each letter of the alphabet). Carve the shape of the letter, back to front, onto a metal punch. Hammer this into a copper sheet to make your mould. Fill the mould with hot metal, and when it cools, you have your metal type.

02. Arrange the pieces of type to make up the words and sentences of the text you want to print line by line in a wooden frame known as a form. When the form is full, ink the letters well with an oil-based ink and place a sheet of paper on top.

03. Place the form on a table and lower a wooden screw so that it presses a board down onto the paper.

04. Raise the screw, remove the paper, and put in another sheet. Repeat until you have printed all the copies you need.

The sought-after spices

cinnamon

black pepper

cloves

ginger

nutmeg

What started the age of discovery?

The desire of European merchants to control the trade in luxury goods from Asia – silk, cotton, and spices – combined with technological advances in shipbuilding and navigation led to a wave of long-distance voyages of exploration that redrew the map of the globe between the 15th and 18th centuries.

Wrong way!

In 1492, self-taught navigator **Christopher Columbus** attempted to reach the Spice Islands in the east by **sailing west**. His three ships – the *Santa Maria*, *Pinta*, and *Niña* – reached the Bahamas and Columbus mistook America for Asia.

What's in a name?

When Ferdinand Magellan finally made his way safely through the towering waves around Cape Horn on 28 November 1520, he was so relieved to see calm, tranquil water ahead, he called it *Mar Pacifico* – the **Pacific Ocean**. He had no idea how wide the ocean was though. He wouldn't see land again for more than three months, reaching Guam on 6 March 1521.

Blasts from the past

1487–1488
Portuguese navigator Bartolomeu Dias sails down the west coast of Africa and rounds the Cape of Good Hope to enter the Indian Ocean

1492
Christopher Columbus sails west from Spain to discover America

1497
Italian-born John Cabot (Giovanni Caboto) sails from Bristol to Nova Scotia

1497–1498
Vasco da Gama makes the first return voyage from Portugal to India

1499
Amerigo de Vespucci explores the coast of South America

1500
Pedral Alvarez Cabral discovers Brazil while sailing to India

1509–1510
Lopez de Sequeiro is the first European to reach Malacca (the Spice Islands)

1516
Portuguese explorer Rafael Perestrello reaches China

Explorers who came to **sticky ends**

- ✳ Bartolomeu Dias died in a storm off the Cape of Good Hope in 1500

- ✳ **Ferdinand Magellan was killed in a fight in the Philippines in 1521**

- ✳ Giovanni de Varrazano was killed and eaten in Guadeloupe in 1528

- ✳ **Henry Hudson was cast adrift by his mutinous crew in 1611 and never seen again**

- ✳ Sir Francis Drake died of scurvy on a West Indies raiding expedition against the Spanish in 1596

- ✳ **Captain James Cook was murdered by angry islanders in Hawaii in 1779**

- ✳ Sir John Franklin's ship became trapped in thick ice while looking for the Northwest Passage through the Arctic to the Pacific in 1847. He and 105 others died of starvation

Sir John Franklin's ship trapped in Arctic ice

How to: **make ship's biscuit**

01. Mix together four parts of flour with one part of water. Add salt.

02. Roll out the dough and score with a knife to make squares, or cut into rounds. Bake in an oven until rock hard.

03. To eat, bash into crumbs with a handy implement or soak in broth until mushy enough to swallow.

04. Watch out for weevils (tiny black insects)!

Killer at sea!

A lack of fresh fruit and veg on long voyages led many a sailor to fall victim to **scurvy**. It made gums bleed and teeth fall out and victims got weaker and weaker until they died. The British Navy made sailors drink lots of lime juice – that's how they came to be nicknamed "limeys".

I don't believe it!

In 1494 the Atlantic was divided between Spain and Portugal by papal decree (a ruling from the Pope). All new land found west of an imaginary north-south line running down the middle (ie the Americas) would belong to Spain and all land east of it (ie the route to India and beyond) to Portugal. No one knew quite where the line lay, which allowed Portugal to claim Brazil in 1500.

What to pack for a **sea voyage**

 Maps and charts based on discoveries of earlier explorers

 Compass – essential for knowing in which direction you are travelling

Cross-staff – to work out latitude (how far you are from the Equator) by measuring the height above the horizon of the Pole Star (at night) or Sun (at midday). Only works when the skies are clear

 Lots and lots of rope

 Spare canvas for sails

 Water – as much as possible, stored in barrels below decks as ballast to keep the ship stable

 Ship's biscuit – also known as hard tack

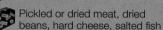 Pickled or dried meat, dried beans, hard cheese, salted fish

Goods to trade with, such as beads and trinkets

 Guns – to keep hostile natives and pirates at bay

maps and charts

compass

cross-staff

rope

1519–1522
Ferdinand Magellan leads the first around-the-world voyage but dies in the Philippines. Sebastian del Cano completes the voyage

1524
Giovanni da Varrazano sails the length of the Atlantic coast of North America

1535–1536
Frenchman Jacques Cartier explores the St Lawrence River of Canada

1606
Dutch explorer Willem Janz explores the coast of Northern Australia

1642–1644
Dutchman Abel Janszoon Tasman reaches Van Diemen's Land (Tasmania) and New Zealand

1767–1768
Louis-Antoine de Bougainville explores the islands of the South Pacific for France

1768–1771
James Cook explores New Zealand and the eastern coast of Australia on the first of three great voyages of discovery in the Pacific

Why did kings become so powerful in Europe?

Before the 1500s, nobles were always plotting revolts against kings. Over time, kings raised the money to pay for full-time armies, putting an end to civil wars. Kings started to believe they had a divine right to rule and that no one could tell them what to do.

Happy families?

The key to power in the 16th century was to marry well. Here's how some royals were related:

Emperor Charles V was the **nephew** of Catherine of Aragon, the first **wife** of Henry VIII of England.

Charles V's **son** Philip II of Spain **married** Queen Mary I of England, who was Catherine and Henry's **daughter**. When Mary died he proposed to her **half-sister**, Elizabeth I, but she turned him down flat.

Mary, Queen of Scots was Henry VIII's **great-niece** and a **cousin** of Elizabeth I. She was the **widow** of King Francis II of France, who was the **brother** of Elizabeth of Valois, who became Philip II's next **wife**. Another **sister** of Francis II, Margaret of Valois, was **married** (for a time) to Henry IV of France.

Who said that? (supposedly)

01. "I speak Spanish to God, Italian to women, French to men, and German to my horse."

02. "You have sent me a Flanders mare!"

03. "I have the heart and stomach of a king, and of a king of England too."

04. "Paris is well worth a mass."

05. *L'Etat, c'est moi.* ("I am the state.")

(answers far left)

Versailles court etiquette

- Only the king or queen (or visiting monarch) could sit on an armchair.
- **The king's brother or children might sit on a chair with a back and no arms.**
- Duchesses were allowed to sit on a *tabouret*, a padded, drum-shaped stool.
- **Everyone else had to stand.**

- Courtiers had to scratch on the king's door with their little finger and then wait for permission to enter – they were not allowed to knock.
- **Around 100 nobles were on hand every day to attend the king's ritual *levée* (rising) and *couchée* (going to bed). They would quarrel for the privilege of holding his shirt or fetching his chamber pot.**

THE SUN KING

King Louis XIV (main picture) of France (1643–1715) insisted all his nobles lived at his vast palace at **Versailles** so they couldn't plot against him. Life revolved around him, gaining him the nickname *"le roi soleil"* ("the sun king").

In numbers

The palace of Versailles, France, is vast.

11 hectares
(26 acres) of roof

67
staircases

357
mirrors in Hall of Mirrors

500 m
(1,640 ft) frontage

800 hectares
(2,000 acres) of grounds

700
rooms

1,250
fireplaces

1,400
fountains

2,153
windows

51,210 sq m
(551,220 sq ft) of floors

Europe's royal households

Bourbon:
France (1589–1792),
Spain (1700–1931,
restored 1975)

Braganza:
Portugal (1640–1910)

Habsburg:
Austria (1282–1918),
Spain (1516–1700),
Portugal (1598–1640)

Hanover:
Great Britain (1714–1901)

Hohenzollern:
Brandenburg-Prussia
(1415–1918);
emperors of Germany
(1871–1918)

Orange-Nassau:
Netherlands (1815–)

Romanov:
Russia (1613–1917)

Savoy:
Sardinia and Piedmont
(1720–1861),
Italy (1861–1946)

**Saxe-Coburg/
Windsor:**
Great Britain (1901–)

Stewart/Stuart:
Scotland (1327–1601)
England and
Scotland (1603–1714)

Tudor:
England (1485–1603)

Valois:
France (1328–1589)

For the chop

Kings might insist on their divine
right to rule, but their subjects did
not always agree – as **King
Charles I** of England found to his
cost. He thought he could govern
without parliament and tried to impose
his religious views on hardline
Protestants – a fatal mistake that
resulted in civil war. Charles lost the
war and his head, which was
chopped off in 1649.

Terrible tsar

☞ Ivan the Terrible (1530–1584) was the first
grand prince of Russia to crown himself tsar.

☞ His nickname in Russian, "*Grozny*", more
accurately translates as "awesome".

☞ He started off terribly well, introducing new
laws, updating the army, and more than
tripling the size of his kingdom.

☞ But then it all went terribly wrong – he used
his army to terrorize his subjects, and had
thousands executed.

☞ His rages got worse and worse until one day
he killed his son Ivan in a terrible fit of anger.
He felt really terrible about it afterwards and
never forgave himself.

The six wives of Henry VIII

**King of England
(1509–1547)**

divorced
Catherine of Aragon

beheaded
Anne Boleyn

died
Jane Seymour

divorced
Anne of Cleves

beheaded
Catherine Howard

survived
Catherine Parr

What is a colony?

A settlement set up by a group of people in a new country, with close ties to the country from where they came. Between 1500 and 1900 the European powers founded colonies all around the world, from America to Africa, Asia and the Pacific. Countries with large numbers of overseas colonies are called empires. Spain was the first European power to create an overseas empire in the 1500s, but by 1900 Britain had the largest empire.

Jewel in the crown

The so-called "Jewel in the Crown" of the British Empire was India. Queen Victoria became Empress of India in 1877, but she never went there. India was ruled by a viceroy representing the British crown until the country won independence in 1947.

Four facts about the British Empire

01: The Empire reached its greatest extent during the reign of Queen Victoria (1837–1901).

02: It covered one-fifth of the Earth's surface and contained one-quarter of its population.

03: The colonies supplied Britain with raw materials – sugar, cotton, tea, bananas, rubber, palm oil – and provided important markets for British goods.

04: The British developed law courts, hospitals, schools, and railways, but they did so with little regard for the traditions, religions, and languages of the people they governed.

Tell me more: 19th-century European empires

Belgium: Congo

Britain: Australia, Canada, New Zealand, South Africa, Gibraltar, India and Burma (Myanmar), Sri Lanka, Egypt and Sudan, west and southeast Africa, Malaya and Singapore, Fiji and other Pacific islands, British Guiana (Honduras), West Indies (Jamaica, Trinidad, and other islands)

France: Algeria, Morocco, French Central Africa, French West Africa, Madagascar, Indochina (Vietnam, Cambodia, and Laos), French Polynesia (Tahiti), French Guiana

Germany: Cameroon, German East Africa (Tanzania), German South-West Africa (Namibia)

Italy: Libya, Eritrea, Somalia

Netherlands: Dutch East Indies (Indonesia), Dutch Antilles (Aruba), Suriname

Portugal: Angola, Mozambique

Spain: Philippines, Puerto Rica, Cuba

Foreign invasion

Colonization was tough on native peoples – their lands were stolen from them, and they were wiped out by diseases such as smallpox, measles, and mumps as they had no natural immunity to them. Resistance was useless as the foreigners had guns.

One lump or two...

Portuguese navigators discover **Madeira** and the **Canary Islands** in the Atlantic. They colonize the islands and begin growing **sugarcane** there.

By 1550 they have established large **sugar plantations** in **Brazil** and are importing **African slaves** as labour.

Sugar cultivation spreads to the **Caribbean islands**, which are now mostly owned by the Dutch, French, and British.

As all the **local people have been wiped out** by disease and war, thousands of **slaves are imported from Africa** to work on the sugarcane plantations.

In numbers

Colonization of the Americas had one terrible consequence. Between 1500 and the early 1880s millions of Africans were forcibly transported across the Atlantic Ocean to work as slaves for European plantation owners.

2,000
The average number of Africans transported each year in the 1550s

10,000
The average number of Africans transported each year in the 1650s

100,000
The average number of Africans transported each year in the 1750s

12 million
The total number of African slaves transported to work on plantations

The original 13 colonies:

Name: **New Hampshire**
Year founded: **1623**
Nickname: **Granite State**

Name: **New York**
Year founded: **1664**
Nickname: **Empire State**

Name: **Massachusetts**
Year founded: **1620**
Nickname: **Bay State**

Name: **New Jersey**
Year founded: **1664**
Nickname: **Garden State**

Name: **Rhode Island**
Year founded: **1636**
Nickname: **Ocean State**

Name: **Connecticut**
Year founded: **1635**
Nickname: **Nutmeg State**

Name: **Pennsylvania**
Year founded: **1682**
Nickname: **Keystone State**

Name: **Maryland**
Year founded: **1634**
Nickname: **Old Line State**

Name: **Delaware**
Year founded: **1638**
Nickname: **First State**

Name: **Virginia**
Year founded: **1607**
Nickname: **Old Dominion**

Name: **North Carolina**
Year founded: **1653**
Nickname: **Tar Heel State**

Name: **South Carolina**
Year founded: **1663**
Nickname: **Palmetto State**

Name: **Georgia**
Year founded: **1732**
Nickname: **Peach State**

Colonial America

■ Many early settlers were Puritans (Protestants) who came to avoid religious persecution in England. They created the patchwork of small farms and rural communities that makes up the landscape of New England (the northeastern states of the USA) today.

■ Thanksgiving Day, celebrated on the fourth Thursday of November, is said to date from 1621 when the settlers of New Plymouth celebrated their first harvest.

■ Life was hard for the Jamestown settlers in Virginia until they hit on the idea of growing tobacco and exporting it to England – put that in your pipe and smoke it!

■ American beaver furs became all the rage for fashionable hats in Europe. French traders travelled far into the interior to obtain pelts (furs) from Native American trappers.

I don't believe it!

In 1667 the Dutch agreed to a swap with the English – their settlement of New Amsterdam on Manhattan Island for the tiny island of Run in the Spice Islands and Suriname, a swampy area of forest on the coast of South America. The English renamed the settlement New York – and got themselves a chunk of prime real estate!

...in your tea?

☕ **Portuguese traders** in China bring **tea** back to Europe.

☕ **British** begin growing **opium** in India to **sell to China** in exchange for tea. They also introduce **tea plantations** to **India** and **Sri Lanka**.

☕ The British put **a tax on tea** in their North American colonies. The **Americans don't like it** and dump a cargo of tea in Boston Harbor – no wonder they develop a taste for coffee!

Countdown to independence

1776
The 13 American colonies rebel against British rule

1810–1823
South America is liberated from Spanish rule

1922
Ireland (previously British) becomes a Free State

1946
Philippines gain independence from USA

1947
India and Pakistan gain their independence

1949
Indonesia wins its independence from the Netherlands

1957–1975
Former colonies around the world from the Caribbean to the Pacific gain independence

1990
Namibia is the last country in Africa to gain independence (from South Africa)

What are revolutions?

Periods of rapid or dramatic change when the world is turned upside down. Political revolutions take place when people become so fed up or unhappy with their rulers they overthrow them and set up a new government. The outcome is often bloody and violent – this happened in France in 1789 and in Russia in 1917.

Tell me more: political revolutions

✪ **American Revolution (1775–1783)**
13 colonies throw off British rule to become the United States of America

✪ **French Revolution (1789–1793)**
Antiroyalist uprising leads to the setting up of a republic; the king loses his head

✪ **Year of Revolutions (1848)**
Revolutions break out across Europe

✪ **Chinese Revolution (1911)**
Popular uprising topples Qing Dynasty

✪ **Russian Revolution (1917)**
The tsar (king) is forced to abdicate (resign) and a Bolshevik (communist) government seizes power

Cuban revolutionary Che Guevara

✪ **Cuban Revolution (1959)**
Fidel Castro overthrows a right-wing dictatorship and sets up a communist state in Cuba

✪ **Cultural Revolution (1966–1976)**
Mao Zedong launches a terror campaign to eradicate the "enemies of socialism" in China

✪ **Khmer Rouge (1975)**
Communist guerrillas seize power in Cambodia. Their hardline regime causes the deaths of more than 3 million people

✪ **Iranian Revolution (1979)**
The shah (king) is overthrown and an Islamic republic set up in Iran (Persia)

✪ **Velvet Revolution (1989)**
Peaceful protests topple Czechoslovakia's communist regime as communist rule collapses in Eastern Europe and Soviet Union

How to: have a revolution in France

01. Have the King and Queen lead a life of luxury in the palace of Versailles while the rest of France starves.

02. Get the King to call a meeting of the Estates General (parliament) so he can raise taxes. This will cause the Third Estate, who represent commoners, to storm out and set up a rival assembly.

03. Start a rumour that the King is sending his army to close down the assembly. Rioters in Paris will storm the Bastille, a royal fortress, in protest and release all seven prisoners inside. It's 14 July 1789 and the French Revolution begins!

04. Have bands of revolutionary citizens (the *sans-culottes* or "people without breeches") roam the streets demanding an end to aristocratic power under the slogan "Liberty, Equality, Fraternity!"

Five **revolutionary leaders**

George Washington
(1732–1799) After winning the war against British rule, this Virginian farmer was elected the first president of the United States.

Maximilien de Robespierre *(1758–1794)* Unleashed a wave of terror against French aristocrats and political opponents before losing his head on the guillotine.

Vladimir Lenin
(1870–1924) Led the Russian Bolsheviks to power in October 1917 and became the first leader of Soviet (communist) Russia.

Leon Trotsky
(1879–1940) Key figure in the Bolshevik revolution who fell out with Stalin (Lenin's successor) and ended up with an ice pick in his head.

Mao Zedong
(1893–1976) Chinese communist leader who masterminded the creation of the People's Republic of China in 1949.

Industrial Revolution (1760–1900)

A period of rapid social and economic change when people left the countryside to live in towns and work in factories.

WHAT'S IN A NAME?

The **guillotine** – bloody symbol of the French Revolution – takes its name from Dr Joseph Guillotin, a professor of anatomy who championed its use as a speedy, clean and humane method of **execution**. The **razor-sharp blade**, falling from a height, separated the victim's head from the body in less than a second, much quicker than hanging or beheading with an axe.

05. When the King tries to flee the country, arrest him and put him on trial for plotting to betray France. Send him to the guillotine, along with his hated wife.

06. Now that France is a republic, it is time for the revolutionary leaders to turn on each other in a frenzy of political feuding. Paris is awash with blood as thousands of people lose their heads on the guillotine.

FAST FACTS

Industrial Revolution

01: New machines are invented in Britain to speed up the spinning of wool and cotton. At first, they are powered by waterwheels, but later steam engines are developed.

02: Iron becomes cheaper and stronger as iron-making techniques improve.

03: Thanks to changes in farming fewer people are needed to grow food, forcing them to leave the countryside to find work in mills and factories. Industrial towns grow rapidly.

04: Canals are dug to carry coal from the mines, and to transport finished goods.

05: Within 50 years railways replace the canals. The first public railway opens in 1825.

06: In the United States, the first coast-to-coast railroad is completed in 1869, opening the way to rapid industrial expansion. Mass-production techniques are developed to drive down costs.

Scientific Revolution (c.1550–1800)

Laid the foundations of modern science. Starting with the discovery that the planets move around the Sun, and not the other way around as the medieval Church had taught, scientific advances revolutionized the way people thought about the world.

Agricultural Revolution (1700–1850)

Brought sweeping changes to the countryside. Fewer people were needed to work on the land thanks to more efficient ways of farming.

I don't believe it!

Russian revolutionary leader Lenin's body has been on public display in a marble mausoleum (tomb) in Moscow's Red Square since his death in 1924. The mausoleum is closed every 18 months so his corpse can be treated with special embalming fluids and given a change of clothes.

Information Revolution (1980s onwards)

Computer technology and the microchip have revolutionized our world. The Internet is re-inventing the way we do business and politics, study, and access entertainment.

Trench fighting in World War I

Which century has seen the most wars?

10 major 20th-century wars

01: World War I (1914–1918)

02: Russian Civil War (1918–1921)

03: Chinese Civil War (1927–1949)

04: Spanish Civil War (1936–1939)

05: World War II (1939–1945)

06: Arab-Israeli Wars (1948–1973)

07: Korean War (1950–1953)

08: Vietnam War (1964–1973)

09: Iran–Iraq War (1980–1988)

10: Gulf War (1991)

During the 20th century a war was being fought somewhere on the planet every year and there were at least 165 major conflicts. About 40 million soldiers died, nearly 75 per cent of them in the two World Wars. Millions of civilians also lost their lives in the conflicts.

RECORD BREAKER

The **shortest war** on record lasted just 38 minutes. It was fought between Britain and Zanzibar, an island off the east coast of Africa, in 1896.

Danger! More than 110 million APLs (Anti Personnel Landmines) litter war-torn countries of the world. These **deadly devices** kill or maim thousands of people a year.

For 40 years superpower rivalry between the USA and the USSR (communist Russia) brought the world close to conflict. During this Cold War, the superpowers amassed enough nuclear weapons to destroy the planet.

1945–1948 The USSR takes control of Eastern Europe, imposing communist regimes

1949 China becomes a communist Republic and forms a pact with the USSR

1950 Communist North Korea invades South Korea and is pushed back by a US-led force

1952–1953 A nuclear arms race begins

1956 Soviet troops put down an uprising in Hungary

1961 The Berlin Wall is built sealing off communist East Berlin from West Berlin

1964 USA enters war against communist North Vietnam

1970 The USA and USSR begin talks to reduce nuclear weapons

1979 USSR invades Afghanistan

1985 Mikhail Gorbachev becomes the leader of the USSR and introduces reforms

1988–1991 Communist rule collapses in Eastern Europe and USSR

Blasts from the past

Guess how long it lasted?

❓ Hundred Years' War
(1337–1453)* Fought (with interruptions) between England and France

❓ Thirty Years' War
(1618–1648) Bitter struggle between Catholics and Protestants fought mostly in Germany

❓ Seven Years' War
(1756–1763) European conflict that spilled over to become the first global war

❓ Seven Weeks' War (1866)
Prussia made a smash-and-grab raid on Austria, aided by Italy

❓ Six Day War (1967) The time it took Israel to defeat Egypt and Syria and occupy the West Bank

❓ Hundred Hours' War (1969)
Fought between Honduras and El Salvador after rioting broke out at a football match

*well spotted – it was actually 116 years!

War stories

In medieval sieges it was quite usual to hurl dead plague victims over the wall at your enemy – an early form of germ warfare.

The first use of chemical weapons came in World War I when the Germans released mustard gas (a yellow oily liquid that attacks the lungs) into the Allied trenches.

German and British troops fighting in the trenches called a temporary truce on Christmas Day 1914 to play a football match.

The Soviet army trained dogs to crawl under tanks with explosive devices strapped to their backs in World War II. The explosives were then triggered, destroying the tanks – and the dogs.

I don't believe it!

The Thirty Years' War started when some Protestants chucked two Catholic envoys out of a castle window in Prague on to a heap of poo. It caused quite a stink!

US President George W Bush declared a **"War on Terror"** after Al-Qaeda Islamic terrorists flew two airliners into the Twin Towers of the World Trade Center in New York City on 11 September 2001, killing nearly 3,000. It led to military action in Afghanistan and Iraq.

Feeling peckish? Try these food wars

Potato War (1778)
This conflict got its strange name because both sides (Prussia and Austria) spent more time combing the countryside for food supplies than fighting.

War of the Oranges
(1801) This war is named after a present of oranges sent to the queen of Spain by her lover after he'd invaded Portugal on Napoleon's orders. Sweet!

Pastry War (1838)
Some Mexican soldiers wrecked a shop belonging to a French pastry cook. The Mexican government refused to compensate him, so a French army invaded.

Cod War (1975)
This was a clash between the United Kingdom and Iceland over fishing rights in the North Atlantic. There was not much actual fighting, but a lot of net cutting!

10 famous military leaders

Alexander the Great
Macedonian empire-builder who never lost a battle

Hannibal
Led his men (and several war elephants) across the Alps and beat the Romans

Julius Caesar
Conquered Gaul (France) and made himself master of Rome

Saladin
Organized Muslim resistance to the Crusaders

Genghis Khan
Mongol warlord who ruled an empire from the Black Sea to the Pacific

Napoleon
Took on all the armies of Europe and beat them – until he faced…

Duke of Wellington
British general who defeated Napoleon at the Battle of Waterloo

Robert E Lee
Successful Confederate (southern states) general in the American Civil War

Erwin Rommel
Led the World War II German army in North Africa, but later fell out with Hitler

Georgi Zhukov
Most successful Soviet general of World War II

→ 1903: The Wright brothers achieve the first powered flight at Kitty Hawk, North Carolina

↓ 1906: Finland is the first European country to give women the vote

← 1902: The teddy bear becomes a popular toy. It is named after US President Theodore (Teddy) Roosevelt

↓ 1908: Henry Ford launches the Model-T Ford, the world's first mass-produced car

1900s

→ 1912: SS *Titanic* hits an iceberg and sinks on its maiden voyage

↓ 1914: World War I begins (ends 1918)

↑ 1916: Easter Rising against British rule in Ireland

↑ 1917: Russian Revolution

← 1918: Spanish flu epidemic kills millions of people worldwide

1910s

↓ 1923: Charleston dance becomes all the rage

1920s

↓ 1951: Colour TV introduced in the United States

↓ 1955: African American woman Rosa Parks refuses to give up her seat on bus to a white person, triggering the start of the civil rights movement in the USA

↓ 1953: DNA is discovered by scientists at Cambridge University, England

↓ 1956: Ghana is the first former British colony in Africa to gain independence

← 1959: The Barbie doll is launched (wearing a black and white zebra striped swimsuit)

1950s

← 1961: The Berlin Wall (separating communist East from the West) is built

↓ 1964: The Beatles take the United States by storm

1968: Street riots in Paris. US students hold sit-ins to protest against Vietnam war

→ 1969: Two US astronauts become the first humans to walk on the Moon

↓ 1963: US President John F Kennedy is assassinated

↓ 1967: First heart transplant

1960s

→ 1972: Pocket calculators are introduced

↑ 1978: The first test tube baby born

→ 1979: Islamic Revolution brings regime change in Iran

1970s

← **1920:** Women win the right to vote in the United States

← **1922:** Archaeologists discover Tutankhamun's tomb in Egypt

1926: First pictures transmitted by television

↑ **1927:** First talking movie, *The Jazz Singer*

← **1928:** Alexander Fleming discovers penicillin

→ **1931:** The Empire State Building opens in New York City

↓ **1933:** Adolf Hitler becomes Chancellor of Germany and passes the first anti-Jewish laws

← **1934:** Start of Stalin's "Great Terror" in Russia. Millions die in labour camps

↓ **1935:** Nylon invented

↓ **1936:** African American athlete Jesse Owens wins four gold medals at the Berlin Olympics. Hitler walks out in disgust

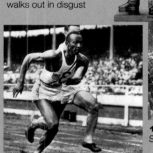

↑ **1939:** Hitler invades Poland. Start of World War II (ends 1945)

1930s

1940: The first McDonald's restaurant opens in San Bernardino, California, USA

→ **1941:** Japanese bomb the US naval base at Pearl Harbor, Hawaii. The United States enters World War II

← **1942:** Soft (two-ply) toilet paper goes on sale for the first time

↓ **1945:** US drops atomic bombs on the Japanese cities of Hiroshima and Nagasaki

↑ **1948:** State of Israel founded

→ **1949:** Communists win the civil war in China

1940s

↑ **1973:** The United States pulls out of the war in Vietnam

← **1975:** Pol Pot becomes the communist dictator of Cambodia and kills millions

← **1980:** The World Health Organization declares that smallpox has been eradicated

↓ **1982:** Michael Jackson's *Thriller* becomes the best-selling album ever

↓ **1984:** AIDS virus is discovered

↑ **1986:** The world's worst nuclear disaster occurs at Chernobyl, Ukraine

→ **1989:** Cold War comes to an end as communism collapses

1980s

→ **1990:** Nelson Mandela is released from jail after 27 years. He is elected president of South Africa four years later

← **1991:** Communist rule in Russia comes to an end

→ **1992:** War breaks out in Balkans as Yugoslavia falls apart

↓ **1994:** Genocide in African state of Rwanda

↑ **1996:** Dolly the sheep is the first cloned animal

→ **1997:** J K Rowling publishes the first Harry Potter novel

1990s

Index

Credits

DK would like to thank:
Steven Carton, Jenny Finch, and Fran Jones for additional editorial work, Stefan Podhorodecki for additional photography, and Lee Ritches for additional design. Peter Pawsey for creative technical support. Nick Deakin of www.spaceboosters.co.uk and Carole Stott for mission patches. Charlotte Webb for proofreading. Jackie Brind for preparing the index.

The publisher would like to thank the following for their kind permission to reproduce their photographs:

Key: a–above; b–below/bottom; c–centre; f–far; l–left; r–right; t–top

1 Corbis: Andrew Brookes (ftr/light bulb); Jason Horowitz / Zefa (ftr/ganesh); Images.com (tl/heart); Fred Prouser / Reuters (cra/tutankhamun). Getty Images: Philippe Body / Hemis (bc/pyramids); Photographer's Choice RR / Steve McAlister (clb/brain). **3** Corbis: Andrew Brookes (ftr/light bulb); Jason Horowitz / Zefa (ftr/ganesh); Images.com (tl/heart); Fred Prouser / Reuters (cra/tutankhamun). Getty Images: Philippe Body / Hemis (bc/pyramids); Photographer's Choice RR / Steve McAlister (clb/brain). **4** Corbis: Andrew Brookes (ftr/light bulb); Images.com (tl/heart) (bl/ganesh). **5** Corbis: Jason Horowitz / Zefa (ftl/ganesh); Images.com (br/heart). **6–7** Getty Images: Stocktrek Images (c). **7** Getty Images: (tr); Digital Vision (br); Ian McKinnell (c); NASA – digital version copyright Science Faction (cb); National Geographic (ca); Stocktrek (cr). **8** NASA: HST (bl); SOHO (tr). Science Photo Library: NASA (cl); Victor de Schwanberg (cr). **9** NASA: HST (bc) (br); SOHO (bl). Science Photo Library: Mark Garlick (clb); Pascal Goetgheluck (tr); David A. Hardy (cla); Max Planck Institute for Astrophysics (fbr). **10** ESA: (cl). NASA: HST (tr) (bc) (bl) (br) (c) (fbl) (fbr). NOAO / AURA / NSF: (cra) (cr) (crb). **10–11** NASA: HST. **11** 2MASS: J. Carpenter, T. H. Jarrett, & R. Hurt (cl). Galaxy Picture Library: NASA/JPL-Caltech (t). Science Photo Library: Magrath Photography (cr). **12** Anglo Australian Observatory: Royal Observatory, Edinburgh/David Malin (bl). NASA: (bc) (br); HST (l) (cl). **12–13** NASA: HST. **13** Galaxy Picture Library: DSS1 (tr); Gordan Garradd (tl); Gordon Garradd (tc). NASA: HST (ftl) (cr) (fcl); JPL-Caltech/K. Su (University of Arizona) (ftr); SST/IRAS (fcr); X-ray: NASA/CXC/PSU/S.Park & D.Burrows.; Optical: NASA/STScI/CfA/P.Challis (bl). **14** NASA: SOHO (c) (cb). Science Photo Library: Lawrence Berkeley National Laboratory (b). **15** Science Photo Library: Pekka Parviainen (tl); Eckhard Slawik (c). **16** NASA: (bl). Science Photo Library: John Sanford (t). **17** Corbis: Roger Ressmeyer (br). NASA: (t). **18** Corbis: NASA/Roger Ressmeyer (tl). **18–19** Corbis: epa/Gerhard Neukum. **19** Corbis: NASA/Roger Ressmeyer (br). NASA: JPL (c) (t). **20** Corbis: Araldo de Luca (bl). Galaxy Picture Library: NASA / JPL / University of Arizona (br). **21** Galaxy Picture Library: NASA / ESA / E.Karkoschka (tl). NASA: (c) (br) (bl/iron). **22** DK Images: Colin Keates / courtesy of the Natural History Museum, London (fbl/stony) (br/io) (br/titan) (cb/miranda) (fcrb/phobos). NASA: (cl). **22–23** Galaxy Picture Library: Robin Scagell (background). **23** Galaxy Picture Library: Robin Scagell (c). NASA: (fcr). **24–25** Alamy Images: Ian McKinnell (c). **25** Corbis: The Gallery Collection (bc). **26** Corbis: Roger Ressmeyer (l). Jodrell Bank Observatory, University of Manchester: (crb). NASA: (br). **26–27** NASA: HST. **27** akg-images: (tr/Archimedes). Alamy Images: Wiskerke (b). ESA: (tl). European Southern Observatory: H. Zodet (crb). W.M. Keck Observatory: UCLA/Ian McLean (cra). NASA: HST (clb); JPL-Caltech/STScI (cl); SOHO (cla); X-ray: NASA/CXC/CfA/M.Markevitch et al; Optical: NASA/STScI; Magellan/U.Arizona/D.Clowe et al Lensing Map: NASA/STScI; ESO WFI; Magellan/U.Arizona/D.Clowe et al (tr). Science Photo Library: Kapteyn Laboratorium (cr). **28** NASA: JHUAPL/CIW (tr); JPL (l). **28–29** NASA: ESA/Johns Hopkins University; JPL/Cornell University/Maas Digital (br). **29** NASA: JPL (tl) (tr); JSC (cr); KSC (bc). **31** Corbis: Bettmann (tl); Hulton-Deutsch Collection (tl); Reuters (ftr/Dennis Tito). Science Photo Library: Ria Novosti (tr/Leonov). **33** DK Images: NASA (fbr). **34** Corbis: NASA Handout/CNP (cr). NASA: (tc); KSC (c). **34–35** NASA. **35** Corbis: NASA TV/epa (tl); Roger Ressmeyer (cr). NASA: KSC (tc). Science Photo Library: NASA (cb); The Image Bank / Andy Rouse (ftr); The Image Bank / Philippe Bourseiller (cra). **36** Getty Images: The Image Bank / Matthew